全国高等教育自学考试指定教材

国际贸易专业（独立本科段）

外刊经贸知识选读

（附：外刊经贸知识选读自学考试大纲）

全国高等教育自学考试指导委员会　组编

主　　编　史天陆

副 主 编　徐　伟

主编助理　邹　丽

编　　著　史天陆　徐　伟　邹　丽

张　霞　闫建涛

中国人民大学出版社

图书在版编目（CIP）数据

外刊经贸知识选读/史天陆主编.
北京：中国人民大学出版社，2000
全国高等教育自学考试指定教材
附：外刊经贸知识选读自学考试大纲

ISBN 978-7-300-03417-1
Ⅰ. 外...
Ⅱ. 史...
Ⅲ. 英语-对照读物，经济-汉、英
Ⅳ. H319. 4：F

中国版本图书馆 CIP 数据核字（2000）第 04225 号

全国高等教育自学考试指定教材
国际贸易专业（独立本科段）
外刊经贸知识选读
（附：外刊经贸知识选读自学考试大纲）
全国高等教育自学考试指导委员会　组编
主　　编　史天陆
副 主 编　徐　伟
责任编辑　李　滢　孟　超
版式设计　王坤杰

出　　版：中国人民大学出版社
（北京海淀路 157 号　邮编 100080）
E-mail：rendafx@263. net
印　　刷：北京市鑫霸印务有限公司

开本：880×1230 毫米　1/32　印张：17. 5
2000 年 9 月第 1 版　2021 年 3 月第 27 次印刷
字数：499 000

定价：36. 00 元
官方淘宝店网址：http://shop136348527. taobao. com
本书如有质量问题，请与教材供应部门联系。

组　编　前　言

当您开始阅读本书时，人类已经迈入了21世纪。

这是一个变幻难测的世纪，这是一个催人奋进的时代。科学技术飞速发展，知识更替日新月异。希望、困惑、机遇、挑战，随时随地都有可能出现在每一个社会成员的生活之中。抓住机遇，寻求发展，迎接挑战，适应变化的制胜法宝就是学习——依靠自己学习、终生学习。

作为我国高等教育组成部分的自学考试，其职责就是在高等教育这个水平上倡导自学、鼓励自学、帮助自学、推动自学，为每一个自学者铺就成才之路。组织编写供读者学习的教材就是履行这个职责的重要环节。毫无疑问，这种教材应当适合自学，应当有利于学习者掌握、了解新知识、新信息，有利于学习者增强创新意识、培养实践能力、形成自学能力，也有利于学习者学以致用、解决实际工作中所遇到的问题。具有如此特点的书，我们虽然沿用了“教材”这个概念，但它与那种仅供教师讲、学生听，教师不讲、学生不懂，以“教”为中心的教科书相比，已经在内容安排、形式体例、行文风格等方面都大不相同了。希望读者对此有所了解，以便从一开始就树立起依靠自己学习的坚定信念，不断探索适合自己的学习方法，充分利用已有的知识基础和实际工作经验，最大限度地发挥自己的潜能以达到学习的目标。

欢迎读者提出意见和建议。

祝每一位读者自学成功。

全国高等教育自学考试指导委员会

1999年10月

编者的话

英语外刊经贸选读这一课程随着我国改革开放的不断扩展，在高等教育相关专业的教学中显得日益重要。这是因为这门课程符合了对外经贸工作不断发展的需要，能够直接地、多方面地服务于国际商务活动。通过这一课程的学习，可以初步掌握阅读和理解西方报刊经贸文章的方法与技巧，为从事国际商情调研做好准备；可以熟悉大量当今经贸领域惯用的词语和句式，不但可用于阅读，还可提高业务写作和口语；同时通过选文的内容还可帮助了解当前世界的经贸形势和主要特点。

《外刊经贸知识选读》这部教科书是为了实现上述课程的教学目标，按照国家高等教育自学考试教学的要求而编写的，其主要组成部分及其安排和特点简介如下：

1. 课文。课文的选用首先保证文字的典型性。典型的文章才能体现这类文章共有的特点，这样的文章学通了就可以较好地独立解读同类的写作而达举一反三之效。

同时，选取课文也充分注意了文章内容的时新，要传送现实有用的经贸信息：有的展现最近一两年情况变化，有的反映近年来一个阶段的国际和中国的经贸发展情况；特别选用了一批表现最新情况的辅文（练习用文和补充阅读用文）与前期文章组成系列展示某一课题的事态的演变过程和不同方面。

文章的选题，力求做到广泛而精要，宏观、微观领域并重，能够反映世界经济和贸易发展的主流和大趋势。涵盖的主题有：中国外贸和利用外国直接投资的演进、现状和政策，世界各地近年的经贸概况，特别是美国与日本的贸易动向和策略及欧盟的发展与前景，亚洲经济的崛起和问题，GATT－WTO与国际贸易，易货贸易的滞存，日益激烈的市场竞争和变化无常的初级产品市场等。

选文的文体包括：新闻述评、评论、报道、特写、电传稿以及国际组织编制的年度经贸形势报告与政府部门的市场调研报告等。

本书用文主要选自美、英、欧陆和香港地区的主要报刊，包括《经济学家》（The Economist）、《金融时报》（Financial Times）、《财富》（Fortune）、《华尔街日报》（The Wall Street Journal）、《国际先驱论坛报》（International Herald Tribune）、《远东经济评论》（Far Eastern Economic Review）、《新闻周刊》（Newsweek）、《商业周刊》（Business Week）、《基督教科学箴言报》（The Christian Science Monitor）、《纽约时报》（New York Times）、《华盛顿邮报》（Washington Post）、《读者文摘》（Reader's Digest）、《时代》（The Times）、《亚洲周刊》（Asiaweek）等。

2. 课文的注释。根据理解课文的需要提供了充分的经贸专业词语的说明、背景资料和有关国际组织及大企业的介绍，既可帮助理解课文又可充实、丰富经贸知识。注释对课文中出现的语言上的艰深之处也做了必要的解释。

3. 课文的提问。大体上总结了注释以外的课文内容和语言上的要点和难点，应该是学习中钻研和教学中讲解的重点。这些问题大部分要求以理论联系实际，用理论解释实际，通过对已有知识的运用，认真思考来解决，必要时再加以适当的指导。

本书后部备有 1 课～15 课课文问题中较难部分的答案或提示，可以参考。

此外，为了锻炼归纳、总结整段整篇资料的能力，部分课后设有“总结题”。

4. 课后练习。配有用以练习读解的文章，多种测试题和答案。练习的目的是锻炼和检验分析、理解能力，同时扩大眼界增长知识。

大部分课后还提供了“自由阅读用补充材料”，其用意在于鼓励学习或浏览更多、更新、内容更丰富的资料，阅读的要求不宜划一，应可多可少，可深可浅，量力而行，各有所得。

本书所选文章主要出自西方报刊，西方世界的经济、政治、社会观必然在文章中得到大量反映。因此，在使用当中应注意以马克思主义的观点有分析有批判地研究吸收，使之“洋为中用”。

由于编者的水平所限，不当之处一定不少，衷心希望使用本书的教师和同学及时指正，不胜感谢！

2000年2月，北京

Contents

外刊经贸知识选读

附　外刊经贸知识选读自学考试大纲

外刊经贸知识选读

Lesson 1

China's Foreign Trade

Text

China in the Market Place

(Excerpts)

Barry Coulthurst examines the development of China's trade policy and the present state of the overseas economic links

The pattern of China's foreign trade has changed substantially since the founding of the People's Republic. During the 1950s China exported agricultural products to the USSR and East European countries in return for manufactured goods and the capital equipment required for the country's industrialisation programme which placed emphasis on the development of heavy industry. The Great Leap Forward of 1958—1959 initially produced gains in agricultural and industrial production, but subsequently resulted in serious economic imbalances. Economic problems were exacerbated by three bad harvests (1959—1961) with the result that national income and the volume of foreign trade contracted during 1960—1962.

The withdrawal of Soviet economic and technical aid in the early—1960s caused trade to shift away from the USSR and its Comecon partners towards Japan and Western Europe. A consistent theme of China's foreign trade policies has been the strong emphasis which has been placed on developing trade relations with the Third World countries.

The growth of foreign trade was disrupted again during the Cultural Revolution(1966—1976) when agricultural and industrial production fell sharply and transportation constraints became more serious.

Foreign trade, which has a major role in the Four Modernizations programme, has grown rapidly over the past few years. A major trade agreement with Japan, under which China exports coal and oil in return for industrial equipment and technology was signed in February 1978. China also signed a long-term trade agreement with the EEC in 1978 while trade with the USA has increased rapidly in the wake of the normalisation of diplomatic relations at the beginning of 1979. The Sino-USA agreement on trade relations, which came into force in February 1980, accords China most-favoured nation treatment.

Breakdown

A commodity breakdown of China's trade shows that fuels accounted for 24 per cent of total exports in 1982, food products for 13 per cent, textile fibres and mineral ores for 7 per cent and manufactured goods (the most important products were textiles, chemicals and machinery and transport equipment) for 55 per cent. Since the founding of the People's Republic strong emphasis has been placed on importing capital equipment in order to strengthen the industrial sector. But the leading categories of imports in 1982 were food, which accounted for 22 per cent of the total, light manufactured items with a share of 20 per cent and machinery and transport equipment with 17 per cent.

During the past few years a major objective of the Chinese authorities has been to reduce the proportion of agricultural exports, while increasing that of industrial and mineral products. A wide variety of industrial goods are now exported and Chinese capital equipment has been used by a number of developing countries to establish projects in areas such as agriculture, forestry, light industry, food processing, water conservation and transport and communications.

The Balance Shifts

The US dollar value of Chinese exports increased at an average rate of almost 18 per cent per annum between 1978 and 1983, while imports increased by approximately 11 per cent pere annum. As a result, the visible trade surplus rose sharply from US $1.4 billion in 1981 to US $4.4 billion in 1982 and US $3.7 billion in 1983. Exports grew much faster than imports during this period not only because of the strong emphasis placed on exporting by China's economic planners, but also because a number of industrial projects were postponed in 1979. Official recognition that foreign technology could play a major role in modernising the Chinese economy had caused imports to rise by more than 50 per cent in 1978 placing undue strain on the national economy. Grain imports have fallen sharply over the past few years —— China became a net grain exporter in 1984 —— and in 1983 the country started to export soyabeans and cotton.

The pattern of foreign trade growth was reversed in 1984: the value of exports increased by 10 per cent, but imports jumped 38 per cent with the result that the visible trade account was in deficit by US $1.1 billion. The strong increase in imports last year is attributed to buoyant economic activity as well as to the success of the Government's trade and foreign investment policies.

Direction of Trade

Hong Kong is China's major export market accounting for approximately 26 per cent of total exports in 1983 (though much is re-exported to other destinations from there). Other important markets include Japan, with a share of 20 per cent in 1983, and the USA with approximately 8 per cent. The EEC's share of China's exports has generally been around 11—12 per cent over the past few years (the leading export markets within the European Community are Germany and the United Kingdom), while the proportion destined for the Comecon countries declined from almost 15 per cent in 1978 to 6 per cent in 1983. The non-oil developing countries (excluding Hong Kong) accounted for 23 per cent of China's total exports in 1983.

In sharp contrast the developing countries provided less than 15 per cent of China's imports in 1983. The most important suppliers among the industrial countries were Japan, with a share of 26 per cent, and the USA with 13 per cent. The EEC's share in 1983 was 15 per cent and that of Comecon 8.2 per cent.

The successful outcome to negotiations between Britain and China about the future of Hong Kong will strengthen Sino-British relations and is expected to boost trade between the two countries. A large British economic and trade delegation, headed by Lord Young, Minister without Portfolio, visited China in March. The value of Chinese exports to Britain, which rose rapidly between 1977 and 1980, declined in 1981—1982, but recovered strongly in 1983; imports from the United Kingdom followed a similar pattern. The most important Chinese exports to Britain in 1983 were clothing, textile fibres, tea and food products while the leading British exports included iron and steel, machinery and transport equipment, scientific instruments, chemicals and textile fibres.

Chinese officials stress the importance of introducing advanced technology to domestic industry, but the need is for technology of varying degrees of sophistication, not necessarily for advanced technology as that term is understood in the West.

Reserves Rise

There are no official statistics covering the invisible account of the balance of payments, but the size of the visible trade surplus during 1981—1983 and a pronounced increase in earnings from tourism suggest that the current account has been in surplus over the past few years.

Foreign exchange reserves have risen rapidly from approximately US $2.5 billion at end—1980 to US $17.0 billion (sufficient for approximately eight months' imports) by October 1984. Approximately US $12 billion of the country's reserves are held by the central bank, the People's Bank of China, while the balance is controlled by the Bank of China which specialises in foreign exchange business. Individual cities must try to balance their foreign exchange earnings and requirements, but there is some scope for purchasing additional foreign exchange with Renminbi yuan. The authorities are willing to permit a run-down in the country's international reserves over the next few years as a means of accelerating the introduction of foreign technology.

China has shown a much more flexible approach to foreign trade over the past few years and has adopted a series of measures designed to strengthen international economic co-operation. Foreign countries are encouraged to mount exhibitions of their goods and China itself has participated in a number of trade fairs and exhibitions held abroad. Since the late 1970s China has also adopted foreign trade practices long-established in many other countries. Goods are produced according to a sample provided by the customer, while strong encouragement is given to compensation trade whereby a foreign seller supplies raw materials and equipment and receives manufactured goods, produced by the equipment provided, in return. Compensation trade differs from barter or countertrade insofar as there is a direct link between the equipment supplied from abroad and the manufactured product. Assembly manufacturing began in 1978 and particular forms of foreign trade are eligible for exemption from customs duties and taxation.

Investment Encouraged

A series of polices designed to encourage foreign investment have accompanied these trade reforms. A law adopted in 1979 defines the principles governing the rights and interests of participants in joint ventures. The China International Trust and Investment Corporation (CITIC), established in 1979, co-ordinates incoming foreign investment, promotes joint ventures by assisting Chinese and foreign enterprises to find suitable business partners and also has responsibility for negotiating contracts relating to 100 per cent foreign-owned enterprises. When negotiations are complete and a joint venture contract has been agreed, it is submitted to the Ministry of Foreign Economic Relations and Trade for final approval.

China's cautious approach to foreign borrowing is to be maintained, at least for the time being. The debt problems confronting a number of developing countries have reinforced China's determination to introduce foreign technology by means of direct investment and concessionary finance rather than by raising substantial sums of money on the international capital markets. Foreign investment is advantageous insofar as it facilitates the transfer of technology and skills and avoids creating an overhang of debt. The authorities do not consider it appropriate to incur large amounts of external debt until a number of practical bottlenecks in the economy, such as an inadequate transport network and energy constraints, have been tackled. China's access to substantial sums of money from the World Bank also reduces the need to borrow on commercial terms.

China has borrowed almost US $2 billion from the World Bank and its affiliates, but a substantial proportion of these loans are still to be disbursed. Figures compiled by the OECD and the Bank for International Settlements show borrowings from western commercial banks of approximately US $2 billion, but also show that the bulk of China's foreign obligations consist of non-bank traderelated credits which exceed US $4 billion.

While there are limited lending opportunities in the short-term, there appears considerable scope for foreign banks to undertake profitable business over the longer term. The need to develop business relationships with Chinese enterprises and government officials have persuaded a large number of foreign banks to open representative offices in Beijing or other parts of China.

—From *China Now* • Spring 1985, No. 112

Words and Expressions

initially	*ad.*	最初;开头
subsequently	*ad.*	随后;后来;接着
exacerbate	*v.*	使加剧;使恶化
contract	*v.*	收缩;缩小
disrupt	*v.*	扰乱;使中断
constraint	*n.*	约束;限制
in the wake of	紧紧跟随;在…后	
accord	*v.*	授予;给予
breakdown	*n.*	分类
sector	*n.*	部分;部门
category	*n.*	种类,类
item	*n.*	项目;项
balance	*n.*	(收支等的)平衡;均衡
per annum	(拉丁语)每年	
undue	*a.*	过度的;不应有的
strain	*n.*	重负;过度的要求
reverse	*v.*	倒转;反向
in deficit	赤字;逆差	
attribute	*v.*	把…归因于;把…归于
buoyant	*a.*	趋于上升的
destination	*n.*	目的地;终点
destine	*v.*	预定;指定
decline	*v.*	下降;减少

outcome	*n.*	结果;结局
boost	*v.*	推动;提高
Lord	*n.*	(英)勋爵
recover	*v.*	恢复;复苏
instrument	*n.*	仪器
introduce	*v.*	引进
varying	*a.*	不同的;有差异的
sophistication	*n.*	(技术、产品等的)精密;高级;尖端
term	*n.*	术语;词语
statistics	*n.*	统计资料
pronounced	*a.*	显著的;明显的
earning(s)	*n.*	收益;赢利
tourism	*n.*	旅游业
suggest	*v.*	(间接地)表明;暗示
in surplus	盈余;顺差	
specialize	*v.*	专门从事
scope	*n.*	余地;机会
run-down	*n.*	减少;减缩
accelerate	*v.*	加快;增速
flexible	*a.*	灵活的
approach	*n.*	(处理问题的)方式;方法
mount	*v.*	举办;进行(活动等)
fair	*n.*	商品展览会,商品交易会
practice	*n.*	惯常做法;惯例
compensation	*n.*	补偿
assembly	*n.*	装配;组装
eligible	*a.*	在法律上合格的
exemption	*n.*	免税;免除
customs duties	关税,海关税;进口税	
taxation	*n.*	税;税收
govern	*v.*	(法律、规律、准则等)适用于;指导

approval	*n.*	批准;核准
raise (money, funds)	*v.*	筹集(款项,资金)
facilitate	*v.*	使变得(更)容易;使便利
overhang	*n.*	威胁
incur	*v.*	招致;引起
bottleneck	*n.*	阻碍进展的人(或事物、情况等);障碍
tackle	*v.*	对付;处理
access	*n.*	接近(或进入)的机会;权;享用权
affiliate	*n.*	附属机构
loan	*n.*	贷款
disburse	*v.*	支付,支出
bulk	*n.*	绝大部分;主体
obligation	*n.*	债务
credit	*n.*	信贷
enterprise	*n.*	企业单位;公司

Notes to the Text

1. China Now

由英中了解协会(the Society for Anglo-Chinese Understanding)出版的季刊。该组织成立于1956年,目的在于加强英国人民和中国人民之间的了解和友谊。

2. Barry Coulthurst 英国经济学家

他曾作为银行经济学家工作过十年,近年把研究目标转向亚洲地区。他曾于1984年随商业经济学家学社来北京参观。

3. national income 国民收入

一国从事物质生产的劳动者在一定时期(如一年)内新创造的价值或体现这部分价值的产品。劳动者在一定时期内创造出来的全部产品或价值中,扣除已消耗的生产资料或其价值,就是国民收入。其实物形式是全部消费资料和用作扩大再生产和增加后备等的生产资料。从实物形式看，国民收入因社会劳动生产率的提高和物质生产部门劳动者人数的增长而增长，是国民经济发展的总指标。

4. Comecon　经互会

Council for Mutual Economic Association（经济互助委员会）的简称，苏联和东欧国家于 1949 年 1 月成立的国际组织。其总部设在莫斯科，有 10 个成员国，即：苏联、保加利亚、波兰、民主德国、捷克斯洛伐克、罗马尼亚、匈牙利以及古巴、蒙古和越南。1991 年苏联解体，经互会失去其支柱也随之很快解散。

5. EEC (European Economic Community)　欧共体

欧洲经济共同体的简称，又名"欧洲共同市场"(European Common Market)，是西欧国家于 1958 年成立的一个经济联盟，为欧洲共同体(European Community，现改称 European Union)的组成部分。现有成员国为西德、意大利、法国、比利时、荷兰、卢森堡、丹麦、爱尔兰、英国、希腊、西班牙、葡萄牙、奥地利、瑞典和芬兰等 15 国。

6. most-favored nation treatment (status)　最惠国待遇

最惠国待遇是指在国际贸易条约中，缔约国双方在通商、航海、关税、公民法律地位等方面相互给予的不低于现时或将来给予任何第三国的优惠、特权或豁免待遇。根据关贸总协定的原则，最惠国待遇是缔约国之间贸易自由的核心，是规范缔约国之间贸易关系的基石。这一条款现也称为"正常贸易待遇(地位)"(the normal trade treatment [status])，该名称更为确切地表达了其实际内容。

按优惠待遇的给与是否附有条件，最惠国待遇可以分为"无条件"和"有条件"两种。"无条件"是指不得附加条件，避免因附加条件而使最惠国待遇失效。因此，这种最惠国待遇又称"无歧视待遇"。一般来讲，国际间采用的多是无条件最惠国待遇。"有条件"是指给最惠国待遇附加一定的条件。例如，目前美国执行中美双边贸易协定给予中国的就是有条件的最惠国待遇。

7. visible trade account　有形贸易收支

是国际收支(见注 9.)统计中经常项目(见注 11.)下的最重要的子目，也是整个国际收支统计中最重要的项目。它反映商品进出口的货币收支，具体分为进口和出口两个指标。

8. minister without portfolio　不管部长

亦称"无任所相"、"不管部阁员"、"不管大臣"、"不管部长"。不专管某一个部的事务的部长。通常是内阁阁员或部长会议成员之一，出席内阁或部长会议，参与决策，处理会议决议或总理（首相）交办的特种重要事务。

9. balance of payments　国际收支

一国对所有其他国家在一定时期内所发生的全部对外支出与收入的对比，通常包括以下各项：贸易项目，比重最大，也叫有形项目；其次是劳务收支，包括运输、保险费及银行费用等，也叫无形项目；此外还有资本项目，主要包括长期和短期的资本流动。

10. invisible account　无形贸易收支

是国际收支统计中经常项目的一个子目。指由于商品的贸易、资本往来和其他交易活动而发生的不属于有形商品收支方面的各种劳务收支。非贸易收支的内容繁多，主要包括进出口商品中的运输、保险、通讯等收支，旅游收支，投资生产的利息、股息和利润收支，以及其他一些劳务收支，如银行手续费等。

11. current account　经常项目

国际收支统计平衡表中最基本、最重要的一个项目。它包括商品进出口及劳务项目的收支。

12. central bank　中央银行

指一国银行体系中居于主导地位，负责制定和执行国家的货币信用政策，实行金融管理和监督，控制、调节货币流通与信用活动的中心金融机构。中央银行具有特殊职能：垄断银行券的发行权；集中商业银行的存款准备金，并向它们提供信贷；执行国家金融政策，代理国库，代理国家发行债券，并向国家提供贷款。

13. "Approximately US $12 billion of the country's reserves are held by the central bank, the People's Bank of China, while the balance is controlled by the Bank of China which specializes in foreign exchange business. Individual cities must try to balance their foreign exchange earnings and requirements, but there is some scope for purchasing additional foreign exchange with Renminbi yuan."

自1994年起以上所述中国外汇体制已有很大变化，取消了外汇留成和上缴实行银行结汇、售汇制，即要求外商投资以外的企业将外汇收入按当日汇价卖给银行，而当企业需要外汇时，可以持有效凭证（如进口合同）到银行用人民币兑换。

14. barter　易货贸易

不需要用货币而进行的商品和劳务的直接交换。

15. counter-trade　反向贸易

指出口人承担从进口方购买等值或其出口货值一部分金额的货物。反向贸易可以分为反向购买、补偿贸易、易货贸易以及转手贸易四种不同做法。

16. "Assembly manufacturing began in 1978 and particular forms of foreign trade are eligible for exemption from customs duties and taxation."

- "Assembly manufacturing"来件组装，是吸引外资的一种做法。如，中国企业接受外国企业提供的零部件，然后按照后者的要求将零部件组装为成品，将成品交给外方，中方获得组装费。组装产品所需的机器设备通常由外国企业提供，其成本费从组装费中扣除。
- "particular forms of foreign trade"特殊的贸易做法，这里指组装所需的零件的流入和成品的流出。
- "taxation"（入境后的）税收，在此处主要指当时征收的工商统一税。

17. joint venture　合资企业

在国际经济活动中，指两国或两国以上的投资者在一国境内根据所在国（东道国）的法律，共同投资设立的股份制企业，共同管理、共享利润、共担风险及亏损。这是一种目前在跨国公司中非常流行的所有权分享形式。

18. concessionary finance

指中国进口大型工程项目经常采用的由卖方提供某些方便的付款方式，如延期付款。延期付款主要用于进口整个工厂或用资巨大的设备，用于购买工厂和设备的大部分款项可以在交货几年之后再付。

19. the World Bank and its affiliates　世界银行及其附属机构

国际复兴和开发银行通称为世界银行。世界银行与其两个附属机构，即国际开发协会和国际金融公司，合称为世界银行集团。

世界银行成立于 1945 年 12 月，1946 年 6 月开始营业，是联合国的一个专门机构。世界银行总部设在美国华盛顿，主要业务活动是对成员国政府或经政府担保的私人企业提供贷款和技术援助。银行成立初期，贷款重点放在欧洲经济复兴，后转向以发展中国家为重点的各种开发项目。在对发展中国家提供贷款方面，主要是通过提供长期贷款资助他们兴建某些建设周期长，利润率偏低但又为该国经济和社会发展所必需的建设项目。世界银行的资金主要通过在国际市场上发行债券以及成员国按比例认缴股金来筹集。

国际金融公司主要是向发展中国家在经济上具有重要意义的私营生产性企业进行直接投资，而不需其本国政府担保。

国际开发协会主要是向发展中国家的公共工程和发展项目提供优惠贷款。

20. OECD (Organization for Economic Co-operation and Development)　经济合作和发展组织

西方国家政府间的联合组织，1961 年成立，会员国近 30 个，包括美、英、法、德、日等。该组织旨在研究、规划会员国经济增长、充分就业和发展贸易等问题，有多种出版物，总部设在巴黎。

21. Bank for International Settlements　国际清算银行

国际清算银行是英、法、德、意、比、日六国的中央银行与美国摩根保证信托公司、纽约花旗银行和芝加哥花旗银行组成的银行集团投资合办的国际金融机构，开业于 1930 年 5 月 20 日，行址设在瑞士巴塞尔，现有 30 个国家的中央银行和其他金融机构参加。银行主要是同各国中央银行往来。其主要业务项目是办理存款、放款、贴现业务、买卖黄金、外汇和债券，和有关国家的政府或中央银行签订特别协议，代办国际清算业务等。

国际清算银行成立时最初的目的是帮助处理德国和第一次世界大战中的其他战败国向战胜国的赔偿事宜，并以此命名。

22. non-bank trade related credits　指买方信贷，卖方信贷等

为了促进出口，解决出口商以延期付款方式卖出设备时所遇到的资金周转困难，由出口商所在国银行向出口商所提供的低利优惠贷款，即为卖方信贷。在大型机械及成套设备等资本货物出口贸易中，由出口商所在国银行为进口商或通过进口商所在国银行向进口商提供的旨在扩大贷款国资本货物出口的低利优惠贷款，即为买方信贷。两者都是政府鼓励出口政策的部分。

Questions on Content and Language Points

(for preview, discussion and review)

1. What's the meaning of "the pattern of China's foreign trade"? (Please go through all the first section before giving your answer.)

2. What kind of clause is introduced by "when" in the sentence of the third paragraph, section 1? An adverbial clause or an attributive one?

3. "Official recognition that foreign technology could play a major role in modernising the Chinese economy had caused imports to rise by more than 50 per cent in 1978 placing undue strain on the national economy."

Why did the more than 50% rise in imports of 1978 place undue strain on China's national economy?

4. What's "a net grain exporter"? Does it mean one who has never done any imports?

5. "The strong increase in imports last year is attributed to buoyant economic activity as well as to the success of the Government's trade and foreign investment policies."

What did China's foreign investment policies have to do with her strong increase in imports?

6. "Chinese officials stress the importance of introducing advanced technology to domestic industry, but the need is for tech-

nology of varying degrees of sophistication, not necessarily for advanced technology as the term is understood in the West."

What's the implication of the underlined part of the paragraph quoted above?

7. "The authorities do not consider it appropriate to incur large amounts of external debt until a number of practical bottlenecks in the economy, such as an inadequate transport network and energy constraints, have been tackled."

Why did China refuse to borrow more until their transport capacity and energy supply have further increased?

8. "China's access to substantial sums of money from the World Bank also reduces the need to borrow on commerial terms."

What does "borrow on commercial terms" imply here? And why does China prefer loans from the World Bank?

Topics for Summary

1. What were China's major achievements in foreign trade in the 1978—1984 period, according to the text?

2. What were the problems during this period?

3. What would be your suggestions to further improve the situation?

Exercises

Read the article and do the following true-and-false questions:

China Leaps Towards Top 10 Traders

Tony Walkeer looks at the pressures accompanying rapid export growth

China this year is expected to enter the "top ten" of the world's trading nations, leapfrogging Taiwan and South Korea in the process. But China's extraordinary export growth is also bringing increased pressures for liberalisation and improved access to its markets.

Sensitive to these pressures, emanating mainly from the US, whose trade deficit with China in 1992 reached $18bn, Chinese officials have promised to quicken the pace of reform. One of China's main aims is to rejoin the General Agreement on Tariffs and Trade as soon as practicable, perhaps this year.

The Chinese see early Gatt membership as one way of dealing with bilateral pressures from its main trading partners—the US, Japan and Germany—all of which are restive about their yawning trade gaps with China.

China's powerful Ministry of Foreign Economic Relations and Trade will be monitoring trade signals from the new Clinton administration, expected to be less tolerant of the imbalance than its predecessor. Congress has also signalled a growing restiveness on the China trade issue.

An early indication of the state of China—US trade relations is likely to come in the next few weeks when officials of the office of the Special Trade Representative—the first high-level Clinton team to come to Beijing—sit down to discuss GATT-related issues.

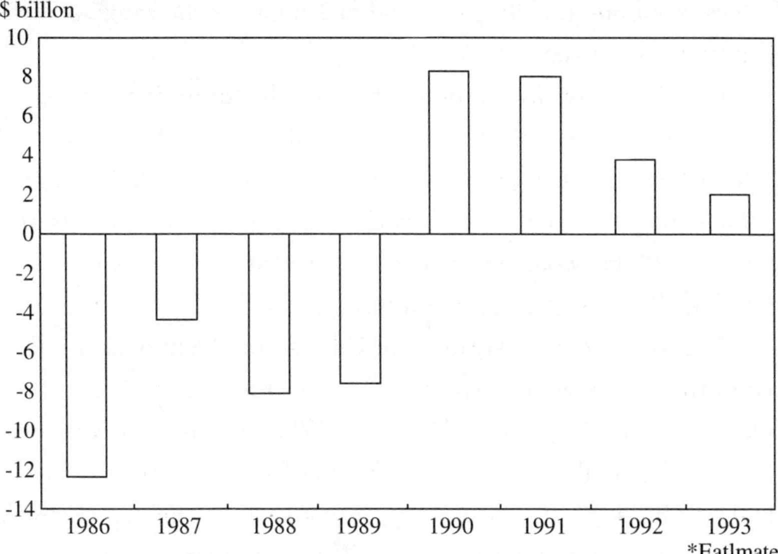

Japan and China have agreed to start bilateral negotiations on tariffs on Japanese goods, to help Beijing's re-entry into the General Agreement on Tariffs and Trade (GATT), a Foreign Ministry official said, Reuter reports from Tokyo.

This is the first time China will have such negotiations with a G7 country, the official said. Date for the talks is not yet fixed. Officials from the two governments met in Beijing over the weekend for a regular two-day meeting to exchange views on bilateral trade issues.

The US officials are certain to press their Chinese counterparts to speed liberalisation in line with the US-China market agreement reached last October. Under this, Beijing agreed over the next few years to remove about 75 per cent of its non-tariff barriers on a global Most Favoured Nation (MFN) basis.

US trade representatives are also reporting that China is making a special effort to discuss new projects. Since the end of 1989, American businessmen have been returning to China with "zest", according to a US official.

But the larger deals in the petrochemical, power and transport sectors will take time to bring to fruition. In the meantime, the Chinese continue rapidly to expand and improve the range and the quality of their exports.

Progress made by China in the past decade is impressive. A decade ago, China ranked 20th as a world trader. Then exports of $18bn represented 4 per cent of Gross Domestic Product (GDP) and less than one per cent of world trade. Projected exports this year of $100bn would represent 20 per cent of China's GDP and more than 2.5 per cent of world trade.

The growing sophistication of Chinese products is also reflected in the shift towards exports of manufactured items from 50 per cent in 1980 to 80 per cent last year. While China's success owes much to cheap labour costs—textiles and footwear accounted for one third of 1992's $85bn in exports—exports of machinery, electronic products and transport equipment are the fastest growing areas.

High foreign investment in capital intensive areas spawned an increase of about 86 per cent in exports of machinery and transport equipment in the first nine months of 1992, compared with 1991. Trade in these items accounted for 16 per cent of exports last year, compared with just 6 per cent in 1988.

The contribution to China's booming trade in 1992 of Special Economic Zones andcoastal cities opened to foreign investment was also notable. Industrial output in these areas increased by 72 per cent in the first half of 1992 compared with 1991 and the bulk or this was directed towards exports.

In their difficult discussions with representatives of their main trading partners, Chinese officials are certain to point out that in spite of China's export boom, the country is also coping with a surge in imports. Imports are expected to grow by 19 per cent this year to $96bn, compared with projected growth in exports of 16 per cent to around $98.5bn.

Western trade officials say the Chinese are becoming more concerned about their shrinking trade surplus, down to $4.4bn last year, and its impact on the country's reserves. Curbing import growth is certain to be linked to problems associated with an overheating economy, which registered 12 per cent growth last year, and a risk of inflation.

However, curbs on imports would run counter to Chinese undertakings to further liberalise its trade regime in preparation for its re-entry to GATT.

——From *Financial Times*. Feb. 16, 1993

True—and—false questions:

1. Before entering the "top 10" of the world's trading nations, China was behind Taiwan and South Korea. ( )

2. China concerned a great deal over her trade surplus with the U.S. ( )

3. As China is a developing country, her main trading partners wouldn't care much about their trade imbalance with China. ( )

4. The Clinton administration acted more friendly than the previous one though it had harsh words about China. ( )

5. The U.S. officials would require their Chinese counterparts to open China's markets for American goods at a more rapid pace. ( )

6. Years after 1989, most American businessmen refrained themselves from coming to China. ( )

7. Big deals in the petrochemical, power and transport sectors would see little progress in a long time if improvement in exports' quality didn't take place. ( )

8. Textiles and footwear had accounted for quite a large percentage of China's total exports and were still growing the fastest. ( )

9. Most of the goods produced in the special economic zones

and the coastal open cities were sold abroad. ( )

10. Chinese officials might use the increasing volume of imports as an effective means to defend China in the negotiations with her main trading partners. ( )

11. China entered the "top 10" of the world's trading nations in 1997. ( )

Supplementary Material for Free Reading

A. China's Import Growth Rate Exceeds Export Growth in 1998

1. Review of foreign trade in 1997

In 1997, China's foreign trade realized a rapid growth rate of 12.1 per cent after low-speed growth in 1996. An export growth rate of 20.9 per cent combined with an import growth rate of 2.5 per cent led to a favorable trade balance of US $40.34 billion, but produced new problems related to an imbalance in trade activities. The export structure has been effectively adjusted, spurring new development trends in foreign trade. China entered the top 10 trading nations in the world last year.

The development momentum of China's foreign trade is the result of improvements to the foreign trade management system and enterprise operation mechanisms. The unitary and closed foreign trade operation pattern has been changed. Pluralisticoperations are stimulating foreign trade. Global economic development is creating many opportunities for growth in China's foreign trade.

During the past few years, especially in 1996, China's foreign trade experienced unsteady development, slow structural adjustments, and a lack of high-tech and high added-value products. Problems in the quality of imports and exports are driven by a faulty foreign trade control and operation mechanism. The financial crisis in East Asia, economic growth in South Asia, and rapid expansion in Latin America has altered the global economic pattern and brought massive new challenge to China's exports. Trade and investment liberalization will aggravate the competition on the domestic and international markets.

2. Analysis and forecast of export situation in 1998

In terms of export policy environments in 1998, the reform of China's foreign trade mechanism required by the socialist market economy will progress with new changes in the administrative functions of the government and service functions of nongovernmental market coordination organs, including foreign trade intermediate organs, industry associations and chambers of commerce, thus enhancing reform and coordinating the development of management, operations and services. Related laws and regulations concerning exports will be improved. More productive enterprises will enjoy foreign trade autonomy. Policies that encourage active, rational and effective use of foreign investment will guide foreign-funded enterprises to make full use of their export superiority to expand exports. Under this circumstance, pluralistic competition patterns and various foreign trade bodies will develop, bringing about more new growth points. Also, industrial policies set to optimize industry structure will be strengthened and further implemented. By means of support and preferential policies, the State will encourage the development of backbone industries that display strong competitiveness in international markets, hi-tech industries and capital-intensive industries. Policies that encourage exports will be further implemented. Under these premises, the State will adjust export policies in line with its macroeconomic development program. New foreign trade policies are beginning to play active roles. They have raised tax rebates for textiles and will continue the effort to bring about a zero-rate terminally so as to reduce export costs. The policy environments in 1998 will work to foster growth in exports. International and domestic markets are revealing the following favorable factors. First, importing countries are continuing to raise demand for Chinese products. Second, domestic production capacity has been upgraded although domestic investment and consumption are still limited. Foreign markets are currently the only outlet for some elements of Chinese production. Third, inflation was kept under control in 1997. All indications are that prices will continue to be stable during 1998. The costs of production, and therefore the costs of exports, will not rise much, allowing Chinese enterprises to improve competitiveness on the international scene. However the international market has given rise to some negative impacts on China's exports. The financial crisis that shock Southeast Asia in July of 1997 has caused many natoins in the region to devaluate their currencies. This has led to a new level of competition within the region. China's traditional mainstay exports are being threatened since 40 per cent of China's exports are to East Asia. The devaluation of the Yen has hurt Chinese exports to Japan. A large share of the processing and assembling activities in China and around East Asia will be seriously affected by the currency devaluation. The financial turmoil has had a massive impact on many sectors of the economy, leading to reductions of economic growth in many countries. The impact on export growth is still uncertain. Therefore, China cannot afford to be optimistic about the short-term situation. Thailand, Indonesia, and the Philippines seem to be recovering. However, China's export growth rate of 24. 5 per cent in the first half of 1997 fell to an annual average of 20. 9 per cent. In January of 1998, export growth dropped further, with an increase of only 8. 8 percentage points over the same period in 1997. The reductions are expected to continue. The export growth rate is expected to hover at 5 per cent in 1998. Normal trade will decrease greatly although processing trade will continue to rise. The State-owned foreign trade enterprises will lag behind foreign-funded enterprises in exports. However, the export of electrical machinery produced through assembly and processing will maintain its development momentum, and exports to Europe, North America and South America will experience an increase.

3. Analysis and forecast of import situation in 1998

The policy environment for imports in 1998 is evidently better than in 1997. First of all, the slump in import brought about a favorable trade volume and the situation will progress, thus further intensifying trade friction between China and its main trade partners. China pays close attention to keeping a balance and so adopted effective policy measures to stimulate import demand. On October 1, 1997, China's average import tariff was lowered to 17 per cent, a move that will surely effect trade in 1998. In 1998, China will not rule out the possibility of further lowering tariffs to an average of 15 per cent in developing countries as it promised the international community so as to meet the demands of the global economy. Beginning on December 31, 1997, China canceled control efforts over 13 import categories and reduced non-tariff trade barriers. After canceling exemptions for foreign-funded enterprises and reducing tariffs on their imported equipment and value-added taxes on import in April of 1996, new foreign-funded projects decreased sharply. In order to actively and effectively utilize foreign capital and encourage investment in hi-tech, infrastructure and export-oriented enterprises in China, the government resumed those preferential policies towards foreign-funded projects that complied in the national industrial policy and the Directory of Foreign-Funded Industries. These moves went into effect on January 1, 1998. Reductions in equipment imports by foreign-funded enterprises in 1997 have impacted development trends. Against the background of currency devaluation in East Asia. China will continue to stabilize Renminbi as a means of stimulating imports from Japan, South Korea and throughout East Asia.

The exports by the processing trades have developed rapidly. This will surely stir an increase in demand for imports. To lower export prices in East Asia will also benefit import growth. But the negative factors hindering import may actually play a positive role. Weak demands on the domestic market, especially weak investment demands, will lead to slow growth in imports. If the policy works effectively, the market factors hindering import growth will be controlled in a certain extent. It is predicted that the import growth rate will reach 10—15 per cent in 1998, a little higher than the export level.

4. Forecast of foreign trade balance in 1998

Calculated on the basis of 5 per cent for export growth and 10 per cent for import growth, China's export volume will reach US $192 billion while imports rise to US $158 billion. The gross foreign trade volume will be US $350 billion, an increase of about 7.7 per cent over 1997. The favorable trade volume will be US $34 billion, falling 15.7 per cent from the level in 1997. The trade balance between China and its principal trading partners will also change. It is possible that trade with Japan may actually shift to a marginal unfavorable balance. The favorable balance with the United States will be expanded, as will trade with European Union in the wake of the first year of favorable trade with that region — US $4.62 billion in 1997. The unfavorable balance will be exacerbated between China and South Korea and Taiwan. On the whole, the favorable trade balance with the United States may cause new trade friction, leading to low growth rate of export in 1998. This will be the main feature of China's foreign trade development in 1998.

Zhao Jinping
Development Research Center of the State Council
——From *China's Foreign Trade* • June, 1998

B. "Greater China" on the March

Without fanfare or formality, southern China, Taiwan and Hong Kong are forming an informal regional trading block. This Chinese Economic Area(CEA), or greater China, is a little-noticed but fast-growing power in world trade. It threatens to become an even mightier one.

China's economy is two and a half times as big as Taiwan's and more than six times bigger than Hong Kong's, but all three are equally mathched as traders with developed countries. Stripping out their trade with each other, the trio now collectively accounts for 4. 5 per cent of world trade—about the same share as France or Britain. Only the United States, Germany and Japan have a substantially bigger share. In 1980 greater China accounted for just 1. 8 per cent of world trade. Thanks to fast growth of its manufactured exports, the CEA is the third largest supplier to the United States, after Canada and Japan. It has also become a leading market for the United States and Japan. Other Asian dragons, such as Singapore and Thailand, are having to cut their export prices to stay competitive.

If the CEA can maintain its rapid growth for another generation—which Asia's other dragons managed at a similar stage of development—then it will likely have a bigger share of world trade than Japan by the end of the century—and be a bigger trading nation than even the United States in less than 40 years. Do not, though, get carried too far ahead of events by such extrapolations. Today, California is a larger economy than greater China.

Unlike the negotiated trade blocks of Europe and North America, greater China is being knitted together by businessmen rather than politicians. One third of the trio's total trade is now among themselves, triple the level 15 years ago when China embarked on its economic reforms. Investment, financial and technological links have grown even faster. China and Hong Kong are the biggest direct investors in each other; Taiwan is the fourth biggest investor in China. Hong Kong is both a source of debt and equity capital for China. Even a 40-year ban on Taiwanese sending money to China was lifted in 1990.

Potent mix: Taiwan's capital and technical and managerial knowhow, China's cheap labor and natural resources and the skilled financial and commercial middlemen of Hong Kong—all held together by strong family and cultural ties—make for a potent mix. They have also helped make China's transition from a planned economy so much smoother than in the former Soviet Union. What next? A common currency, perhaps? Well, 20 per cent of Hong Kong's currency is already circulating in southern China.

——From *News Week* • Feb. 15, 1993

Three Become One

- Trade: China was an $8 billion export market for Hong Kong in 1992. China-Taiwan trade rose from $50 million in 1978 to $7 billion in 1992.
- Investment: Hong Kong and China are the biggest direct investors in each other at $9 billion each. Taiwan firms have put $3 billion into China.
- Finance: Four fifths of China's big commercial loans are raised in Hong Kong. Taiwanese have remitted $120 million to China since 1990.
- Jobs: Hong Kong firms employ up to 3 million workers in Guangdong.

Lesson 2

China's Absorption of Foreign Direct Investment

Text

The Curtain Goes up

Peking permits foreign investment all along its coastline —creating differing rules and added confusion

By Mary Lee in Beijing

A clearly confident China has rolled up a large section of its bamboo curtain, declared itself "open to the outside world" and hung signs on nearly all its cities inviting foreign investors to come and do serious business.

The four special economic zones (SEZs) in Guangdong and Fujian provinces, 14 coastal cities (all former treaty ports) and Hainan island (19 "open" areas in all) have specifically designed tax and other incentives for the foreign investor. But every provincial capital is doing its best to attract foreign investment.

The foundation for all this was assembled in piecemeal form, beginning in mid—1979 with the State Council's decision to set up four SEZs in the south. Then a joint-venture law was published for the first time (albeit one full of holes), quickly followed by procedures for "compensation trade"——both of which were designed to attract foreign investment to these four zones. The following year, a tax law for joint ventures was promulgated.

But even as businessmen battled with bureaucracy in an effort to fulfil their hopes of doing business with a potential market of 1 billion people, Chinese leaders were growing impatient with the rate of progress in the showpiece SEZ—Shenzhen.

In April 1984, after the country's top leaders had visited the Shenzhen, Zhuhai and Xiamen SEZs, the State Council declared 14 cities along the entire coast plus Hainan island open to foreign investment, thus introducing a real element of competition into the country's economic-development programme. Then came the much-publicised "decision on reform of the economic structure" and suddenly, the race to get foreign technology and funds was on.

For foreign investors, the prospect of having access to a market of 1 billion consumers no longer seems like a pipedream. The Chinese—in particular the rural population—are getting richer and now want visible improvements to their standard of living: they aspire to own colour TV sets, refrigerators, trucks, washing machines and better radios, bicycles and clothing. Even local factories are taking note of the vast potential sales in their own domestic market.

Recently, State Councillor Gu Mu, head of the China Coastal Cities Economic and Technical Development Corp. (CCETDC)—the policymaking and coordinating body for the 19 "open areas"—reportedly pronounced the entire coast open to foreign investment. Taken literally, this does not make much sense as the parts of the coast which have not been "opened" are simply not ready for the demands of foreign businessman. In fact, Shantou among the SEZs, and some of the 14 coastal cities plus Hainan are not even equipped with administrative support or infrastructure to cope with the responsibilities which the central government has placed on them.

A well-placed source within the CCETDC said Gu in fact was referring to the 19 areas which had been officially opened. The strategy, he said, was a long-term one, to transfer the SEZs' experience with new industry to the 14 cities and Hainan, at the same time as this experience was being shared with the country's inner regions. *

The central government's determination to raise the level of industrial technology is clearly behind the decision to open the 14 coastal cities. In addition, China is now ready to spend US $14.2 billion of its foreign-exchange reserves (which stood at US $16.5 billion in June 1984) to buy foreign technology. The Bank of China has also said that new and more flexible loan policies will enable "thousands" of domestic enterprises to borrow foreign exchange to import equipment and repay in Renminbi.

The need to upgrade industrial equipment is great: official figures show that in 1980, 20% of China's capital stock was already 10—20 years behind that of the West. Another 20%—while technologically backward—worked well, but the remaining 60% should have been scrapped or renovated. The combined industrial output of the 15 coastal areas is reportedly equal to a quarter of the nation's total.

But while the reasons for throwing 19 areas and cities open to foreign investment and technology transfer are clear, how the preferential systems will operate is not. This is due largely to the intensity of competition among the 19, coupled with the inexperience of most local authorities both in making decisions and in dealing with the outside world. However, there are important differences between the SEZs and the coastal cities and even among the coastal cities themselves.

In the SEZs, which are being built almost from scratch, for-

---

* Further to the establishment of the 4 SEZs and the opening of the 14 coastal cities and Hainan island, the Yantze River and Pearl River deltas and the triangular area in southern Fujian Province were declared open in 1985, and in 1988 China's coastal open region was extended once more with the cities and counties encircleed therein increased from 144 to 284 and the population from 90 million to 160 million, including Shenyang, Nanjing, and Hangzhou.

With the rapid and brilliant progress in pursuing her reform and open-door policy, China continues opening more areas for absorbing foreign direct investment. Till 1995, the zones added covered the inland border areas with 5 690 000 sq. kilometers in area and over 200 million in population, the belts along the Yangtze River (ranging from Pu Dong, Shanghai via Wuban to Chongqing), the regions along the country's trunk railway lines, and the inland 14 central cities (all provincial capitals).

eigners can invest in anything which the state deems useful for the country, be it, for example, production of goods for export or construction of private-housing estates. These can be joint ventures, co-operative enterprises or wholly foreign-owned operations. Because every factory or business established in the SEZs is new, imports of capital and consumer goods (except cigarettes and liquor) are exempted from customs duties, and a uniform 15% income-tax rate is applied.

In the coastal cities, only factories where plant is being upgraded by foreign investment, enjoy the 15% tax rate (or less for target projects such as transport, energy and telecommunications). Only "key equipment and other materials necessary for technical transformation which cannot be readily obtainable in China" will enjoy exemptions from customs duties prior to 1990, according to Gu.

However, each coastal city also has been granted the right to establish an Economic and Technical Development Zone (ETDZ) outside the city centre, which will offer a uniform tax rate of 15% for all projects and waive the usual 10% profit-remittance tax.

Only the ETDZ in Shanghai (one of the 14 coastal cities) enjoys the same status as the four SEZs. This means that if an enterprise is within the zone, it will enjoy the preferential tax rate of 15%. A joint venture outside the Zone—involving the setting up of a new factory, and not the upgrading of an existing one—is liable to the standard 33% tax rate. Tourist enterprises and any other service industry outside the zone—as with similar projects outside the SEZs—are not entitled to any special status.

The major source of confusion for foreign investors, however, is not the tax rate but who has the authority to approve projects. The municipal governments of Tianjin and Shanghai have the power to approve projects each costing no more than US $30 million. Dalian and Canton have the power to approve projects of less than US$10 million each, and the other 10 cities may approve projects involving less than US $5 million.

One official who is well aware of the confusion afflicting both local authorities and foreign investors is Jing Shuping, president of China International Economic Consultants Inc. which is the consultancy arm of the China International Trust and Investment Corp. The various cities and zones, he said, must discover their own special characteristics, strengths and weaknesses.

"We want to stir up the enthusiasm of the grassroots units—the enterprises—to get things done," he said. "We are only just beginning, so the confusion is natural. But if we start putting too many rules and regulations (in an effort to introduce some order to the situation) they will get discouraged. The time will come when the cities and zones will ask for help in coordinating their efforts."*

Another source of confusion for the investor lies in the fact that in Guangdong, for instance, there are three SEZs and two "open" areas, Canton and Hainan island. There have been recent complaints from the Hainan government on interference from Canton (the provincial capital) on the exercise of its authority.

So, while a comprehensive framework for the country's modernisation has been provided by the central committee's 21 October 1984 decision to reform the economic structure, it will be some time before the dust settles and local authorities and foreign investors can deal with one another in a systematic way. The mountainous bureaucracy facing foreign businessmen has yet to be reduced effectively, despite promises by government.

What foreign businessmen find encouraging is that ideology is no longer in the driver's seat, having been deftly removed with the slogan

---

* In addition to Shanghai and Tianjin, many more local governments are authorized to approve projects each costing as much as US $30 million since 1988. They include Liaoning, Hebei, Shandong, Jiangsu, Zhejiang, Fujian, Hainan, Guangdong, Guangxi provinces (all the coastal ones) and Beijing.

"Socialism with Chinese characteristics" and replaced by entrepreneurship. Enterprises wholly owned by foreigners are now allowed. Even the oft-repeated phrase "public ownership of the means of production" has been amended with the passage of a law on inheritance which protects private ownership of capital equipment—another way of saying that individuals can now own the means of production.

Stock-taking of the open policy will come later this year when the National People's Congress discusses the seventh five-year plan, which will run to the end of the decade.

——From *Far Eastern Economic Review* · 31 Jan., 1985

Words and Expressions

section　　*n.* 部分
former　　*a.* 以前的;旧时的
specially　　*ad.* 明确地;特别地
tax　　*n.* 税
incentive　　*n.* 刺激;鼓励
attract　　*v.* 吸引
assemble　　*v.* 汇集;形成
piecemeal　　*ad.* 一件一件地;逐渐地
State Council　　国务院
joint-venture　　合资企业
albeit　　*conj.* 尽管
procedure　　*n.* 程序;手续
promulgate　　*v.* 颁布;公布
potential　　*a.* 潜在的
showpiece　　*n.* 优秀样品;展出之事物
publicize　　*v.* 引起公众对…注意;(尤指用广

	告)宣传
fund	*n.* 资金
prospect	*n.* 前景
pipe dream	*n.* 白日梦;幻想
aspire	*v.* 渴望
vast	*a.* 巨大的
state councilor	国务委员
pronounce	*v.* 宣布;宣告
administrative	*a.* 管理的;行政的
infrastructure	*n.* 基础设施
cope (with)	*v.* (成功地)应付;(妥善地)处理
strategy	*n.* 战略
long-term	*a.* 长期的
transfer	*v.* 搬;使转移
inner regions	内地
foreign-exchange reserves	外汇储备
repay	*v.* 偿还;付还(钱)
upgrade	*v.* 提高;改善
remaining	*a.* 剩余的;其余的
scrap	*v.* 刮(擦)净;除掉
renovate	*v.* 革新;更新
technology transfer	技术转让
intensity	*n.* 强烈;激烈
(to start) from scratch	从零(开始)
deem	*v.* 认为;相信
estate	*n.* 地产;财产
wholly foreign-owned	外商独资拥有的
operation	*n.* 企业
business	*n.* 工商企业
capital goods	资本货物
consumer goods	消费品

liquor	*n.* 酒类
uniform	*a.* (税收、法律等)一样的;一致的
plant	*n.* 全套设备
readily	*ad.* 无困难地;容易地
prior (to)	*ad.* 在…之前
grant	*v.* 给予;授予
waive	*v.* 放弃;不坚持要求
profit-remittance	利润汇款
status	*n.* 地位
preferential tax rate	优惠税率
be liable to	有义务的;应付(税)的
entitle (to)	*v.* 给…权利;给…资格
authority	*n.* 权;权利
approve	*v.* 批准;核准
municipal	*a.* 市(政)的
afflict	*v.* 使苦恼;折磨
consultant	*n.* 顾问
consultancy	*n.* (承接咨询业务的)顾问服务公司
strengths and weaknesses	优缺点
stir (up)	*v.* 激起;鼓励
grassroots	*a.* 群众的;基层的
complaint	*n.* 抱怨;抗议
interference	*n.* 干预;扰乱
exercise	*v.* (官能、力量、权利等的)行使;运用;执行
comprehensive	*a.* 广泛的;综合的
framework	*n.* 准则
has yet to	有待
ideology	*n.* 思想意识

in the driver's seat	处于统治(或控制)地位
deftly	*ad.* 机敏地
remove	*v.* 移开;挪走
entrepreneurship	*n.* 企业家精神
oft-repeated	反复说的
means of production	生产资料
amend	*v.* 修改;修订
inheritance	*n.* 继承权
protect	*v.* 保护
stock-taking	盘货;评估、估量
National People's Congress	全国人民代表大会

Notes to the Text

1. Far Eastern Economic Review 《远东经济评论》

报道和评论东亚和东南亚政治、商业、金融及其他新闻的周刊,为远东最具权威性及影响最大的新闻周刊之一。该杂志于1946年创刊,在香港出版,主要刊登关于这一地区发展的文章和关于地区以外影响本地区的发展的文章。该杂志评论的立场明显倾向于自由贸易市场经济,大体上类似于英国的《经济学人》和《华尔街日报》的观点。

2. bamboo curtain 竹幕

第二次世界大战后,西方某些政客、报人曾以"铁幕国家"(iron curtain country)称呼苏联和其他东欧社会主义国家,意指这些国家为阻止本国人民同西方进行交流,特别是政治和意识形态的交流,设置了障碍。后又以"竹幕"污蔑中国,用意相同。

本文句"China has rolled up a large section of its bamboo curtain"中的"bamboo curtain",意指中国多年来由于各种历史原因造成的经济上闭关自守的状况。

3. The Special Economic Zone (SEZ) 经济特区

国际上通常把自由贸易区、自由港、出口加工区、自由边境区、边境区等凡属各国在对外经济贸易中采取特殊政策的地区统称为经济特区。

我国的经济特区是兼有自由贸易区和出口加工区功能的综合性特定地区。

为了与世界各国发展贸易、经济合作和技术交流，中国政府在1979年7月划定广东省深圳、珠海、汕头和福建省厦门为经济特区。1988年海南省又被辟为第五个经济特区。在这些经济特区内，中国政府给予投资者在税收、土地的使用和出入境管理等方面以特殊的优惠。

4. "14 coastal cities (all former treaty ports)" 沿海开放城市

1) 1984年，中共中央国务院决定将大连、秦皇岛、天津、烟台、青岛、连云港、南通、上海、宁波、温州、福州、广州、湛江、北海14个沿海港口城市列为对外开放城市。上述沿海开放城市是我国沿海对外开放的前沿地区。其主要任务是把自身具有的工业基础较好、生产技术水平较高、科技力量较强的优势，同吸收外资、引进国外的先进技术结合起来，改造老企业，更新传统产品，开发新技术，推动科技进步和经济发展。

2) all former treaty ports 在此文章中指那些在清代末年被迫对外开放并按照帝国主义强加于中国的条约进行贸易的港口。事实上，并不是所有14个城市都是以前的通商口岸，其中大多数是。

5. "The four special economic zones ..., 14 coastal cities ... and Hainan Island ... have specially designed tax and other incentives for the foreign investors."

这些适用于开放地区外资的特别规定包括：1) 低率征收企业所得税；2) 降低或全部免除进出口税，工商统一税以及其他投资所需器材及材料和投资商私人所用物品及汇出利润等方面应征的税；3) 降低土地使用费，等等。

1993年中国的税制金融改革取消了原为外商专设的"工商统一税"，从1994年1月1日起，内外资企业统一实行增值税、消费税和营业税。但原有的鼓励外商投资的税收和优惠政策原则上保留不变，继续施行。

6. capital stock

capital stock 在不同的情况下意思也不尽相同。在这里指的是实际资本(非货币资本)——用于从事物质生产的各种资本货物，和"全部实际资本"(capital stock, real)同义。一个国家的实际资本包括它所有的铁路、公路、港口设备、发电站、水坝、工农业机器设备、工具及原料等，全部实际资本是上述各种设施、设备及物资的总和。在本文中其具体所指是工业机器设备。

7. cooperative enterprise　合作(经营)企业

外国和本国投资者根据东道国有关法律以各自法人的身份共同签订合作经营合同，在合同中规定合作各方的投资条件、风险方式、经营方式、收益分配等权益和义务的投资方式，亦称契约式合营。与合资经营企业(joint venture)不同，在合作经营中，决定双方权益和义务的基础是合同，而不是股权，而合同条款均由合作者自行商定，故具灵活多样，适应性强的特点。契约式合营通常有两种基本方式："法人式"合作经营和"非法人式"合作经营。前者指合作各方通过契约组成统一的合营经济实体，具有东道国的法人资格，并拥有独立的财产处置权(合作各方的投资归独立的法人所有和支配)；后者是指合作各方通过契约仅组成一个松散的合作经营联合体，不具有东道国单一的法人资格。这种合作经营组织有自己独立的财产所有权和处置权，资产所有权仍然归合作各方自己所有。

8. "... only the ETDZ in Shanghai enjoys the same status as the four SEZs."

1) ETDZ (Economic & Technical Development Zone)经济技术开发区：指以中外合资、合作和外商独资企业为主，重点发展知识密集型和技术密集型工业项目，对投资者实行类似经济特区优惠政策的国家设立的开发经济技术的区域。

2) 引文所指为当时上海已然成立的如：闵行、虹桥、漕河泾开发区等。

3) 1990 年国务院批准上海市开发和开放浦东新区，为吸引外资提供更为优厚的条件。浦东迅速成为国内外资本投向的热点。其优惠政策主要是:第一,允许外国企业在浦东新区开办百货商店、超级市场等第三产业。第二,允许上海设立证券交易所,为浦东开发自行审批发行人民币股票和B种股票。第三,在浦东新区外高桥设立中国开放度最大的保税区。在这个区域内,实行免关税,免许可证,允许设立内资、外资国际贸易机构,企业外汇全额留成,各国货币自由流通等特别优惠的政策。第四,在浦东新区兴办生产性或非生产性项目,及企业自营进出口业务等方面,中央给予上海更大的自主审批权。浦东新区对合资企业和外国企业税收方面的优惠包括:免征关税,免征和减征所得税,利润汇出和再投资的优惠。中国其他地区向浦东投资也享有税收方面一定的优惠。

9. "There have been recent complaints from the Hainan government on interference from Canton (the provincial capital) on the exercise of its authority."

1987年9月,全国人民代表大会常务委员会同意了国务院将海南地区划为一个独立省份的提议并决定将此提议交第七届全国人民代表大会通过。1988年4月,七届全国人民代表大会第一次会议采纳了此项提议,自此海南以省建制。

10. entrepreneurship 企业家的特性、精神

所谓企业家,就是自主地作出经营决策并承担经营风险的企业管理者。一个企业家必须在以下几个方面有坚持不懈的创新:(1)新产品的创造,(2)新技术的运用,(3)新市场的开拓,(4)新资源的开发,(5)新文化的培养,(6)新产业的组建。

Questions on Content and Language Points

(for preview, discussion and review)

1. "A clearly confident China has rolled up a large section of its bamboo curtain, declared itself 'open to the outside world' and hung signs on nearly all its cities inviting foreign investors to come and do serious business."

In what is China confident in opening the country to the

outside world?

2. "The four special economic zones (SEZs) in Guangdong and Fujian provinces, 14 coastal cities (all former treaty ports) and Hainan island (19 "open" areas in all) have specifically designed tax and other incentives for the foreign investor."

What part of the sentence is the word tax here?

3. Why was foreign direct investment considered "a real element of competition" in "the country's economic-development programme"?

4. Could you find a substitute for the word race in "the race to get foreign technology and funds"?

5. "The Chinese ... aspire to own color TV sets, refrigerators, trucks, washing machines and better radios, bicycles and clothing."

What is implied by using the word "better"? (Does "better" refer merely to the quality of goods here, or something more?)

6. "Even local factories are taking note of the vast potential sales in their own domestic market."

In what sense is the word sales used in the sentence?

7. How would you paraphrase "taken literally"?

8. What does "administrative support" in the text refer to?

9. What is "a well-placed source"?

10. "The central government's determination to raise the level of industrial technology is clearly behind the decision to open the 14 coastal cities."

What's your paraphrase of the above sentence? Does it mean that the "determination" was the reason for the decision?

11. "The combined industrial output of the 15 coastal areas is reportedly equal to a quarter of the nation's total."

What is the meaning of "combined" in the sentence?

Could you find another word to replace it? What is that?

12. "But while the reasons for throwing 19 areas and cities open to foreign investment and technology transfer are clear..."

"Throwing ... open" basically means having ... open, doesn't it? Then what is the difference in meaning between "throwing 19 areas and cities open" and having ... open? What more does it mean when the word throw is used?

13. "... , how the preferential systems will operate (in the 19 open districts) is not (clear). This is due largely to the intensity of competition among the 19 ..."

How could "the intensity of competition among the 19", if there was one, lead to some confusion in absorbing foreign direct investment?

14. "This is due largely to the intensity of competition among the 19, coupled with the inexperience of most local authorities both in making decisions and in dealing with the outside world."

What does "coupled" mean here? Could you find some substitutes for it?

15. What are "target projects"?

16. "One official who is well aware of the confusion afflicting both local authorities and foreign investors is Jing Shuping, president of China International Economic Consultants Inc. which is the consultancy arm of the China International Trust and Investment Corp."

What is the meaning of the word "arm" here? Could you find some other word to substitute?

17. "The time will come when the cities and zones will ask for help in coordinating their efforts."

What kind of clause does "when" introduce? An attributive or an adverbial one? Why?

18. "... , while a comprehensive framework for the country's modernization has been provided by the central committee's 21 October 1984 decision to reform the economic structure, it will be some time before the dust settles and local authorities and foreign investors can deal with one another in a systematic way."

What's your understanding of "the dust settles"?

19. What's "stock-taking of the open policy"?

Topic for Summary

You would find in the text that some foreign investors were more or less confused about certain China's arrangement for foreign direct investment, such as different duty and tax rates for different areas, and limits of the authority to approve investments differing from place to place.

Do you agree that the arrangement was totally a "confusion"? Could you find reasons for these policies?

Exercises

Ⅰ. Read the article given below and then answer the following questions in brief English.

China Tries Guiding Foreign Investment

BEIJING—For years China has been not only the world's fastest-growing economy but a magnet to many international companies, with foreign investment rising to a record of around $30 billion in 1994.

Now, both Chinese government officials and foreign executives are telling a slightly different story: The welcome mat is still out, but economic planners in Beijing are determined to channel foreign money more explicitly to the projects and regions that meet their own needs.

"We need to guide foreign investment so that it goes to sectors that are conducive to our economic growth plans," said Wu Jie, a leading architect of economic reforem and vice chairman of the State Commission for Restructuring the Economic Systems.

This does not necessarily mean that investing in China will become unattractive. But it does mean that direct foreign investment in China is likely to be transformed in the coming months and years. China is expected to require total foreign investment of more than $80 billion between now and 2000.

"Obviously the Chinese feel they are in a very strong position and can manage foreign investment to their advantage," said Ramgopal Agarwala, the World Bank's chief economist in Beijing.

In the late 1980s and early 1990s, as China experienced booming annual growth rates of more than 10 per cent and stepped up its move toward a market economy, billions of dollars of foreign investment went mainly into lucrative, short-term property development and fairly basic, low-technology manufacturing plants.

But the urban real estate sector has become thoroughly overheated. As a result of Beijing's greater emphasis on managed investment, foreign investors will now be encouraged to move away from speculative property development and toward selected high-tech and infrastructure projects.

In an interview Tuesday, Mr. Wu said priority areas for investment would include the energy, transportation, telecommunications, biotechnology, environmental technology and automated machine tools sectors. Agriculture is also a priority.

Chinese officials said here this week that many of these targets would appear more attractive to foreign investors after the National People's Congress passed a series of policies providing tax, investment and import-export benefits this spring.

The total amount of foreign funds flowing into China in 1995 may not decline by much, analysts say, but foreign investors will find themselves asked to adjust their plans to fit China's next five-year plan of economic reform, which begins in 1996.

Apart from channeling the flow of capital, the Chinese authorities are keen to reap benefits that go beyond money. They want more technology transfer, help in improving management at state enterprises and employee training.

"The bottleneck now is people, not technology, not capital, not bureaucracy," said Percy Barnevik, chairman of ABB Asea Brown Boveri Ltd. "that is why we invest in training of thousands of Chinese managers, engineers and skilled workers."

In telecommunications, one of China's priority investment areas, Beijing has until recently limited foreign investment to the manufacturing sector, allowing selected Western firms into the market to build much-needed technology, often in joint ventures.

But, while the need and cost of installing telephone lines across the country threatens to eclipse China's resources, Beijing will continue to refuse to allow foreigners to directly invest in operating networks.

But the potential market is huge. Investment in telecommunications in China this year will reach 80 billion yuan ($9. 52 billion), Mr. Wu said.

——From *International Herald Tribune* • April 12, 1995

1. What does the author mean by saying that China has been a magnet to international companies?
2. Why do you think the government should encourage foreign investors to put their money into high-tech and infrastructure projects such as telecommunications and transportation?
3. What did the Chinese officials imply when they said the targets would appear more attractive to foreign investors after NPC passed a series of policies?

Open question:

Do you agree with Mr. Percy Barhevik, chairman of ABB Asea Brown Boveri Ltd. that "the bottleneck now is people, not technology, not capital, not bureaucracy"? Why or why not?

Ⅱ. Read the article given below and do the exercises as required.

Era of the Multinationals

The development of communications and a change in political climate is altering the face of global manufacturing, writes Tony Jackson.

Direct investment by multinational corporations is becoming a hugely important force in the world economy. A recent study from the United Nations estimated that multinationals now control a third of the world's private productive assets. Their stock of foreign investments is now worth $2 000bn. The turnover generated by these assets in 1992 was bigger than total world exports. In other words, direct investment abroad is now a bigger economic force than world trade.

Although investment worldwide has dropped sharply from its peak in 1990, it seems likely that the upward trend will resume. As the UN report points out, growth in foreign direct investment in the past couple of decades has averaged 13 per cent a year. In the period 1986—1990 the rate was 28 per cent. That brief and unsustainable spurt was due partly to the economic boom of the late 1980s, partly to one-off changes such as the introduction of the European single market.

The underlying arguments for growth in foreign direct investment remain unchanged. In essence, a combination of factors, such as the development of global communications and a change in the political climate towards multinationals, is bringing in an era of true global manufacturing.

A company such as Siemens, the German electronics giant, may now start making a product in Germany, where precision and automation are required, then ship it to Malaysia for the labour-intensive final stages of manufacture. At the same time, much of its software research is undertaken in India, which has an abundant supply of cheap computing talent.

Foreign direct investment is also proving an important force in the integration of national economies. Ford is developing its "world car", known as the Nondeo in Europe and to be sold in North America next year as Ford Contour and Mercury Mystique. Components such as engines and transmissions for the car will be made at single locations and shipped worldwide.

In semiconductors, Siemens, IBM and Toshiba have formed an alliance to develop the next generation of memory chip. The chip will be supplied to the world market from a single factory, in a country yet to be determined.

As the UN report argues, such integration is also important at the regional level. The strategy by Japanese companies of locating production in cheaper Far Eastern countries such as Thailand and Malaysia has done much to integrate the economies of the region. US companies were setting up production in Mexico, for similar reasons, before negotiations on the North American Free Trade Agreement had even started.

There is an important distinction to be made between the kind of integration based on trade, which is relatively simple, and the far more complex links involved in global manufacturing. The report says that "as integration moves from shallow trade-based linkages to deep international production-based linkages under the common governance (of multinationals), the traditional division between integration at the corporate and country levels begins to break down."

As a result, the multinationals "encroach on areas over which sovereignty and responsibilities have traditionally been reserved for national governments. This raises new issues of direct concern to the formation of national laws and regulations."

Foreign direct investment tends to transfer assets from the developed world to the developing world. But the pattern is not entirely simple. Last year, of a total of $126bn in foreign direct investment worldwide, $10bn—32 per cent—went to developing countries. This represents an advance on the 26 per cent going to developing countries in the period 1981—1985, but the change is not dramatic.

In part, this is accounted for by the fact that big shifts have occurred in the composition of foreign direct investment by sector. Increasingly, investment is going into services and high-tech manufacture, rather than basic manufacture and natural resources. As might be expected, foreign direct investment in the developed world is mostly in the former category, whereas in the developing world the emphasis is on the latter. Increasingly, it seems, countries have to reach a basic level of sophistication before they can get in on the act.

This is borne out by the fact that last year, the $40bn of foreign direct investment going to developing countries was spent almost wholly in two regions: east, south and south-east Asia got $21bn, while Latin America and the Caribbean got $16bn. The whole of Africa got a pitiful $2bn, while the sum invested in the least developed countries was too small to measure.

Changing this pattern may prove a long job. Simple cash incentives to set up production in a country have little effect, other than on the margin. As any international businessman will tell you, if that is the best reason for going to a country you had better not go at all. In addition, the increasing sophistication of global production means that cheap labour is often not a deciding factor either.

What companies often look for are threefolds: a skilled local workforce, good infrastructure (especially telecommunications) and a welcoming attitude by government. Acquiring the first two is a haul. But at least, something can be done about the third.

The dangers of antagonizing international investors can be illustrated by the case of an economy as sophisticated as that of South Korea which has a real need for inward investment primarily as a means of getting hold of technology. But a streak of xenophobia in the Korean character shades into downright antagonism when it comes to their former colonial masters, the Japanese. Korea traditionally has made things awkward for foreigners in terms of its financial systems, its real estate laws and so forth.

Last year, Korea saw a net outflow of foreign direct investment, a fact which seems to have brought the government to its senses. A concerted attempt is now being made to be nicer to foreigners.

Whether it will reverse the damage remains to be seen. Across the world, the days when it paid to reveil the multinationals are long gone. Like it or not, too much depends on them.

From *Financial Times* • Sept. 24, 1993

Ⅰ. Elaborate on the nature of the multinationals mentioned in the article.

Ⅱ. Find out from the article what encourages multinationals to invest in a foreign country. Give your own opinions.

Ⅲ. Translate the following into Chinese:

1. Direct investment by multinational corporations is becoming a hugely important force in the world economy.

2. (The whole of Paragraph 3.)

3. Foreign direct investment tends to transfer assets from the developed world to the developing world. But the pattern is not entirely simple.

4. What companies often look for are threefolds: a skilled local workforce, good infrastructure (especially telecommunications) and a welcoming attitude by government. Acquiring the first two is a haul. But at least, something can be done about the third.

Supplementary Material for Free Reading

A. China's Foreign Investors Stake Claim to the Interior

By Tony Walker in Beijing

Growth in foreign direct investment in China is slowing after surging in the mid—1990s. However, investors are spreading to China's interior, helping to balance development with coastal areas, according to a report by the Australian embassy in Beijing.

The survey* found that contracted foreign direct investment was 20 per cent lower in 1996 than in the previous year. Utilised investment was up 12. 2 per cent.

US and Japanese investment rose sharply while that of Hong Kong and Taiwan grew more slowly after leading the charge in the early stages of China's opening to the outside world.

The study also identified movement away from traditional investment in export processing to larger capital-intensive investments aimed at the local market. The average value of investment projects has more than doubled since 1992 to $2. 45m, reflecting this trend.

Foreign investors are showing an increasing preference for wholly foreign-owned ventures, where investment in 1995 was twice that of 1992. Joint venture investment increased by only a third over the same period.

"If those rates of investment have continued in 1996 and 1997, investment in wholly foreign-owned enterprises will already have exceeded investment in joint ventures," the report says.

---

* Foreign investment in China. published by the Australian Embassy, Beijing. April 1997.

China:foreign direct investment

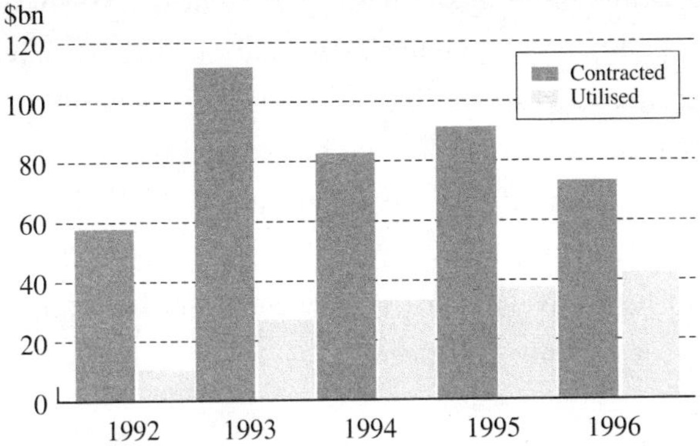

Source: Chinese Statistical Yearbook. State Statistical Bureau

Utilised foreign direct investment reached an accumulated total of $177. 2bn by 1996 while contracted foreign investment stood at a total of $469. 3bn. China received about a quarter of all foreign direct investment to developing countries between 1979 and 1997, according to the World Bank's Global Finance report.

Some 200 of the world's 500 largest transnational corporations have established a presence in China since 1990. This is reflected in growing investment in larger infrastructure projects and in such industries as petrochemicals and motor vehicles.

The study found there had been a "shift northward and westward in foreign direct investment" in the past two years. Foreign investment growth has risen sharply in Shanghai and coastal provinces north of Fujian.

Rates of investment in the interior grew by 27. 2 per cent in 1995 compared with 11. 1 per cent growth along the coast, but poor infrastructure constituted a "considerable barrier" to investment in China's hinterland.

The study also noted that between 1979 and 1994, 81. 9 per

cent of contracted investment was committed to coastal areas, but special economic zones in southern China appeared to "have reached saturation point and will be unable to continue to absorb high levels of foreign direct investment".

Hong Kong's share of foreign investment had slipped to 54 per cent in 1995 compared with 68 per cent between 1979 and 1993. Japanese and US utilised investment in 1995 rose by 52 per cent and 24 per cent respectively over the previous year, but Hong Kong investment rose by only 2 per cent.

—From *Financial Times* · April 30, 1997

B. FDI Flood Meets Barriers

Tax reform and policy changes are setting new conditions for overseas investors

The flood of foreign investment that has buoyed China's economic expansion over recent years is now at a watershed. A more selective stance from Beijing, combined with fiscal and tariff reforms, is changing the conditions for direct investment and the destination of capital inflows.

"We are still encouraging foreign investment, but we are trying to divert it to bottlenecks and high-technology areas," says Mr Li Zongzhou, director general of the department of international trade and economic affairs at China's foreign trade ministry. Mr Li cites infrastructure, energy and advanced manufacturing among the priority areas.

Such a shift raises challenges not only for investors but also for the Chinese authorities, which must seek to develop new means of financing and guarantees for projects and try to resolve concerns about the investment environment. It may also herald a trend of fewer, bigger projects and a cooling in the rate of investment growth.

Foreign direct investment in China

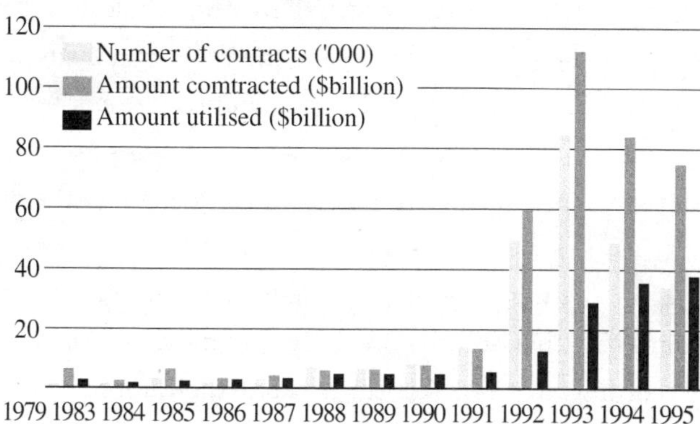

Source: Jetro, 1995 projections based on Jan-Sept 1995 growth over same period in 1994

Recently, the rate has been frenetic. Statistics show that in the first quarter of the year, foreign investment contracts rose by 87 per cent to US$27bn, underlining China's position as the dominant recipient of direct investment among developing countries. This came on top of existing commitments of more than US$390bn and actual investment of more than US$135bn by the end of last year.

Behind the first quarter surge, however, lay some special factors. In particular, investors were rushing to beat the April 1 elimination of tax and tariff breaks on imports of capital equipment. A longer-term picture (see chart above) shows a fall in the number of investment contracts alongside a continued rise in the value of utilised investment.

The elimination of these import incentives is part of the broader shift away from all-out investment promotion policies. A parallel shift is the reduced interest in labour-intensive and small-scale projects that dominated the early years of China's economic liberalisation. "They are not interested by $10m projects any more," Mr Alfred Shum, executive partner for China at the accountants Ernst & Young, says.

There are plenty of big projects on the table, many in the power and infrastructure sector targeted by the Chinese authorities. But the bigger the project, the bigger the risk, and many investors remain to be reassured about the terms and conditions for committing their funds. At the top of their list of anxieties are rates of return, management controls, guarantees for loans and the ability to transfer revenue streams into foreign currency.

Mr Li at the ministry of trade and foreign economic co-operation is confident that solutions will be found. Of particular significance, according to Chinese officials and their foreign investment counterparts, is the development of a Build Operate Transfer power plant project (See the note at the back of the article.) in the southwestern province of Guangxi. The project, which is now in the bidding stage, is touted as a potential model for future big projects and a yardstick for financing and rates of return.

The terms of such big projects are not the only concerns of investors. The US—China business council cites "opaque and unpredictable" methods used to enact regulatory changes as a problem in business planning. The scaling back of investment incentives, it adds, is likely to dampen investor enthusiasm and make marginal projects unfeasible.

At Jetro, the Japanese trade and investment promotion agency, there are misgivings about the pace of change. "We understand their intention to move to high technology but they are very much in a hurry," says one official. He believes the changes in tax and tariff incentives will represent "a big handicap" to foreign investors.

An additional worry is the growing influence of domestic companies in protecting their markets. "A lot of the state-owned enterprises are bleeding red ink and they have pushed for limits on foreign presence," says one businessman. Profitable state enterprises have also exerted influence. Foreign insurance companies, for instance, have seen glacial movement in market liberalisation, partly because of pressure from state insurers seeking to limit inroads into their business.

Foreign Direct Investment into China by Countries and Regions (US $ 10 000)

Country and Region	1988	1989	1990	1991	1992	1993	1994	1995
HK and Macau	209 520	207 759	191 342	248 687	770 907	1 786 125	2 017 481	2 049 900
Hong Kong	206 760	203 690	188 000	240 525	750 707	1 727 475	1 966 544	2 006 000
Taiwan	2 244	15 479	22 240	46 641	105 050	313 859	339 104	300 400
US	23 596	28 427	45 599	32 320	51 105	206 312	249 080	308 300
Japan	51 453	35 634	50 338	53 250	70 983	132 410	207 529	310 800
Singapore	2 782	8 414	5 043	5 821	12 231	49 004	117 961	185 100
Korea	—	402	1 267	3 960	11 948	37 381	72 283	104 300
Thailand	610	1 268	672	1 962	8 303	23 318	N/A	28 800
UK	3 416	2 848	1 333	3 539	3 833	22 051	68 884	91 400
France	2 267	460	2 106	988	4 493	14 141	19 204	28 700
Canada	602	1 695	804	1 076	5 824	13 688	21 605	25 700
Others	22 878	36 871	27 967	38 390	56 074	153 206	263 519	340 200
Total	319 368	339 257	348 711	436 634	1 100 751	2 751 495	3 376 650	3 773 600

Source: Jetro

Many, however, see positive steps, citing accelerated moves towards currency convertibility which will facilitate the repatriation of profits. And it is a rare voice in the business community that claims the difficulties of access or operation outweigh the potential. "It remains one of the few markets with huge growth prospects, so there is no lack of interest, says Mr Shum of Ernst & Young.

Over recent months, this interest has been focused increasingly on new markets within China, in terms of both products and location. Mr Victor Chu, chairman of the Hong Kong-based First Eastern Investment Group, argues that the consumer sector is poised for sustained and robust expansion as China's developing economy produces a broadening middle class. His group recently forged an agreement with Sinochem of China and several international chemicals groups with an eye on the plastics and by-products required for consumer products. Goldlion of Hong Kong has seen rapid profits growth on the back of rising expenditure on its garments, ties and related consumer products.

Foreign Direct Investment into China and Regions (US $ 10 000)

Year	China	Guangdong province	% share	Shenzhen City	% share	Shenzhen S. E. Z	% share
1987	231 353	60 299	226	27 379	12	226 486	11
1988	319 368	95 786	30	28 716	9	25 870	8
1989	339 257	115 644	34	29 252	9	27 144	8
1990	348 711	146 000	42	38 994	11	34 920	10
1991	436 634	182 286	42	39 875	9	33 487	8
1992	1 100 751	355 150	32	44 879	4	32 166	3
1993	2 751 495	749 804	27	98 900	4	67 221	2
1994	3 376 650	939 708	28	125 046	4	62 870	2
1995	3 773 600	1 018 028	27	130 989	3	N/A	N/A

Source: Jetro

At the same time, investor focus has shifted somewhat from the traditional magnet areas. Guangdong remains the largest recipient of foreign investment, supported by funds from Hong Kong, the largest source and the main conduct of investment into China. But the share of funds flowing to the southern province has fallen from more than 40 per cent in 1991 to less than 30 per cent last year. Stronger growth has been seen in Shanghai, the Yangtze River Delta, eastern coastal provinces such as Shandong and industrial areas around Beijing.

"By 2005, I believe that Hong Kong investors' attention will have shifted from Guangdong and the Pearl River Delta to Shanghai and the Yangtze River Delta," says Mr Vincent Lo, chairman of the Shui On property and construction group. Mr Lo cites rising costs in Guangdong and Shanghai's traditional importance as a business base as the motors for change.

China's leaders would like investment to flow further fields, helping to develop the western and inland regions and to reduce disparities with the coast. So far, investors have been cautious, wary of the lack of infrastructure and logistical limitations. "There are opportunities, but it is certainly more difficult," says one French engineering executive. Given Beijing's more rigorous stance, it is an assessment that could be applied to China as a whole.

—From *Financial Times* · June 27, 1996

注：

Build Operation Transter contract

简称"BOT合同"。业主与承包人签订的共同出资，单方建设，共同经营一定时期后，将项目所有权和经营权全部转移给业主的一种国际承包工程合同。这是一种新兴的承包形式，它既适应发展中国家建设技术、资本密集型大型开发项目的需要，又能解决资金短缺、技术落后、经营管理水平不高等问题。

C. Globalization's Depredations Are Real and Brutal

By William Pfaff

PARIS—The United States came under much criticism at the Hong Kong joint meeting of the World Bank and International Monetary Fund because many in Asia hold Washington responsible for the crisis that has struck the region's currencies and markets.

When leaders such as Prime Minister Mahathir bin Mohamad of Malaysia accuse Western speculators of responsibility for the crisis, Mr. Mahathir is usually held not to understand today's global economy. And it is true that Malaysia, Thailand and other Asian countries have brought many of these problems onto themselves through real estate speculation, uncontrolled bank credit, grandiose state projects and insider profiteering. They also have had considerable encouragement from abroad in their profligacy.

Nonetheless it is indispensable to understand that the United States is promoting a revolutionary remaking of international trade and markets, which in the short term mainly profits the West, and the long-term consequences of which remain profoundly uncertain. We do not known where this revolution will take us.

The politically correct description of this says that Washington's drive to reduce trade barriers and open up still more markets to international trade will eventually produce advantages for everyone, including the people in countries that may suffer a brutal short-term introduction to the international competition to drive manufacturing costs down and corporate profits up.

A politically incorrect description would say that globalization is an American-inspired drive toward universal economic deregulation.

The result of this deregulation not only lifts tariffs meant to protect local markets and producers, but subjects small-country producers to an international competition they often are incapable of withstanding, tending to destroy the power of smaller governments to regulate their own economies, not to speak of their fiscal systems.

The latter is what the Malaysian prime minister is saying.

Globalization universalizes the labor market, thereby undermining labor unions and labor standards in the advanced countries. It tends to render environmental regulations in those countries irrelevant by promoting the transfer of production and pollution to poorer countries or regions where environmental standards are weak or nonexistent.

I am putting this very polemically, I know. But it is necessary to call a spade a bloody shovel when those who are promoting globalization ignore the damage it does.

Obviously trade produces benefits, above all when the countries exchanging goods are at roughly the same level of industrial development and have sophisticated economic structures and legal systems. The obvious examples of this mutually beneficial process include the European Single Market and trade between the United States and Europe and Japan.

But trade does not produce only benefits, and this is what people in Southeast Asia, and also in the less-developed Third World, are attempting to say. Dominant opinion in the West tends to dismiss the downside of trade deregulation by describing it as mere "creative destruction" (Schumpeter's expression is a favorite one). In the future all will be well. Alas, it seems, in a very distant future.

The economic transformation taking place today is extremely complex, and in social and political terms. It could produce very destructive international consequences. The immense variety of humanity's economic societies are being violently annexed into a Western economic monoculture, dominated by enormously powerful Western economic actors, whose motivation is simply to maximize return on investment.

Trade between the West and countries in the non-Western world may destroy subsistence agriculture, co-opting Third World farmers into production for the international marketplace while their societies are made dependent on imported foods. The social and cultural consequences of this may be very serious.

Resources may be pillaged, as is happening in Asia's forests. Local artisanal production can be wrecked by international competition, causing more unemployment than the new employment produced by international investment. When barriers between advanced and backward economies are destroyed, a new form of human exploitation can follow, resembling that of colonialism in the 19th and early 20th centuries, complete with new forms of indentured labor.

Listening to President Bill Clinton as he asks Congress for

"fast track" negotiating powers, one would think that nothing but positive effects will follow the expansion of free-trade zones and further deregulation.

It is time to recognize that the trade, labor and environmental regulations that globalization undermines were put there in the past for a reason. Much of this regulation came about as a direct result of the rampant abuses and exploitation of the industrial and colonial systems of the 19th century. Do we really wish to restore the conditions for such abuses?

It is time for Congress to call a halt and to think. It is time to let the free trade groupings we already have come to maturity, so that we understand their longer-term implications. It is time to consider whether economic interest is our only interest.

——From *International Herald Fribune* • Sept. 25, 1997

Lesson 3

China's Opened Economy

Text

Beijing Rising

(Excerpts)

China's emergence as an economic heavyweight after more than a decade of fast growth makes it likely to supplant Japan as the West's main trade worry in Asia

By Frank Gibney Jr.

If there is a road to China's future, Highway 204 out of Shanghai is it. Along its two dusty lanes, local trucks and buses jockey with Cadillacs driven by financiers from Taiwan and Hong Kong investors. Migrant workers crowd the narrow shoulders. Factories line the highway, producing sneakers, toys, plastics, clothes, aircraft components and medical equipment. Eventually industry gives way to ricefields, which is being dug up to build still more factories. Cranes turn overhead as dump trucks and cement mixers nose onto the road. Outside the town of Jiading, one tractor-trailer leaves Asia's largest container plant every three minutes, carrying goods bound for the Shanghai docks. The traffic on Highway 204 is so thick that the trip from Shanghai to Zhangjiagang—only 115 kilometers away—takes five hours.

Zhangjiagang is a commercial hub of Jiangsu, the fastest-growing province in China. China has the most dynamic economy in the world today. Its boom radiates from Guangdong, its richest province, but it has spread as far west as Xinjiang, where foreign investors are searching for oil and other natural resources. It is creeping inland, from Jiangsu to the cities of Congqing and Wuhan, where businessmen from Hong Kong and Taiwan are starting to spend billions of dollars to build factories. And it has penetrated the northeast, where the city of Shenyang, long a moribund center of state industry, is bustling with new private business, from trading companies to prostitution. Back in Beijing, officials at China's state council, or cabinet, are giddy with excitement — and exhaustion. "We don't have people, we don't have time," says one. "Things are moving too fast."

After a slowdown through 1990, China's economy bounced back mightily, reaching a recent peak of 13 per cent growth last year. Now, some Western experts are predicting that China could become the world's dominant economy early in the 21st century. Many economists believe a standard estimate of China's per capita gross national product ($370) is already two to three times too low. And former World Bank chief economist Larry Summers recently argued that China could surpass both Japan and the United States to become the world's largest economy by 2020.

A farfetched prediction? The new American administration doesn't think so. Bill Clinton has appointed China hands to top Asia posts at the State and Treasury departments. When critics called the appointments a slight to Japan, the leading Pacific economic power, U. S. Deputy Treasury Secretary Roger Altman explained the administration's reasoning: by early in the next century, he said, China may replace Japan in importance to the U. S. as an economic partner. Japan recognizes the rise of China. As a warning shot in an intensifying rivalry, Tokyo last week put punitive import tariffs on Chinese steel.

China is reaping the rewards of reforms first launched by Deng Xiaoping in 1979. Foreign investment is now welcome. Special Economic Zones are booming. The opening of securities and real-estate markets have created new opportunities. Growing ties between China's traders and their partners in Taiwan and Hong Kong are creating an unofficial but formidable "greater China" trade bloc. Expansion has transformed places like Jiangsu province, where GDP grew 26 per cent last year. Six years ago Zhangjiagang was part of another town and did not even have its own name. Now it's China's seventh largest port and a tumultuous construction zone of half-built office buildings and hotels.

Clearly, China's economy is a work in progress, nowhere near realizing the potential of its billion-plus population. Its gross domestic product last year was, according to the official measure, $420 billion — no more than that of southern California. China remains primarily a nation of farmers, and the transition to an industrial free market is much like the traffic on Highway 204 — unpredictable. Few state-owned firms have been sold, and most are laggard behemoths. Growth is driven by new joint ventures, collectives and private businesses, which now account for more than 50 per cent of China's industrial production.

For China's newly-rising enterprises, profits are up throughout the region — thanks largely to low wages. Last year the BeiBei company in Zhangjiagang cleared $14 million on exports of 10 million pairs of shoes to U. S. department stores. At the BeiBei plant, women huddle over a conveyor belt in frigid temperatures, gluing rubber sneakers together. Typically, Chinese workers in a plant like this make about 34 cents an hour, compared with $3. 50 for Korean workers, according to South Korean estimates. That gives China a huge competitive advantage. Just two years ago South Korean manufactures were flourishing on contracts from western athletic footwear giants like Nike, Reebok and Adidas. Since then much of the business has shifted to China, dealing a hard blow to the South Korean shoe industry. This is a blow to Seoul, but it also reflects the fact that South Korea is moving to a high-tech, high-wage economy — leaving China behind.

China is now reaching for the next rung on the economic ladder. Last fall Beijing agreed to open its markets to more U. S. goods, including everything from Polaroid film to automobiles. In return, Washington would support China's membership in the General Agreement on Tariffs and Trade. Membership in this club, which includes all the world's leading economies, could provide a huge boost for a low-wage export economy. Already though, China's commercial strength is starting to worry competitors. Last year China's trade surplus surged, buoyed by exports of toys, textiles and consumer electronics. Its trade surplus with the Unied States hit a record $18 billion. Only Japan's was larger. With the U. S. Congress due to consider the renewal of China's most-favored nation trade status in June, officials in Beijing fear the trade imbalance could surpass human rights as a source of U. S. opposition to preferred status for China. "The trade surplus itself will be the No. 1 problem this year," says one Chinese official. "After Japan, we'll be first in line for retaliation."

At the same time, America has an increasingly large stake in good relations with China. In 1992 American companies led a rush of foreign investors who signed more than $30 billion worth of contracts in China. (That is 30 times more than the 1987 record for annual foreign investment in South Korea.) In Shanghai, Tianjin and other urban centers, China is trying — with considerable success — to attract hightechnology firms that will modernize its economy. McDonnell Douglas has built 35 MD—80 series aircraft in Shanghai — and has contracted to build 40 more. General Motors and Ford are rushing to establish a beachhead there. Throughout China, foreign firms are building plants for copiers, computers and industrial machinery.

Even more striking, China's entrepreneurs are starting to hunt for opportunities abroad. In the last year Capital Steel, a state-owned conglomerate with 205 000 employees, purchased steel operations in the United States and announced plans to build semiconductor chips in cooperation with NEC of Japan. In December Capital outbid a Japanese-Mexican-Chilean consortium to buy Peru's leading iron-and-steel complex, Hierroperu. The $312 million purchase makes Capital the second largest foreign investor in Peru. Other state-affiliated companies, including CITIC and China Resources, Inc., are branching out from Hong Kong to establish overseas posts as varied as diamond-trading operations in Sri Lanka and brokerage services in New York.

However, even as the party promotes growth as a national priority, it worries about going too far. Inflation has recently climbed back into double digits, and the party press is issuing strident warnings, urging restraint on buyers and sellers alike. Rapid development is overwhelming China's antique transport networks. Energy brownouts are a regular occurrence in Guangdong and Shanghai.

Now Beijing has cut this year's growth target from 10 to 8.5 per cent, in an effort to keep the economy from careering out of control just as it was cut back in 1989 and 1990 when it overheated. "We need a smooth transition into another system," says the head of a research institute in Shanghai. "But no one in the world has a design we can use, so we just have to experiment." Even 8.5 per cent growth a year doubles an economy in 10 years, China's "new man" may well find himself astride one of the world's largest economies in the 21st century. And the rest of the world will look foolish if it lets itself be caught by surprise.

With Kari Huus in Beijing and
Robin Bulman in Seoul

——From *Newsweek* • Feb. 15, 1993

Words and Expressions

emergence	*n.*	出现
heavyweight	*n.*	有影响的人物;要人;大人物
economic heavyweight	举足轻重的经济强国	
supplant	*v.*	取代
jockey	*v.*	驾驶;移动;变换位置
financier	*n.*	金融(资本)家
migrant	*a.*	迁移的
sneaker	*n.*	[常用作复数]运动鞋;旅游鞋
crane	*n.*	吊车
dump truck	翻斗车	
nose	*v.*	小心翼翼地行驶
tractor-trailer	*n.*	牵引拖车
container plant	集装箱工厂	
commercial hub	商业活动的中心	
dynamic	*a.*	有生气的;有活力的
radiate	*v.*	辐射状发出;从中心向各方伸展出
creep	*v.*	潜行;在…上面爬行
penetrate	*v.*	渗透
moribund	*a.*	停滞不前的;凋敝的
bustle	*v.*	喧闹;活跃
prostitution	*n.*	卖淫
cabinet	*n.*	内阁
giddy	*a.*	头晕的;眼花缭乱的
exhaustion	*n.*	筋疲力尽
bounce	*v.*	反弹
farfetched	*n.*	牵强的;勉强的
slight	*n.*	忽视;冷落

warning shot	鸣枪示警
intensifying rivalry	不断增强的竞争,对抗
formidable	*a.* 令人生畏的;巨大的;可怕的
tumultuous	*a.* 喧闹的;骚动的
measure	*n.* 尺度,标准
laggard	*a.* 落后的;迟钝的
behemoth	*n.* 庞然大物
huddle	*v.* 挤成一团
conveyor belt	输送带;传送带
frigid	*a.* 寒冷的;严寒的
rung	*n.* 阶;梯
buoy	*v.* 浮起;支持
source	*n.* 原因
preferred status	优先权
retaliation	*n.* 报复
have a stake in	与…有利害关系
beachhead	*n.* 滩头堡;藉以扩张势力的据点
outbid	*v.* 出价高于
consortium	*n.* 财团;综(联)合企业
complex	*n.* 综(联)合企业
strident	*a.* 刺耳的;尖声的
overwhelm	*v.* 使…不知所措;使受不了
brownout	*n.* 部分停止供电
career	*n.* 事业
astride	*prep.* (跨)在…上;跨骑

Notes to the Text

1. "Beijing Rising"

报刊文章的题目称之为"标题"(headline),"Beijing Rising"即

是本文的标题。

2. “China's emergence as economic heavyweight after more than a decade of fast growth makes it likely to supplant Japan as the West's main trade worry in Asia.”

报刊文章除了标题之外通常还有一组“导语”(lead)附于标题，简要介绍文章主要内容。以上引文即本篇之导语。

3. Cadillac　卡迪拉克牌轿车

一流名牌轿车，美国通用汽车公司(General Motors, GM)制造。Cadillac原仅是这种轿车的品牌，现用指这种品牌的轿车。以品牌代指商品是报刊英语中一种常见的用法。

4. Per capita　按人均计算的，人均

源自拉丁文，原意“by heads”。

5. Gross national product (GNP)　国民生产总值

指一个国家的国民在一定时期内，在国内和国外所生产和提供的最终产品和劳务的总量。

6. Punitive import tariff　惩罚性进口关税

由于进口商品本身或其来源国方面的原因，海关所征收的惩罚性的额外进口税项，如：针对蓄意低报进口商品价值以图偷税的“低估税”，与反倾销和反补贴税等。

7. Securities and real estate markets　证券及房地产市场

Securities有价证券，指股票、公债券及公司债券等证明所有权或借贷关系的书面凭证。证券市场则是对可以上市的有价证券进行交易的公开市场。在西方国家也有无组织的场外市场。房地产市场是指从事土地及土地上的房屋，设施(又称“不动产”)交易的市场，包括房地产的开发、经营、管理及服务等。

8. “Greater China” trade bloc　“大中华”贸易集团，又称“华人经济区”(Chinese Economic Area, CEA)

指出中国大陆、台湾和香港的经济力量合作组合形成的非正式的区域性贸易集团。这一地区经济发展迅速，在世界贸易中所占地位也越来越重要。目前其贸易额占世界总贸易额的4.5%。这三个地区各有优势：台湾拥有充裕的资本，较先进的技术和管理方面的经

验；大陆拥有廉价的劳动力和相对丰富的自然资源；而香港是世界金融及商业中心。由于中国大陆、台湾和香港近年来在经济上展现整体强势增长，世界银行及国际货币基金组织顺应国际经贸学界及媒体的言论趋势，在正式报告里把大陆、台、港视为一个整体的分析单元，并预期他们所称的“华人经济区”力量将在今后 10 年内壮大到足以与德国、日本、美国分庭抗礼，成为全球经济的“第四极”。

9. Nike Inc.　耐克公司

是一家公开招股的公司(a public company)，成立于 1964 年，名为 Blue Ribbon Sorts(蓝缎带成套铅字行)，1972 年更名为 Nike Inc.。总公司设于美国俄勒冈，起初以进口日本鞋为主，现已发展成为世界最大的运动鞋和运动服制造商之一。耐克公司多年来一直靠产品设计的不断革新和一贯重视促销来推动业务在美国和海外市场的发展。

10. Reebok International Ltd.　锐步国际有限公司

世界主要运动鞋和服装制造商之一，公司起源可追溯到英国 19 世纪 90 年代，其母公司为世界生产运动鞋的最早厂家。锐步首先推出了样式和功能俱佳的增氧健身运动鞋，吸引了大批女性顾客而崭露头角，继而在这个基础上向其他运动用品和别的产品市场扩展业务并努力开拓国际市场。

11. Adidas　阿迪达斯

德国运动鞋制造厂家，大约创立于 1922 年。目前该公司是欧洲最大的供应商，并跻身于本行业全世界的三大公司之列，产品行销近 200 个国家，以其“彪马”商标著名于世。

12. high-tech, high-wage economy　高技术，高工资经济

指主要由技术方面的投资和技术人员及技术工人的使用占主要地位的产业构成的经济。这些产业部门包括如计算机工业、生物工程工业等。由于技术员工在这类工业当中的地位和作用，他们通常被付以高额的工资。

13. Polaroid (Corporation)　宝丽来公司

世界最大的即拍即现摄影器械生产企业。该公司是这种摄影技术的创始者，并一直以研究开发带动经营而著称。公司总部设于美

国马萨诸塞州。

14. General Agreement on Tariffs and Trade (GATT)　关税及贸易总协定

第二次世界大战后，1947年美、英、法等23个国家政府间缔结的关于关税与贸易政策的多边国际协定，亦指执行这个协定的国际经济组织。该组织设于日内瓦，成立于1948年。我国是23个创始缔约国之一。当前缔约方之间的贸易已占世界贸易的90%以上。关贸总协定的基本目标是通过实施无条件的多边最惠国待遇，削减关税及其他贸易壁垒，促进贸易自由化，以充分利用世界资源和扩大商品生产与交换。关贸总协定的基本原则包括无歧视待遇原则，互惠平等的关税减让原则，关税为惟一保护手段原则，公平贸易原则等等。此外还有一些在特殊情况下免除缔约国其他义务的例外原则，如国际收支平衡例外，幼稚工业的保护例外，安全例外等。由于历史的原因，中国与关贸总协定中断关系40余年，近年来一直在为恢复其关贸总协定缔约国地位和加入其后继机构"世界贸易组织"(WTO, World Trade Organization)而进行努力。

15. McDonnell Douglas　麦克唐纳—道格拉斯(飞机制造公司)

美国公司，主要生产军、民用飞机、空间飞行器和导弹、能源系统、电子系统、数据处理系统等。公司建于1939年，总部设在密苏里州圣路易斯。该公司1992年销售额为175.13亿美元，在全美排行第23位。资产137.81亿美元，排行第33位。1997年夏与美国和世界最大的飞机制造商，波音公司(Boeing Company)合并。合并后的波音—麦道公司国际竞争能力大为增强。

16. General Motors　美国通用汽车公司

世界上最大的制造商之一，也是最大的汽车生产商。主要制造、装配和销售马达驱动产品。除汽车外，该公司还生产柴油机和各种发电机。公司成立于1916年，总部设在底特律。1992年销售额为1 327.749亿美元，全美排行第一。资产为1 910.128亿美元，排行第二。

17. Ford　美国福特汽车公司

主要生产、装配和销售轿车、卡车、拖拉机、各种有关零部件、零配件，并开发和制造家用电器和太空工业用电子产品，工业和化工产品，建筑工程玻璃以及供政府部门使用的空间防御产品，此外还从事财经和保险业务。公司成立于1903年，总部设在密歇根州第伯恩。1992年销售额为1 007.856亿美元，全美排行第三。资产有1 805.452亿美元，全美排行亦为第三。

18. conglomerate　跨行业公司

同时从事多种多样经营活动的企业。这种企业的形成是多年来陆续买进不同行业的附属机构或子公司的结果。出现这种类型的企业，主要是为了减少和分散业务风险而从事多种经营。

19. semiconductor chips　半导体集成电路芯片

是高科技电子产品如计算机集成电路的载体，被视为“电脑的心脏”。

20. NEC (Nippon Electric Company)　日本电气公司

主要生产电讯设备（包括电话、电视和收音机系统）和计算机。在纽约、伦敦和新加坡都有分公司。

21. Consortium　国际财团

指由多家公司组成的一个集团，从事由单一公司难于承担的大项目的投资与建设。

22. CITIC (China International Trust and Investment Company)　中国国际信托投资公司

成立于1979年，为国务院直接领导下经营的国有企业。该公司主要是授权协调来华外资，促进中外合资企业的建立和协助建立外国独资企业，并通过其业务活动促成先进技术及最新设备的引进。

23. China Resources Inc.　香港华润（集团）有限公司

成立于1948年12月，1952年划归对外贸易部，是我国经贸部所属各外贸专业总公司在香港的总代理。华润公司是一个以贸易为主，多元化经营的大型企业集团。主要经营范围包括：各类商品进出口及转口；香港本地的批发和零售业务；承办陆空运输及仓储业务；提供广告宣传、商品展览、贸易咨询等服务；投资企业，兴办工厂，从事合资经营，合作生产等；并在海外设有一些企业，从事贸易、生产及房地产开发等。

Questions on Content and Language Points

(for preview, discussion and review)

1. "If there is a road to China's future, Highway 204 out of Shanghai is it."

1) What is the exact meaning of "out of" here in the sentence?

2) Why does the author compare Highway 204 to the road to China's future? (you may answer the question after you've studied the whole article.)

2. "Migrant workers crowd the narrow shoulders"

What does "shoulders" refer to?

3. "Eventually, industry gives way to rice fields, which is being dug up to build still more factories."

1) What does the phrase "to give way to something" mean in the above sentence?

2) What does the author mean to convey to the readers when he used the word "eventually"?

4. Please explain the following phrases as they appear in their respective contexts:

"dynamic economy" (paragraph 2)

"the world's dominant economy" (paragraph 3)

5. "We don't have people, we don't have time," says one. "Things are moving too fast."

What is the meaning of "We don't have people" in the above sentence?

(Don't the officials think we've already had the largest population in the world?)

6. "Many economists believe a standard estimate of China's per capita gross national product ($370) is already two to three times too low."

According to the information given, could you figure out the economists' idea about China's per capital GNP?

(How much do these economists believe the estimate of China's per capita GNP should be?)

7. "Bill Clinton has appointed China hands to top Asia posts at the State and Treasury departments."

Please translate the above sentence into Chinese and explain the implication of Mr. Clinton's action.

8. Can you paraphrase the following sentence in your own words, especially the phrase <u>a work in progress</u>?

"Clearly, China's economy is a work in progress, nowhere near realizing the potential of its billion-plus population."

9. "China remains primarily a nation of farmers, and the transition to an industrial free market is much like the traffic on Highway 204—unpredictable."

1) What does the author mean by comparing the transition to "the traffic on Highway 204"?

2) According to the information from the article (given in the next two sentences following the above one), what changes does China need in order to realize the market economy in the author's opinion? Is it totally acceptable to Socialist China?

10. "Last year the BeiBei Company in Zhangjiagang <u>cleared $14 million on exports</u> of 10 million pairs of shoes to US department store."

Please explain the underlined part in the above sentence.

11. "Just two years ago South Korean manufacturers were flourishing <u>on</u> contracts from western athletic footwear giants ...."

What does "on" mean? Can you give some more examples?

12. "Since then much of the business has <u>shifted</u> to China, dealing a hard blow to the South Korean shoe industry."

1) Please explain the meaning of "shift" and find a synonym?

2) What part of the sentence is the phrase introduced by dealing? What does it show?

13. "Membership in this club, which includes all the world's leading economies, could provide a huge boost for a low-wage export economy."

How many reasons are mentioned in the sentence for "a huge boost"?

In what way could low wages promote the export?

14. "Already though, China's commercial strength is starting to worry competitors."

What part of speech is the word "though"? What part of the sentence is it? And what is the meaning it implies?

15. "The trade surplus itself will be the No. 1 problem this year," says one Chinese official. "After Japan we'll be the first in line for retaliation."

Can you find out why trade surplus would be a problem and for what reason(s) or on what excuse "we might be retaliated?"

16. "And the rest of the world will look foolish if it lets itself be caught by surprise."

What does the author imply by the above words?

Exercises

Ⅰ. Say whether the following is true or false according to the text.

1. The traffic on Highway 204 is very slow according to the author. ( )

2. As China's economic boom started in Guangdong Province, the foreign investors paid attention only to that part of China and poured their money into the area. ( )

3. The fact that President Bill Clinton appointed China hands

to top Asia posts at the State and Treasury departments reflects the important position China now occupies in the minds of the decision makers of the USA. ( )

4. The transition of China from an agricultural nation to an industrial country will be very slow and difficult. ( )

5. The private sectors of China's economy feel unsafe because relative laws and regulations have not been well established yet. ( )

6. The low cost labour force enabled China to have a great competitive advantage over some of her Asian neighbors. ( )

7. The strategy of opening markets to more U. S. goods is adopted by Chinese leaders in the hope of obtaining Washington's support in winning back China's membership in GATT. ( )

8. The Americans would not care so much as the Chinese in keeping good relations between the two countries. ( )

9. The Chinese corporations, either state-owned or state-affiliated, are energetically searching for opportunities abroad. ( )

10. There is the opinion that China's economic development has been going too fast, resulting in a sharp increase in inflation. ( )

Ⅱ. Read the article and explain the picked sentences using your own words.

The Outlook

China's Economic Role In Asia Is Burgeoning

——*SHANGHAI, China*

In this endless megalopolis, Japanese factories crowd against Hong Kong office towers, Taiwanese pay cash for apartments, and Singaporeans scour for trade opportunities.

Asia's dynamos are accustomed to competing—for capital, for technology, for markets—but in China they are varying for position. They seek to weave ties with an economy that not only transfixes but may transform Asia.

With 1. 2 billion people and an economy growing more rapidly than any other in the region, China's rising importance as a trader, manufacturer and investor offers neighbors once heavily dependent on U. S. trade a fast-growth cushion against slowdowns in the West, says Shan Li, China economist at Goldman, Sachs & Co. Countries such as tiny Singapore, bordered by Indonesia and Malaysia, also gain regional reassurance through closer ties to Asia's political and economic giant, he notes.

"China is becoming Asia's economic engine," proclaims Tian Zhongqing, an economist at a state-funded think tank here. Although the U. S. remains by far Asia's largest export market and Japan the No. 1 Asian economy, China is so intertwined with regional investment and trade flows that many in Asia believe its importance soon may rival that of the old economic powers.

And most signs point to a healthy relationship between China and its neighbors. Trade between China and the rest of Asia is soaring, up nearly a quarter last year alone and more than a third in the first half of 1995. "You show me where people are investing, and I'll show you where trade will follow," says Andrew Freris, chief Asian economist for Salomon Brothers Inc. Last year, the investments pouring into China totaled about $34 billion, a record.

More than one-third of China's exports come from foreign—mainly Asian—owned factories. The big beneficiaries are Hong Kong and Taiwan. By integrating Chinese factories into production strategies, their companies can compete globally. Factory wages on the mainland—less than $1 000 a year—are a 10th those in Taiwan. Companies from Hong Kong, a trading port of six million people, now employ more than three million workers in China.

For Japanese businesses grappling with the strong yen, China

Growing Links

China's trade flows with Asia, In blllons of dollars

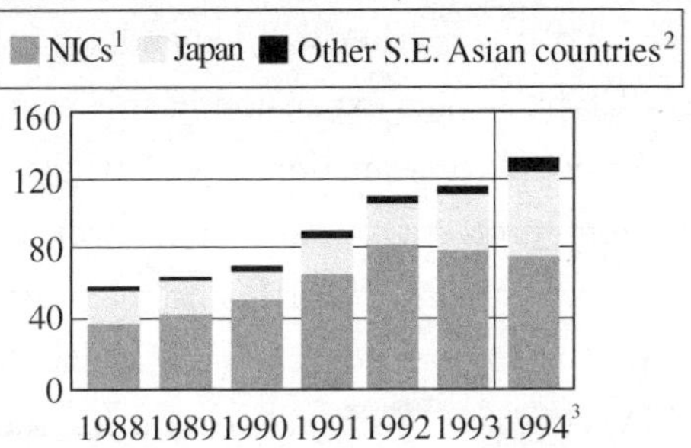

1. Newly Industrialized Countries South Korea Taiwan Hong Kong, Singapore
2. Indonesia Malaysia. Phillppines, Thailand
3. Estimate

Source: Develapment Bank of Singapore Ltd.

is especially attractive. Japan's domestic market is sagging, and yen-based costs are pricing its exports too high. China offers a thriving market and a cheap production base. Nearly one of every 10 yen that Japanese companies invest this year will end up in China, by one estimate. The latest move: Akai Electric Co. pledged $230 million for 81% of a Hong Kong company that is South China's biggest maker of consumer electronic goods. It then laid off 40% of its Japanese work force.

But it isn't just manufacturing that links China to Asia. China's huge appetite for everything from grain to top-of-the-line technologies helps, too. South Korea's auto industry and Japan's steel industry, both dragging, get a big lift from China, according to Lehman Brothers Inc.

And China's market could grow even more important, and not just to Asia. Deputy U. S. Trade Representative Charlene Barshevsky, in recent testimony to Congress, noted that although Sino-American trade surged to $40 billion last year from only $2 billion when Beijing began its economic reforms in 1979, trade in some areas, notably services, is still generally closed. As it opens, and if China succeeds in a campaign to join the World Trade Organization, other areas of the market will expand.

To be sure, China's trade expansion hasn't been smooth. This year, Beijing averted U. S. sanctions by settling a dispute over copyright and patent protection. And China won't be joining the WTO unless it opens its markets further to meet global standards.

But by the year 2010, according to the Organization of Economic Cooperation and Development, Asia will account for one-third of global demand— and China will almost certainly be the largest component. Asia's other giant, India, is shackled by poorer infrastructure, complex regulations and latent economic nationalism and isn't likely to match China despite increasing popularity with foreign investors.

China reciprocates Asian interest with regional interests of its own. Friedrich Wu, chief economist at Development Bank of Singapore Ltd., says at least 120 Chinese companies have set up shop in the island republic since 1990. Even China's state oil-products giant, Sinochem wants a Singapore stock-market listing by year end.

Marcus W. Brauchu

From *Wall Street Journal* · July 24, 1995

Ⅲ. The picked sentences for paraphrasing exercise:

(1) They seek to weave ties with an economy that not only transfixes but may transform Asia.

(2) China is becoming Asia's economic engine. Although the U. S. remains by far Asia's largest export market and Japan the No. 1 Asian economy, China is so intertwined with regional investment and trade flows that many in Asia believe its importance soon may rival that of the old economic powers.

(3) "You show me where people are investing, and I'll show you where trade will follow."

(4) Japan's domestic market is sagging, and yen-based costs are pricing its exports too high. China offers a thriving market and a cheap production base.

Ⅳ. Translate the following paragraphs and sentences into Chinese.

1. With 1.2 billion people and an economy growing more rapidly than any other in the region, China' rising importance as a trader, manufacturer and investor offers neighbors once heavily dependent on U. S. trade a fast-growth cushion against slow-downs in the West,...

2. For Japanese businesses grappling with the strong yen, China is especially attractive. Japan's domestic market is sagging, and yen-based costs are pricing its exports too high. China offers thriving market and a cheap production base. Nearly one of every 10 yen that Japanese companies invest this year will end up in China, by one estimate.

3. To be sure, China's trade expansion hasn't been smooth. This year, Beijing averted U. S. sanctions by settling a dispute over copyright and patent protection. And China won't be joining the WTO unless it opens its markets further to meet global standards.

Supplementary Marterial for Free Reading

A. Market Plays Important Role

Interview Li Peng, premier

The prime minister speaks about the subjects that dominate Chinese thought and policy.

Mr Li Peng, China's premier, spoke to the Financial Times in Beijing recently. What follows are his observations on key issues facing the country.

Economic reform: "We think that the market plays a fundamental role in the allocaion of resources. In China, a socialist country, this role can only be brought into full play under the government's macro-regulation and control. The Chinese government will resort to multiple means to exercise macro-control over the economy, such as through the plan, through fiscal policies, and through monetary policy."

Economic growth and monetary policy: "We practise a moderately tight monetary policy and this will remain unchanged. However, we will somewhat ease controls over working capital for the production of marketable goods."

Entry to the World Trade Organisation: "China maintains that if it is not able to join the WTO, that is of course a loss for it; but if the WTO rejects China, then that will also be a loss for the WTO. However, I cannot see the prospect of China's trade with other countries being affected if it is not a member of the WTO because China itself is a huge market. That is the reality. When I was in France, we signed the contract with Airbus to buy 33 Airbus planes; we did not do it through the WTO."

Preferential tax policies for special economic zones: "Our basic policy towards the state-owned enterprises in China remains unchanged. Corporate income tax for the foreign-invested enterprises is 15 per cent. I think this is fairly low compared with other countries in the world."

Foreign investment: "We want more investment in infrastructure; we also welcome co-operation in the technical transformation of small and medium-sized enterprises in light industries. In the services sector we are also ready to co-operate. But in the area of banks and insurance companies we are not ready to open on a large scale."

Relations with the US: "The United States has tried various means to interfere in China's internal affairs. The core issue in Sino—US relations is the question of Taiwan. If the United States can observe in deed not just in word the three Sino—US joint communiqués then it will be possible to further improve and develop relations between the two countries."

Participation in the Three Gorges hydro-power project: "China's biggest project is the Three Gorges project. But the EximBank of the US on the instruction of its government has said it will not provide loans to American companies that want to bid on the project. This policy of the United States actually kills the opportunities of American companies to participate. But it will lead to no loss to China because it can obtain the same technology from the Europeans or from the Russians."

Relations with Eurorpe: "The Europeans have more favourable terms, more lenient terms. They do not attach political strings to co-operation with China—unlike the Americans who arbitrarily resort to the threat of sanctions or the use of sanctions. This is the reason that has prompted China to enter into close co-operation with the Europeans. If the Europeans adopt more co-operation with China—not just in economic areas but also in political and other areas—then I believe they will get more orders from China."

Policy towards Taiwan: "So long as the Taiwan authorities can abandon pursuit of 'two Chinas' and can return to the position of 'one China' not just in word, but also in deed, then cross-straits relations will be improved and strengthened in a peaceful manner."

Resumption of sovereignty over Hong Kong: "There are less than 400 days before Hong Kong's sovereignty will return to China. The die is cast. This also accords with the aspirations of the people. The basic policy of China is to ensure a stable transition and smooth transfer of government in Hong Kong. I can say that for all Hong Kong people —for each and every Hong Kong person—so long as he or she loves Hong Kong, loves the motherland, abides by the Basic Law, he or she can have a role to play in the future of Hong Kong."

Political reform:"Apart from our economic reform we will continue to promote our political reform. The purpose of political restructuring is to make the government more efficient and to enable the people to play a bigger role to serve as masters of the state so that the capacities for developing the country can be mobilized. Some people in the west believe that along with economic development China will evolve more into a western democracy, but we think it is not possible here."

Interview conducted by Tony Walker, Peter Montagnon and John Ridding

—From *Financial Times* • June 27, 1996

B. Bullish Firms Clamor for China Market

(Excerpts)

By Robert Cameron

China is a country with big opportunities. Witness the enthusiasm of international corporations pouring enormous amounts of direct investment into China and the crowds of companies clamoring to do business there.

The ever-bullish William Overholt, a director of Bankers Trust in Hong Kong and a veteran China watcher, speaking at the Hotel Okura in Tokyo recently, wanted to put in perspective some of what he considers dangerous misperceptions and shed some positive light on China's drive for modernization.

The U. S. and Japan, for example, can in the foreseeable future expect growth of 2 per cent a year, if they are managed well, Overholt said, whereas China is expecting between 8 per cent and 9 per cent a year, in the same league as the most vigorous of the Asian "tiger" economies. China will hugely overshadow Japan's economy and will catch up with that of the U. S. very soon.

The China numbers are enormous, but so are the stakes for businesses wanting to compete globally. For example, China is today the world's largest purchaser of civil aircraft, so if Boeing wants to be a global force, it has to be in China. If it loses the China market it doesn't just lose sales in China; it loses the economies of scale that make it possible to compete globally.

The same is true of power plants and other industrial machinery, right down to basic consumer goods like soft drinks and cosmetics.

Overholt points to an investor-friendly business environment that has prompted a flow of direct foreign investment of unprecedented proportions. In 1994, China got $34 billion in direct foreign investment, in 1995 $39 billion; last year the figure was $40.5 billion.

To provide a sense of how big these numbers are, Overholt cites the No. 2 economy in the developing world, Brazil. Between World War II and 1994, Brazil got less foreign direct investment than China got in 1994 alone.

The money is flooding in for a specific reason. Other Asian nations, such as Japan, financed their postwar growth using primarily debt financing. Official development banks borrowed from foreign banks and then lent the money to big corporations, mostly keeping the direct investor out.

"The Chinese added up the numbers of how much money they were going to need," Overholt said, "and there wasn't enough debt in the universe" to finance their modernization. Hence the openness to foreign investment and the emphasis on stability and reform.

Overholt warns naysayers against judging from a snapshot perspective a 30-year process that is only three to five years along and cites some reliable indicators.

China has foreign exchange reserves of $110 billion. That

puts it about second in the world, after Japan. Three years ago that figure was $21 billion, and "by end of this year it will be much bigger because they're trying to keep the Renminbi from getting too strong and undermining their export sector. They're going to be buying a lot of dollars."

At the same time, it has brought inflation down from 24 per cent in 1994 to about 6 per cent today (the difference largely attributable to a large trade surplus), while keeping growth at around 10 per cent.

All this is in addition to the world's most ambitious banking reform, which has also just begun, the world's most ambitious tax reform and a very ambitious legal reform.

The process could still sour. A lot of painful restructuring is in store for China, and the social upheavals could prompt a backlash from the millions of state enterprise workers with a strong interest in maintaining the status quo.

Overholt counsels patience. "You have to give them a little credit for this kind of progress. If you take a snapshot of China, it looks unideal." But look at where it was five years ago and where it is today: nobody in human history has done what it has done.

—From *The Japan Times* • Feb. 17, 1997

Appendix to Lesson 1—3

The following article is provided to help readers gain a full and deep understanding of the significance and guiding principles of China's reform and opening to the outside world.

Deng Calls for Speedup in Reform

Following is part of Deng Xiaoping's remarks on June 12, 1987 to Stefan Korosee, member of the Presidum of the Central Committee of the League of Communists of Yugoslavia. Subtitles are Beijing Review's.

No Reform, No Way Out for China

China is now carrying out a reform. I am all in favour of that. There is no other solution for us. After years of practice it turned out that the old stuff didn't work. In the past we copied foreign models mechanically, which only hampered the development of our productive forces, induced ideological rigidity and kept people and grass-roots units from taking any initiative. We made some mistakes of our own as well, such as the "great leap forward" and the "cultural revolution," which were our own inventions. I would say that since 1957 our major mistakes have been "left" ones. The "cultural revolution" was an ultra-left mistake. In fact, during the two decades from 1958 through 1978, China remained at a standstill. There was little economic growth and not much of a rise in the people's standard of living. How could we go on like that without introducing reforms? So in 1978, at the Third Plenary Session of the 11th Central Committee, we formulated a new basic political line: to give first priority to the drive for modernization and strive to develop the productive forces. In accordance with that line we drew up a series of new principles and policies, the major ones being reform and the open policy. By reform we mean something comprehensive, including reform of both the economic structure and the political structure and corresponding changes in all other areas. By the open policy we mean both opening to all other countries, irrespective of their social sysytems, and opening at home, which means invigorating the domestic economy.

Great Achievements In Rural Reform

We introduced reform and the open policy first in the economic field, beginning with the countryside. Why did we start there? Because that is where 80 per cent of China's population lives. An unstable situation in the countryside would lead to an unstable political situation throughout the country. If the peasants did not shake off poverty, it would mean that the majority of the people remained poor. So after the Third Plenary Session of the 11th Central Committee, we decided to carry out rural reform, giving more decision-making power to the peasants and the grass-roots units. By so doing we immediately brought their initiative into play. And by adopting a policy of diversifying agriculture, we substantially increased not only the output of grain but also the output of cash crops. The rural reform has achieved much faster results than we had anticipated. Frankly, before the reform the majority of the peasants were extremely poor, hardly able to afford enough food, clothing, shelter and transportation. Since the rural reform began they have shown their initiative. Bearing local conditions in mind, they have grown grain and cash crops in places suited to them. Since the peasants were given the power to decide for themselves what to produce, they have brought about a dramatic change in the rural areas. The reform was so successful that in many places it yielded tangible results within just one year. The peasants' income has increased substantially, sometimes even doubling or quadrupling.

Of course, not everyone was in favour of reform at the outset.

At the beginning two provinces took the lead: Sichuan and Anhui. We worked out the principles and policies of reform on the basis of the experience accumulated by these two provinces. For one or two years after we publicized these principles and policies, some provinces had misgivings about them and others didn't know what to think, but in the end they all followed suit. The Central Committee's policy was to wait for them to be convinced by facts.

Generally speaking, once the peasants' initiative was brought into play, the rural reform developed very quickly. Our greatest success—and it is one we had by no means anticipated—has been the emergence of a large number of enterprises run by villages and townships. They were like a new force that just came into being spontaneously. These enterprises engage in the most diverse endeavours, including both manufacturing and trade. The Central Committee takes no credit for this. The annual output value of these village and township enterprises has been increasing by more than 20 per cent every year. Their output value has been greater than in the corresponding period last year. This increase in village and township enterprises, particularly industrial enterprises, has provided jobs for 50 per cent of the surplus labour in the countryside. Instead of flocking into the cities, the surplus farm workers have been building up a new type of villages and townships. If the Central Committee made any contribution in this respect, it was only by laying down the correct policy of invigorating the domestic economy. The fact that this policy has had such a favourable result shows that we made a good decision. But this result was not anything that I or any of the other comrades had foreseen; it just came out of the blue. In short, the rural reform has produced rapid and noticeable results. Of course, that doesn't mean all the problems in the countryside have been solved.

The success of the reform in the countryside emboldened us to apply the experience we had gained from it to economic restructuring in the cities. That too has been very successful, although it is more complicated than rural reform.

Urban Reform and Our Open Policy

In the meantime the policy of opening China's doors to the outside world has produced the results we hoped for. We have implemented that policy in various ways, including setting up special economic zones and opening 14 coastal cities. Wherever the open policy has been implemented there have been notable reaults. First we established the Shenzhen Special Economic Zone. It was the leaders of Guangdong Province who came up with the proposal that special zones be established, and I agreed. But I said they should be called special economic zones, not special political zones, because we didn't want anything of that sort. We decided to set up three more special zones in addition to Shenzhen—Zhuhai and Shantou, both also in Guangdong Province, and Xiamen in Fujian Province. I visited Shenzhen a couple of years ago and found the economy flourishing there. The Shenzhen people asked me to write an inscription for them, and I wrote: "The development and experience of the Shenzhen Special Economic Zone prove the correctness of our policy of establishing such zones." At the time, a number of people of different political persuasions, from Hong Kong journalists to Party members, were sceptical about that policy. They didn't think it would work. But the Shenzhen Special Economic Zone has achieved remarkable successes since it was established almost eight years ago. This zone is an entriely new thing, and it is not fair for the people who run it not to be allowed to make mistakes. If they have made mistakes, they were minor ones. The people in Shenzhen reviewed their experience and decided to shift the zone's economy from a domestic orientation to an external orientation, which meant that Shenzhen would become an industrial base and offer its products on the world market. It is only two or three years since then, and already the situation in Shenzhen has changed greatly. The comrades there told me that more than 50 per cent of their products were exported and that receipts and payments of foreign exchange were in balance.

I am now in a position to say with certainty that our decision to establish special economic zones was a good one and has proved successful. All scepticism has vanished. Recently a comrade told me that the Xiamen Special Economic Zone is developing even faster than Shenzhen. When I visited Xiamen in 1984, there was only an airport surrounded by wasteland. Great changes have taken place there since then. Now we are preparing to make all of Hainan Island a special economic zone. Hainan Island, which is almost as big as Taiwan, has abundant natural resources, such as iron ore and oil, as well as rubber and other tropical and subtropical crops. When it is fully developed, the results should be extraordinary.

Our achievements in the last few years have proved the correctness of our policies of reform and of opening to the outside world. Although there are still problems in various fields, I don't think they'll be too hard to solve, if we go at it systematically. Therefore, we must not abandon these policies or even slow them down. One of the topics we have been discussing recently is whether we should speed up reform or slow it down. That's because reform and the open policy involve risks. Of course we have to be cautious, but that doesn't mean we should do nothing. Indeed, on the basis of our experience to date, the Central Committee has been considering to accelerate the reform and our opening to the outside world.

So much for reform of the economic structure.

Reform of Political Structure

Now a new question has been raised, reform of the political structure. This will be one of the main topics at the 13th National Party Congress to be held next October. It's a complicated issue.

Every measure taken in this connection will affect millions of people, mainly cadres, including the veterans.

Generally speaking, reform of the political structure involves democratization, but what that means is not very clear. The democracy in capitalist societies is bourgeois democracy—in fact, it is the democracy of monopoly capitalists. It is no more than a system of multi—party elections and a balance of the three powers. Can we adopt this system? Ours is the system of the people's congresses and people's democracy under the leadership of the Communist Party. The greatest advantage of the socialist system is that when the central leadership makes a decision it is promptly implemented without interference from any other quarters. When we decided to reform the economic structure, the whole country responded; when we decided to establish the special economic zones, they were soon set up. We don't have to go through a lot of repetitive discussion and consultation, with one branch of government holding up another and decisions being made but not carried out. From this point of view, our system is very efficient. We should neither copy Western democracy nor introduce the system of a balance of three powers. We should uphold socialist democracy, so as to retain the advantages of the socialist system. The efficiency I'm talking about is not efficiency of administration or economic management, but overall efficiency. We have superiority in this respect, and we should keep it. In terms of administration and economic management, the capitalist countries are more efficient than we in many ways.

China is burdened with bureaucratism. Take our personnel system, for example, I think the socialist countries all have a problem of ageing cadres, so that leaders at all levels tend to be rigid in their thinking. But we think that to reform our political structure we can't copy the Western system, the capitalist system. We socialist countries have to work out the content of the reform and take specific measures to implement it in the light of our own practice and our own conditions. The particular reform to be carried out in each socialist country is different too, and that is true of the East European countries. Since each has a different history, different experience and different current circumstances to confront, their reforms cannot be identical. Take China, for instance. We have a different point of view from yours on the question of reform. But we have in common the desire to retain our superiority and avoid the defects and evils that exist in capitalist societies.

What is the purpose of political restructuring? Its general purpose is to consolidate the socialist system, the leader ship of the Party and the development of the productive forces under that system and that leadership. So far as China is concerned, the reform should also make it easier to implement the line, principles and policies laid down by the Party since the Third Plenary Session of its 11th Central Committee. To this end we have to do the following, I believe:

(1) revitalize the Party, the administrative organs and the whole state apparatus, so that they are staffed with people whose thinking is not ossified and who can bring fresh ideas to bear on new problems;

(2) increase efficiency; and

(3) stimulate the initiative of the people and of the grass-roots units in all fields of endeavour.

Revitalization. Here, the biggest problem is the need for younger cadres. In China the problem of ageing cadres with rigid ideas is more serious than it is in your country. For example, in our Central Committee the average age of members is higher than it is in the cental committee of any other Communist Party in the world. The average age of the members of our Political Bureau, of its Standing Committee and of the Secretariat of the Central Committee is also quite high. There was no such problem when the People's Republic of China was founded. At that time the leaders were young. The problem of ageing leaders in the central organs didn't manifest itself until the 11th National Party Congress. There was an objective reason for this: a great many veterans who had been brought down during the "cultural revolution" were now rehabilitated and were resuming their posts at an advanced age. Take myself for example. I was only 52 when the Eighth National Party Congress was convened in 1956, but I was 72 when the "cultural revolution" ended in 1976. I was 73 when the 11th National Party Congress was held in 1977, and I will be 83 when the 13th National Party Congress meets later this year. Some comrades are younger than I, but only by a few years: they are elderly too. This problem exists in leading organs at all levels and in all fields of endeavour. It is the outstanding problem in China.

In general, old people tend to be conservative. They all have one thing in common: they consider problems only in the light of their personal experience. In today's world things are moving with unprecedented rapidity, especially in science and technology. There is an old saying in China. "Progress is made everyday," and that's the way things are today. We must keep abreast of the times; that is the purpose of our reform. We must firmly carry out the policy of promoting younger cadres, but we must be cautious and proceed gradually. We are bound to meet with obstacles and we will have to overcome them. It's going to take a lot of effort. Of course, youth is not the only criterion for promoting cadres. They should have political integrity and professional competence, broad experience and familiarity with conditions, so as to form a reliable echelon of leaders of different years of age.

Increasing efficiency and eliminating bureaucratism. This includes, among other things, streamlining Party and government organs.

Stimulating people's initiative. The main idea is to delegate power to lower levels. The reason our rural reform has been so successful is that we gave the peasants more power to make decisions, and that stimulated their initiative. We are now applying this experience to all fields of work. When the people's initiative is aroused, that's the best manifestation of democracy.

These are the three objectives for our reform of the political structure. Democracy is an important means of carrying out our reform. But the question is how to put it into practice. Take general elections for instance. We run general elections at the lower levels, that is for county and district posts, and indirect elections at the provincial and municipal and the central levels. China is such a huge country, with such an enormous population, so many nationalities and such varied conditions that it is not yet possible to hold direct elections at higher levels. Furthermore, the people's educational level is too low. So we have to stick to the system of people's congresses, in which democratic centralism is applied. The Western two-chamber, multi-party system won't work in China. China also has a number of democratic parties, but they all accept leadership by the Communist Party. Ours is a system under which we make decisions after consulation with all the other parties. In this connection, even Westerners agree that in a country as vast as China, if there were no central leadership many problems would be hard to solve, first of all, the problem of food.

Our reform cannot depart from socialism, it cannot be accomplished without the leadership of the Communist Party. Socialism and Party leadership are interrelated; they cannot be separated from each other. Without the leadership of the Communist Party, there can be no building of socialism. We shall never again allow the kind of democracy we had during the "cultural revolution". Actually that was anarchy.

In short, so far as economic reform is concerned, the principles, policies and methods have been set. All we have to do now is to speed up their implementation. As for reform of the political structure, we are still discussing what its goals should be. We will work that out before the 13th National Party Congress and launch the reform after that. It took three years for the rural economic reform to achieve good results, and it should take from three to five years for the urban economic reform to produce the visible results we expect. Reform of the political structure will be more complicated. In certain aspects, results can be obtained in from three to five years, but in certain others it may take ten.

—From *Beijing Review* · Aug. 24, 1987

Words and Expressions

Presidum	*n.*	(共产党国家政府的)常务委员会
hamper	*v.*	阻碍,束缚
rigidity	*n.*	僵硬,僵化
standstill	*n.*	停止,停顿
standard of living	生活水平	
formulate	*v.*	规划;制定
priority	*n.*	优先,重点
give priority to...	最优先考虑…	
invigorate	*v.*	激励;使生气勃勃
diversify	*v.*	使多样化
dramatic	*a.*	引人注目的;给人印象深刻的
tangible	*a.*	实际的;非想象的
quadruple	*v.*	成为四倍的
accumulate	*v.*	积累
misgiving	*n.*	(常作～s)(尤指对未来事件的)疑虑;担忧
township	*n.*	镇

spontaneously	*ad.* 自然地;自发地
corresponding	*a.* 相应的;对等的
surplus labour	剩余劳动力
implement	*v.* 实施;执行
inscription	*n.* 题词
political persuasion	政治派别
abundant	*a.* 丰富的;富裕的
accelerate	*v.* 使加快;使增加
democratization	*n.* 民主化
interference	*n.* 干涉,干预
bureaucratism	*n.* 官僚主义;官僚体系
confront	*v.* 勇敢地面对;正视;对抗
apparatus	*n.* 机构
the state apparatus	国家机器
ossify	*v.* 僵化;使极端保守
manifest	*v.* 使显露;使显现
rehabilitate	*v.* 恢复…的职位;恢复…的名誉
unprecedented	*a.* 无前例的;空前的
keep abreast of	(使)不落后于;与…齐头并进
echelon	*n.* 领导(或指挥)系统中的等级
streamline	*v.* 精简;使效率更高
anarchy	*n.* 无政府(状态)

Notes to the Text

1. productive forces 生产力

亦称“社会生产力”。人们征服自然、改造自然的能力。表示人们在生产过程中对自然界的关系。它和生产关系是社会生产不可分割的两个方面。生产力主要包括:(1)具有一定的科学技术知识、生产经验和劳动技能的劳动者;(2)同一定的科学技术相结合的、以生产工具为主的劳动资料;(3)劳动对象。劳动者是生产力的首要的能动的要素,因为只有劳动者才能制造和改进生产工具,掌握和使用生产资料。

2. cash crops　经济作物

亦称"工业原料作物"、"特用作物"、"工艺作物"。指收获主要供作工业原料的一类作物。按用途可分为:纤维作物、油料作物、糖类作物、淀粉作物、嗜好作物、饮料作物、橡胶作物、染料作物、药用作物、鞣料作物、芳香油料作物等。

3. "... Hainan Island, which is almost as big as Taiwan."

海南是中国第二大岛,面积 32 200 平方千米。台湾面积为 35 780平方千米。

4. multi-party election　多党竞选

在西欧及许多资本主义国家一般都有两个或两个以上的政党并存、对抗。这些政党都通过选举得到国家权力。在选举活动中,各党派展开竞选活动,特别是在野党,宣传各自的政策以达到赢得选举的目的。

5. "... a balance of the three powers..."

在资本主义国家,国家权力一般以三种形式体现。议会负责立法,政府搞行政管理;而法院掌握司法大权。权力的均衡使这三方在管理国家时互相制约,没有三方的合作,国家大事则无法有效地进行。

6. "The western two-chamber ... system"　西方的两院(议会)制

议会由两院组成——上议院和下议院

英国称为上议院(House of Lords)和下议院(House of Commons);美国称为参议院(the Senate)和众议院(House of Representatives)。从宪法的角度来说,下议院可以用其法案约制上议院的行动。

7. anarchy　无政府状态

Questions on Content and Language Points

(for preview, discussion and review)

1. "... After years of practice it turned out that the old stuff didn't work..."

1) What does "stuff" mean in the text?

2) What does "the old stuff" refer to in the given context?

2. "I would say that since 1957 our major mistakes have been left ones."

What does "I would say" mean? What's its usual translation?

3. "In accordance with that line we drew up a series of new principles and policies, the major ones being reform and the open policy."

What is the underlined part of the sentence in grammar (the syntax)? Is it a loose descriptive attributive clause, or something else?

4. What is meant by "reform"? (See the last few lines of Section 1.)

5. What is meant by "the open policy"? (See the last few lines of Section 1.)

6. "We introduced reform and the open policy first in the economic field, beginning with the countryside."

In what sense is the verb "introduce" used here?

7. "Frankly, before the reform the majority of the peasants were extremely poor, hardly able to afford enough food, clothing, shelter and transportation."

Paraphrase the underlined part of the sentence.

8. "The peasants, income has increased substantially, sometimes even doubling or quadrupling."

Suppose the original income were RMB ¥100, how much would it be when it's doubled, and quadrupled?

What's the usual Chinese translation of quadruple in a case

like this?

9. "It was the leaders of Guangdong Province who came up with the proposal that special zones be established, and I agreed. But I said they should be called special economic zones, not special political zones,..."

Why did Comrade Deng Hsiaoping insist that the word economic be made prominent in naming the zone?

10. "... The comrades there (in Shenzhen) told me that more than 50 per cent of their products were exported and that receipts and payments of foreign exchange were in balance."

1) What do the enterprises there receive foreign exchange for?

2) What do they pay foreign exchange for?

11. "There is an old saying in China. 'Progress is made everyday,' and that's the way things are today."

What is the old Chinese saying?

12. "They (the cadres to be promoted) should have political integrity ..."

1) What is the meaning of "integrity" in the context?

2) What is the Chinese original of the English translation—"political integrity"?

13. What are the 3 objectives of the reform of the political structure?

Lesson 4
The World Economy

Text

The Economic Scene: A Global Perspective

(Excerpts)

In 1991, for the second year in a row, the economies of low-income and middle-income countries virtually stagnated, as measured by an increase in per capita gross domestic product (GDP). Aggregate output for developing countries advanced by slightly less than 2 per cent during 1991 (similar to the weak performance of 1990), implying an easing in per capita income of 0. 1 per cent.

Aggregate statistics for 1991 were influenced by the sharp decline in output in Central and Eastern Europe, as well as by the adverse effects of the Gulf crisis on several economies in the Middle East. Excluding Central and Eastern Europe, growth in developing countries in 1991 was 3. 4 per cent, compared with 3. 8 per cent during the 1980s. Estimates of GDP growth by major geographic region show an acceleration in Latin America and in sub-Saharan Africa; an increase in China's growth rate helped to sustain high rates of growth in the East Asia region.

International conditions for growth in developing countries deteriorated in 1991. The seven major industrial countries (the G—7) experienced a significant slowdown in GDP growth—from 2. 8 per cent in 1990 to 1. 9 per cent during 1991 as recession gripped Canada, the United Kingdom, and the United States and growth rates slowed in continental Europe and Japan. In important respects, the slowdown was different from those that occurred during the 1970s and 1980s. Rather than reflecting the effect of disinflationary policies, weakness in demand was more closely related to the loss of momentum that had built up during the long period of expansion that began in 1983. In addition, a common factor underlying the slowdown in many industrial countries was the cyclical deceleration in investment spending.

Although the weakness in demand in the United States led to a sharp decline in short-term dollar interest rates—a positive development for many developing countries—it also contributed to a drop of over 6 per cent in nonoil commodity prices and to a slackening, to 3 per cent, in the growth of world trade. These trends were compounded by worsening economic conditions in the Soviet Union and its successor states, where a growing shortage of foreign exchange led to a compression of imports from Eastern Europe and an acceleration of certain commodity exports (aluminum, gold and lead, for instance) to earn hard currencies.

Against this deteriorating global background, the improvement in economic performance in a few developing regions in 1991—which carried over into 1992—was especially noteworthy. This improvement is attributable, in part, to the implementation by many governments of measures to stabilize their economies and restructure incentives to encourage private initiative and international trade. Policy reforms in Latin America helped to moderate inflation and domestic demand; East Asian economics, supported by growth in export volume in the range of 10 per cent and by robust domestic demand, continued to grow rapidly. Sub-Saharan Africa raised its real GDP growth rate from 1. 3 per cent in 1990 to 2. 4 per cent in 1991.

Also noteworthy was the implementation by the Paris Club of a new menu of enhanced concessions in debt reschedulings for the severely indebted, low-income countries. The menu was introduced in agreements with Benin and Nicaragua, and was subsequently applied in agreements with Bolivia and Tanzania. Nonconcessional but special extended rescheduling terms were also accorded to ten severely indebted middle-income countries.

In the commodity market, prices of all major categories declined in 1991. The index of nonoil primary commodity prices in nominal dollar terms decline for the third consecutive year, and the index in real terms hit an all-time low. Growth in the volume of world trade in constant dollar terms declined from 5 per cent in 1990 to 3 per cent in 1991, mainly the result of the slowdown in industrial countries' import demand. There were no breakthroughs in the Uruguay Round of GATT negotiations on key elements, and the outcome remains in doubt.

In matters relating to the environment, the United Nations Conference on Environment and Development, held in June 1992 in Rio de Janeiro, produced an "Earth Charter," or declaration of basic principles for the conduct of nations and peoples with respect to environment and development; agreements on specific legal measures, including conventions on climate change and biodiversity, and principles for a framework agreement on forests; and an agenda for action ("Agenda 21"), establishing the environmental work program agreed by the international community for the period beyond 1992 and into the twenty-first century.

Major Industrial Countries

Growth in the G—7 countries decelerated from 2.8 per cent in 1990 to 1.9 per cent in 1991 (see Table 1). The broad trend was the outcome of largely unexpected setbacks to recovery in the United States and the United Kingdom and the apparent onset of a slower period of economic growth in Japan and Germany. A cyclical slowdown of investment was apparently a major component of the slowdown: In-**Table 1. G-7 Countries: Output, Inflation, Investment, and Unemployment, 1981—1991**

(average annual percentage change: unemployment rates in per cent)

G-7 country	1981—1991[a]	1990	1991[b]	1981—1991[a]	1990	1991[b]
	Real GNP or GDP[c]			GNP or GDP deflator[c]		
Canada	3. 2	0. 5	−1. 5	3. 9	3. 0	2. 7
France	2. 5	2. 2	1. 3	5. 1	3. 1	3. 0
Germany[d]	2. 5	4. 5	3. 1	2. 7	3. 4	4. 6
Italy	2. 6	2. 2	1. 4	8. 7	7. 6	7. 3
Japan	4. 4	5. 2	4. 5	1. 4	2. 1	1. 9
United Kingdom	3. 0	1. 0	−2. 2	5. 6	6. 4	6. 9
United States	2. 9	1. 0	0. 9	3. 8	4. 2	3. 6
Aggregate weighted average[e]	3. 0	2. 8	1. 9	3. 5	3. 8	3. 8
	Gross fixed investment			Unemployment rate		
Canada	4. 5	−3. 3	−3. 5	9. 5	8. 1	10. 3
France	3. 2	2. 9	−0. 6	9. 3	8. 9	9. 4
Germany[d]	3. 2	8. 8	6. 7	5. 7	4. 9	4. 3
Italy	2. 8	3. 3	0. 9	10. 7	11. 1	11. 0
Japan	6. 4	9. 5	3. 5	2. 5	2. 1	2. 1
United Kingdom	5. 3	−2. 4	−10. 3	9. 5	5. 9	8. 3
United States	2. 5	−1. 6	−7. 6	7. 1	5. 5	6. 7
Aggregate weighted average[e]	3. 7	3. 5	−0. 9	6. 5	5. 4	5. 9

Note: a. Ordinary least squares trend.

b. Preliminary.

c. GNP for Germany, Japan and the United States; GDP for others.

d. The part of Germany corresponding to the western *L!? nder*.

e. Aggregates are weighted on the basis of 1987 values of GNP or GDP converted to US dollars at 1987 exchange rates.

Source: Organization for Economic Co-operation and Development (OECD).

vestment decelerated or fell during 1991 in all the G—7 countries. In Japan, the cyclical slowing of investment was probably the dominant factor in weaker growth, but a slump in construction of rental housing and the fading of a tax-cut-induced boom in auto sales also contributed. In Germany, the role of investment was dominant, as well. Unification further boosted investment, which then appeared to diminish, as expectations of profitability were dampened by higher wages and high short-term nominal and real interest rates. Upward pressures on wages and interest rates generally dampened economic activity in Germany during 1991. The special factor there was the pressure on interest rates that arose from the financing of unification and from anti-inflationary monetary policy. Inflation as measured by the GDP deflator slackened in most of the G-7 countries. It continued to decelerate in North America and edged down in Japan. The record in Europe was mixed, however, inflation eased somewhat in Italy and in the smaller economies such as Spain and Portugal, but accelerated by about one half of a percentage point in the United Kingdom (the result of statistical anomalies) and by more than a point in Germany.

The slowdown of the industrial countries in 1991 partly originated in structural problems inherited from the 1980s. Slower growth in Europe in 1991 revealed that unemployment, for instance, was still a structurally problematic area. The unemployment rate in the four largest European economies was 7. 8 per cent in 1990, near the peak of the business cycle, and rose to 8. 3 per cent in 1991. Financial stress brought on by excessive debt in the household and corporate sectors was an example of another kind of structural problem, in particular for the economies of Japan and the United States. Financial institutions in these two countries adopted more conservative lending policies, curtailing financing of higher-risk projects such as commercial construction and highly leveraged corporate transactions. A number of weaker institutions were also consolidated through bankruptcy, merger and reorganization. These developments played some part in the general tightening of credit during 1991, which may have helped to slow the pace of investment in the United States and Japan. Weak growth of credit and a fall in some asset prices probably slowed consumption, as well.

A notable development in 1991 was a narrowing of current-account imbalances of most major industrial countries (see Table 2): The

U. S. current-account deficit moved to near balance (only 0. 2 per cent of gross domestic product). The trade component of the deficit narrowed as lower inflation and earlier dollar depreciation improved competitiveness, while the transfers component moved into substantial surplus because of war-related payments. Moreover, there was a remarkable swing in the German current account—from a surplus equivalent to 3. 2 per cent of GDP in 1990 to a deficit of 1. 3 per cnet. A continuation of the surge of imports that followed unification, as well as the earlier appreciation of the deutsche mark, contributed to the swing. The Japanese surplus on current account rose from 1. 2 per cent of gross domestic product in 1990 to 2. 1 per cent in 1991.

Table 2. Current-account Balances of the G-7 Countries, 1984—1991

G-7 country	1984	1985	1986	1987	1988	1989	1990	1991[a]
Billions of US dollars								
Canada	2. 1	−2. 3	−8. 2	−8. 8	−11. 3	−17. 5	−18. 9	−23. 4
France	−1. 2	−0. 2	2. 0	−4. 9	−4. 7	−5. 5	−15. 2	−6. 3
Germany[b]	9. 8	16. 4	39. 5	45. 9	50. 5	57. 2	47. 9	−20. 7
Italy	−2. 3	−3. 6	2. 4	−1. 1	−5. 8	−10. 6	−14. 4	−18. 8
Japan	35. 0	49. 2	85. 8	87. 0	79. 6	57. 2	35. 5	72. 6
United Kingdom	2. 4	3. 5	−0. 1	−7. 1	−27. 4	−33. 4	−25. 5	−7. 8
United States	−99. 0	−122. 3	−145. 4	−160. 2	−126. 2	−106. 3	−92. 1	−8. 6
Total G-7	−53. 2	−59. 3	−24. 0	−49. 1	−45. 2	−59. 0	−82. 7	−13. 0
Percentage of GDP								
Canada	0. 6	−0. 6	−2. 3	−2. 1	−2. 3	−3. 2	−3. 3	−3. 9
France	−0. 2	0. 0	0. 3	−0. 6	−0. 5	−0. 6	−1. 3	−0. 5
Germany[b]	1. 6	2. 6	4. 4	4. 1	4. 2	4. 8	3. 2	−1. 3
Italy	−0. 6	−0. 8	0. 4	−0. 1	−0. 7	−1. 2	−1. 3	−1. 6
Japan	2. 8	3. 6	4. 3	3. 6	2. 7	2. 0	1. 2	2. 1
United Kingdom	0. 6	0. 8	0. 0	−1. 0	−3. 3	−4. 0	−2. 6	−0. 8
United States	−2. 6	−3. 0	−3. 4	−3. 5	−2. 6	−2. 0	−1. 7	−0. 2
G-7 average	−0. 7	−0. 8	−0. 3	−0. 5	−0. 4	−0. 5	−0. 6	−0. 1

Note: Details may not add to totals because of rounding.

a. Preliminary.

b. The part of Germany corresponding to the western *L!?nder* (up to mid 1990).

Source: OECD.

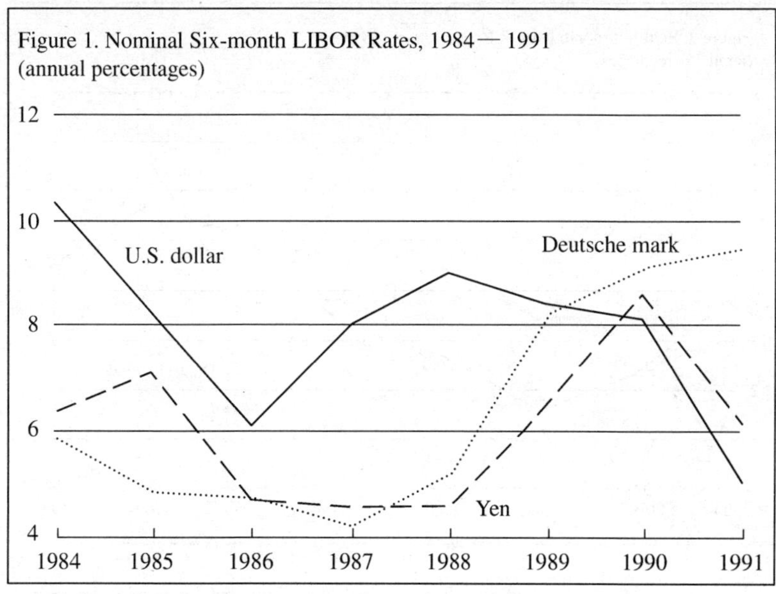

Note: LIBOR: London interbank offered rate (伦敦银行同业优惠利率). LIBOR is the rate applicable to borrowing and lending between London commercial banks. The interest rate for customer borrowers is fixed on that basis with a premium added. It has been highly influential, affecting all capital markets elsewhere, but now the prime rate (优惠利率) of the U. S. (the rate of interest charged the most credit—worthy customers for short—term loans) tends to substitute for it in function.

Source: IMF and OECD.

Several important developments in monetary conditions also took place in 1991. Reflecting more accommodative monetary policy, nominal short-term interest rates fell in the United States and Japan (see Figure 1). In contrast, the increase in German nominal short-term interest rates to postwar highs narrowed the potential of some European Monetary System partners to reduce their rates. The German short-term real interest rate also rose relative to real interest rates in the United States and Japan (see Figure 2). The slope of the Japanese yield curve became less negative and the United States' curve more positive as short-term interest rates fell more

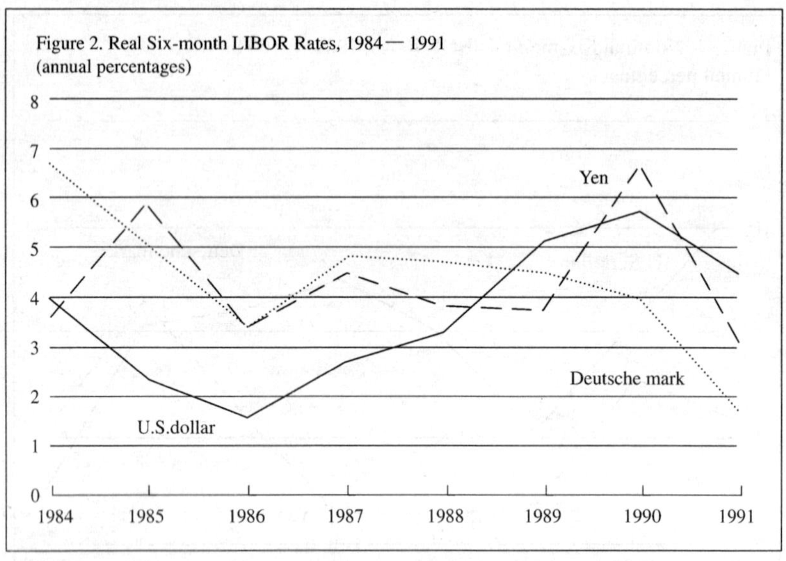

Note: Date are the corresponding nominal rates adjusted by the local-currency GNP deflator for the respective country.

Source: IMF and OECD.

quickly than long-term rates in both countries. In Germany, the slope of the yield curve turned positive.

Developing Countries

Output for the developing countries advanced by 1. 9 per cent during 1991—comparable to the weak performance they registered in 1990 (see Table 3). ① In terms of per capita income, real output in developing countries apparently eased somewhat, by −0. 1 per cent. A number of factors—some broad-based, others more specific—contributed to the weakness of performance:

① Because of date limitations, states of the former Soviet Union are not included.

Table 3. Low-and Middle-income Economies: Growth of GDP and GDP Per Capita, 1981—1991

(average annual percentage change unless otherwise noted)

Region or income group	GDP					1990 GDP
	1981—1987	1988	1989	1990	1991[a]	(US$ billions)
Low-and middle-income economies	3.4	4.0	3.2	2.3	1.9	3 635
By regional group						
Sub-Saharan Africa[b]	1.8	3.9	3.5	1.3	2.4	173
East Asia[c]	8.2	9.6	6.0	6.5	6.8	900
South Asia[d]	5.0	8.3	5.7	5.6	2.8	381
Middle East and North Africa[e]	1.2	−0.8	2.5	2.6	0.8	460
Europe and Central Asia[f]	2.6	2.8	0.8	−3.1	−7.4	522
Latin America and the Caribbean[g]	2.0	0.5	1.2	−0.4	3.0	1 904
By income group						
Low-income economies[h]	6.3	8.1	5.1	4.9	4.3	1 022
Middle-income economies[i]	2.3	2.1	2.3	0.9	1.0	2614
Severely indebted, middle-income economies[j]	2.4	1.1	0.8	−2.0	1.2	1 111

Note: a. Preliminary.

b. Excludes South Africa.

c. American Samoa, Cambodia, China, Fiji, Guam, Indonesia, Kiribati, Republic of Korea. Lao People's Democratic Republic, Macao, Malaysia, Mongolia, New Caledonia and Pacific Islands Trust Territory, Papua New Guinea, the Philippines, Solomon Islands, Thailand, Tonga, Vanuatu, Viet Nam and Western Samoa.

d. Bangladesh, Bhutan, India, Maldives, Myanmar, Nepal, Pakistan and Sri Lanka

e. Afghanistan, Algeria, Bahrain, Egypt, Islamic Republic of Iran, Iraq, Jordan, Lebanon, Libya, Morocco, Oman, Saudi Arabia, Syrian Arab Republic, Tunisia and Yemen.

• Because slowdown in industrial-country growth dampened demand for exports of both primary commodities and manufactures from developing countries, the volume of merchandise exports of developing countries declined by 2 per cent.

• The influence of the Gulf crisis, including the spike in oil prices and dislocations in the Middle East, was widespread; the effects of the crisis on Iraq and Yugoslavia (these two countries alone account for some 4 per cent of developing countries' aggregate GDP) resulted in steep declines in output.

• Structural transformation and the collapse of trade with the Soviet Union and its successor states combined to induce a deep recession in most of Central and Eastern Europe, while the sharp compression of imports by the Soviet Union adversely affected its other trading partners (such as India).

• Weakness of policy implementation affected economic performance in a number of countries.

Aggregate statistics for 1991 were dominated by the sharp decline in output in Central and Eastern Europe and by the severely adverse effects of the Gulf crisis on the economies of Middle Eastern countries. Estimates of GDP by major geographic region reveal that growth of output accelerated in Latin America and in sub-Saharan Africa, while a pick-up in China helped sustain Asian activity. Despite a sharp slowdown in India, where GDP growth fell from 5.5 per cent in 1990 to 2.5 per cent, the population-weighted growth rate of developing countries' GDP—3.5 per cent in 1991—continued to exceed the ordinary measure. ①

Despite the slowdown in the industrial countries—particularly in the United States—improvements in economic performance in Latin America were widespread. The region's GDP rose by 3.0 per cent in 1991, thus reversing the slide in annual per capita income that

---

① Average GDP growth rate for a group of economies is computed as a weighted average of individual economies GDP growth rates. Ordinarily, the weights consist of individual economies' GDP shares, while in population weighted methodology, the weights are individual economies' population shares.

had taken place over the past decade. Growth rates were in excess of 4 per cent in Argentina, Chile, and Mexico and reached a high of 9. 1 per cent in Venezuela. Policy reforms covering fiscal adjustment, trade and investment liberalization, the financial sector, and public-enterprise restructuring and privatization, supported by debt restructuring, have helped to moderate inflation in the region and strengthen domestic demand. Chile has now been growing at an average annual rate of 4. 5 percentage points for the past six years, and since 1989 Mexico has been enjoying a broad-based expansion at rates of 3 per cent to 4 per cent a year. Recent major policy steps undertaken in Argentina have brought a recovery in confidence and growth, and a reflow of capital to a number of countries in the form of foreign direct investment and portfolio investment suggests an increased level of market confidence in the progress achieved to date.

Growth in output in East Asia, supported by the continued vibrant performance of the region's exports, as well as by a firming of domestic demand, particularly in China, accelerated to about 6. 8 per cent in 1991. The sharp acceleration of GDP growth in China, from 4. 5 per cent to over 6 per cent, was supported by improvements in industrial output, higher levels of consumer spending, and significant gains in the export of manufactures. Despite the slowdown in industrial-country markets, export volumes for the group of East Asian countries advanced at double-digit rates, implying gains in market share. A moderate slackening in GDP growth from the rapid 9 per cent-to-10 per cent gains of 1990 occurred in the dynamic economies of the Republic of Korea, Malaysia, and Thailand, in part reflecting a catch-up of imports. The major risk facing this highly trade-oriented region is the potential for sluggishness or disruption in world-trade flows. Economic weakness in some of the region's traditional export markets has underlined the importance of market diversification, including a further strengthening of ties within the region. Increasingly buoyant intraregional trade in East Asia may be viewed as evidence of an ongoing process of "market-oriented" regional integration, a development that could partially offset lackluster progress in the area of multilateral trade agreements.

The GDP growth rate in 1991 of the South Asia region was 2. 8 per cent, down from 5. 6 per cent in 1990. The decline was partly caused by India's reining in of its budget deficit and the short-term effects of the implementation of strong emergency stabilization measures, which, coupled with the collapse of the Soviet market and recession in the U. S. , contributed to a sharp slowdown in industrial activity and exports. The emergency measures included a severe compression of imports, tight credit policies and exchange-rate devaluation.

Output in the Middle East and North Africa region grew weakly at 0. 8 per cent in 1991, reflecting the shocks from the Gulf crisis. Petroleum-price declines reduced revenues in oil-exporting countries, and many countries in the region were adversely affected by declines in workers' remittances and tourism revenues, as well as by the need to increase social spending in support of workers repatriated from Iraq and the Gulf countries.

In Europe and Central Asia, GDP contracted by about 7 per cent, as stabilization and reform programs in several countries had not yet led to a bottoming-out in their economies. Average output of the Central and East European economies, including Yugoslavia, is estimated to have dropped by 14 per cent, following a decline of 8. 7 per cent in 1990. Estimates of economic decline among the five reforming economies in this region range from 7. 5 per cent in Hungary to 26 per cent in Bulgaria. However, efforts to liberalize imports and diversify exports—which followed the disbanding of the Council for Mutual Economic Assistance (CMEA) trading block—led to strong growth in trade between Eastern Europe and the industrialized countries.

Growth accelerated in sub-Saharan Africa to 2. 4 per cent in

1991, in part the result of the indirect stimulation of Nigeria's economy by the Gulf crisis, not only through temporarily higher oil prices but also through its success in exploiting new oilfields quickly. For the past five years, the prices of nonoil commodities exported by most West African countries (robusta coffee and cocoa, for example) have fared worse than those that are particularly important for East and Southern African countries (mild arabica coffee and copper, for example). Such sustained losses in terms of trade have contributed to growth performance in West Africa that is poorer than in East and Southern Africa.

—From *The World Bank Annual Report*, 1992

Words and Expressions

in a row	连续
as	*conj.* 以…方式,像…一样
stagnate	*v.* (经济等)不发展;停滞
aggregate	*a.* 合计的
easing	*n.* (限制等)放松;缓和;(价格)下降趋势;(利率)降低
per capita income	人均收入
acceleration	*n.* 加快;增速
sustain	*n.* 保持;使持续不息
high rates of growth	高增长率
deteriorate	*v.* 恶化;变坏;(质量或价格的)下降;
underlying	*v.* 根本的;基本的
cyclical	*a.* 循环的;周期的
slacken	*v.* 变缓慢;减弱
compound	*v.* 加重
compression	*v.* 压缩

moderate	*n.*	使缓和;减轻;减弱
robust	*v.*	强健的;强有力的
domestic demand	国内需求	
concession	*a.*	让步
debt rescheduling	重新安排债务的偿还计划	
breakthrough	*n.*	突破性的进展
onset	*n.*	开始
slump	*n.*	暴跌
rental housing	出租房屋	
fading	*n.*	逐渐消失;渐弱;衰退
tax-cut-induced boom	由减税引发的繁荣	
diminish	*v.*	减少;降低;缩减
dampen	*v.*	使扫兴;减少;降低
anomaly	*n.*	反常之事物;异例
excessive	*a.*	过多的;过分的;极度的
curtail	*v.*	消减;
leverage	*v.*	(使)举债经营
consolidate	*v.*	把…联合为一体;统一;合并
merger	*n.*	兼并
accommodative	*a.*	肯通融的
comparable(to)	*a.*	可比较的;相似的
register	*v.*	达到;取得;获得
pick-up	*n.*	好转;恢复;进步
reverse	*v.*	使倒转
portfolio investment	证券投资	
vibrant	*a.*	充满生气的
dynamic	*a.*	有活力的
catch-up	*n.*	竞争
sluggishness	*n.*	萧条
disruption	*n.*	混乱
diversification	*n.*	多样化

intra-regional	地区内的
buoyant	*a.* 活跃的;有生气的
integration	*n.* 结合,合并;统一,整体
lackluster	*a.* 无生气的;灰暗的
rein in	抑制
couple with	并提;把…联系起来,加之…
workers' remittance	工人侨汇(在国外工作的工人汇回本国的外汇收入)
repatriate	*v.* 把…遣返回国
contract	*v.* 收缩;减少
bottoming-out	(经济衰退局面等)降至最低点后即将复苏
robusta	*n.* 粗壮咖啡豆
arabica	*n.* 咖啡籽

Notes to the Text

1. 本文选自世界银行 1992 年年度报告第二章《经济概况:全球总览》。1992 年的《年度报告》叙述了 1991 年 7 月 1 日至 1992 年 6 月 30 日期间各方面的详细情况,是由国际复兴开发银行和国际开发协会的执行董事会按照这两个组织的附则编制的。

2. GDP (Gross Domestic Product) 国内生产总值

国民生产总值[一国经济在特定时期内(通常为一年)所生产的最终产品与劳务的总市场价值]减去国外收入部分即为该国的 GDP。

3. "Aggregate statistics for 1991 were influenced by the sharp decline in output in Central and Eastern Europe..."

1991 年东欧中欧一些国家经历了一场大变革,大动荡。首先是苏联的解体,随后是前南斯拉夫联盟共和国分解。经互会——东欧社会主义国家所依赖的地区性经济联盟也随前苏联的消失而失去其存在的意义和作用。德国正被两德统一后出现的许多问题所困扰。

中、东欧的原社会主义国家都处在从计划经济转向市场经济的过程中，普遍出现通货膨胀，失业人口增加，工厂倒闭，致使其产出大幅度下降。

4. "Central and Eastern Europe"

在本文中实指地处中、东欧的前社会主义国家，是一种政治上的提法，包括波兰、捷、匈、罗、保等。地理上，本地区应含更多的国家。

5. Gulf Crisis　海湾危机

1990 年 8 月 2 日凌晨，10 万伊拉克大军顷刻之间越过边界，朝邻国科威特席卷而来，2 万科威特士兵尽管进行了最顽强的抵抗，但终因寡不敌众，机场、港口以及国防部、电视台等政府大厦相继失落。伊军在一天之间完成了占领科威特全国的行动。伊拉克入侵科威特的行为遭到了世界许多国家的谴责，同时各国对伊拉克的经济制裁接踵而来。联合国安理会连续通过决议，要求伊拉克撤军，恢复科威特的主权，以期和平解决海湾危机。但联合国在伊入侵科后在海湾地区派有部队的 28 个国家及世界其他一些国家所尽的一切努力斗争未能使伊拉克总统萨达姆·侯赛因同意从科威特撤军。五个多月之后，在联合国作出的让伊拉克从科威特撤军的最后期限——1991 年 1 月 15 日已经过去了一天多之后，1 月 17 日凌晨 2 点 35 分(伦敦格林威治时间 23 点 35 分)以美国为首的英国、沙特阿拉伯和科威多国部队空军飞机对伊拉克实施了大规模的空袭，开始了"沙漠风暴"行动，揭开了海湾战争的幕布。

石油是世界经济的中枢神经，也是工业化社会的命脉，石油危机可以给世界带来灾难性后果。海湾地区的石油产量约占 OPEC 成员国全部产量的 68%，蕴藏着世界石油产量的 60%。海湾危机及随后海湾战争的爆发，特别是伊拉克威胁欲摧毁海湾油田后，造成工业化国家极大恐慌，也引起世界石油市场的惊恐不安，石油价格不断上涨，本来已经处于低速增长的世界经济增长速度普遍放慢，出现了一定程度的经济衰退。危机不仅使西方股票市场价格大跌，对外汇市场也产生了重要影响。

6. Latin America　拉丁美洲

美国以南所有美洲地区的通称。包括墨西哥、中美、西印度群岛和南美洲。因曾长期沦为拉丁语族的西班牙和葡萄牙的殖民地，现有国家中绝大多数通行的语言属拉丁语族，故被称为拉丁美洲。这个地区的主要经济部门是农牧业、渔业和采矿业等。

7. the G-7——the Group of Seven　七国集团

指美国、日本、英国、法国、德国、意大利和加拿大七个工业国。近些年来，这七个国家经常召开首脑会议，就国际经济贸易形势及各国之间的贸易进行磋商。

8. Continental Europe　欧洲大陆

位于东半球的西北部。欧洲大陆是亚欧大陆伸入大西洋的一个大半岛。其面积占亚欧大陆的五分之一。在地理上习惯分为南欧、西欧、中欧、北欧和东欧五个地区。在本文中实指不包括英国在内的欧洲大陆上的发达资本主义国家。

9. deinflationary policies　反通胀政策

通过限制需求抑制通货膨胀的政策，措施是降低货币流通量(货币政策)和减少开支(财政政策)。所采取的方法和紧缩通货(deflation)政策相似，但要更温和，其目的在于尽量避免措施带来的消极后果。

10. "In addition a common factor underlying the slowdown in many industrial countries was the cyclical deceleration in investment spending."

周期性的投资下降。指的是商业周期引起的投资下降。在商业周期进入不景气(衰退)阶段，整个经济活动呈低水平，这时的需求及消费水平很低，厂商商品销售不力，对资金需求减少；而投资商无利可图，投资活动也随之减少。

11. hard currency　硬通货

价值稳定，在国际贸易支付中求过于供，成为争相获得的货币通称为硬通货。第二次世界大战后至今，美元和英镑都是硬通货，目前德国马克、瑞士法郎、日元也被认为是硬通货。

12. "Also noteworthy was the implementation by the Paris Club of a measurement of enhanced concessions in debt rescheduling for the severely indebted low-income countries."

主语和谓语语序颠倒的倒装句子。有时倒装是由于主语较长，以避免句中表达主要概念的词语相隔过远，影响句意的连贯；有时也为了强调谓语部分的意思。此句倒装，主要是因为主语太长。

13. Paris Club　巴黎俱乐部

正式名称为十国集团（the Group of Ten）。1961 年 12 月，美国、英国、法国、意大利、荷兰、比利时、西德、瑞典、日本、加拿大十国在巴黎开会成立的。从 1964 年起，瑞士以联系国身份参加活动。此外，瑞士国民银行、国际货币基金组织、经济合作及发展组织、欧洲经济共同体委员会也都派代表参加。

20 世纪 60 年代初期，美元和英镑相继发生危机，于是美、英向西欧、日本等国建议并在 1962 年签订《借款总安排》，决定在国际货币基金组织正常贷款之外，设置一笔 60 亿美元的信贷基金，由十国分摊，供国际货币基金组织成员国借用，以维持各成员国的货币稳定。西欧各国尽管同意了这一建议，但不赞成由美国操纵国际货币基金管理，因此成立了十国集团来管理这笔基金：对基金的动用须经七个成员国的同意；借款国须在五年内偿还；同时十国中任何一国如本身发生国际收支危机，可随时抽回自己的股份。

14. Benin

贝宁人民共和国地处西非中南部，首都为波多诺夫。实际上政府所在地为科托努，这一新兴港口城市是贝宁的商业和政治中心。90％的人口以农业为主。出口棕油、棕仁及其他棕榈产品、棉花、花生、金刚石等；进口纺织品、机械、化学品、粮食等。

15. Nicaragua　尼加拉瓜

拉丁美洲国家，中美洲最大的国家，首都马那瓜。尼加拉瓜经济处在发展阶段，主要以服务业、轻工业和农业为基础。

16. Bolivia　玻利维亚

拉丁美洲国家，位于南美洲西部内陆，首都拉巴斯。经济以采矿为主，矿产品占出口总额的 80％左右。全国有采矿、石油、铁路、航空四大国家公司。输入食品和工业品。

17. Tanzania　坦桑尼亚

正式称坦桑尼亚联合共和国，东非国家，首都达累斯萨拉姆。坦桑尼亚经济处在发展阶段并实行统一计划：主要以农业为基础；铁矿、石油和天然气的开发正在进行中，工业仅占国民生产总值的八分之一，进口额为出口额的两倍多。主要贸易国有英国、德国、日本、荷兰和意大利等。

18. commodity market 商品市场

有时指一般商品市场，但更多情况下是指初级产品市场，如玉米、小麦、大豆、咖啡、可可、棉花、羊毛、猪羊牛肉、蛋类、钢、铁、铜、银、木材等大宗买卖的市场。

19. nominal (dollar) terms 名义(美元)价

商品(初级产品)交易所中卖主和买主提出的但尚未得以实际成交的价格。常用其平均值表示。

terms(复数)，在商务英语中常作“价格”之意使用。

20. constant (dollar) terms 不变(美元)价格

意同 constant price，不变价格，也称“固定价格”或“可比价格”。是以某一时期产品的价格作为一段长时期内各年计算产品产值的价格。按不变价格计算产值的目的在于消除不同时期价格变动的影响，使各年的产品的产量具有可比性，用以反映生产的实际发展水平和速度。

21. “There were no breakthroughs in the Uruguay Round of GATT negotiations on key elements, and the outcome remains in doubt.”

关贸总协定乌拉圭回合谈判在本文发表之时还未结束，而且当时谈判各方互不相让，毫无妥协之意。有人预测乌拉圭回合前景渺茫，几年的努力可能会付之东流，但后来在各方的努力下，这一轮谈判最终在 1993 年 12 月 15 日落下帷幕，并在许多方面达成一致。详情请参阅第十课课文有关注解。

22. “In Japan... a tax-cut-induced boom in auto sales...”

近年来，日本的经济长衰不振。日本政府为了刺激消费，恢复市场活力，以求早日复苏，不时地采取减税措施，通常是阶段性的(暂时的)。在减税期间，手里有了更多的可支配收入，消费者对汽车之类的物品会更感兴趣。

23. “unification”

指1991年东西德的统一。统一后的德国延用原西德的政治、经济及社会体制。

24. anti-inflationary monetary policy　反通货膨胀货币政策

西方国家为了抑制或减轻通货膨胀所采取的控制货币数量和信贷规模的政策，有时也称紧缩银根政策。主要措施有：中央银行或其他金融主管机构提高商业银行准备金的比例，提高贴现率和在公开市场上抛售政府债券等。

25. GDP (GNP) deflator　消除国内(民)生产总值通货膨胀因素指数

在通货膨胀的条件下，为了反映国内(民)生产总值的实际变动情况，要剔除价格上涨的因素。其办法是把国内(民)生产总值的各个组成部分用有关的价格指数消除掉价格上涨的成分，以求得无价格变动的产值。例如，以消费价格指数除总的消费支出，以批发价格指数除企业对资本设备、原料及半制品的总支出等。各个有关的价格指数的总和，就是消除国内(民)生产总值中通货膨胀因素的指数。

26. structural problems

structure的基本意思是“结构”，现在在经贸英语中常引伸为“体系”、“安排”、“制度”等义。structural problems在这里指的是由于社会体系或管理制度不完善而引起的问题，如欧洲的失业问题。目前一些经济学家认为，欧洲劳务市场过分僵化，管制过严，最低工资规定得过高，以及过分慷慨的失业救济金和对在职劳工征收高税都是导致高失业率的主要因素。欧盟欧洲委员会的《增长、竞争能力和就业》白皮书提出一系列改善结构(改进制度)的建议，如创建一种普遍通用的职业教育培训进修制度，适当削减失业救济金，放宽过于严格的不正当解雇保护条例，实行灵活的工作时间等。

27. “Highly leveraged corporate transactions”

公司用大量借来的钱进行的交易，一般这些交易具有投机性质，并指望赚取大量利润以支付利息有余。这类交易风险很大。

28. current account　经常项目

参第一课此条注释。

29. “transfers (component)” 资本转移(部分)

即国际资本转移。资本的国际运动一般出自投资、借贷或寻求安全庇护等目的,影响一国国际收支情况的变化。

30. war-related payments 战争费用的支付

海湾战争的费用在战争期间大部分是由美国支付的。根据约定,这笔费用应由所有同盟国负担。战后,其他国家逐渐履行责任,偿付美国垫付款项。

31. “... the increase in German nominal short-term interest rates to post-war highs narrowed the potential of some European Monetary System partners to reduce their rates.”

European Monetary System (EMS):欧洲货币体系。欧共体于 1979 年 3 月建立,旨在促进其成员国之间的经济与货币合作。该体系最为突出的特点是设有“汇率管理机制”(the Exchange Rate Mechanism),用以在预定的幅度内稳定各参加国的汇率。

按照约定,任何参加国首先要对本国货币汇率的稳定负责,一旦一国货币的汇率上下浮动超出所限,该国的中央银行就要出面干预直到恢复正常。这就是为什么创战后新高的德国利率约束了一些 EMS 参加国降低本国利率的力。因为在这些国家任何明显的利率下调都会使得资本外流投资德国并且因此可能造成本币汇率下降超出约定所限范围。

32. real output

以不变价格(constant price)计算的产品价值,剔除了价格变化的影响,其目的在于使不同期间的经济发展情况有可比性。

(参考本课第 22 注解。)

33. “The influence of the Gulf crisis, including the spike in oil prices and...”

由于各石油进口国忧虑海湾战争可能引起石油短缺,许多国家积极买进原油储存,使石油价格一度急剧上升,而这却促使石油输出国大幅度提高石油产量,从而导致石油产量过多结果使油价失去控制,不断地下滑。

spike 于此用作“猛跌”之意,就好像一枚长钉被猛力敲下,这个意思是以该字的原意引申而来，请参看字典。

34. Yugoslavia　南斯拉夫联盟共和国

位于欧洲中南部，是巴尔干半岛最大的国家。南斯拉夫是一个多民族的国家，主要民族有塞尔维亚人、克罗地亚人、波斯尼亚穆斯林、斯罗文尼亚人等，民族问题至关重要，但由于历史上的原因，南联盟各民族之间形成了一种以血还血、以暴抗暴的恶性循环，民族矛盾积怨已久。第二次世界大战后，民族问题有所缓解，但是铁托总统逝世后，民族矛盾日趋激化。1991年6月25日，南联盟共和国的两个主要共和国——斯罗文尼亚共和国和克罗地亚共和国正式宣布独立，南联盟陷入解体之中。原六个共和国之一的波黑共和国由于领土划分和种族归属问题上产生巨大分歧，又无法协商解决，波黑战火由此点燃。三派民族武装相互攻击，最终战火烧至萨拉热窝。波黑战火燃烧至今已两年多，其规模之大、争战之惨烈、伤亡之严重，都是第二次世界大战以来所罕见，联合国安理会已通过了二十多项有关决议，进行了无数次调停。波黑三方达成了30多次停火协议，但往往是墨迹未干，炮声又响。波黑的复杂局势仍在继续发展中。

35. the population-weighted growth rate (of developing countries' GDP)　人口加权增长率

加权平均是统计学中一种计算方法，即在计算若干个数量的平均数时，为了考虑到每个数量在总量中所具有的重要性不同，可分别给予不同的权数。按不同权数计算的各个数量的平均数就是加权平均数。（权数：在统计中计算平均数等指标时，对各个变量值具有权衡轻重作用的数值。例如，计算工人的平均工龄时，各种工龄的工人人数影响着平均工龄的大小，各种工龄的工人人数就是权数。）

"The population-weighted growth rate of developing countries' GDP"就是把发展中国家各自人口数量考虑在内的并加以适当表现的各国GDP增长的总和的平均值。

36. debt restructuring　债务调整

至1991年，发展中国家的全部外债已达15 000亿美元以上。债务的还本付息对他们本来有限的经济发展资金是一个巨大的消耗。为了帮助他们摆脱困境，最终还是为了促进国际贸易，作为债权国的发达国家会同他们的商业银行与一些负债国做出安排豁减债务，延期归还，这些债务国主要是东欧某些前社会主义国家，一些非洲和拉美国家。

37. direct investment　直接投资

一国政府、企业或私人为了取得控制权而对另一国的厂矿企业进行全部或部分投资。直接投资主要形式有：

(1)投资者在外国建立全部属其所有的独资企业；(2)在外国与少数合伙者举办合资经营企业，拥有特定的经营管理权；(3)购买外国当地市场上的外国企业股票，达到一定比例或拥有该外国企业相当一部分的经营管理权。

38. portfolio investment　证券投资

购买股票和债券(证券的主要形式)从而获取利息或红利的投资行为。

39. the Gulf countries　海湾国家

指波斯湾周围的一些国家，包括：伊朗、伊拉克、科威特、沙特阿拉伯、巴林、卡塔尔、阿拉伯联合酋长国和阿曼等。

Questions on Content and Language Points

(for preview, discussion and review)

1. What's the meaning of aggregate in "Aggregate output" and "Aggregate statistics"?

2. Put the following sentence into Chinese and see what part of the sentence the underlined part is.

"Excluding Central and Eastern Europe, growth in developing countries in 1991 was 3.4 per cent, <u>compared with 3.8 per cent during the 1980s.</u>"

3. "Estimates of GDP growth by major <u>geographic</u> region show an acceleration in Latin America and in sub-Saharah Africa,..."

What does the report mean to emphasize using the word "geographic"? (Is there any other way in dividing the world?)

4. How did international conditions for growth in developing countries deteriorate in 1991? (In what way could the slowdown in industrial countries affect developing countries?) (Read paragraph 3 and 4)

5. "The seven major industrial countries (the G-7) experienced significant slowdown in GDP growth—from 2.8 per cent in 1990 to 1.9 per cent during 1991 as recession gripped Canada, the United Kingdom, and the United States and growth rates slowed in continental Europe and Japan."

What does the word "grip" imply in this sentence?

6. What were the main reasons for the recession, according to Paragraph 3?

7. "Against this deteriorating global background, the improvement in economic performance in a few developing regions in 1991—which carried over into 1992—was especially noteworthy."

Can you find what "which" stands for?

8. "Also noteworthy was the implementation by the Paris Club of a new menu of enhanced concessions in debt reschedulings for the severely indebted, low-income countries."

What does the word "menu" in the above sentence mean? Can you find some other word to replace it?

9. "It continues to decelerate in North America and edged down in Japan."

Can you tell the difference between decelerate and edge down?

10. What does structural mean in the "structural problems" discussed in the second paragraph of the section under the title of "Major Industrial Countries"?

11. What are "the four largest European economies" mentioned in the same paragraph?

12. "Weak growth of credit and a fall in some asset prices probably slowed consumption, as well."

1) Did "a fall in some asset prices" have anything to do with "weak growth of credit"?

2) What does "consumption" refer to here? Is it consumption of the consumer goods or that of the capital goods?

3) How could "weak growth of credit and a fall in some asset prices" slow down consumption?

13. "The trade component of the deficit narrowed as lower inflation and earlier dollar depreciation improved competitiveness,..."

1) What is your paraphrase of "the trade component of the deficit"?

2) In what way could lower inflation and earlier dollar depreciation improve competitiveness?

14. Read carefully the information on Germany in Paragraph 11 of the text and answer the following question:

Why could the appreciation of the deutsche mark cause the German current account to swift from a surplus to a deficit?

15. What is an "accommodative monetary policy"?

16. Read the first paragraph of the section with the title of "Developing Countries" and answer the following questions:

1) What does "output" refer to in the first sentence? Could you think of some more common wording for the same idea?

2) What does "ease" mean in "... real output eased..."?

3) How do you understand "broad-based (factors)" and "more specific (factors)" in the third sentence?

17. "Because slowdown in industrial-country growth dampened demand for exports of both primary commodities and manufactures from developing countries, the volume of merchandise exports of developing countries declined by 2 per cent."

What is "merchandise exports"? What is the other kind of trade?

18. "Structural transformation and the collapse of trade with the Soviet Union and its successor states combined to induce a deep

recession in most of Central and Eastern Europe, ..."

What does the author mean by "structural transformation"?

19. "... a pick-up in China helped sustain Asian activity."

In what way could the pick-up in China help sustain Asian activity?

20. What is market diversification?

21. "The GDP growth rate in 1991 of the South Asia region was 2. 8 per cent, down from 5. 9 per cent in 1990. The decline was partly caused by India's reining in of its budget deficit and the short-term effect of the implementation of strong emergency stabilization measures."

1) What is the meaning of "reining in" in the context?

2) What is the main content of the "emergency stabilization measures"?

Find the answer in the fourth paragraph of the section from the bottom.

3) Why are the two underlined parts of the sentence quoted above counted as causes of the decline in the GDP growth rate of the South Asia?

22. "Such sustained losses in terms of trade have contributed to growth performance in West Africa that is poorer than in East and Southern Africa."

In what sense is the word "contribute" used in the given context? Does it mean to add something positive or helpful to the "growth performance", or just the opposite?

Exercises

I. Translate the following passages from the text into Chinese.

1. Rather than reflecting the effect of disinflationary policies, weakness in demand was more closely related to the loss of momen-

tum that had built up during the long period of expansion that began in 1983.

2. These trends were compounded by worsening economic conditions in the Soviet Union and its successor states, where a growing shortage of foreign exchange led to a compression of imports from Eastern Europe and an acceleration of certain commodity exports (aluminum, gold, and lead, for instance) to earn hard currencies.

3. The broad trend was the outcome of largely unexpected setbacks to recovery in the United States and the United Kingdom and the apparent onset of a slower period of economic growth in Japan and Germany.

4. Financial institutions in these two countries adopted more conservative lending policies, curtailing financing of higher-risk projects such as commercial construction and highly leveraged corporate transactions.

5. Policy reforms covering fiscal adjustment, trade and investment liberalization, the financial sector, and public-enterprise restructuring and privatization, supported by debt restructuring, have helped to moderate inflation in the region and strengthen domestic demand.

Ⅱ. Read the following article carefully and translate Paragraphs 5, 9 and 12 into Chinese.

For World Economy, the Worst of Recession Has Passed

For many nations, the worst of the economic slump is over.

"The world economy has bottomed out," notes Rudi Dornbusch, a Massachusetts Institute of Technology (MIT) economist who takes a monthly look at global economic trends for a number of corporations.

After a slow first half, the United States recovery has accelerated. Some economists are talking of a real 4 per cent or better growth rate this quarter. The monthly survey of members of the National Association of Purchasing Management found a "healthy increase" in both manufacturing and the overall economy in November. There is something of a debate among forecasters as to whether the growth in the first half of 1993 will remain vigorous or slow down as it did in the winter of 1993. Mr. Dornbusch is cautious, suggesting 2.75 per cent to 3 per cent real growth in the next 12 months.

"Easy money will countervail fiscal restraint", he says.

Business is picking up in Canada and Britain also. Canada should have around 2.7 per cent real growth this year. The new British budget, announced this week, assumes a real growth rate next year of 2.5 per cent.

But on the European continent, the situation is less happy. "The economic climate has deteriorated further, albeit at a declining rate," a European Community report commented recently. "There are still few signs of a cyclical turning point being reached."

"The Bundesbank continues to call the shots," Dornbusch says, referring to Germany's central bank. It has been gradually lowering interest rates all year, but not fast enough to satisfy its neighbors. Dornbusch argues that real interest rates, which take into account inflation, are too high in Germany. Producer prices have fallen for six months there, so interest rates of 6.4 per cent are "extremely high for an economy that is not growing," he says.

For 18 months economists have been revising their forecasts down for continental Europe. Dornbusch figures, "The bottom may have been reached, but a strong upswing is implausible."

The MIT economist criticizes the French government for strangling the economy with high interest rates in order to keep the franc strong against the German deutsche mark. As a result, Dornbusch predicts, France will experience rising unemployment in 1993, 1994 and 1995. And mass unemployment will worsen France's budget deficit and the prospect for tax cuts or more government spending to boost the economy. "France will do very poorly," he concludes.

By contrast, Dornbusch describes Italy as "the most promising economy in Europe." That is because it abandoned its effort to keep parity with the deutsche mark and the European Monetary System in 1992. The resulting devaluation of the lira has made Italian business "highly competitive." But growth is slack because of major political and industrial restructuring.

Canada's new Liberal government "has to start rebuilding the economy," Dornbusch writes. "Public finance is rotten; industry is dull. But... there is an understanding of what has to happen."

Inflation is lower in Canada than in the US, allowing the Bank of Canada to lower interest rates over the next year without much risk of a rout for the Canadian dollar on foreign exchange markets.

The Japanese economy remains in trouble, with output falling two quarters in a row for the first time in decades. An appreciation of more than 15 per cent in real terms in the yen over the past two years has hurt Japanese competitiveness, Dornbusch notes. The fiscal package to stimulate the economy, to be implemented next April, "will help some but not much".

At best, Dornbusch predicts, the Japanese economy will grow a real 1 per cent next year. "Japan is in a situation which business is singularly ill-equipped to handle. The entire belief system of decades—superiority of the Japanese culture and business system, sustained growth, social cohesion, lifetime employment, accommodating finance, the US can be managed—are all up for grabs. Bad news!"

Outside Japan, Asia booms. China tried to slow down its economy, but apparently abandoned that effort at a Communist Party meeting last month. Growth in national output is expected to run at an astonishing 13 per cent this year.

South Korea has its woes, and so do a few other economies, Dornbusch notes. But "there are no major obstacles to continued growth in Asia: savings rates are high, access to external capital is plentiful, and the world trading system is staying open. Asia cannot fail to do well."

—From *the Christian Science Monitor* • Dec. 3, 1993

Ⅲ. True or false test on the above article.

1. Rudi Dornbusch has noticed that the world economy has fallen to its record lows of the recession. ( )

2. Governments' deflationary efforts will not bear the expected fruits due to inflation. ( )

3. The economic situation in Europe has worsened, and there is no sign of a strong recovery yet. ( )

4. According to Rudi Dornbusch for an economy that is not growing the interest rates should be relatively low. ( )

5. France's decision to keep parity with German Deutsche mark is not a wise one. ( )

6. The present economic situation in Canada presents nothing to be optimistic about. ( )

7. The high value of the Yen has contributed to the incompetitiveness of Japanese manufacturers. ( )

8. The Japanese people have lost their total confidence in the belief system built up over many years. ( )

9. Asian countries, having solved all their problems, are going to fare through 1993. ( )

10. China's national output growth running at 13% is considered very high and implausible. ( )

Supplementary Material for Free Reading

The Net is Open for Business-Big Time

E-commerce is "an absolutely unstoppable force". In less than a decade, it would account for as much as 6% of GDP.

Tim Stojka was just a toddler in 1967 when Benjamin Braddock, Dustin Hoffman's Character in *The Graduate*, was offered the now-classic career tip: "Plastics!" So it's no surprise that Stojka added a 1990s cybertwist. Three years ago, he and brother Nick took time off from running their dad's Chicago plastics company to start the Plastics Network, a Web site that connects buyers and sellers of plastic materials and equipment.

Now, a year after Stojka started conducting transactions on the site, 40,000 visitors a month shop for products from 150 sellers. Commerx Inc., Stojka's holding company for PlasticsNet, takes a 5% cut of transactions, far less than existing distributors, who charge up to 50%. The result: Sales are expected to jump over 300% this year, to about $7.5 million. That's just a tiny fraction of the worldwide plastics market, but the Net's potential to electrify commerce is jolting his industry. Says Joseph J. Liccese, who runs a Web site for Bayer Corp.'s Polymers Div., a PlasticsNet partner: "It's becoming an electronic world much faster than anybody in our industry thought."

Less than a decade after it opened for commercial activity in 1991, the Net is poised to turbocharge E-commerce into a blockbuster economic force. Market researcher Forrester Research Inc. figures that by 2002, (Internet commerce among U.S. businesses alone will hit $327 billion, equal to 23% of gross domestic product.) By 2005, Net commerce could jump to as much as 6% of GDP, reckons Forrester CEO George Colony.

Analysts see E-commerce making up a huge portion—20% to 60% or more—of such industries as computers and software, catalogs, energy, and books. As a result, E-commerce seems certain to provide much of the fuel that will power the 21st Century Economy. Says USWeb Chief Executive Joe Firmage, who sets up Web sites for companies such as NBC and Harley-Davidson: "Electronic commerce is an absolutely unstoppable force."

Already, there are glimpses of incredible efficiencies to come. Starting in early 1999, Canadian Imperial Bank of Commerce in Toronto will start aggregating orders among departments for greater discounts and sending them electronically to suppliers using an Internet procurement program from Ariba Technologies Inc. The bank expects to save almost $100 million on its $1.3 billion in annual purchases.

And it's not just big companies that can take advantage of such savings. Now that the Net lets even small manufacturers communicate intimately with outside suppliers and subcontractors, they're eager to farm out more tasks, such as inventory management and customer service—freeing them to focus on what they do best, such as product design or marketing. "Companies are asking: 'Do I really need to do that part of the business?'" says Malcolm Frank, senior vice-president at Boston consultant Cambridge Technology Partners.

SCALE SAVINGS. One early sign: Some 1,000 food-service operators have turned to Instill Corp. in Palo Alto, Calif., as their virtual order desk. Instill automates and tracks purchases for restaurants, eliminating the time and error of phone and fax orders. CEO Mack Tilling, ex-operations manager for a brewpub chain, expects to process some $1 billion in orders this year, from $180 million last year.

Established companies are starting to use the Web to reinvent themselves, too. One pioneer: W. W. Grainger Inc., a 71-year-old supplier of maintenance, repair and operating supplies from motors to light switches. Since 1995, when it put its entire 80,000-product catalog online, its Web sales have risen 60% to 100% a quarter, with an average transaction of $250, nearly double the offline average. Hoping to capture a broader array of customers Group President Donald E. Bielinski is designing a site to gather outside suppliers as well.

But the next wave of Internet commerce will present as much of a threat to such middlemen as it offers opportunity for startups. After all, warns Steve Johnson, co-director of Andersen Consulting's global electronic-commerce program: "Your competition is always going to be just a click away." The new wave will not just save money but create new electronic marketplaces—quickly turning business models on their heads.

It's hard to find a more agile somersaulter than online bookseller Amazon. com Inc. Even though it's still losing money during its expansion phase, analysts say it's successfully busting the rules of bookselling. Despite offering 3 million titles, vs. 175,000 for a Barnes & Noble superstore, Amazo carried only $17 million in inventory last quarter—2% of Barnes & Noble's. And while buyers pay Amazon instantly with their credit cards, it doesn't pay publishers for the books until about 46 days later—a tidy float that reverses the economics of physical stores.

The result: $240,000 in sales per employee, vs. $100,000 at Barnes & Noble. "Amazon isn't about technology; it's about changing the business model," says venture capitalist Ann Winblad of Hummer Winblad Venture Partners in San Francisco. Indeed, the Net's unique economics may well allow a host of upstarts to commandeer wide stretches of their industries. Winblad's partner J. William Gurley calls them vortex companies: Once a site gathers a mass of buyers by offering useful product information, in swirl sellers, whose products draw more buyers in a fast-moving cycle that leaves rivals high and dry. Presto: One dominant player emerges. Sound familiar? Think Microsoft. Suddenly, it's software economics all over again, but in every industry. The leaders see increasing, not diminishing, returns as they expand.

It is these kinds of opportunities that help exphain why onetime mortgage-brokerage owner Christian A. Larsen started E-Loan Inc. in Palo Alto three years ago. The goal: to enable homebuyers to bypass mortgage agents, who he says do little but add $1,500 to the cost of a mortgage. Last month, Larsen processed

$ 70 million worth of loans, and E-Loan is growing 25% a month. "We take out all the steps in between the buyer and the mortgage-capital markets," he says. "The Internet accelerates this consolidation."

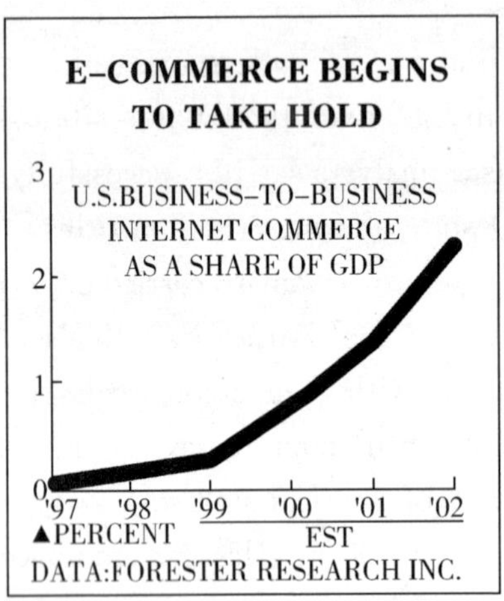

As the Net brings interaction costs to near-zero, experts say there's little reason not to have competitive bidding on almost any product. FreeMarkets OnLine Inc. in Pittsburgh runs an auction for suppliers and buyers of such industrial products as steel parts and printed circuit boards. It doesn't take possession of goods but does everything else: identifies suppliers, finds buyers and runs the auction. CEO Glen Meakem expects to handle $ 500 million in deals this year, up fivefold from 1997, and to post gross sales of $ 7 million.

Just emerging are exchanges such as Energy Marketplace, a site started last year by Southern California Gas Co. to let energy buyers shop for deals among a host of small and midsize gas providers. And in a few years, automated "bots" or programs that search the Net for the best prices on particular products, may even set off rampant price wars. Says Esther Dyson, chairman of EDventure Holdings: "You'll see more real-time pricing."

And maybe even real-time marketing and product design. Amazon. com, for instance, uses software that collects information about consumers' preferences and buying histories to offer instant recommendations on other books. Says Amazon. com CEO Jeffrey P. Bezos: "We want to be like a small-town bookseller who knows your tastes." Book distributor Ingram Book Group, Amazon's chief supplier, is even developing technology to print books one by one as orders come in—potentially changing the economics of publishing.

Given the rapid pace of change, nobody really knows how deep an impact E-commerce will make. But they're about to find out.

By Robert D. Hof in San Mateo, Calif.

——From *Business Week* • August 31, 1998

Lesson 5

On the US Strategy & Policy in Trade

Text

U. S. Is Prepared to See Trade Relations Worsen

By Peter Behr

Washington Post Service

WASHINGTON—The Clinton administration is drawing the first lines of a tougher U. S. policy on trade, signaling to Europe and Japan that it will demand fairer treatment for American exports and is prepared to see relationships with U. S. trading partners get worse before they get better.

The strongest signal came last week, when Mickey Kantor, the U. S. trade representative, moved quickly to cite the 12-nation European Community for "intolerable" discrimination against U. S. companies seeking government contracts within the Community. The administration will begin retaliating in six weeks if EC policies remain unchanged, Mr. Kantor said.

The opening themes of the new administration's trade policies e-merged this week in interviews with officials and congressional sources familiar with the administration's thinking. Among the highlights:

- An insistence that Europe and Japan create a "level playing field" for trade by agreeing to give U. S. exporters the same access to their markets as foreign companies receive in the United States. This push to expand U. S. manufacturing exports is considered essential politically to fulfill President Bill Clinton's campaign promise of more "high-wage, high-skill" jobs for Americans.

• A willingness to impose sanctions on major trading partners to reduce trade barriers abroad, with less patience for drawn-out negotiations. Administration officials see little risk that this more aggressive policy could escalate into a full-fledged trade war that would shock the world's fragile economies. Thus, the administration will not be deterred by complaints that it has moved to "protectionism".

• Serious misgivings about some main parts of the preliminary agreements in Geneva to expand the General Agreement on Tariffs and Trade. Although the administration will ask Congress to renew its negotiating authority, which expires in June, it has moved slowly on this front, leaving the future of the negotiations much in doubt.

• A possible negotiation with Japan seeking a step-by-step reduction in its nearly $50 billion trade surplus with the United States. To the administration, Tokyo appears more "results-oriented" than the Community, prompting hopes that bargains can be reached with Japan to ease frictions on a range of issues.

• A pledge to Mexico and Canada to seek rapid congressional approval of the North American Free-Trade Agreement as the highest trade priority.

Some of the Clinton administration's tough talk appears tactical, intended to pressure trading partners into offering concession and to unblock stalled negotiations on several fronts. But it appears that officials are prepared to turn up the temperature on trade — and live with the consequences.

In some ways, Mr. Clinton and his advisers are following the same well-trod path as the Bush administration, which threatened sanctions against the Community last year and walked away from GATT negotiations rather than sign an agreement that would provide only small gains for U. S. companies. The same political pressures from trade hawks in Congress that the Bush officials felt are now bearing down on the Clinton team.

Mr. Kantor acted immediately on the EC procurement case Monday to demonstrate that the new administration's patience would be shorter than its predecessor's.

"I think it clearly indicates a resolve to stick by our guns," a government official said.

A broad review of trade policy issues is just beginning within the administration, but officials said the underpinnings of Mr. Kantor's decision were plainly found in Mr. Clinton's trade speeches during the campaign, particularly the demand for open markets abroad.

The reactions to these first signals from the Clinton team has been sharply divergent.

EC officials were peeved by Mr. Kantor's action and accused the administration of bullying and instigating trouble at a time when careful negotiations are vital.

"It is time now to tell the Americans they are on the wrong track," Foreign Minister Niels Helveg Petersen of Denmark said.

Balanced against that criticism is the positive reaction in Latin America to Mr. Clinton's embrace of the free-trade agreement. Enrique V. Iglesias, president of the Inter American Development Bank said in an interview that Mr. Clinton's meeting with President Carlos Salinas de Gortari of Mexico a month ago and the promise of fast action on the trade agreement was "a very important statement".

Some representatives of U. S. business, seething over what they view as protectionist EC policies, praised Mr. Kantor's action.

"Whenever the United States starts to act like all the other countries in exercising its trade rights, everybody gets mad," said William Archey, a senior vice president of the U. S. Chamber of Commerce. "That's absurd."

But some economists stressed the risks that a more aggressive U. S. policy poses. C. Fred Bergsten, director of the Institute for International Economists and a prominent member of the free-trade establishment, said he saw little evidence of a strategy, except for "a willingness to listen to protectionist appeals" from the automobile, semiconductor, steel and energy industries, among others, and a desire to mollify these industries' powerful congressional protectors.

Mr. Bergsten warned that if the dispute with the European Community over government procurement is soon followed by clashes with Europe over steel, with Canada over lumber and with Japan over minivans and semiconductors, then the Clinton policy will end up being defined by a flurry of battles.

"Unless they have something else in mind, they will be cut to death by these cases and the policy will be and will appear to be very protectionist," Mr. Bergsten said. The "something else" should be a plan to revive broad negotiations to liberalize trade, he said.

Gordon Ritchie, a trade consultant who was Canada's trade ambassador during negotiations of the U. S.-Canada free-trade agreement, said, "Some of the administration's leading lights are persuaded that confrontation can succeed. Anyone who thinks Europe and Japan will be bullied into meeting American deadlines and priorities isn't awake to the changes that have occurred."

Although some administration officials hope that Japan is amenable to market-opening agreements, the Clinton team is getting off to a ragged start there, as well, said Hiroshi Hirabayashi, a veteran trade official who now is deputy chief of the Japanese Embassy in Washington.

The world needs to hear from new president what his trade signals mean and where they are leading, Mr. Hirabayashi said.

"Mr. Clinton should speak out on the trade issue," he said. "Without his explicit intervention, the speculation will be going on and most of it is going in a negative direction."

A more combative U. S. trade policy may not be dangerous, perhaps, unless it goes too far, said Helmut Maucher, the chairman of Nestle SA.

"Everybody understands that you defend your interest," he said.

—From *International Herald Tribune* • Feb. 8, 1993

Words and Expressions

news service	通讯社
cite	*v.* 提出,举出
intolerable	*a.* 无法容忍的;过分的
push	*n.* 推销运动
campaign	*n.* 运动;战役
drawn-out	*a.* 冗长乏味的;使人厌烦的
escalate	*v.* 逐步上升,逐步增强
full-fledged	*a.* 羽毛丰满的;充分展开的(文中指全面贸易战)
fragile	*a.* 脆弱的;虚弱的;易损坏的
deter	*v.* 威慑住,吓住
misgiving(s)	*n.* 疑虑(尤指对棘手之事)
friction	*n.* 不和;抵触;争执;摩擦
to ease frictions	缓和争执;减少摩擦
tough	*a.* 强硬的;固执的
tough policy	强硬的政策
a tough negotiator	不妥协的谈判者
unblock	*v.* 扫除…障碍
stall	*v.* 使…拖延
consequence	*n.* 结果;后果

trod	*v.*	(原形 tread)践踏;踩
sanction(s)	*n.*	国际制裁(常用复数)
trade sanctions	贸易制裁	
impose against	对…实行制裁	
(trade) hawks	*n.*	主张强硬路线的鹰派人物,本文中指在贸易中主张实行制裁的人
predecessor	*n.*	前任
resolve	*n.*	决心
underpinning(s)	*n.*	基础;根据(常用复数)
divergent	*a.*	有分歧的;不同的
peeve	*v.*	惹恼,使恼怒
bully	*v.*	威吓
instigate	*v.*	煽动;挑动
embrace	*n.*	(欣然)接受
seethe	*v.*	(内心中)发怒;激动
absurd	*a.*	荒谬的;荒唐的
pose	*v.*	摆姿势;在形成
appeal	*n.*	呼吁;恳求;申诉
mollify	*v.*	使平静;抚慰
define	*v.*	为…特色
flurry	*n.*	一阵;混乱
confrontation	*n.*	对抗;冲突
amenable	*a.*	顺从的;易从启导的;易作出反应的
ragged	*a.*	不协调的
explicit	*a.*	明确的
combative	*a.*	好斗的;好事的

Notes to the Text

1. US policy on Trade　美国贸易政策

美国总统克林顿上台后，为了扭转当时美国经济不景气的状况，制定了新的对外贸易政策，变自由贸易为“公平贸易”，尽力扩展海外市场，为美国经济振兴创造条件。美国的新政策强调“公平互惠”和“机会均等”，即美国在欢迎外国产品和劳务进入美国市场的同时，也要让美国产品和劳务进入他们的市场。作为实现“公平”的保证，美国政府同时反对国内两种倾向：一是贸易保护主义倾向，一是“放任自流”的倾向，即主张政府面对国外的竞争而无所作为。

克林顿政府的贸易政策有以下几个特点：

(1)在原则上，单方面强调维护美国的经济利益，对其盟国也不例外。

(2)在手法上，采取执行美国贸易法规和单方面制裁的措施。

(3)在策略上，迫使贸易伙伴增加进口美国的产品以平衡贸易。

2. “The Clinton administration is drawing the first lines of a tougher US policy on trade, signaling to Europe and Japan that it will demand fairer treatment for American exports...”

在句中 signaling 是现在分词，引导一分词短语，用作状语，表示结果或效果。本文中第六段第二句中的 leaving 是同样用法的另一个例子。现在分词在句中也可作定语用：作定语的分词如果是单词，一般放在它所修饰的名词之前，如果分词短语作定语时，放在它所修饰的名词的后面，如本文第二段第一句中的 seeking government contracts.

现在分词作定语和状语的用法在报刊经贸文章中经常出现。

3. be prepared to do something

be prepared to do，有准备的、准备好的(尤指在思想或心理上)，有时还带有愿意做某事的意思。如：

US is prepared to see trade relations worsen.

美国已做好准备任凭其贸易关系恶化。

But it appears that officials are prepared to turn up the temperature on trade.

但是看上去官员们准备(愿意)让贸易问题升级(升温)。

4. Mickey Kantor　米奇·坎特

克林顿第一届总统任内(1992—1996)的贸易谈判代表。现任为巴尔舍夫斯基女士(Charlene Barshefsky),系米奇·坎特任上的副职。

5. the US trade representative　美国贸易谈判代表

美国贸易谈判代表不是临时的任命,而是一个常设的部长级职务,专司美国对外贸易谈判。

6. President Bill Clinton　比尔·克林顿总统

美国第42和第43届总统。克林顿1946年生于阿肯色州,早年曾就读于乔治敦大学、英国牛津大学、耶鲁大学法学院。后应聘到阿肯色州大学出任法学教授。1974年宣布参加州议会选举,虽未成功(年轻、资历浅),但其知名度大大提高。1976年当选阿肯色州司法部长,1979年当选州长,成为美国当时最年轻的任此职者。1980年连任州长竞选中失败,1982年再次当选,此后一直连任。1992年11月3日在美国第42届总统大选中克林顿战胜布什,入主白宫。1996年,克林顿在连任总统竞选中再次获胜。

7. "Administration officials see little risk that this more aggressive policy could escalate into a full-fledged trade war that would shock the world's fragile economies."

这是一个同位语从句,risk为先行词,由连词that引导。同位语从句的作用是说明它的先行词(一般是名词)的内容,连词that在从句中不做任何句子成分。又如:To the administration, Tokyo appears more "results-oriented" than the Community, prompting hopes that bargains can be reached with Japan to ease friction on a range of issues.

American hopes that pressure from the US will force Japan to suddenly dismantle its trade barriers are almost certain to evaporate in disappointment.

8. "results-oriented"　以结果为导向的,(只)强调结果的

to orient 的一个基本含义是 to place something in a specific direction。在这个基础上,to orient 使用在一些复合形容词里,意思有所延伸变化。results-oriented 的意思是 results 得到特别的强调,被看作为最重要的或给予最优先的考虑。orient 用作类似意思的复合词还有 export-oriented, growth-oriented, market-oriented 等等。

9. NAFTA (North America Free Trade Agreements) 北美自由贸易协定

建立北美自由贸易区的设想系由美国、加拿大和墨西哥三国总统于 1991 年共同提出的。经过谈判,于 1992 年 8 月正式决定签定北美自由贸易协议。此协议于 1994 年 1 月 1 日起生效。美国、加拿大和墨西哥三国将按照协定要求在 15 年内逐步取消三国间的几乎所有贸易的关税和其他非关税壁垒,实现商品、劳务及技术的自由流通,从而成为世界上最大的、拥有 3.7 亿人口的,平均产值 6 万多亿美元的共同市场。美、加、墨三国互有需要,但美国的期望更高。一位经济学家认为美国积极推动建立北美共同市场,这不过是第一步,其目标是把北美自由贸易区逐步扩建为一个西半球自由贸易协议,最后发展成为一个与欧洲和亚洲相抗衡的经贸实体。

10. "... Bush administration ... walked away from GATT negotiations (rather than) sign an agreement that would provide only small gains for US companies."

rather than 连用时作并列连词,它所连接的两端应是同类的词或成分。

可表示主观愿望的抉择,即"宁愿……而不……","不是这样……而是那样……"

例:He went "rather than" stay at home.

the policy of more "rather than" less involvement in a neighboring country's affairs

或反映客观上的差异,即表示"与其说是……不如说是……","倒不如说"之意。

例:You should help them "rather than" they should help you.

They are engaged in designing an engine "rather than" (in) repairing the machine.

11. "... at a time when careful negotiations are vital."

这里 when 是关系副词,引导一个定语从句而非状语从句,常放在 day, year, time 这类名词后面。

12. "Balanced against that criticism is the positive reaction in

Latin America to Mr. Clinton's embrace of the free-trade agreement."

"拉丁美洲对克林顿先生欣然接受自由贸易协定的积极反应弥补了那些批评。"

这是一个使用倒装语序的句子,主、谓位置颠倒。使用倒装句的原因多种多样,上面这一句主要是由于主语太长,使用正语序反而会使句子中表达主要意思的词、语相隔远,不利于理解;同时倒装也使此句和上文紧密衔接。

13. (government) procurement　政府采购

政府采购这里指国际贸易中歧视性的政府采购政策,是非关税壁垒的一个重要手段。一些发达资本主义国家制定法令,规定政府机构在采购时优先购买本国产品,从而导致对外国产品进口的限制。政府在采购中可以采取有利于国内供应者而不利于外国供应者的差别待遇,或者在外国供应者那采取有利于某些国家而不利于其他国家的差别待遇。这种差别待遇可以采取对本国供应者给予价格优惠的方式,亦可以是对本国供应者或某些国家在做法上和程序上给予各种优惠待遇的方式。

14. "... then the Clinton policy will end up being defined by a flurry of battles."

句中划线部分可以看成:不及物动词短语作谓语与主语补足语合用,这种现象也称做双重谓语,后一部分用来说明主语的性质、状况等。

例:His remarks passed unnoticed.

他的讲话没有人注意。

15. Nestle SA　雀巢股份有限公司

瑞士最大的产业公司,也是世界上主要的食品公司之一。其跨国经营活动遍布世界各主要市场;其经营额的98%来自瑞士以外,但绝大部分集中在欧美。雀巢公司主要经营饮料、矿泉水、乳制品、婴幼儿营养品、烹饪用品、冷食和冰淇淋、冰冻食品、巧克力和粮果等。近年来该公司开始拓展其业务到旅馆饭店、制药以及化妆品等领域。

雀巢公司十分注重发展海外业务,在欧洲、北美以及拉美的许多国家拥有大量子公司和分支机构。近年来，雀巢公司开始向东方开展其业务，在日本、印度、中国、香港等国家和地区都设有分支机构。

Questions on Content and Language Points

(for preview, discussion and review)

1. "The Clinton administration is drawing the first lines of tougher U. S. policy on trade, signaling to Europe and Japan that it will demand fairer treatment for American exports and is prepared to see relationships with U. S. trading partners get worse before they get better."

What would happen (how would they react) if the U. S. demand for "fairer treatment" were rejected, according to the context?

What's the implication of their being "prepared to see relationship with U. S. trading partners get worse before they get better?"

2. "An insistence that Europe and Japan create a 'level playing field' for trade by agreeing to give U. S. exporters the same access to their markets as foreign companies receive in the United States."

What did the U. S. mean by a "level playing field" for trade?

3. "This push to expand U. S. manufacturing exports is considered essential politically to fulfill President Bill Clinton's campaign promise of more 'high—wage, high—skill' jobs for Americans."

In what way could this push help "fulfill President Bill Clinton's campaign promise"?

4. Why would the administration not be deferred from exercising the more aggressive policy by complaints that it had moved to "protectionism"? (See Paragraph 5.)

5. What attitude did the U. S. administration take towards the new General Agreement on Tariffs and Trade according to Paragraph 6?

6. "To the administration, Tokyo appears more 'results-ori-

ented' than the Community, prompting hopes that bargains can be reached with Japan to ease frictions on a range of issues."

1) What does "bargains" mean in the above sentence? Deals, agreements, lower prices, or something else?

2) What is the meaning of "results-oriented"?

7. Read Paragraph 9 of the text and answer the following questions.

1) "Some of the Clinton administration's tough talk" is described as being "tactical" in the text. What is the implication of tactical in the given context?

2) Was the U. S. really as tough as it looked on trade questions according to the text? Why?

Try to find some information within the paragraph to support your viewpoint.

8. Read the Paragraph 10 and try to explain "the . . . well-trod path" and see what "the well-trod path" specifically refer to.

9. "'I think it clearly indicates a resolve to stick by our guns,' a government official said."

Paraphrase the official's words in plain language according to the context (Paragraph 11).

10. Could you make a brief summary of the divergent reactions to the Clinton administration's trade policies? (Information on the reactions is given in Paragraph 14—19)

11. "Whenever the United States starts to act like all the other countries in exercising its trade right, everybody gets mad. . ."

What can you find in reading between the lines of the above statement by a U. S. business representative?

12. What exactly does the word "lights" mean in the following sentence?

"Some of the administration's leading lights are persuaded that confrontation can succeed."

13. Translate the following sentence into Chinese so as to get a clearer meaning.

"Anyone who thinks Europe and Japan will be bullied into meeting American deadlines and priorities isn't awake to the changes that have occurred."

May we say from the above words that the speaker didn't believe that the United States could succeed by taking a tough stand in the negotiations?

14. "The world needs to hear from the new president what his trade signals mean and where they are leading ..."

What does "they" stand for in the sentence?

Exercises

Read the article below and then answer the following questions:

U. S. as Self-appointed Global Hall Monitor

America imposes its standards of behavior on rest of the world.

By Jessica Mathews

The Washington Post

WASHINGTON—Congratulations, says the letter, your country has been certified by the United States as having acceptable sea-turtle conservation practices. You may continue to sell shrimp in our market.

"That's good, I suppose," shrugs the ambassador to whom it is addressed, adding with some bitterness, "I didn't even know we were being judged on sea turtles. Where does it end?"

Not with fishing. As self-appointed global hall monitor, the United States unilaterally judges other countries' environmental practices, human-rights policies, anti-terrorism, the fairness of elections and the adequacy of anti-drug efforts (though its own elections are noteworthy for minuscule turnout and massive special-access money, and its efforts to shrink the world's largest pool of drug users have been strikingly ineffective).

Simultaneously, Washington pushes a widening set of rules of international behavior and claims a growing number of exemptions. We have made it an increasingly common practice to lead negotiations to a U. S. —defined outcome and then to reject the result, including several human-rights treaties, the Law of the Sea treaty and, perhaps, the Chemical Weapons Convention, just sent into limbo by the Senate.

At the United Nations, we specify financial and management reforms as the price of our support and, when they are adopted, move the goal posts. Our nonpayment of dues violates a formal, legal obligation. We expect a prominent role even when we decide not to play, as at the International Court of Justice, which includes American jurists though we reject the court's jurisdiction.

Recently imposed secondary boycotts against Cuba, Iran and Libya are a practice Washington loudly condemned when exercised by the Arab states against Israel. The assertion of domestic legal jurisdiction outside our borders infuriates our closest allies. We'd be even madder in their place. The air strikes against Iraq for actions taken in its own territory may be the only way to deal with Saddam Hussein but are of questionable legitimacy.

Rather than debate, as we have for years, how much multilateralism we should indulge in, the real question for U. S. foreign policy is how unilateral it can afford to be and still be effective and publicly supported.

One superpower, it turns out, is harder to swallow than two, especially when it counts Hollywood, McDonald's and CNN in its arsenal. For anyone outside the United States, says former Canadian Prime Minister and self-described friend of the United States Joe Clark, "It's pretty hard to persuade yourself that your destiny lies exclusively in your own hands. Not to put it too subtly, the stars and stripes are in your face—on your television, in your markets, on every question of foreign policy and many of domestic policy."

In your face or not, the world is lucky to have us. We have reason to expect special treatment. Without us there would have been no response to the invasion of Kuwait, no peace in Bosnia and no deal to halt North Korea's nuclear ambitions.

Europeans would have lifted the sanctions against Iraq long before its chemical, biological and missile programs were rooted out. There would have been no bailout of the Mexican peso, and any number of nonproliferation, environmental and human-rights standards would be a far cry from what they are today. Many fewer people would have tasted liberty.

But we should not kid ourselves that others don't notice that our leadership is oddly incomplete. In the Gulf War and the North Korean deal, we spent other countries' money. In the percentage of wealth or per capita income that goes for aid, the United States ranks last among industrialized nations, and it is the only significant debtor at the World Bank. We are both a smaller piece of the global economy and less willing to spend what we have.

We are less willing to spend blood, too. As the margin of our military superiority climbs, our willingness to accept risk has dropped. We shun any but U. S. -designed and —led peackeeping, while our unpaid U. N. bills mean that poor countries that do commit troops go unreimbursed. Our military pre-eminence means less to others than it used to because so few feel threatened.

Our rising demands on others, in fact, are uncomfortably matched to a smaller pool of leadership assets. Those Americans who make foreign policy have an undiminished—if not enlarged—sense of the need for the United States to decide everything from the conflict in Northern Ireland to the balance of power in Asia. This is not shared by a public that overwhelmingly prefers international burden-sharing. We are in the habit of asserting a rhetorical imperative for U. S. leadership that we don't intend to provide. It leads us into trouble and encourages others to sit back and wait on us.

What can only the United States do in the world? How much do we need others and exactly what for? How much can we go our own way and still command support when we want it from friends and allies? Are we too often, or too intrusively, the arbiter of global good conduct? Is our belief that only we have the capacity for leadership a self-fulfilling prophecy?

We don't so much need a new single idea to replace containment of communism as we do a consensus on a workable unilateralism tolerable to others and understood, supported and adequately funded by Americans.

Jessica Mathews is a senior fellow at the Council on Foreign Relations.

—From *The Japan Times* • Sep. 19, 1996

Questions:

1. In Paragraph 9, the author lists the U. S. performances in some international events as their contributions to the world peace and development. From what motive(s) do you think they did that if there was something good done by them?

2. What is the writer's attitude toward the role of "global hall monitor" assumed by the United States? Does he hold that the U. S. should give up (completely and thoroughly) hegemoniosm?

3. On which points of the article do you agree with the author? And on which not?

Supplementary Material for Free Reading

A. Clinton Reaffirms Asia-Pacific Role

CANBERRA (reuter) U. S. President Bill Clinton, in his first major foreign policy speech since his re-election, called Wednesday for a deeper engagement with China and reaffirmed Washington's commitment to the Asia-Pacific region.

"The direction China takes in the years to come, the way they define its greatness in the future, will help to decide whether the next century is one of conflict or co-operation," Clinton told the Australian Parliament.

Striking a reassuring tone aimed directly at Beijing, he added: "The United States has no interest in containing China. That is a negative strategy."

"What the United States wants is to sustain an engagement with China... in a way that will increase the chances that there will be more liberty and more prosperity," Clinton told a joint session of both Houses of Parliament.

Clinton's comments come only four days before he meets Chinese President Jiang Zemin in the Philippines ahead of the Asia-Pacific Economic Cooperation summit.

But Clinton said Washington and Beijing would continue to have important differences, especially in the area of human rights.

"We will continue to discuss them candidly, but by working together where possible and dealing with our differences openly and respectfully where necessary we can deepen our dialogue and add to Asia's stability," he said.

"I look forward to doing just that when I meet for the fourth time with President Jiang in the Philippines next week."

In a wide-ranging speech, Clinton said the United States, even though it retained close ties with Europe, must look to the East no less than to the West.

(Excerpts)

—From *The Japan Times* • Nov. 21, 1996

B. Why I'm Going to Beijing

The White House View: America's future will not be secure if Asia's is in doubt.

By Bill Clinton

This week, I will become the first American president to visit China in a decade. I am going for one reason: to advance America's interests. America's future will not be secure if Asia's is in doubt. On the Korean Peninsula—where nearly 40,000 Americans patrol a militarized fault line—the prospects for reconciliation are matched by the danger of miscalculation. Indonesia's ongoing political and economic transformation is hopeful but uncertain. When markets tremble in Hong Kong or Tokyo, we feel the tremors on Wall Street—and Main Street. And just when the world is making real progress in reducing the nuclear danger, India and Pakistan's tests threaten to spark a dangerous arms race.

Our ability to resolve these challenges will be deeply affected by the policies pursued by China—home to one fourth of the earth's population. Beyond Asia, the role China chooses to play in preventing or abetting the spread of weapons of mass destruction, combating or ignoring international crime, protecting or degrading the envirronment, tearing down or building up trade barriers and respecting or abusing human rights will help shape the next century.

In short, America has an interest in a stable, secure and open China that embraces political pluralism, free markets and the rule of law and joins us in working to build a secure international order. The question: what is the best way to encourage the emergence of that kind of China?

Some Amereicans believe China's interests and our own inexorably are in conflict and that we should work to contain China before it becomes stronger. But in isolating China, we would only encourage China to turn in ward and to act in opposition to our interests and values.

We have chosen a pragmatic and principled course: expanding our areas of co-operation with China while dealing directly with our differences, especially over human rights.

Working with China serves our interest in a stable Asia. China has joined us in condemning India and Pakistan for their nuclear tests and urging peaceful solutions to their differences. It has supported the Four Party Peace Talks on the Korean Peninsula and our successful efforts to freeze North Korea's dangerons nuclear program. It has been a firebreak in the Asian financial crisis. And China is once again pursuing cross-strait discussions with Taiwan, contributing to a significant reduction in tensions.

Working with China serves our interest in stopping the spread of nuclear, chemical and biological weapons. China once was a major exporter of sophisticated technologies. Over the past decade, it has joined almost all of the major arms-control regimes. And China has agreed to stop assistance to Iran for its nuclear program, terminate its assistance to unsafeguarded nuclear facilities such as those in Pakistan, tighten its export-control system and sell no more anti-ship cruise missiles to Iran. Each of these steps was the product of our engagement.

Working with China serves our interest in combating international crime and drug trafficking. Bordering more than a dozen countries, China has become a transshipment point for drugs and money laundering. At the Washington Summit, President Jiang and I established a high-level group of American and Chinese lawenforcement officials to increase our co-operation against organized crime, alien smuggling and counterfeiting. This month, the Drug Enforcement Administration will open an office in Beijing.

Working with China serves our interest in preserving the environment. Poisoned air or polluted water within China's borders can do grievous harm beyond them. Last year, Vice President Gore launched talks with the Chinese aimed at protecting their environment while pursuing development. We will keep working to bring American clean-energy technology to China.

Working with China serves our interest in open trade. Access to its markets remains far too restricted. We could retaliate and spark a self-defeating cycle of protectionism. Or we can keep pressing China to open its markets and to join the World Trade Organization on commercially meaningful terms. And we can renew normal trade treatment for China, as every president has done since 1980.

Our engagement with China is also the best way to advance our ideals. The more we bring China into the world, the more the world will bring freedom to China. The number of Internet accounts in China is projected to jump from about 400,000 this year to 20 million early in the next decade. One in five residents of Beijing has access to satellite TV.

But China's leaders must understand that China will only reach its full potential if its people are allowed to reach theirs. The true wealth of a nation lies in its people's ability to create, communicate and innovate. To develop that capacity, people must have the freedom to speak, publish, associate and worship without fear.

America will continue to urge China's leaders to move to the right side of history when it comes to human rights and freedom of religion. Over the past year, we have seen some real progress—though far from enough. China has released several prominent dissidents. It announced its intention to sign the International Covenant on Civil and Political Rights. And President Jiang received a delegation of prominent American religious leaders.

In my meeting with Chinese leaders, I will press ahead on human rights, with one goal in mind: making a difference. Dealing directly with and speaking forthrightly to the Chinese is the best way to do just that. And when it comes to advancing America's interests in China, Asia and around the world, we are better off working with China than without it.

——From *News Week*. June 29, 1998

C. Uneasy Together

Hopes of a "strategic partnership" are dead, but a new Cold War is not a viable alternative. China and the United States are fumbling towards a new relationship where national security will be paramount—but shared interests will survive.

By Bruce Gilley in San Francisco, with Trish Saywell in Shanghai and Lorien Holland in Beijing

In mid-May, Li Yi was organizing protests at the University of California at Berkeley against the American bombing of the Chinese embassy in Belgrade. A few weeks later, he put away his banners and headed for Silicon Valley to begin work at Maxtor Corp., a Nasdaq-listed hi-tech firm in Milpitas, California, where he is helping to develop the next generation of central-processing units.

A countradiction? Li embodies the forces that simultaneously attract the United States and China to each other and push them apart. As chairman of Berkeley's main pro-Beijing student group, Li vented the patriotic anger and suspicion that have dominated Chinese attitudes towards the U. S. recently. But with a brand new doctorate in electrical engineering in his pocket, his decision to stay and work in the U. S. is proof of how closely economic and cultural ties have woven the two countries together.

"The company I have joined has nothing to do with the U. S. government," says Li, explaining his move. "There is no contradiction."

If only the two governments could resolve the dilemma as easily. In the past month, both Chinese and American leaders have been confronted with the question of what to do when a leading trade partner is suspected of being a threat to national-security interests. The embassy attack has convinced many Chinese that the U. S. is a bully that has no respect for the lives of non-Americans and wants to keep China from becoming a world power. In the U. S., allegations of Chinese espionage and attempts to buy political influence have caused critics of engagement to argue that Beijing can't be trusted.

China's long-awaited entry to the World Trade Organization is likely to be further delayed and both sides may start pouring more money into defensive weapons systems unless relations are quickly put on a surer footing.

Signs are emerging that U. S. and Chinese leaders want to do just that. Analysts say that a new realism appears to be creeping into Sino-U. S. relations that could set the tone for years to come. This approach abjures both Cold-War hostility and the excessive optimism of the "constructive strategic partnership" that Beijing and Washington have struggled to patch together over the past two years. Under this new dispensation, both governments will promote trade, investment and popular exchanges. But they also will acknowledge that a rising power and an already dominant one are not natural allies, and give serious attention to protecting their respective strategic interests. When the interests of trade and national security conflict, security will come first.

"If you're asking these two countries to be friends then you're asking the impossibility," says Robert Ross, a Sino-U. S. relations specialist at Boston College. "But if you're asking them to manage difficult issues to prevent any deterioration in the relationship, then that is what they are learning to do."

The implications for business are mixed. Chinese and American leaders will encourage trade and investment because it is in their interest to do so. But the political risks of doing business may grow because of heightened attention to the strategic rivalry. "As long as our customers keep expanding in China we will follow them," says David Beatson, chairman and chief executive of San Francisco-based logistics company Circle International, which counts U. S. companies in China such as 3M and IBM among its customers. "But the political turmoil of Sino-U. S. relations will be a unique shallenge."

Chinese—U. S. relations have swung wildly ever since Nixon and Mao first met in 1972. Three times in the past decade alone relations have plunged dangerously: in 1989, in 1993 after China lost its bid for the 2000 Olympics and the U. S. Navy searched a Chinese cargo ship en route to Iran, and in 1996 when China lobbed missiles towards Taiwan and the U. S. floated two aircraft-carrier groups off the island. Each time, relations rebounded with greater resilience and speed. That is a stark contrast to the worst days of the Cold War: Soviet-U. S. relations took a decade to recover from the Cuban missile crisis of 1962.

A major reason is the extensive economic and social ties that have created powerful lobbies for good relations in both the U. S. and China. In 1989, U. S. companies had invested only $1. 7 billion in China. Today the figure stands at $21 billion. Both sides rank the other among their top trade partners. Tens of thousands of Chinese engineers like Li Yi help keep the U. S. hi-tech sector humming, while hundreds of American non-governmental organizations work in China on projects ranging from legal reform to wetlands preservation.

TANGLED WEB

U.S. exchanges with China are extensive and diverse, spanning business, culture, tourism and family relations. By contrast, U.S. exchanges with the Soviet Union were sparse right up until its collapse

● U.S. exports to China in 1998:	$18.9 billion
● China exports to U.S. in 1998:	$55.8 billion
● Two-way U.S. Soviet trade at its peak in1989:	$5 billion
● Share of goods in Target warehouse stores in the U.S. that are made in China:	one-quarter to one-third
● Number of McDonald's outletsin China:	225
● Number of weekly direct flights by U.S.airlines to China:	27 currently scheduled to reach 54 in 2001
● Number of weekly direct flights by U.S. airlines to the Soviet Union in 1990:	15
● U.S. investment in China,1979-1998:	$21 billion
● U.S. investment in the Soviet Union When it collapsed in 1991:	$300 million
● Number of Chinese studying in U.S. in 1999:	60 000
● Number of Chinese who became U.S. citizens, 1992-1997:	276 610

Source: REVIEW Data

"Breaking off relations is simply not an option. We are engaged at every level whether we like it or not," says Wang Yong, director of the international political-economy programme at Beijing University and himself a part of the mesh as a visiting fellow at the University of Southern California. But he agrees that pressure is building in the U. S. "for a long-term change in policy towards China that will put higher value on strategic interests."

China, in turn, "doesn't trust the United States to be the world's policeman," says Col. Monte Bullard, interim director of the East Asia Non-Proliferation Project at the Monterey Institute of International Studies and a former U. S. military attached in Beijing. "We cannot expect the PLA to limit its modernization process. We can tighten our security and, through research, development and deployment, maintain our current huge military advantage."

Rebuilding ties on a more security-conscious basis means first getting over the current impasse. The top item is the embassy bombing. The Chinese have put other aspects of relations on hold—including talks on entering WTO—pending a detailed U. S. explanation of the bombing. While Chinese President Jiang Zemin has accepted U. S. President Bill Clinton's apology for the attack, major newspapers still run articles accusing the U. S. of targeting the embassy in order to test China's mettle or throw it into chaos. Many of the articles spring from military conferences. "It is stunning what the Chinese military is saying these days," says Yu Maochun, a historian of Sino-U. S. relations at the U. S. Naval Academy in Annapolis, Maryland. (Yu is another part of the mesh; he came to the U. S. from China as a student in the 1980s and is now a naturalized citizen.)

In Washington, the espionage and influence-buying revelations have sapped patience for further kowtowing to Beijing over the embassy bombing. "China has to come to grips with the fact that we had a tragic accident," State Department spokesman James Rubin said bluntly on May 28.

Fortunately for both sides, there are signs that the freeze will soon end. A June 3 editorial in the Communist Party newspaper, the *People's Daily*, said China must co-operate with the U. S. for mutual benefit and world peace. Chinese leaders have stressed that the door remains open to U. S. investment and trade. A senior official has reaffirmed the government's support for a global forum of chief executives from 350 multinationals—a third from the U. S.—to be held in Shanghai in September. "We even received separate assurances that President Jiang was strongly committed to coming to our conference," says organizer John Needham.

At the same time, Beijing is insisting that it will never allow any foreign country to infringe on China's sovereignty. "We must both oppose hegemonism and develop relations with the United States," the editorial explained. "We cannot give up developing relations in order to oppose hegemonism. Nor can we give up our opposition to hegemonism because we are developing relations." That duality has already been accepted by Chinese consumers, who have slipped back into McDonald's and Kentucky Fried Chicken restaurants. "American products aren't made by the people who bombed our embassy," says a 57-year-old man browsing the goods with his wife at the Number One Department Store in Shanghai.

In Washington, the Clinton administration has been quick to reaffirm the policy of "engagement" with China and quash suggestions that a new Cold War may emerge. "We believe that China is not the Soviet Union. China has a billion people with a thriving market-based economy in many respects," Rubin of the State Department said on May 28 when asked whether the U. S. and China were moving toward a Cold War.

Each side must now placate domestic opponents who, while lacking the clout to derail bilateral relations, can slow the mending process. China and the U. S. came close to agreeing on terms for China's entry to the WTO during Premier Zhu Rongji's U. S. visit in April, but in the end Clinton rejected Zhu's offer, then blundered by making it public.

Clinton is now trying to wrench more concessions—especially on telecoms ownership and agriculture—out of a less-willing China. "Washington's floor is now Beijing's ceiling," says one U. S. —based trade analyst. Chinese leaders have postponed resuming WTO talks while working to re-establish a domestic consensus. But time is running out if China is to be included in a new round of global-trade-liberalization talks that begins in December.

For his part, Clinton will be hampered by Congress and partisan politics as Washington prepares for the 2000 presidential election. Congress is weighing legislation that would authorize expanded weapons sales and other military assistance to Taiwan—measures sure to outrage Beijing. Congress already has approved a bill that calls for America to deploy a missile-defence system as soon as it is "technologically possible." The Cox report's claim that China has acquired the know-how to significantly modernize its missile arsenal only adds to support for establishing a theatre-missile defence, or TMD, umbrella for U. S. allies in Asia.

Legislators also are likely to use the annual June debate over renewing China's normal trade status as an opportunity to excoriate Beijing over the alleged spying and illegal campaign donations. But in the end, under pressure from U. S. business, Congress is expected to vote in favour of continued trade ties. A key factor: The three leading Republican candidates for president all have come out in support. They have suggested greater vigilance over Beijing through export controls and improved counter-espionage—a position similar to the one the Democratic administration is taking.

The New York Times summarized the emerging consensus in a May 30 editorial: "Working ties will have to be rebuilt, but on more realistic foundations than before. While it makes sense to encourage China to open its economy and play a constructive role in international affairs, Washington must give clear priority to protecting American security."

That may hurt business. The White House is likely to expand U. S. statellite-launch capabilities so that fewer U. S. —made satellites need be launched by China. And U. S. controls on technology exports to China—especially in the areas of computers and encryption technologies—may well be strengthened. "I understand the concerns, but they need to be flexible," says John Chen, chairman and chief executive of Sybase, a computer-systems provider based in Emeryville, California. Sybase, whose clients include China's railways and taxation bureaus, wants to bid for a new Chinese government project to put information such as pension and credit records onto the Internet in restricted-access form. But that would require a waiver of current rules on the export of encryption technology to China. "It's probably the wrong time to be asking for relaxing export controls," says Chen.

The good news for business is that the fallout will be largely isolated to hi-tech areas. A Cold War that would wipe out two decades of patiently built trade and investment ties is not in the cards. In the 27 years since Nixon and Mao met, "hardliners have never taken over the Sino-U. S. relationship in either country," notes Ross of Boston College. "That calls for some degree of optimism."

—From *Far Eastern Economic Review* • June 17, 1999

D. A Series on International Responses to the US Helms-Burton Act

a. EU Unites to Retaliate Against Helms-Burton

LUXEMBOURG (Reuter) EU foreign ministers agreed on Monday to make it illegal for Europeans to obey Washington's anti-Cuban Helms-Burton Act.

Daylong negotiations persuaded Denmark that tit-for-tat countermeasures to the U. S. legislation would not compromise its sovereignty.

Trade Commissioner Sir Leon Brittan said the decision was "a historic break-through which shows we have the will and capacity to defend our interests."

The Helms-Burton Act was passed earlier this year to a chorus of indignation from some of America's closest friends and largest trade partners.

Among other things, it allows naturalized Americans to sue in U. S. courts foreign companies or individuals deemed to have gained from investments in property confiscated in Cuba since Fidel Castro's communist revolution of 1959.

The EU law will prohibit European individuals or companies from complying with the act—which has been suspended by U. S. President Bill Clinton until January—and allow them to reclaim damages in EU courts.

EU diplomats believe Clinton—ahead in all polls to retain the U. S. presidency—passed the act only because of congressional pressure in an election year and is likely to further suspend it further in the new year.

Brittan said he hoped that now "the EU has leveled the playing field," he would be able to negotiate an equitable solution to the trade row.

The European Commission—the EU's executive—has also filed a complaint on the matter with the World Trade Organization. A dispute panel is due to convene on Nov. 20.

Danish reservations had threatened to scupper the EU's response but Brittan said amendments made to bring Denmark on board were minor.

"We have convinced all the partners that the legal and constitutional novelty (of the EU measures) does not affect sovereignty," Brittan said. "We have achieved this without the regulation being in any way weakened."

Demmark had objected to a catch-all clause in the law which it said handed national powers to the EU. The Danish government is embroiled in a court case with 11 of its citizens who have complained that Copenhagen is giving away sovereignty.

Legal experts from the commission trawled through EU legislation on Monday and unearthed a little-used treaty declaration dating back to 1968 which was included in the final wording of the anti-Helms-Burton regulation.

Among other things, it says the circumstances of using the clause to which Denmark objects are exceptional and only to be used on specific occasions.

The wording of the final resolution appeared to laymen to be little different from that originally proposed, and diplomats said the spirit of the EU's opposition to the act was undiluted.

"We had to practically break their thumbs to get them to agree," said one diplomat, "but we have been aware all along that Denmark is against the act as the rest of us. It was the means rather than the end that counted for them."

—From *The Japan Times* • Oct • 30, 1996

b. U. S. Seeks to Calm Angry EU

Anti-Cuba enforcement linked to rights promotion

COPENHAGEN (Reuter) The United States sought Thursday to calm European anger over a controversial anti-Cuba law, hinting that planned lawsuits against European firms could be dropped if EU states visibly promoted Cuban human rights.

Visiting Denmark on a swing through European capitals, President Bill Clinton's special envoy, Stuart Eizenstat, said that relatively modest steps could make it easier for Clinton to shelve implementation of the Helms-Burton law, already delayed since July.

"The president has to make a decision no later than the 16th of January about whether to continue to suspend the lawsuits under Helms-Burton," Eizenstat said at a news conference.

"The president, in order to continue the suspension of those suits has to make the finding that a further suspension would be in the security interest of the country and would expedite the transition to democracy in Cuba," he added.

"That's why we look to our European friends . . . to elevate the human rights issue so that the president will be in a position—if he wishes to do so—to consider to exercise that waiver," Eizenstat said.

He added that in talks Thursday with Danish Foreign Minister Niels Helveg Petersen he suggested that Denmark give someone in its embassy accredited to Havana responsibility for human rights activities, disseminating outside news, and channeling more European assistance through local agencies.

He said he also proposed that European firms make a point of using the same standards of pay, safety and environmental concern in their Cuban operations as they would elsewhere and that nongovernmental agencies channel aid through similar Cuban bodies rather than through the Havana government.

They could also speak out on political prisoners and work on judicial and penal reform, he said, adding that such actions would help encourage a change to democracy in Cuba.

"It would also have the additional benefit of helping to alleviate and reduce, and perhaps eliminate, the trade tensions that have resulted from the passage of the Helms-Burton Act."

"It is not in any way shape or form an effort to extend our trade embargo to the rest of the world, it doesn't prevent any Danish company from trading with Cuba, it doesn't prevent any Danish company from investing in Cuba so long as they don't use expropriated U. S. property," he said.

The act, which has triggered a rare show of cohesion among EU members united in anger, allows lawsuits to be filed in U. S. courts against foreign firms that own or operate properties seized by Cuba from naturalized U. S. citizens since Fidel Castro's communist revolution of 1959.

An EU countermeasure agreed Monday will prohibit European individuals or companies from complying with the act and allow them to reclaim damages in EU courts.

Asked if Washington was taken by surprise by the intensity of European opposition to the Helms-Burton Act, Eizenstat said it had been "an eye-opener."

EU diplomats believe that Clinton passed the act only because of election year pressure and is likely to further suspend it if re-elected, but Eizenstat warned that a waiver was not a foregone conclusion.

"I've said this today to (Danish) government officials, and I've said it throughout this week in Europe. It is a mistake to assume that on Nov. 6, if the president's re-elected, that this act is going to disappear—it isn't."

—From *The Japan Time* • Nov. 2. 1996

c. Ibero-American Summit Slams U. S. Law on Cuba

VINA DEL MAR, Chile (Reuter) Leaders of 19 Latin American nations, Spain and Portugal condemned the Helms-Burton law tightening the U. S. trade embargo Monday on Cuba while pointedly saying democracy must include free and fair elections.

In the final statement at an Ibero-American Summit in Chile, the leaders urged the United States to reconsider the Helms-Burton law which "ignores the fundamental principle of respect for the sovereignty of states."

In a thinly veiled reference to the last nonelected government in the hemisphere — Cuba — the leaders said "free, periodic and transparent elections are an essential element of democracy."

"Freedom of expression, association and assembly, full access to information, free, periodic and transparent elections are essential elements of democracy," said the 37-page consensus statement.

The document also cited the "essential role in democratic development" played by political parties, called for "open and transparent debate in public life" and said citizens should demand authorities make public and periodic accounting of their actions.

Speculation that Castro would not sign the document did not end until he actually did, along with the other leaders.

Venezuelan President Rafael Caldera, host of next year's summit, said allusions to Cuba could plainly be read between the lines of the document.

"The issue of Cuba was not treated in an explicit manner. But any observer realizes that it was treated implicitly in the statements and deliberations," Caldera said, when asked about the document dubbed the Declaration of Vina del Mar.

Some kind of condemnation of Helms-Burton had been expected. The document, however, went much further in stressing elections and political freedoms, both lacking in Cuba, than diplomats had originally suggested.

The summit, the sixth of its kind since the first Ibero-American meeting in Mexico in 1991, moved from Santiago to the seaside city of Vina del Mar on Monday for its third and final day of talks.

Castro, who has worn a conservative blue suit for the entire summit instead of his usual fatigues, fired up the summit Sunday with an impassioned speech attacking free market economics, big foreign capital and the U. S. mass media.

Yet he heard steady calls for reforms to Cuba's one-party political system. Spanish Prime Minister Jose Maria Aznar offered to help Cuba through its economic straits if he began reforms, while the widow of late Chilean socialist President Salvador Allende also urged Castro to call elections.

"If Cuba decides to move toward economic modernization, democracy and human rights, Spain will also make a move," Aznar told a news conference, adding that Spain would ask the European Union to aid Cuba in exchange.

Argentine President Carlos Menem compared Castro unfavorably to former Chilean dictator Augusto Pinochet.

"Pinochet ... made the Chilean people's access to democracy possible and left the country economically stable. Commander Castro has led Cuba for 37 years, with all the problems we know about," said Menem.

In a new diplomatic victory for Castro against the U. S. embargo, the statement lambasted the law which "ignores the fundamental principle of respect for the sover-eignty of states" and violates the U. N. Charter.

—From *The Japan Times* • Nov. 13, 1996

d. Clinton Delays Enforcing Anti-Cuba Business Law

WASHINGTON (Reuter) President Bill Clinton on Friday once again delayed implementation of a law that would allow U. S. citizens to sue some foreign companies doing business in Communist-ruled Cuba.

Clinton ordered a further six-month suspension of the controversial provision of the so-called Helms-Burton law "to consolidate and build on the momentum we have generated for democratic change in Cuba."

Clinton issued a statement while on vacation in the U. S. Virgin Islands. He said he would keep on suspending the law as long as U. S. allies, who have been angered by the law, continued efforts to promote democracy and human rights.

The provision would allow U. S. citizens, including Cubans who left after Fidel Castro took power in 1959 and are now naturalized U. S. citizens, to sue foreign companies benefiting from their property seized by the Communist government.

The law, enacted in March, enraged Europeans, Canadians and Mexicans who argued that the United States was trying to impose its anti-Cuba trade sanctions on them. They moved to counter Helms-Burton and filed trade complaints to the World Trade Organization.

Clinton, seeking to calm tensions, in July suspended the lawsuit provision for six months. He appointed Under-secretary of Commerce Stuart Eizenstat as a special envoy to work with U. S. allies to find common ground in trying to bring democracy to Cuba.

After a flurry of diplomatic activity by Eizenstat, who traveled to Mexico, Canada and all major European capitals, members of the European Union in December agreed to press Cuba on human rights and democracy.

That move gave Clinton room to suspend the law for at least another six months.

"The United States seemed for too long to be singing solo on the need for human rights and democracy in Cuba," Eizenstat said at a State Department news conference.

"Today, there is more international pressure on Castro than at any time since his coming to power to initiate real democratic reforms."

World reactions mixed

European Commission President Jacques Santer called Clinton's decision a "constructive move" that was a "step in the right direction."

But he said the European Union remains "firmly opposed to all extraterritorial legislation" and will continue to defend its interests.

Cuba dismissed Clinton's move, with Foreign Ministry spokesman Miguel Alfonso in Havana saying the Helms-Burton law remains unchanged.

"It's a negotiating weapon so that other countries adapt their policies to those of the United States," he told reporters.

In Ottawa, Canada shrugged off Clinton's suspension and criticized Washington for continuing to try to influence other countries' relations with Havana.

"I think this decision is disappointing," International Trade Minister Art Eggleton said.

In Mexico City, the Mexican Foreign Ministry was cautiously upbeat about Clinton's suspension of the law, but reiterated that the law should be scrapped. Mexican companies have burgeoning business interests on the caribbean island.

Clinton originally objected to key parts of the law, but agreed to sign it last year after Cuban MiG jet fighters shot down two civilian aircraft flown by anti-Castro activists in February. Four Miami residents were killed.

The law also would bar executives of foreign companies doing business with confiscated property and their families from entering the United States. That provision went into effect and has been used against executives of a Canadian mining company and a Mexican telecommunications firm.

Eizenstat said some 12 other firms stopped using confiscated property or shelved planned investments because of the law. The United States recently told an Israeli sugar and citrus firm it might be in violation of the U. S. law, he said.

Helms disappointed

Senate Foreign Relations Committee Chairman Jesse Helms of North Carolina, who along with Republican Rep. Dan Burton of Indiana authored the law, said he is "extremely disappointed" by the decision.

"By declaring his intention to waive this provision indefinitely, the president has given up the best leverage the United States had to pressure Canada and Mexico to change their ways," Helms said in a statement.

"And he has sent a signal to Europe that they have done enough, just as they have taken their first, small steps in the right direction."

—From *The Japan Times* • Jan. 5, 1997

Lesson 6
The Development of EU

Text

Economic Troubles Cloud New Market's Future

By Howard Lafranchi
Staff Writer of *The Christian Science Monitor*

When the European Community's vast single market officially takes effect on Jan. 1, there will be no balloons and brass bands, and holiday fliers between EC cities will still face passport checks at airports. Europeans will wake up new year's day with the same 10 per cent unemployment and doubts about European unity.

"There won't be the big bang some might have expected," says Ricardo Perissich, EC director-general for the single market.

Yet in its current dour mood, Europe risks almost overlooking the revolutionary step forward it has taken in creating the world's largest and wealthiest barrier-free market — and on a continent where, for centuries, economic battles have led to some of history's bloodiest wars. Moreover, a failure to reinforce the single market by pushing forward with European integration could lead to an unraveling of what the internal market program has achieved, some observers say.

"The single market is central to the community's progress, but it is by no means certain that it could stand alone," says one senior EC official here, "if the political will to continue moving forward fails, we can anticipate more strains in the marriage contract that ultimately would strike at what we've accomplished."

The EC's languishing Maastricht Treaty for deeper political

and economic integration is the obvious example cited. Without the prospect of a single European currency, as called for in Maastricht, the single market risks experiencing more of the damaging monetary instability of the past few months, some analysts note. And without the promise of deeper political integration, those EC countries looking for more than a glorified free-trade zone could tire of the single market's free-market philosophy.

As Europe's economy has soured, free-market ideas that are new to much of Europe face new challenges. "It's worth remembering that a majority of the questions asked during the debate in France on the Masstricht referendum actually had nothing to do with Maastricht at all, but with measures already taken under the single market." says Perissich. "We are not safely beyond a backlash against the new world of competition."

If Europeans aren't bursting to give the single market a coming-out party, it may simply be that markets aren't the kinds of things people gush about, as EC commission president Jacques Delors has often noted. The fact that free movement of people—an aspect of the market that will be most evident to the average person—is not yet a reality also plays a role.

Another explanation is that many of the market's orginal 282 directives have already been implemented.

"By Jan. 1 we will have passed 95 per cent of what we sought in 1986 to create the single market, and much of that will already have been translated into national law," says Perissich. "Adjustment to the market has been going on for years and won't be expected over-night."

But perhaps the major reason is the dark economic clouds now hanging over Europe. One of the central justifications for the single market was its ability to create greater prosperity, but it is making its debut just as Europe traverses one of its roughest economic storms in years.

"We're going to wind up 1992 with just about the same level of unemployed—nearly 10 per cent community wide—that we had before this project," says an aide to Mr. Delors. In addition, economic growth is skidding to an anticipated 1 per cent next year. All of which adds up to consumer and business confidence sinking to the same lows recorded during the pre-single market days of Europessimism.

Both EC and independent analysts say that business anticipated the economic benefits of the single market, so that much of the burst of economic activity in preparation for the new market has already occurred.

Business investment, which had been flat for the five years preceding the decision in 1985 to create the single market, soared to a 7 per cent annual growth rate from 1985—1990. GNP growth over the same five years averaged 3. 5 per cent; mergers, joint ventures, and plant modernizations took off; and the moribund economies of new EC members, Spain and Portugal jumped with new life.

But beyond the short-term statistics, many analysts say the real revolution of "1992"—Brussels shorthand for the single market project—is how it has changed the way Europe works and how it approaches business.

"Adoption of the 1992 program led to [national] budget cuts, deregulation, privatizations, and a general cutback in the excess role of the state," says Jaeques Pelkmans, a researcher at the center for European policy studies here and author of an upcoming book on "how 1992 changed European integration."

Mr. Pelkmans is not among those who believe that the EC's single market is threatened by the doubt building over Europe's continued integration. "1992 is a set of laws, and because of the mutual stakes no one would take a breach of those laws lightly," he says.

But he also acknowledges that further progress opened up by 1992 will be more difficult because the strong leadership that existed across the EC as the single market was being implemented is no longer present.

"Leaders five years ago had the courage and the political strength to take some very difficult decisions, but today that's no longer the cast," he says. "Everyone is politically weak back home, which leads to fighting instead of compromise over Europe."

Perissich agrees that the current weakness of European leadership is a problem, but he adds that the single market is now largely in the hands of all Europeans. "What the community has completed rather well is the legal framework, but it is not a blueprint for how the single market will actually work," says Perissich. "They have to invent their own single market according to their tastes, imagination, and ambition," he adds. "That's not for us to say from here."

—From *The Christian Science Monitor* • Dec. 30, 1992

Words and Expressions

staff writer	本报记者	
holiday fliers	乘飞机外出渡假的人	
big bang	大爆炸	
dour	*a.*	抑郁的
barrier-free market	自由市场(无壁垒市场)	
unravel	*v.*	(口语)破坏(计划)等
strain	*n.*	紧张(情况)矛盾和争斗
languishing	*a.*	衰弱无力的;失去活力的
glorified	*a.*	使美化了的;吹嘘
sour	*v.*	恶化;变坏
referendum	*n.*	(对立法机构以通过或拟通过法案的)公民复决投票

backlash	*n.*	强烈抵制;集体反对
evident	*a.*	明显的;明白的
directive	*n.*	指令
implement	*v.*	实施;执行;使生效
justification	*n.*	正当的理由
debut	*n.*	(法语)首次出现;初次露面
traverse	*v.*	渡过;穿过
traverse the ocean	横渡重洋	
rough	*a.*	剧烈(颠簸)的
wind up	把(事务)料理停当	
aide	*n.*	助手
skid	*v.*	急剧下降
flat	*a.*	(市场等)呆滞的;无增减的
moribund	*a.*	不进展的;停滞不前的;奄奄一息的
shorthand	*n.*	简略的表达方式
deregulation	*n.*	撤消(价格,费用方面的)管制规定
excess	*a.*	过量的;过多的
breach	*n.*	违反
cast	*n.*	班子;一套人马
blueprint	*n.*	蓝图;行动计划

Notes to the Text

1. the Christian Science Monitor　基督教科学箴言报

1908 年美国基督教科学派创始人玛丽·贝克·艾迪在波士顿创立的报纸,以其精心处理新闻报道和对政治、社会和经济的发展具有高瞻远瞩和深入分析的能力而闻名。

2. European Community　欧洲共同体

西欧主要工业化国家于 20 世纪 60 年代建立和发展起来的一个政治经济集团,总部设在比利时的布鲁塞尔。1951 年 4 月 18 日法国、联邦德国、意大利、比利时、荷兰、卢森堡六国在巴黎签订了为期50年的《欧洲煤钢联营条约》，即《巴黎条约》，并于1952年7月25日生效。1957年3月25日六国又在罗马签定了《建立欧洲经济共同体条约》和《建立欧洲原子能联营条约》，通称"罗马条约"，1958年1月1日生效。这三个组织原各有单独的执行机构，1967年7月1日合并为单一的执行机构，统称"欧洲共同体"。1973年1月1日，英国、爱尔兰、丹麦正式加入。1981年1月1日希腊成为正式成员国。1986年1月1日，西班牙和葡萄牙成为正式成员国。

欧共体的进步和成长，以及共同体成员国的繁荣，使得更多的国家希望加入共同体联盟。土耳其、匈牙利、塞浦路斯、马耳他、瑞典、芬兰、瑞士等国家纷纷提出加入共同体的申请。

1986年通过的《欧洲一体化文件》以及1992年通过的《马斯特里赫特欧洲联盟条约》成为共同体进一步发展的基本条文，把其成员国更加紧密地联系在一起。几十年来欧洲一体化的进程对欧洲大陆及其人民有着极大的影响。所有的政府都承认：只有为了一个共同的目标共同努力，欧洲才能够继续其经济、社会进步，才能够保持其在世界上的影响。

共同体的主要组织机构有：

欧洲共同体委员会：提出政策并负责欧共体的管理

欧洲共同体成员国部长会议：决定共同体委员会所提出的政策的正式通过

欧洲会议：确定预算，在立法方面起重要作用

欧洲共同体法院：负责监督共同体成员国与共同体机构正确实施欧洲共同体法规。

3. the Single Market　统一大市场

1993年1月1日，欧洲共同体正式成为一个没有内部边界的统一大市场。从即日起，人员、货物、服务以及资本可以在大市场内自由流动。大部分边境控制将被取消；对于人员来说，欧洲统一大市场意味着他们能够在共同体成员国内部自由旅行，而不需要办理任何超出他们本国所需的手续。资本限制的取消将使银行、个人以及公司自由选择货币及市场进行投资。欧洲统一大市场的建立能够降低

由于各种因素如边境检查，各国之间不同的技术规定及标准，贸易保护主义，市场分割等等造成的成本开支，从而刺激经济增长，增加就业率，开展更大的规模生产。根据欧共体委员会的报告，大市场启动后，运作正常，市场稳定。但大市场还不完善，存在着一些问题，而人员流通障碍是大市场最突出的特点。为了保证大市场的正常运转，欧共体在当年上半年专门成立了由12国政府代表组成的“内部市场协调委员会”和各国雇主代表参加的“公司听证委员会”，负责对大市场的协调和监督。

欧共体统一大市场启动后，它的对外贸易格局没有根本变化，依然有区别地对待关贸总协定成员国、发展中国家和“非市场经济国家”。

4. “... and on a continent where, for centuries, economic battles have led to some of history's bloodiest wars.”

……并且是在一个大陆上几世纪以来那里经济上的争斗曾几度引发了历史上最血腥的战争。

5. Maastricht Treaty　马斯特里赫特条约(欧洲联盟条约)

马斯特里赫特条约是于1991年12月在罗马制定，1992年2月中旬由12个成员国在荷兰马斯特里赫特城签定通过的(英国和丹麦对个别条款保留例外权)。马约原订于1993年1月生效，但由于各种原因而推迟，最后于1993年11月1日正式生效，由此诞生了新的欧洲联盟。

建立欧洲联盟的马约的主要内容是:

实现欧洲经济货币联盟，建立欧洲中央银行，最迟在1999年实行单一欧洲货币。

实行共同的外交和安全政策——政府间进行更多的合作，但这种合作不受欧洲委员会的中央控制。

欧洲公民权利:欧洲联盟成员国的公民将有权在联盟中任何其他国家工作，参加当地的欧洲议会选举，并最终参加地方选举。

欧洲议会权利增加——在涉及单一市场、教育、文化、健康和消费以及环境保护，跨欧洲网络规划等法律上有否决权。

6. “... the single market risks experiencing more of the dama-

ging monetary instability of the past few months,..."

这里"the ... monetary instability of the past few months"指：1992 年 9 月由于处于欧洲货币体系核心地位的德国马克汇率坚挺，利率高居不衰，严重地影响了资本流向，对西欧的弱币形成压力，致使其反复下跌，触发了一场货币危机，尽管欧洲货币体系的汇率机制(见第四课注 31)促使有关国家做出了艰苦的努力，英镑和意大利里拉还是被迫暂时游离出了这一旨在稳定欧洲汇率的体制。

7. free-trade zone　自由贸易区

是国家领土的一个组成部分，或位于国家某个港口内，或是整个城市。其地理界线被明确划定。在这界线内，国家放弃行使其主权的某些方面，但又不许其他国家在这一界线内行使主权。在海关管辖方面，自由贸易区被认为如同位于国家领土之外，但国家对自由区行使其他主权管辖权和立法权。自由贸易区的产生，最初是为服务于转口贸易而设立的，后为吸引大量国际资本投资于该国的工业，自由贸易区不仅仅经营贸易，而且经营出口工业。现在自由贸易区不再只是赋予一些贸易项目以某些特权，而且还经营储存、改装、修理、加工及制造，各种劳务、旅游、科技和其他各项事业。对于发展中国家来说，宗旨也由过去的服务于宗主国的利益转变为它们手中的一个实现经济、社会发展的手段。

8. "... without the promise of deeper political integration, those EC countries looking for more than a glorified free-trade zone could tire of the single market's free-market philosophy."

"……没有进一步的政治上一体化的承诺，那些寻求比一个备受称颂的自由贸易区更为理想的共同体的成员国可能会对这个统一大市场的自由市场理论感到厌倦。"

经济上的联合离不开政治上的联合。欧洲统一大市场的启动是通向政治联盟的先决条件，而反过来它则需要政治一体化的支持才能得到巩固和发展。因此，欧共体很多成员国不满现状，期望实现政治上进一步的联盟，以给统一大市场注入新的推动力。

9. Masstircht referendum

referendum，复决权，选民对政府的政策或法案表示意见的方式。法国和意大利在第二次世界大战后制定的宪法规定公民有修改宪法的复决权。在爱尔兰和澳大利亚,对宪法的一切修改都需经过复决投票。

Masstircht referendum 是指欧共体一些成员国对马斯特里赫特条约进行的公民复决投票。丹麦在 1992 年 6 月 2 日进行了投票,结果由于 50.7%的反对票没有通过马约。当时由于欧洲金融市场混乱,对马约的问题争论也很多,同年 9 月 20 日的法国全民复决投票中,也仅以 51.1%的多数通过了马斯特里赫特条约。

10. "We are not safely beyond a backlash against the new world of competition."

"我们并非会安全无恙,处于对以竞争为特点的新世界的强烈抵制之外。"

beyond,介词,(指范围)越出,处于……之外

例:Even if Mr. Nakasone's upcoming pump-priming program ultimately proves successful *beyond* his wildest dreams, it would not bring a tremendous decline in Japan's huge annual trade surplus.

即使中曾根先生即将出笼的刺激经济复苏的方案最终被证明是超出实际想法之外的成功,它也不可能大幅度地降低日本巨大的年贸易盈余。

11. "By Jan. 1, we will have passed 95 per cent of what we sought in 1986 to create the single market."

近年来,为对付欧洲的经济衰退而各自采取果敢的行动使各国政府承受着越来越重的压力。欧共体成员国认识到他们面临着共同的问题,他们决定联合解决这些问题。越来越多的商人、经济学家、政治家以及欧洲议会议员开始认识到欧洲的复兴依赖于内部大市场的建立。事实上,许多人已逐渐把这件事看成是共同体未来成功的基本的先决的条件。

针对这些情况,所有成员国的国家元首或政府首脑们多次声明要致力于完全统一的内部市场的建设,并于 1985 年特别提请欧委会拟出一份具体提案以期在 1992 年实现这一目标。

欧委会于 1985 年 6 月发布了白皮书,列出了必要的计划以及一

份明确的行动时间表。这一白皮书力求做到全面彻底:它试图一步一步地建立一个一体化的、互相联系的经济结构;它试图找出所有为边界控制辩护和阻碍市场自由运作的物质的、技术的以及税收方面的障碍,并为排除这些障碍提出282项立法提案。本文中所说的"... pass 95% of what we sought ..."就是指这282项立法提案。

12. community wide 合成词,作形容词或副词用,表示"全共同体范围内的(或地)"

相似的有:nationwide, statewide 全国范围的,worldwide 全世界范围的。

13. merger *n.* 并入,兼并

这里指一个公司把另一个公司并入,被并入的公司不再是一个独立的公司。通常并入的方法有两种:(一)公司甲把公司乙的股票买进或用自己的股票与公司乙交易,成为公司乙的控股公司;而公司乙则成为公司甲的附属公司。(二)公司甲把它自己的股票发给公司乙的股东,并接受公司乙的一切资产和债务,公司乙即解散。

14. "... 1992 program..."

指在1992年完成一切准备工作,继而成立欧洲统一大市场的宏伟计划。

Questions on Content and Language Points

(for preview, discussion and review)

1. What more does the word trouble mean than difficulty in the title?

2. What are "holiday fliers"?

3. What conclusions could you draw from the pictures presented in the 1st paragraph?

4. "Yet in its current dour mood, Europe risks almost overlooking the revolutionary step forward it has taken in creating the world's largest and wealthiest barrier-free market—and on a continent where, for centuries, economic battles have led to some of

history's bloodiest wars."

1) In what sense is revolutionary used here?

2) What did the writer worry about for Western Europe in the article?

5. "... those EC countries looking for more than a glorified free-trade zone could tire of the single market's free market philosophy."

Do you think that the single market means the same thing as a free trade zone in the sentence?

How do you know?

6. "... we are not safely beyond a backlash against the new world of competition."

How do you understand "the new world of competition" according to the context?

7. "If Europeans aren't bursting to give the single market a coming-out party, it may simply be that markets aren't the kinds of things people gust about,..."

Explain the underlined words and phrases and then find out what the writer really wants to convey to his readers?

8. Please find out the reasons from the text why Europeans may not be very enthusiastic about the coming out of the Single Market?

9. "The fact that free movement of people—an aspect of the market that will be most evident to the average person—is not yet a reality also plays a role."

1) How many subordinate clauses does this sentence contain?

2) What kinds of clause are they respectively? And what parts of the sentence?

10. How would you interpret the word "translate" in the sentence "By Jan. 1 we will have passed 95 per cent of what we sought in 1986 to create the single market, and much of that will already have been translated into national law"?

Can you find an appropriate Chinese equivalent for it?

11. "Adjustment to the market has been going on for years and won't be expected over-night."

Paraphrase the above sentence.

12. "Both EC and independent anaylsts say that business anticipated the economic benefits of the single market,..."

What does the word *business* represent here?

13. Define the word "approach" in the following sentence according to its context.

"But beyond the short-term statistics, many analysts say the real revolution of '1992'... is how it has changed the way Europe works and how it approaches business."

14. "1992 is a set of laws, and because of the mutual stakes no one would take a breach of those laws lightly."

1) What's the implication of "1992" here?

2) What do *stake* and *lightly* mean respectively in the sentence?

15. "Everyone is politically weak back home, which leads to fighting instead of compromise over Europe."

Why could the weak positions of EU countries' leaders at home lead to fighting instead of compromise over Europe?

16. "What the community has completed rather well is the legal framework, but it is not a blueprint for how the single market will actually work."

Is there any difference between "a legal framework" and a "blueprint"?

What is that?

17. When you finish the article, have you got an idea of the viewpoints of the European people on the single market and the EC? Make a summary of your gains.

Topic for Discussion

Exchange with your classmates what you know about the latest developments of the single market and the EU.

Exercises

Read the article given below and do the following exercises as required.

Eastern Europe has focused most of its trade efforts on the west, but new restrictions have raised concerns.

East Europeans Fear Protectionism

By Colin Woodard
Special to The Christian Science Monitor

With the collapse of the Comecon trading systems two years ago, the countries of Eastern Europe cut ties with one another and reoriented their trade to West European markets. Now leaders in Poland, Hungary, and the Czech and Slovak Republics are wondering if that was a good idea.

Helped by the lifting of many European Community and European Free Trade Association (EFTA) trade barriers, the four Central European countries conduct 60 to 75 per cent of their trade with Western Europe. Eastern leaders had hoped that the signing of free trade agreements with the EC and EFTA earlier this year would further integrate their economies with the West.

But a spate of measures restricting imports from the East has raised concerns across the region that Western Europe has no intention of letting the East compete on an equal footing.

"Europe uses a sort of double-speak," says Laszlo Csaba of Hungary's Kopint-Datorg economic research institute.

"It's all very good when they're talking in very general terms," he adds. "But when it comes down to substantive things it gets very petty-minded, especially in areas where we have a competitive advantage."

West European measures

In April, the EC imposed a ban on livestock, meat and dairy products from 18 eastern countries following an outbreak of hoof and mouth disease in Croatia. Hungarian Foreign Minister Geza Jeszenszky told EC leaders that the "entirely unwarranted (move) smacks of a most regrettable survival of the notion of an Eastern bloc."

The EC followed with antidumping duties and "voluntary" export restraints on certain steel products from Hungary and Poland. And just days after signing the EFTA free-trade agreement in early April, Austria introduced import quotas on chemicals, cement agricultural machinery, and steel from Eastern Europe. West Europeans claim that their eastern neighbors have an unfair advantage because of low wages, state subsidies and low environmental standards.

Although the EC and EFTA agreements are supposed to lift tariffs and trade barriers on most industrial goods over 10 years, most agricultural products are not included in the agreements. This is critical for Hungary, with its extensive farm sector.

"The EC is never going to let Hungary achieve its potential output," says Iowa farmer David Andres, who has studied Hungarian agriculture firsthand. "They're already afraid of Hungary."

"The stronger player always calls the shots in the gray areas and we're certainly weaker than they are," says Ladislav Derian, first secretary of Slovakia's embassy in Budapest.

"Europe could afford to make more lavish concessions because we're insignificantly small compared to them," says Casaba, who estimates the East-Central European share of imports to the EC at less than 5 per cent.

Diversifying ties

Trade experts say the four central European countries should seek new markets to reduce their dependency on Europe. "Most East Europeans don't understand that if you diversify your economic ties you're not leading yourself away from the EC," a Western trade official says.

"Europe is not eager to let (its) markets be swamped with cheap Eastern imports," he adds. "If these (Eastern) countries traded more elsewhere and with one another it would help relieve the pressure on the EC and EFTA."

Continued recession in Europe and a severe regional drought in Eastern Europe are largely responsible for a sudden downturn in the four countries' exports in the first half of this year.

"This underlines the necessity of cultivating other, fast-growing markets," a document of the Organization for Economic Cooperation and Development (OECD) states. "Continued strong export growth will be essential to sustain the transformation to a market economy and avoid balance of payments constraints."

The OECD says the six "Asian Tigers"—Malaysia, South Korea, Taiwan, Thailand, Singapore and Hong Kong—could make excellent trading partners for the Central Europeans, as they undergo rapid economic growth.

Others say the first step should be for East European states to conduct more trade among themselves. "We traded freely (between ourselves) for 40 years, and now we have quotas and duties blocking the way," Mr. Derian says.

Barriers to trade

In March 1993, with EC prodding, hungary, Poland, and the Czech and Slovak Republics set up a free-trade zone of their own. But member states have shown little interest in promoting the development of this Central European Free Trade Association(CEFTA), besuse of concerns that it might undermine bids for EC membership.

In May, CEFTA representatives failed to ratify an agreement that would have reduced the timetable for trade liberalization from eight to five years.

Instead, some CEFTA countries have started adopting temporary import quotas and imposing indirect barriers to intraregional trade.

"People are reluctant to drop barriers because the other East European countries are the only ones from which we can protect ourselves," Derian says. "All our other trading partners are so much stronger than we are."

—From *The Christian Science Monitor* • Nov. 8, 1993

Ⅰ. Answer the following questions:

1. Why do the East European countries fear the trade protectionism of the Western Europe so much?

2. Why should some East European countries adopt temporary import quotas and impose indirect barriers within their own block?

Ⅱ. Choose one most appropriate answer to each of the following multiple choice questions according to the article:

1. The collapse of the Comecon trading systems.

A. has helped the Eastern European countries to change their direction of trade.

B. has had a positive effect on the economic development of the Eastern European countries.

C. has destroyed the friendly relationship between the Eastern European countries.

a. A & B are correct　　b. All of them are correct

c. B & C are correct　　d. Only A is correct

2. According to the first section of the article,

a. while welcoming the Eastern European countries to join them in trade, Western Europe would not bear a real competition from the East.

b. the four central European countries have benefited a lot from doing business with Western Europe.

c. for some reason, Western Europe had banned imports from the countries of Eastern Europe.

d. western Europe has been quite generous with Eastern Europe but when it comes to doing business, it gets very petty-minded.

3. "In April, the EC imposed a ban on livestock, meat, and dairy products from 18 eastern countries following an outbreak of hoof and mouth disease in Croatia." The underlined phrase means

a. levied a high tariff

b. adopted quota system

c. limited the import volume

d. shut out imports

4. With the EC and EFTA agreements,

a. the Eastern Europe would be allowed to increase their exports to the West.

b. there will be fewer tariffs and barriers on industrial goods from Eastern Europe.

c. there would hardly be any improvement in exports of Eastern Europe's agricultural products.

d. the Eastern Europe countries will see a great leap forward in the production of industrial products.

5. "The stronger player always calls the shots in the gray areas." The underlined expression means

a. have a control in a highly developed areas.

b. is in command in less developed areas.

c. make experiments in poor areas.

d. make profits in less developed areas.

6. According to some experts the four Central European countries need to diversify their economic ties because

a. Europe has continued recession.

b. this would help themselves become more independent.

c. their exports have fallen sharply.

d. decreasing export volumes will cause them balance of payments constraints.

7. To have a successful transformation to a market economy the East European states should

A. seek more help from west Europe

B. turn to the NICs

C. do more trade among themselves

D. have quotas and duties on imports

a. A & C　　b. B & D

c. A, C & D　　d. B & D

8. The barriers to the promotion of trade in the four Central European countries include 3 of the following but

a. concerns that they might not obtain EC membership.

b. import quotas and barriers to trade within their own areas.

c. the establishment of CEFTA.

d. each one's determination to protect themselves.

Supplimentary Material for Free Reading

A. After 40 Years, EU Arrives at Crossroads

By Tom Buerkle

International Herald Tribune

BRUSSELS—Forty years after the founding fathers of European integration launched an idealistic experiment in cooperation among governments, Europe is struggling to adapt the cohesive policies of the past to the divisive challenges of the future.

The Treaty of Rome, signed on March 25, 1957, when Europe was striving to heal the physical and emotional wounds of World War II has fulfilled most of its framers' grandest ambitions. War has become so unthinkable among the countries of Western Europe that this primordial objective is often overlooked today.

Notwithstanding mounting social pressures, the European Union is the world's wealthiest group of countries and remains a pole of attraction to its neighbors to the East and South.

But Europe increasingly looks like the victim of its own success, raising questions about the treaty's fundamental goal of an "ever closer union." The extension of integration into such sensitive areas as a common currency and border controls has prompted a nationalist backlash, while expansion from the six original members to the current 15 has frayed the consensus over policy objectives, a trend likely to worsen when the EU opens its doors to the 11 candidates on its doorstep.

Britain's opposition to deeper integration in current negotiations on EU reform are widely shared in Denmark and Sweden, for example. In Germany, meanwhile, the record rise in joblessness has led populist politicians such as Gerhard Schroeder, the Social Democratic leader of Lower Saxony, to begin to question Chancellor Helmut Kohl's vision of binding Germany into a European economic and political union.

Economically, meanwhile, many Europeans question whether the progression from common tariffs to a common market and ultimately the common currency will provide solutions to mass unemployment, or merely worsen the problem. Persistent joblessness "would be dangerous for the future of the Union," Lamberto Dini, the Italian foreign minister, warned in an interview. But the EU itself can do little directly to combat Europe's economic rigidities because welfare systems and labor rules remain in the hands of national governments, he said.

It is emblematic of the struggle to redefine Europe's role that Wim Kok, the Dutch prime minister and EU president who is leading the negotiations on EU reform, shuns Mr. Kohl's argument that European integration is a question of peace or war.

"We should not just look back at World War II," Mr. Kok said. "For young people, that is not a very realistic thing anymore. We are not talking about war between France and Germany. We are talking about giving hope to Eastern Europe."

This wider Europe will inevitably be less federal than the architects of the Maastricht Treaty on European Union envisaged at the start of this decade, Mr. Kok said, and the Union will have to be more selective about launching new common policies. But, he added, "In my view, there is no alternative to the further development of integration." The tensions and doubts prevalent today reflect the far-reaching nature of the imminent decisions on a single currency and constitutional reforms, which will shape Europe into the 21st century.

Monetary union, warns Malcolm Rifkind, the British foreign secretary, will be a radical and divisive departure from 40 years of common policies. "Europe will be divided between those countries that are part of economic and monetary union, and those countries that are not," he said. "This is not what the founding fathers had in mind."

Hints of a potential rupture are already apparent in the strained relations between Germany and southern EU members. While many Germans fear the inclusion of the lira and the peseta will produce a weak euro, leaders of Italy, Spain and Portugal have stepped up their campaign to join monetary union at the outset.

This southern campaign, moreover, underscores the potential for competing regional alliances as Europe expands.

"There is a tendency for the Mediterranean countries to consult among themselves and try to establish a common position on many subjects," Mr. Dini said. "We don't like to see the balance of the Union shift northeast."

EU reform could be equally divisive. On Tuesday, when EU foreign ministers meet in Rome to celebrate the anniversary of the treaty's signing, France and Germany will present a proposal for incorporating the Western European Union, the fledgling defense group, into the European Union. But a merger is opposed by the EU's four neutral countries—Ireland, Sweden, Finland and Austria—as well as by Britain, which fears the plan will undermine U.S. support for European defense through the North Atlantic Treaty Organization.

A separate French-German reform proposal to allow groups of countries to develop common policies without unanimous backing or participation poses a fundamental threat to Europe's cohesiveness, warns Jacques Delors, the former president of the European Commission, the EU executive agency. Rather than forging a coherent avantgarde of countries capable of leading the entire bloc to deeper integration, the so-called flexibility proposal is more likely to spawn a haphazard series of shifting coalitions as some countries co-operate on defense and others on such areas as fighting international crime, Mr. Delors said.

"That's going to complicate the design of Europe and make it absolutely incomprehensible," Mr. Delors said.

While the challenges are immense, few continental politicians question the rationale of integration at a time when economic globalization has reduced the capacity of national governments to act on their own. "The model is more valid than ever, but it's also more difficult than ever," said Jose Maria Gil-Robles Gil-Delgado, the president of the European Parliament.

Karl Lamers, parliamentary foreign policy spokesman for Mr. Kohl's Christian Democratic Union, acknowledged the "regressive nationalism" caused by economic difficulties. "The consensus model is at stake," he said. But he said the budget-cutting reforms being made for monetary union would strengthen Europe's capacity to grow and create jobs.

The long view also inspires optimism, Mr. Dini said. He noted that Europe had progressed a long way from the customs union established by the Treaty of Rome 40 years ago. "No one thought it would work because of productivity differences between countries", Mr. Dini said. "See where we are today with the single market. This is extraordinary. This is historical."

—From *International Herald Tribune* • March 4, 1997

B. Europe Rising

Restructuring and the Euro May Soon Make it America's Equal

It was the kind of corporate coup that leaves coffee mugs rattling in executive suites. Bell Atlantic Corp., the phone Goliath of the eastern U.S., was just about to buy San Francisco's Air-Touch Communications Inc. But at the last minute in early January, London-based Vodafone Group PLC outbid Bell's original offer by \$17 billion, paying \$62 billion for Air Touch. The world's largest cellular-phone operator would be British, not American. Far from concluding that the European company was overreaching, investors quickly bid up Vodafone shares by 17%.

The deal sounded a wakeup call. Long considered a collection of economic has-beens clinging to outdated social systems, Europe is on the rise. The single currency, officially born on Jan. 4, is only the latest milestone in the Continent's long journey back to global prominence. Gradually, over the past 10 years, companies have restructured and governments have dismantled regulations that stifled competition, following a model perfected in the U. S.

TEAMWORK. Indeed, until recently, it seemed safe to assume that Japan, or perhaps China, would become America's closest economic peer. But with Asia, Latin America, and Russia all in deep financial trouble, Europe seems most likely to fill that role, at least in the medium term. Right now, it's one of the main props under the fragile world economy. Although the global crisis is slowing growth, the euro zone's gross domestic product is still projected to expand by 2% this year—about the same as the U. S. rate—and to recover to around 3% growth in 2000.

Monetary union is only part of the story. European companies have painfully cut costs and sold off money-losing businesses to get into fighting trim. Now, the strongest are teaming up with U. S. counterparts to gain even greater market strength. Several recent mergers give a glimpse of the new transatlantic corporation. At Daimler Chrysler, the biggest combination so far, a jet shuttles executives between Stuttgart and Detroit three times a week, and the two companies plan to integrate procurement and share technology. Deutsche Bank bought Bankers Trust to complement its homegrown clout with U. S. -style investment banking savvy.

Media giant Bertelsmann has widened its global presence in publishing by acquiring Random House. And to cash in on the Continent's growing Internet craze. Bertelsmann took a 2% stake in America Online and manages Aol's booming European operations in a joint venture with the U. S. company. Last fall, Bertelsmann poured $ 200 million into a partnership with Barnes & Noble to take on Amazon. com in the U. S. Such deals, along with British Petroleum's $ 53 billion buyout of Amoco and Vodafone's triumph over Bell Atlantic, suggest that America is Europe Inc.'s favorite shopping mall.

Even when they're not snapping up U. S. counterparts, European companies are proving to be global powerhouses. Formerly state-subsidized Airbus Industrie matches giant Boeing order for order in small and midsize jets. Sales of Mercedes and Volks wagens are booming around the world. Finland's Nokia and Sweden's Ericsson, along with Vodafone, have conquered global telecommunications markets.

Another force behind the Continent's growing muscle is deregulation, which has turned "Fortress Europe" into a freer, more efficient market. For instance, since the German and French telecommunications markets were fully deregulated a year ago, they have become among the most competitive in the world. Companies such as France Télécom, Deutsche Telekom, and Mannesmann are being forced to cut costs and expand across Europe to survive. The side effects are already palpable. German telecom companies alone created 40 000 jobs in 1998. And competition has reduced Germany's phone rates by as much as 70%.

Deregulation will set off the same process in banking and finance, media and energy. Once the leaders in these industries gain enough critical mass in Europe, many will strike out abroad, as Vodafone did. No matter which side of the Atlantic they're on, says John J. Studzinski, Morgan Stanley Dean Witter & Co.'s European investment banking chief, "the biggest companies in each industry will drive consolidation."

Indeed, former monopolies trying to hold on to market share as they begin to face private-sector competition are likely to drive more Europe-U. S. mergers. For instance, giant state-owned Deutsche Post in Bonn is getting ready for mail deregulation by teaming up with air carrier Lufthansa to buy a big stake in parcel-delivery company DHL International Ltd. That way, it will have another business to offset falling margins in letter mail.

Yet some European industries are on the ascendant, thanks to what Americans might consider state intervention. That's certainly the case with the Continent's global lead in cellular phones. The early adoption of a single Europewide standard has created a huge platform for its cell-phone companies. By contrast, says Vodafone CEO Christopher C. Gent, the laissez-faire U. S. created "a mess of standards" by letting multiple systems battle it out. Adds Jorma Ollila, Nokia's CEO: "Economic theory would say that (the U. S. approach) is better, but it hasn't worked out that way." In fact, Europe is likely to set the world standard for next-generation video cell phones.

AMBIVALENCE. For all the progress Europe has made toward global competitiveness, its citizens remain committed to policies that mitigate the harsher aspects of the U. S. economy. Voters want to retain state-run health care, retirement benefits, and liberal unemployment and welfare benefits, even if that means setting aside some of their new wealth to pay for them. The left-of-center governments that run 13 of the European Union's 15 nations are beholden to labor, and their new policies could reverse the moderate wage demands that have helped keep unit labor costs in the Euro zone flat for the past two years.

Indeed, Europe's recovery is a two-tiered affair, in which companies often succeed despite government labor and social policies. Decades-old rules that protect workers could hamper further gains. "There is a world of distance between the actions of (European) companies and governments," says Daniel L. Vasella, CEO of Swiss drug giant Novartis.

Still, thousands of companies are tailoring strategies to capitalize on the Continent's new strength. Out of the ferment will come over more Daimlers and Vodafones poising themselves to globalize once they are strong enough in Europe. They present a challenge to the U. S. —and an opportunity. "Americans are and will continue to be ambivalent about what's happening here," says a top EC official in Brussels. "They know they need a stronger Europe. But finding another big guy on the block makes them nervous." If you don't believe him, just ask the excess at Bell Atlantic.

By Thane Peterson in Frankfurt, with William Echikson in Brussels, Stephen Baker in Paris, Julia Flynn in London, and bureau reports

—From *Business Week* • Feb. 8, 1999

C. The Other Foot

Despite warmer ties, the EU targets Asian exports

By Shada Islam in Brussels

The good news for Asian exporters to Europe is that after three years of recession, the 12 European Union economies are creaking back to life. That means consumers are likely to have more money to spend on Asian goods. The bad news is that EU trade officials, under pressure from increasingly strident industry groups, are tightening the screws on Asian imports. These include cars, TV sets, textiles and footwear. The trade friction contrasts with recent efforts by the EU to improve its diplomatic ties with Asia.

Trade between the EU and Asia stood at US$218 billion in 1993. Asian countries exported US$120 billion of goods to the Union during the same period, running up a trade surplus of US$47 billion. Japan accounted for more than half of that, with a trade surplus of US$29 billion.

Officials at the European Commission in Brussels argue this is proof enough of Europe's open-door policy towards Asia. For Asian exporters, however, the devil is in the details. An increasing number of Asian countries are being investigated—and penalized—for selling cut-price goods on European markets. Asian textile exporters, meanwhile, accuse the EU of doing little to free restrictions on textile and clothing imports, as it promised to do in last year's GATT world-trade accord.

On September 30, for example, the EU turned down Japanese requests for a bigger quota for their car exports to Europe. Under a deal struck in Brussels, Japanese car exports to the EU in 1994 will be limited to 993 000 vehicles, a marginal 1.3% rise from last year. The accord is part of an EU-Japan arrangement signed in 1991 under which Tokyo will keep its vehicle exports to the EU within agreed annual levels until the end of 1999, when the European auto market is to be fully liberalized.

The original deal was struck when Europe's car market was booming, with growth rates of around 15% a year. But when growth rates sank to an all-time low of 2% in March this year, the EU slashed Japan's quota to 984 000 cars, down almost 18% from the 1991 level.

This time around, Japanese trade officials went into the talks demanding a higher quota. They argued that the European car market is finally growing again and could expand by 5%~6% by the end of the year. The final agreement, however, reflects the EU's less optimistic forecasts. "Our conclusion is that the market will expand by 4.4% in 1994," says a senior EU trade negotiator. That represents sales this year of roughly 12.3 million cars—and the EU insists that the lion's share be reserved for its own car makers.

Despite the agreement, European makers remain unmollified. The recent upturn isn't strong or durable enough to justify even the 1.3% quota increase for Japan, says James Rosenstein, a spokesman for the European Automobile Manufacturers' Association. He says Tokyo shouldn't get its hopes up for next year, either.

Japanese exporters nevertheless hope to negotiate a larger car quota for next year following the EU's planned enlargement on January 1 to include Austria, Finland, Sweden and Norway. All four countries have told the EU they want Japanese exporters to have unrestricted access to their markets. Austria, which currently slaps a 20% tariff on Japanese vehicles, says it will bring the duty down to the 10% level applied by other EU states.

While Japan frets about cars, other Asian countries are worried about new EU investigations into imports of allegedly below-cost Asian goods. On October 1, the EU announced anti-dumping duties of up to 29.8% on colour TVs from China, South Korea, Malaysia, Thailand and Singapore.

Asian exporters of car radios, videocassette recorders and compact discs are already paying heavy anti-dumping fines. In each case, the EU has argued that Asian firms are selling their products at prices below cost, thus depriving their European rivals of market share, jobs and capacity. The penalties imposed aim to raise the prices of dumped goods to give European producers a chance to compete.

The duties imposed on Asian exporters of colour TVs are still only provisional; EU officials say it will take four to six months to complete their inquiries. Once fixed, the penalties will last for five years.

European consumer organizations say the anti-dumping fines will raise TV prices in the EU and Britain has opposed the penalties. But the remaining 11 countries are backing European TV makers' claims that sales of allegedly under-priced Asian TV sets are forcing them to shed jobs and close production lines.

So far, Thailand's Teletech has been the hardest hit of the Asian TV makers; its exports to the EU face provisional antidumping duties of 29.8%. South Korea's Daewoo, Goldstar and Samsung face duties of 16.8%~18.8%, while Japan's Sanyo faces a 13.1% duty on TVs it makes in Singapore. In all, up to US$800 million of trade is likely to be hit by the EU move.

Asian textile exporters are also worried about the progress of an EU investigation of exports of cotton and polycotton (a mix of polyester and cotton) from India, Pakistan, Thailand, Indonesia and China. European governments insist that the anti-dumping inquiry, which has already lasted nine months, should be extended for another few months. A similar inquiry is being planned into Chinese footwear exports.

The EU has also made clear it's in no hurry to liberalize quotas for any of Asia's sensitive textile and clothing exports. Under the Gatt Uruguay Round accord, the EU and other importers are committed to phasing out quotas on 16% of their textile and clothing imports from next year. This will be the first stage of a decade-long, four-stage phase-out of the Multifibre Arrangement (MFA), which regulates world trade in textiles. Importers, however, can choose the goods to liberalize at each stage—meaning sensitive items will probably be freed last.

The EU plans to select items like hats, umbrellas, car-seat belts and parachutes for the first round of liberalization. Asians counter that these goods are already exempt from MFA quotas. "We'll be getting no additional benefits," says a South Asian trade official. "The EU is keeping to the letter of its Uruguay Round promise, but it's ignoring its spirit."

—From *Far Eastern Economic Review* • Oct. 13, 1994

Lesson 7

On Japan's Position on trade

Text

Japan Says No

TOKYO

America wants Japan to meet import targets for some American goods. An unwilling Japan has decided to draw the line.

Once, when Japan faced pressure from abroad, it would either give in reluctantly or keep quiet and hope that the fuss would die down. No longer, it seems. The Clinton administration strongly believes in exerting such pressure. Its policy is to open some Japanese markets (which it deems to be closed) by setting import targets—an approach to trade policy that supporters call "results-oriented". This ugly term foreshadows uncertain consequences. Far from capitulating to this new thrust of American trade policy, Japan is taking a stand that could lead to a trans-Pacific confrontation.

Japan's government is deeply opposed to what America's trade representative, Mickey Kantor, has called a new policy geared to "quantifiable results" for some products. It fears that the demands and threats which are part of any such policy are bound to spread—both within product groups and to new areas of trade. At the summit meeting last month between Bill Clinton and Japan's prime minister, Kiichi Miyazawa, America insisted that Japan should come up with specific measures that would enable it to meet new import targets. Japan's government will refuse.

Instead, Japan is undertaking a detailed defence of its record on trade. This will first appear in the annual white paper on trade developments, due to be published on May 21st by the Ministry of International Trade and Industry (MITI)—its definitive statement on trade matters. In addition to the customary dry analysis, this year's edition will put Japan's side of an argument that has, until now, been dominated by American and European critiques. It follows another MITI report, published this week, that takes America, the European Community and other large trading partners to task for their "unfair trading practices". Both reports argue for trade governed by multilateral rules and call for the completion of the Uruguay round of trade talks.

Besides making worthy free-trade noises, MITI's defence will also tackle American criticism head on. Naoyuki Haraoka, director of MITI's international trade research office, is at pains to point out that Japan is in fact more open than other countries. Japan's average tariff on mining and manufactured goods is 2.7%, compared with 4.2% in America and 4.6% in the European Community. The report will also reject the argument that Japan needs special trade sanctions because it operates a different sort of capitalism. It will try to do so by explaining the nature and future of the country's trade surplus.

It is this persistent surplus, more than anything, that has provoked anger in Washington—and Mr Clinton's remark that "the possibility of obtaining real, even access to the Japanese market is somewhat remote". This year the surplus has been growing fast. Jesper Koll, a Tokyo-based economist at S. G. Warburg, estimates that Japan's trade surplus could reach $200 billion if the yen stays at current levels. That is $68 billion more than last year's figure. Moreover, the bilateral surplus with America is also growing rapidly. Mr Koll reckons it will climb from $44 billion in 1992 to $78 billion this year, an all-time high. With the economy still barely growing, despite two fiscal packages in the past nine months, Japan's crities say that the country is once more exporting its way out of recession.

One defence the ministry will make is that most trade statistics ignore services. MITI estimates, using data from the Bank of Japan, that if Japan's imports of services had been included in its trade statistics, then the trade surplus would have been $84 billion, $48 billion lower than reported. Exclusive attention to trade in goods is therefore misleading. MITI wants to see better collection of statistics for trade in services by international bodies such as the OECD.

Surplus, what surplus?

Analysis by Mr Haraoka's office explains the recent rise in Japan's trade surplus as follows: because of the recession at home, Japan has seen a decline in expensive imports of luxuries, which were enormously fashionable during the second half of the 1980s. This effect has been compounded, thanks to slow growth elsewhere, by low prices for the international commodities that Japanese industry depends upon. Exports of Japanese machinery, on the other hand, withstood the downturn quite well because the Asian economies that buy them continued to boom.

Also, the American and Japanese economies have been out of kilter. America's strengthening economy caused an increase in American demand for Japanese imports, while Japanese demand for foreign goods declined. The effect is amplified, MITI argues, because 35% of American exports to Japan are industrial commodities, which are highly sensitive to the business cycle.

Having argued that criticism of the trade surplus in Washington is misconceived, MITI's forthcoming paper goes on to predict that the surplus will, of its own accord, gradually diminish in size and relevance:

- When Japanese demand picks up again, imports will grow

more quickly than in past recoveries. This is because the volume of Japanese imports has become more sensitive to the domestic economic cycle.

• Parts and components account for a growing share of Japan's exports; 28% of total exports and 36% of machinery exports in 1992 compared with 19% and 28% respectively in 1981. MITI believes that such exports should be of less concern to advocates of managed trade than consumer goods, because components increase the competitiveness—and therefore the export potential—of the industries that buy them. (Advocates of managed trade would doubtless dispute that.)

• From now on, MITI argues, Japan's overseas plants will increasingly export their output back to Japan. Before, they bought Japanese exports of equipment and parts.

• Three years of declining profits have followed the over-investment of the late 1980s. Mr Haraoka predicts that Japanese managers will henceforth act more like Western managers, putting profits before their firms' market share. In the past, that is, Japanese firms have been export-driven; in future they will be less likely to export their way out of trouble.

For these reasons, MITI argues, Japan's trade surplus will fall in due course. However, it says, a persistent surplus (albeit a smaller one) is inevitable as long as Japanese households save more than American ones, and America's budget deficit remains untamed. This is a familiar point: trade balances are determined by macroeconomic factors, not by trade policy. To this, a sophisticated advocate of the import-target approach could reply that the balance is not the issue. What matter is access to Japan's markets, America would be content if Japan increased its imports and exports by the same amount (leaving the trade balance, and the associated accounting identities, undisturbed). This reply is disingenuous. American public opinion demands, in its unsophisticated way, a smaller trade deficit.

On trade and other issues, Japan has caved in to outside pressure countless times before, and may do so again. The White House seems to be counting on this. It, and Congress, would be better advised to concentrate on reducing America's budget deficit. That would reduce the trade deficit regardless of Japan's trade policies. Threats of trade reprisals, even if they force Japan to give way, will not.

—From *the Economist* • May 15, 1993

Words and Expressions

target	*n.*	指标
approach	*n.*	(处理问题的)方式;方法
foreshadow	*v.*	预示
capitulate (to)	*v.*	投降;屈服
(take a) stand	*n.*	立场,观点,态度(采取一种态度;持一种观点)
be opposed to	反对,对抗	
gear to	*v.*	使适应;使适合
thrust	*n.*	要点;目标
customary	*a.*	习惯上的;按惯常的
critique	*n.*	评论文章
argue	*v.*	提出理由;提供理由
argue for	主张	

tackle	*v.* （着手）对付
head on	（副词短语）迎头；正面针对地
at pains	尽力；费尽苦心；努力
trade sanctions	贸易制裁
persistent	*a.* 持久的，持续的；始终存在的
provoke	*v.* 激起；引起；惹
access	*n.* 接近或进入的机会（权）；享用机会；享用权
obtain access to a market	得到进入一个市场的机会（权利）
remote	*a.* 绝少的；微乎其微的
reckon	*v.* 估计；判断
withstand	*v.* 经受；承受
out of kilter	失常；失调
amplify	*v.* 增强；扩大
misconceived	*a.* 设想错误的
accord	*n.* 自愿意志
of one's own accord	出于自愿；主动地
diminish	*v.* 减少
relevance	*n.* 意义
sensitive (to)	*a.* 敏感的
sensitive to environment	对环境敏感
advocate	*n.* 拥护者；提倡者
dispute	*v.* 辩驳；争议
henceforth	*ad.* 从今以后，从此以后
untamed	*a.* 未被驯服的；未被抑制的
issue	*n.* 问题；争论点
disingenuous	*a.* 诡诈的
sophisticated	*a.* 老练的
cave in	屈服

trade reprisal　　　　贸易报复

Notes to the Text

1. "... hope that the fuss would die down."

fuss,名词,异议;抱怨。本文中的 fuss 一词指的是为了促使日本改善与其贸易伙伴(主要是美国)在贸易上的不平衡,其贸易伙伴对日本的谴责,在舆论上施加的压力。

2. "No longer, it seems."

这是一个省略句,避免了重复上句的部分内容,而且利用倒装起到了强调的作用。完整的句子可以写为:

It seems Japan will no longer give in or keep quiet when it faces pressure from abroad again.

3. Kiichi Miyazawa　宫泽喜一

日本自由民主党前总裁、内阁总理大臣。1919 年生于广岛县,1941 年在东京帝国大学法学部政治科毕业。1942 年入大藏省,后进入通商产业省,多次当选参议员,众议院议员,历次进入首相内阁,担任重要职务。1980 年曾随日美欧三边委员会代表团访问中国。1991 年 11 月担任日本自民党总裁和内阁首相,1993 年 8 月 5 日辞职。1998 年宫泽应小渊内阁之邀再次入阁任大藏大臣。

4. "... America insisted that Japan should come up with specific measures that would enable it to meet new import targets."

虚拟语气在一些动词如 insist(作"坚持、要求"讲时),suggest, demand, request, recommend, propose 等后面的宾语从句中使用。这里用 should(用于所有的人称)+动词原形。省略 should 的用法在美国英语中较常见,英国英语在同样情况下习惯加 should。

例:The buyer insists that the manufacturer(should)give a 5% price reduction to bring the business to a close.

为了达成协议,买方坚持要制造商减价 5%。

I request that she go alone.

我要求她自己去。

5. White Paper　白皮书

1) 英国、澳大利亚、新西兰及加拿大等国政府就某一问题采取的政策向国会提出的报告。

2) 任何组织发表的阐明并维护自己立场的官方报告。

本文中的 white paper 指(2),是 MITI 关于贸易发展的年度报告。

6. MITI (the Ministry of International Trade and Industry) 日本通商产业省。

7. "In addition to the customary dry analysis, this year's edition will put Japan's side of an argument that has, until now, been dominated by American and European Critiques."

1) dry 在本句中修饰 analysis。dry 作形容词时可以有许多种意思,在本句中表示:不带偏见的,不加修饰(渲染)的;直截了当的。例如:dry facts, 不加渲染的事实;in dry language,以直截了当的话。

2) "Put Japan's side of an argument"

put: 写上,说,提出,

side: 一派(或一方)的态度(立场、看法)等,

somebody's side of an argument　某人对这个论点的态度。

3) That,引导定语从句用的关系代词,其用法和 which 大致相同,但只引导限制性定语从句。

例:I've read the newspaper that carries the important editorial.

我看了那份登载着重要社论的报纸。

本课句中的 that 引导的定语从句修饰它前面 argument。

全句的大概意思是:今年的(白皮书)除了以往的直截了当的分析外,还要提出日本对这一论点的态度,而在此之前这方面是美欧言论一统天下。

8. "It follows another MITI report, published this week, that takes America, European Community and other large trading partners to task for their 'unfair trading practices'."

take sb. to task, 责备某人,申斥某人,也可以用 call 和 bring

两个字替换 take。

例：I was called to task for being a few minutes late.

我因迟到了几分钟而受训斥。

MITI 的报告斥责美国、欧共体以及其他主要贸易伙伴采用“不公正的贸易做法”。

9. Uruguay round of trade talks　乌拉圭回合贸易谈判（请参考第 10 课注释）

10. free trade　自由贸易

政府施行对进口商不加歧视，对出口商也不加干涉的政策。这种政策并不意味着国家放弃对进出口的一切控制和征税。自由贸易的理论根据是亚当·斯密的论点：国际分工导致专业化、高效率和高度集中的生产。尽管就单独一国而言，特别是如果该国是某种商品的主要购买者或出售者，采取限制性措施可能会有实际好处。但实际上，保护国内工业只是对一小部分人有利，而对其他大多数人不利。第二次世界大战以来，人们为了减少各国间关税壁垒和货币限制作出了很大努力。但各国为了保护本国工业及其他行业，仍采用各种各样的关税及非关税壁垒，如进口配额、捐税、对国内工业的补贴等。

11. “With the economy still barely growing, ...”

前置词 With 的一种用法，由 with＋名词或代词＋分词组成，作状语用。

例：With the tree growing, we get more shade.

He fell asleep with the lamp burning.

12. fiscal packages　财政一揽子计划（方案）

政府为了调节经济使其稳定、繁荣而采取的以“财政政策”为基础的一系列措施。在经济衰退时，政府可在设备、建筑、公共事业或社会保险方面增加支出，通过扩大投资和消费促进经济发展；也可以在预算收入项下减少各种税收，以达到经济扩展的效果。在经济活动处在高水平，物价迅速上涨时，政府可以减少开支，增加税收，使之减缓。

本文所指为前一种。

13. “MITI estimates ... that if Japan's imports of services had been included in its trade statistics, then the trade surplus would have been...”

“如日本的贸易统计数字包括劳务进口,那么日本的贸易盈余则应该是……”

这是表示与过去事实相反使用动词虚拟语气的条件句。这类句子的动词构成是条件从句:had+动词过去分词,主句:should, would, could 或 might+have+动词过去分词。

例:If the manager had taken the suggestion earlier, his company would not have lost the competition.

如果经理早一点接受这个建议,他的公司就不可能在竞争中失败。

14. “Because of the recession at home...”

1993 年,陷入泥沼难以自拔的日本经济已进入连续衰退的第三个年头。日本经济衰退是从 1991 年 5 月开始的,其主要特点是:股票、房地产跌价;工厂库存积压,利润下降;银行呆账高筑,无力扩大信贷。出现这一现象的原因主要有三个方面:(一)生产设备能力过剩,(二)传统刺激经济方法失灵,(三)日元升值。根据官方统计,1993 年第一季度日本国民经济增长 0.5%,第二季度为负增长,第三季度和第一季度一样,上升 0.5%。

15. “... because of the recession at home Japan has seen a decline in expensive imports of luxuries ... This effect has been compounded, thanks to the slow growth elsewhere, by low prices for the international commodities that Japanese depends upon.”

1) 这里 effect 指由于高价奢侈品进口的减少而产生的近期日本贸易盈余上升的效果。而这一结果(贸易盈余)又因为日本工业所依赖大量进口的初级产品(原材料)的国际市场价格低廉而扩大。

2) compound　动词,增加;加重

compound a problem　使问题复杂化

compound difficulties　加重困难

3) thanks to slow growth elsewhere

"由于其他地区的缓慢增长"(经济增长缓慢意味着投资、扩大生产规模小,从而对原材料的需求较低)——这实际上是造成国际市场原材料价格低的因素。

16. "America's strengthening economy caused an increase in American demand for Japanese imports, while Japanese demand for foreign goods declined. The effect is amplified, MITI argues, because 35% of American exports to Japan are industrial commodities, which are highly sensitive to the business cycle.

1) industrial commodities

于此专指资本货物、高技术产品和耐用消费品等。

2) "... industrial commodities ... are highly sensitive to the business cycle."

商业周期的转换对所有商品的市场都有影响,但所谓"工业产品"对其反应更为强烈。在周期的萧条阶段,农产品和非耐用轻工产品的销量也会有所减少,但资本货物和耐用消费品的市场较之会大为萎缩,这是因为前者系日用必需品,而对后者的需求弹性(可调整性)很大,并且后者需用大量的资金。这就是本小节上列引文的含义。

3) "... The effect is amplified, ..."

"The effect"指注题引文中第一句的内容——日本出超、美国入超的两国贸易差额大势已成。

据下文,美国对日出口商品35%之多,又都是资本货物和耐用消费品之类,值此萧条阶段,那就要比其他品种削减得更多,从而日美之间的贸易差额又得以进一步扩大。

17. managed trade　管理贸易

管理贸易是自20世纪80年代中期以来的一种趋势,其特点是美、日、欧盟等各主要贸易国家以限制进口促进出口为目的,就某些敏感商品谈判特别的双边贸易协定来进行贸易。

例如欧盟与日本缔结协定要求日本逐年自动减少对欧盟出口汽车数量以使对方继续开放市场;又如美国以对日本开放自己的电子元件市场换取日本市场对自己电子元件的开放。

18. export-driven 合成形容词,意为:为出口所驱使的、以出口为目标的、大力(拚命)出口的。

19. albeit　连词:尽管,即使

例:a useful, albeit complex device　一个结构复杂但有用的装置

They are still waiting, albeit with growing impatience.

他们还在等,尽管越来越不耐烦。

注意:1) 此词较古,但近几年来多见于英美报刊文字。

2) 一般用来连接短语,而不是从句。

20. trade balance (balance of trade)　贸易差额

一国在一定时期内(如一年、半年或一季度)出口总值与进口总值相比的差额。出口总值超过进口总值时,相差之数叫做"贸易顺差"或称"出超",有时也称之为贸易盈余(trade surplus);反之,进口总值超过出口总值时,相差之数叫做"贸易逆差"或称"入超",有时也称之为贸易赤字(trade deficit)。如果出口总值与进口总值相等叫做"贸易平衡",但这种情况很少出现,即使有,也是短期内的偶然现象。

21. "... However, it says, a persistent surplus (albeit a smaller one) is inevitable as long as Japanese households save more than American ones, and America's budget deficit remains untamed. This is a familiar point: trade balances are determined by macroeconomic factors, not by trade policy."

"宏观经济因素"于此指构成一国经济形势的基本方面,如国民生产总值,国民收入,社会总需求,货币供应量等等。这些情况一般认为是决定外贸形势和贸易差额的根本性的因素。

如上列引文第一句所示,日本通产省坚持认为"宏观经济因素",如日本人的高储蓄率(可以遏制社会需求)和美国失控的预算赤字扩大了社会需求才是两国间贸易出现不平衡的真正原因。

Questions on Content and Language Points

(for preview, discussion and review)

1. "An unwilling Japan has decided to draw the line."

What is the meaning of the underlined part in the above sentence?

2. "Once, when faced pressure from abroad, it would either give in reluctantly or keep quiet and hope that the fuss would die down."

1) Could you guess what sort of pressure the writer refers to?

2) Please give a synonym to the expression "give in".

3) Explain the above underlined part of the sentence, paying special attention to the word "fuss".

3. Translate the following sentence into Chinese:

"Instead Japan is taking a detailed defense of its record on trade."

4. "Both reports argue for trade governed by multilateral rules and call for the completion of the Uruguay round of trade talks."

Find a word to replace "multilateral" for the same idea.

5. "With the economy still barely growing, despite two fiscal packages in the past nine months, Japan's critics say that the country is once more exporting its way out of recession."

Paraphrase "exporting its way out of recession."

6. Read Paragraph 6 and try to sum up in a few words the MITI's defending point on the trade surplus question.

7. Sum up the explanations given in the analysis by Mr. Haraoka's office for the recent rise in Japan's trade surplus. (See paragraph 1-2 of the second section.)

8. "However, it says, a persistent surplus is inevitable as long as Japanese households save more than Americans and America's budget deficit remains untamed."

Please find out the relationship between "a persistent surplus" and the Japanese households' higher savings rate and the America's bigger budget deficit. What effects would the two factors have on Japan's trade surplus?

9. How do you understand the last paragraph of the text? Does the writer believe that America's trade deficit with Japan could be improved once Japan gives in to their pressure?

Exercises

Ⅰ. Read the article given below and fill in the blanks from Paragraph 1 to Paragraph 9 with proper prepositions.

Ⅱ. Fill in each of the blanks in the rest part of the article with an appropriate word.

Surplus Is a "Time Bomb", EC Warns Japan

By Steven Brull

International Herald Tribune

Tokyo—As Japan reported Tuesday a further surge ________ its trade surplus, the European Community's top diplomat in Tokyo warned that the trade imbalance was a "time bomb" that could destroy bilateral relations.

The comment is a sign that European and Asian nations, which now suffer trade deficits ________ Japan of an order once experienced only by the United States, will in their growing frustration move closer to Washington ________ the front lines of trade disputes with Tokyo.

"There is a time bomb, which, if not defused, could derail the continuation of positive developments" between the Community and Japan. Jean-Pierre Leng, ambassador of the EC Commission in Tokyo, said ________ a gathering of businessmen.

Japan's trade surplus expanded by a greater-than-expected 39.4 per cent in January from a year earlier ________ \$5.3 billion. The figure, swollen by exports of office equipment and a sharp fall off ________ imports such as European cars, was the highest ever for January and the 25th successive expansion of the monthly surplus, the Finance Ministry said Tuesday. For 1992, the surplus with the rest ________ the world was a record $107 billion.

Mr. Leng warned that unless Japan did more to achieve its targeted economic growth rate of 3.3 per cent ________ the fiscal year beginning in April, the Community's trade deficit with Japan would grow ________ the 1992 level of $32 billion. Most economists say Japan's targeted goal is out ________ the question.

"We advocate additional measures," Mr. Leng said, echoing the view of the United States. He said these should come "the sooner the better" and "certainly" ________ the summit meeting of the seven leading industrial nations in Tokyo in July.

"It will be very difficult to explain to European public opinion, with unemployment ________ 10 per cent, that Japan, with inflation of 2 per cent and unemployment about 2 per cent, needs to accumulate a huge trade surplus with the rest of the world." the EC envoy said.

Japan's surplus with the Community surged 27.1 per cent to $2.74 billion in January, as a slight decline ________ exports was more than offset by a 20.5 per cent drop in imports of European merchandise.

The fastest expansion in Japan's surplus was with the non-Communist states of Asia, where the imbalance catapulted 96.1 per cent to $1.54 billion, the steepest jump in more than a year. Exports ________ Asia, economically the fastest growing region in the world, grew 6.1 per cent, led by microchips, cars and ships. Japanese imports of petroleum products, meat and other goods, meanwhile, were depressed ________ sluggish demand and dipped 4.9 per cent.

Asian nations are also raising their voices on ________ with Tokyo, although the tone remains tempered by Asian sensibilities.

"ASEAN exporters generally find the Japanese ________ inscrutable and difficult to fathom," said a report issued Tuesday by the Asia side of the ASEAN-Japan Economic Council, a private group.

"________ requirements for product quality and services frustrate genuine efforts by ASEAN to expand experts to Japan." added the report, which was issued after talks at the Foreign Ministry.

The Association of Southeast Asian Nations groups Brunei, Indonesia, Malaysia, the Philippines, Singapore and Thailand.

The ________ with Japan's biggest trading partner, the United States, leaped 21 per cent to $2.95 billion in January, an ________ from last month's single-digit rise. The U. S. Treasury secretary, Lloyed Bentsen, in a meeting last weekend with Finance Minister Yoshiro Hayashi, urged Japan to bolster its domestic demand in ________ to trim its trade imbalance.

As the European Community, Asia and the United States step up their demands, Tokyo is going on the defensive, warning that it will no longer tolerate protectionist moves that run ________ to the spirit of free trade.

Noboru Hatakeyama, deputy minister for international affairs of the Ministry of International Trade and Industry, said Tuesday that Japan would complain to the General Agreement on Tariffs and Trade if the United States ________ the tariffs on minivan imports from 2.5 per cent to 25 per cent, as U. S. automakers want.

"In 1987 we refrained from ________ to GATT." said Mr. Hata-keyama, referring to Tokyo's response after Washington ________ tariffs on several Japanese products in retaliation for alleged violation of a microchip agreement. "But once ________ enough."

He added that the government was discussing rule changes that would "force Japan to retaliate" ________ a GATT panel rule that Japanese exports were treated unfairly. He said the government had not imposed a deadline, but added that "necessity is the ________ of the timing."

Asked whether Tokyo had the nerve to follow through on its threat to retaliate against its biggest trade partner, Mr. Hatakeyama noted that Japan was the ________ importer of U. S. farm products and the No. 2 importer of American manufactured goods. "These two simple facts are ________ for Japan to have leverage," he said.

—From *International Herald Tribune* • Feb. 17, 1933

Appendix to Lesson 7

Text

Why Japan Won't Cave Into U. S. Trade Demands

Tradition, culture and an entrenched bureaucracy all work against any immediate entry into Japanese markets

TOKYO

American hopes that pressure from the U. S. will force Japan to suddenly dismantle its trade barriers are almost certain to evaporate in disappointment.

The fact is that Washington faces an obstacle far more formidable than a few power brokers in Tokyo's government offices. It must buck centuries-old, deeply ingrained Japanese customs. To move the Japanese government, Washington must move an entire nation.

So far, the U. S. has had only limited success despite congressional threats to retaliate. In an April 9 nationwide broadcast, Prime Minister Yasuhiro Nakasone urged the Japanese to buy more imported goods and unveiled a long-awaited three-year plan to ease import restrictions. But his program was far short of what Washington hoped to see.

White House Chief of Staff Donald Regan said the Japanese offered "few new or immediate measures." While the plan did promise fewer curbs on imports of telecommunications gear, medicine and medical equipment, it offered no relief for American forest products—which are among the most contentious trade issues.

Nakasone gives every sign of being sincere in his desire to reduce a Japanese surplus in trade with the U. S. that hit 36. 8 billion dollars in 1984 and could soon top 50 billion. Yet to rely on any one Japanese political leader, no matter how popular he is at home, to reverse trade policies is to underestimate the culture and traditions that weigh heavily against a breakthrough.

Big business and dozens of anonymous bureaucrats have as much power as Japan's top elected leaders.

"The whole concept that we can turn this around right now is patently ridiculous," says an American trader who has lived and worked here since 1952. "The vested interests are being shaken and slowly moved, but at a pace too slow for the eyes to follow."

That view is echoed by a U. S. diplomat closely involved in the efforts to open Japanese markets to American goods, Washington's stock solution to the ballooning trade imbalance.

"Japan is a relationship society rather than a transactional society," he says. "You cannot alter that kind of a system with a television speech or a batch of general proposals, no matter how well intentioned they are."

Beyond specific tariffs or other official barriers to imports, experts here say that the U. S. faces these obstacles:

- Nearly total domination of the Japanese market by a few dozen giant conglomerates that strongly oppose even token competition—be it from abroad or emerging domestic firms.
- An elite, thickly layered bureaucracy that historically has drafted laws and regulations as well as enforced them, and both of these powers would be threatened by trade reforms.
- A longtime relationship between business and government that critics say fosters collusion and hinders foreign entry into domestic markets.
- Adamant support for import restrictions among Japanese farmers, one of the most powerful political forces.

• A highly developed sense of loyalty to established practices and relationships that often outweighs any "duty" to society as a whole or, in some cases, even personal best interest.

• Esteem for caution and consensus in desision making at all societal levels, and, conversely, resentment of governmental fiats or one—man decrees—even if that man is the head of government.

Compounding Washington's problem is Nakasone's weak position within his own party, the Liberal Democrats, who have ruled Japan for 30 years. His standing is so complex and fragile that he has been forced to yield all but three of 21 cabinet positions to rival political factions. His cabinet colleagues are far less committed than he is to trade reforms, making it difficult for the Prime Minister to muscle proposals through either the bureaucracy or the Diet, Janpan's parliament.

The existence of "Japan, Inc."—the concept of an entire nation conspiring to advance economically at any cost—is a topic of debate among both Japanese and outsiders. But there is no dispute over how the system actually works.

Guarding the door. "Forget cultural factors. Forget Japan, Inc.," says one U. S. businessman. "Resistance to market opening basically is a power play by leaders of industry. For them, this is really war. The big companies will not tolerate any competition, no matter how small, no matter from where. They feel they have to stamp it out."

This is done most easily, critics say, through the bureaucracy, where some regulators take senior positions in industry after they leave public service. "Who is going to risk losing his standing in his group, not to mention the possibility of a future, high-level position, for the sake of some foreign exporter?" asks one longtime observer.

Corporate Japan also protects itself by maintaining representatives on committees that recommend legislation or regulations. To most Japanese, this is a high calling. To U. S. trade representatives, it is undisguised conflict of interest.

Still another means of Establishment control criticized by outsiders is Japan's complicated system of commodity distribution. Directly or indirectly, it also is run by corporate giants.

Most retail outlets here are small and rely heavily on a regular source of supply up the distribution ladder. Thus, retailers must maintain relations with wholesalers who need to stay in good stead with big Japanese companies.

Foreign businesses have complained that some retailers who agree to stock imported goods are illegally threatened with a cutoff of domestic supplies. But such heavy-handed tactics usually are unnecessary. Simple loyalty to long-term domestic clients is enough to dissuade retailers from putting foreign products on the front shelves.

Unlike the U. S. , Japan has no formidable consumer movement to press the foreign producers' argument that an open marketplace would lower prices of many domestic products and give buyers a wider choice. Similarly, there is no real tradition for adjudicating consumer cases. When a price-rigging suit was brought against Japanese oil refiners, it languished in the courts for nearly a decade.

In Japan, the bureaucracy is the bulwark for consumers. Officials contend that it is this responsibility, not self interest, that lies behind the rigid regulations about which foreign businessmen complain so often. One example: there are 30 different standards that must be met by foreign producers of telecommunications equipment before it can be sold here.

"The U. S. standard is more lax," explains Norimasa Hasegawa of the Ministry of Post and Telecommunications, which is administering the conversion of the state—owned communications network into a private enterprise. "The American side says we are foot dragging. We say that we—and most of the rest of the world, for that matter—have higher standards of excellence."

Whatever the merits of this argument, many foreign officials question how an appointed bureaucracy can pointedly and publicly obstruct policy direction from the elected head of government. The answer, says former Foreign Minister Saburo Okita, is simple: "In Japan, ministers and vice ministers come and go in two or three years. The bureaucracy is here to stay."

Outside pressure. "Gradually," says Okita, who now heads a commission recommending market opening steps to the government, "the bureaucracy will come to understand. Right now, though, they are frustrated by having to change their system very fast and under pressure by a foreign government. This is very difficult for a group that for centuries has represented the best our society has had to offer."

Although he defends the workings of the Ministry of Post and Telecommunications, Hasegawa acknowledges that the civil service, as much as the country as a whole, still has progress to make before Japan can fulfill its responsibilities as an "international nation".

"We Japanese are traveling abroad more and more these days, learning of other countries," he says. "But we still travel in groups, and we still want to eat sushi."

It is this determination to hang on to Japanese traditions that could delay indefinitely any meaningful removal of trade barriers.

U. S. News & World Report • April 22, 1985

Words and Expressions

cave in *phr.* 屈服,投降
entrench *v.* 使处于牢固地位

bureaucracy	*n.*	官僚,政府机构
dismantle	*v.*	摧毁、拆除
evaporate	*v.*	使蒸发,消失,逝去
formidable	*a.*	难以克服的,难以对付的
power broker		(美)(能影响有权势人物以操纵权力的)权力经纪人
buck	*v.*	反抗,反对
ingrained	*a.*	根深蒂固的
unveil	*v.*	向公众透露,揭示
curb	*v.*	控制,约束,抑制
contentious	*a.*	引起争议的
underestimate	*v.*	低估
breakthrough	*n.*	突破
anonymous	*a.*	匿名的
ridiculous	*a.*	荒唐的,可笑的
vested interests		既得利益
echo	*v.*	被重复,产生回音
stock	*a.*	通常的,常用的
transactional	*a.*	交易的
domination	*n.*	支配,统治,控制
conglomerate	*n.*	联合大企业
token	*a.*	象征性的
elite	*a.*	杰出的,卓越的
collusion	*n.*	共谋,勾结,串通
adamant	*a.*	坚强的,坚定不移的
established	*a.*	已确定的,已被确认的
outweigh	*v.*	在价值(或重要性、影响等)方面超过
esteem	*n.*	尊重,敬重
consensus	*n.*	一致同意
conversely	*ad.*	相反地
fiat	*n.*	命令,法令

decree	*n.* 法令,政令
compound	*v.* 使加重,使复杂化
standing	*n.* 地位,立场
fragile	*a.* 脆弱的
faction	*n.* 派系,派别
conspire	*v.* 合作,协力
power play	强权行为,高压行为
tolerate	*v.* 容忍,忍耐
stamp ... out	*phr.* 扑灭,消灭
for the sake of	*phr.* 为了
undisguised	*a.* 无伪装的,公开的
retailer	*n.* 零售商
wholesaler	*n.* 批发商
heavy-handed	*a.* 严厉的,压迫的
tactic	*n.* 战术,策略,手法
dissuade	*v.* 劝阻,劝止
adjudicate	*v.* 判决,裁定
price-rigging	操纵价格的,垄断价格的
languish	*v.* 被忽视,遭冷落
bulwark	*n.* 保障,支柱
contend	*v.* 声称,主张,认为
lax	*a.* 不严格的,不严密的
conversion	*n.* 转换
foot dragging	(美口)迟疑,拖拉
merit	*n.* 长处,优点,价值
pointedly	*ad.* 有针对性地,直截了当地
frustrated	*a.* 失败的,失望的,失间的
civil service	行政部门
indefinitely	*ad.* 无定期的,无限期的

Notes to the Text

1. U. S. News & World Report　美国新闻与世界报道

美国新闻周刊，在华盛顿特区出版，为美国此类最具影响的刊物之一。刊物创始于 1937 年，名为《美国新闻》，以报导华盛顿特区以及美国的大事深入全面而著称，全文经常刊载源自美国首都的讲话和文件。1945 年刊物所有者又创立了《世界报导》，从事世界和美国新闻的传播。两个刊物于 1948 年合并。

2. White House Chief of Staff　白宫办公厅主任

staff：全体工作人员（集体名词）。

此处指辅助总统处理日常事务的行政班子。

3. "Washington's stock solution to the ballooning trade imbalance"

stock *adj*，过时的，没有新意的，如：a stock joke（陈腐的笑话），stock arguments（老一套的论点）。

4. "... —be it from abroad or emerging domestic firms."

在句中"be it"相当于(no matter) whether it is from...

5. "Compounding Washington's problem is Nakasone's weak position within his own party, ... who..."

1) 由于主语及其所带定语从句过长，本句使用了倒装语序，主语系句中底部画线的部分。

2) compound (*v. t.*)：使……复杂化（更为严重）。

6. "Still another means of Establishment control..."

Establishment：权势集团，幕后统治集团。用作此意时，此字前面常加定冠词，——the Establishment。

7. Saburo Okita　大来佐武郎

Questions on Content and Language Points

(for preview, discussion and review)

1. "To move the Japanese government, Washington must move an entire nation."

1) What does "move" mean in the given context? Could you find a substitute word for it?

2) What of the Japanese government is meant to be 'moved'?

2. "... that (Japan's trade surplus with the U. S.) hit 36.8 billion dollars in 1984 and soon could top 50 billion."

To top 50 billion means to increase to as much as 50 billion, doesn't it?

3. "The vested interests are being shaken and slowly moved, but at a pace too slow for the eye to follow."

Paraphrase "a pace too slow for the eye to follow", and translate the above—quoted sentence into good Chinese.

4. "Japan is a relationship society rather than a transactional society," he says.

What's your understanding of the words?

(Read the lines on Obstacle 5. to the U. S. imports listed in the next paragraph to form an idea.)

5. "'Forget cultural factors. Forget Japan, Inc.,' says one U. S. businessman. 'Resistance to market opening basically is a power play by leaders of industry'..."

What's meant by "Forget cultural factors. Forget Japan, Inc." in the context?

6. "Corporate Japan also ..."

What does "Corporate Japan" refer to?

(Note that the word "also" might help you somewhat in finding the answer.)

7. "This is very difficult for a group that for centuries has represented the best our society has had to offer."

1) What does "the best" that the "group" has represented for centuries refer to?

2) Why is that considered "the best" by the Japanese?

Topics for Summary

1. How do the Japanese giant conglomerates restrain imports through the bureaucracy, according to the text?

2. How do they restrain imports through the distribution system?

Lesson 8

South Korea & Other Fast-developing Asian Countries—Their Progress and Problems

Text

Here Comes Korea, Inc.

Like Japan in the 1960s, the old "Hermit Kingdom" is poised for an assault on the world's markets

The ritual begins shortly after dawn. As the early morning light filters through the windows of Lucky-Goldstar's towering corporate headquarters in Seoul, Koo Cha-Kyung, chairman of the $8 billion conglomerate, issues instructions that echo around the world. In Huntsville, Ala., 200 factory workers are producing a million Goldstar color televisions yearly. In California's Silicon Valley Koo's whitefrocked research scientists delve into the mysteries of state-of-the-art semiconductor technology. In Jubail, Saudi Arabia, the company is putting the final touches on a sprawling new petrochemical complex. It is an impressive display of global reach, and a harbinger of things to come. As one of Koo's lieutenants puts it: "Our future lies in becoming a truly glbtal company."

For South Korea as a whole, that seems as much a prophecy as an ambition. Like Japan in the 1960s, the country is poised for an assault on the world's export markets. Its surging $81 billion economy is churning out a flood of increasingly sophisticated products, from shoes, toys and telephones to video recorders and microprocessors. Korea's mighty conglomerates dominate Middle East construction, and they command key shares of the world's shipbuilding, textile and steel industries. Their affiliates, joint ventures and subsidiaries girdle the globe, stretching from Australia, Indonesia and India to Norway, Spain and Gabon, Hyundai and Daewoo, with annual sales of $10 billion and $6 billion respectively, are pushing into the U. S. auto market, riveting the attention of American and Japanese manufacturers. Another colossus, the $9 billion Samsung, has started marketing a "supertech" 256K computer chip—encouraging some Koreans to speak confidently of the day when they will become the world's second largest manufacturer of basic electronic components, outstripping America and running just behind Japan.

Might: Korea, once known as the "Hermit Kingdom," is plainly on the move. As with "Japan, Inc." before it, the new label "Korea, Inc." may be no more than a trendy buzzword. But South Korea aims to forge just such a national economic machine, using the might of its established giants backed by centralized planners who can mobilize the country's banks and industrial infrastructure. The heady dreams of actually rivaling Japan may never come within reach; Korea's economy, while large by Asian standards, is barely one-fifteenth the size of its island neighbor. And it faces a gantlet of other obstacles, ranging from an unwieldy bureaucracy and a volatile political climate to a chronic shortage of investment capital and heavy commitments to military spending. Still, the comparisons with Japan, Inc. are more than empty flattery; in fact, they signal Korea's gathering clout.

Those signs have not been lost on the West. From Washington to Tokyo, Bonn to Rome, governments are eying Korea's challenge with unease. Justified or not, the view is that the Koreans are aggressively targeting Western markets for an all-out export blitz. Already there are hints of a protectionist backlash. European manufacturers shuddered as $4. 1 billion worth of Korean goods flowed into their home markets last year. And in the United States, 13 antidumping suits were brought against Korean firms. The doubling of the country's trade deficit with South Korea—to a conspicuous, if still relatively modest, $3. 5 billion—touched off a groundswell of concern in Congress and the White House.

Not surprisingly, no country is more worried than Japan. Fearful that rapidly modernizing Korean rivals will intrude on its foreign and domestic markets, Japan has fought to keep the Koreans from appropriating its technologies. Korea's entry into the global video market, for instance, has been delayed for years by an embargo enforced by Japanese licensers. But the Japanese will not be able to keep a lid on their high-tech know-how forever. Sooner or later they will begin to lose their edge, much as the United States did against Japan. "History is repeating itself," says Eji Yamashita, general manager of the Daiwa Securities Research Institute in Tokyo. Adds another Japanese executive: "There is still a 10-year gap (between our countries), but it is quickly eroding."

Strategy: South Korea's emergence as a world-class economic power has been starlingly rapid. Four decades of Japanese colonial rule, followed by the bloody Korean War, left the country psychologically scarred and economically bereft. In 1961, when Gen. Park Chung Hee seized power in a military coup, yearly per capita income hovered at a bare—bones $100. Park committed Korea to exporting its way out of poverty, and his strategy was as simple as it was effective: shower the country's fledging conglomerates with huge subsidies, government-backed loans and official favors and turn them into the world's suppliers of bargain-basement textiles, footwear and light industrial goods.

More recently, Korea has benefited from some unabashed borrowing of Japanese business practices. At the Han Ryuk Electronics Co. on the outskirts of Seoul, for example, all 350 employees wear uniforms, the color and style depending on the job. The plant recently held a competition to come up with a company song, and wall placards exhort workers to "Improve Quality," "Boost Exports" and remember the importance of "Diligence and Sincerity." And true to their Japanese model, employees are grouped into small "quality circles," which meet after work once a week to discuss ways to improve productivity.

The results have been dazzling. For two decades, year in and year out, Korea has sizzled along at an 8 per cent annual growth rate. Exports have surged from $119 million in 1964 to $29 billion last year. Per capita income, now $2,000, could reach $5,000 by the end of the century. All this has been accompanied by a near-revolutionary improvement in living standards. Korea boasts a literacy rate of 95 per cent, a standard met by only a few of the most advanced Western nations, and a recent poll showed that nearly two-thirds of all Koreans consider themselves to be members of the middle class. The once provincial capital of Seoul teems with energy and sophistication. Beyond any doubt, Korea's expectations for a better life are high and rising fast.

Income Gap: In fulfilling those hopes, however, Korea faces some potentially disruptive problems. Some are social. For all the progress, deep pockets of poverty exist throughout the country. In Seoul, glistening high-rise apartment houses jostle with warrens of slum housing; in remote rural communities people are still eking out subsistence livings. As a result, conspicuous consumption by a nouveau riche elite has become a real source of friction. In contrast to Japan, which has managed to spread its postwar wealth relatively evenly, Korea is beset by a widening income gap between rich and poor. Prosperity has flowed most readily to the large cities, and to those who founded—or work for—the country's largest industrial companies. Small businessmen and their employees are still waiting for a bigger cut of Korea's newfound bonanza.

Equally unsettling has been the political price paid for economic progress. For much of its postwar history, South Korea has been governed by authoritarian figures who seized power by force. And while Koreans today have more money and more leisure time than ever before, they are also pressing for greater democratic freedoms. President Chun Doo Hwan recently eased human-rights restrictions and adopted a less heavyhanded attitude toward his political opposition. He has also repeated his pledge to step down from office in 1988, just before Seoul hosts the Olympic Games. But these signs of political liberalization pose another dilemma. South Korea's short history has been long on turbulence; while most Koreans welcome the new moves toward democracy, they worry that a major political change could upset their economic apple cart.

Defense: That picture is complicated by South Korea's huge military commitments. Unlike Japan, which spends less than 1 per cent of its gross national product on defense, South Korea has committed more than 6 per cent of its GNP to military expenditures—primarily to meet the threat of an unremittingly hostile North Korea. But while that has bolstered the South's security, it has also detracted from its economic growth. For now, South Korea can only hope that its border with the North will remain tranquil; if so, the country's attention can continue to be focused mainly on growth and material prosperity.

If South Korea is to carry its momentum into the next decade, however, it will have to achieve a huge economic leap forward. For years, relatively cheap labor has been the driving force behind Korea's export boom. Today, with wages rising, the price advantage that Korean products enjoy world wide is shrinking. To preserve its markets and continue to grow, Korea must now change gears by moving up the high-tech ladder, much as Japan did when its labor-cost advantage began to erode in the 1970s. It must improve the quality and sophistication of its products, and in many cases, compete toe-to-toe with the United States, Western Europe and Japan. If it does not, Korea risks being overtaken by new low-wage rivals, including China, Pakistan and Malaysia.

Such challenges and opportunities are to be expected as Korea enters a new era. To negotiate the transition, President Chun's brain trust of American-trained technocrats is busily charting a new economic course. The goal: to leapfrog many of the traditional bottlenecks to development. To begin with, the advisers aim to catapult the country's still-fledgling electronics industry into the outer frontiers of high technology. Over the next five years, say South Korean officials, the country's 50 largest companies will spend more than $3.5 billion to develop everything from state-of-the-art microprocessors and video recorders to advanced telecommunications equipment. That figure is dwarfed by the $28 billion that Japan spends each year on research and development, but it is a start. And the commitments made by Korea's largest industrial groups are much more competitive than the countrywide figures would indicate. For example, Hyundai, the country's largest company, has been spending $700 million a year on electronics factories and research facilities. In time, company executives hope, the company and its sisters will be as widely known and respected as Sony or Mitsubishi.

Revamping: Seoul's ambitious planners have other changes in mind. In fact, they envision nothing less than a wholesale revamping of the country's basic industries. Their main target is the chaebol, the closely held businesses that, like Japan's leviathan zaibatsu, have long powered Korea's growth. While such companies as Daewoo, Samsung and Dong Ah helped put Korea on the word's corporate map, many Koreans view their unbridled growth with misgivings. "We won't advance unless we change our industrial structure." explains Lee Kyu Uck of the Korea Development Institute. "The real question is whether the conglomerates can cope with the world economy in the coming century."

The debate boils down to whether Korea's industrial giants wield too much power and influence, both for their own and their country's good. They are clearly an awesome force. Last year sales from the 50 largest chaebol equaled more than a half of South Korea's gross national product. They account for an overwhelmingly large share of both the country's exports and its $46 billion foreign debt. Their often helter—skelter expansion has created monopolies in many industries and resulted in widespread inefficiency; some companies are run by managers whose qualifications are limited to their family ties to the founder. And because most of this expansion has been financed through borrowed money, the chaebol have grown increasingly vulnerable to business setbacks and changes of economic climate. As a Western banker in Seoul bluntly puts it: "It's a house of cards."

Stakes: The challenge for Chun is to rein in the chaebol without damaging their absolutely essential contribution to the Korean economy—and without stepping on the toes of the chaebol's enormously powerful chieftains. Among them: such rugged empire builders as Hyundai's Chung Ju—Young and Samsung's Lee Byung Chull. Given the stakes involved, it's not surprising that the issue has become politically volatile. The outspoken opposition leaders of the National Asembly routinely criticize the government for granting special tax breaks to the chaebol, which they argue have impeded the growth of small businesses and stymied entrepreneurship. Even worse, they say, the lion's share of the nation's new wealth has gone to the chaebol—a charge that even the conglomerates' owners find hard to deny. "We have to change," acknowledges one senior chaebol executive. "If we don't share the fruits of our success better, the system won't survive."

But Seoul is proceeding cautiously in hunting a remedy. The

government has already eliminated direct subsidies for such industries as steel and shipbuilding. It has also imposed a partial freeze on new loans to the chaebol, mainly in a bid to channel more bank credits to small and medium-size businesses. In addition, South Korean bureaucrats pointedly declined to bail out the Kukje industrial group, the country's sixth largest chaebol, when it was declared insolvent three months ago. The giant footwear, textile and construction conglomerate had been battered by losses on its Middle East building projects, and Chinese and Pakistani textile makers had begun to eat into its markets elsewhere. Since those problems were by no means unique to Kukje, the lesson of the bankruptcy was clear: South Korea's chaebol had better learn to swim on their own—or sink. "We'd like to see the big conglomerates concentrate their activities rather than extend everywhere," says Sakong II, President Chun's chief economic adviser. "They are getting the message."

Seoul's born-again faith in market forces shows up in other areas as well. For one thing, the government is trying hard to reform its cumbersome financial system, now so antiquated and inefficient that it could threaten the country's future prosperity. By far the most pressing problem is a chronic shortage of development funds. After a decade of heavy international borrowing—and increasingly burden-some interest payments—Seoul now hopes to become more self-sufficient in capital. It has allowed official interest rates to float more freely, largely in an effort to siphon funds out of the country's illegal but sprawling "curb money" market. And it has already sold off all state-owned banks in the expectation that private managers can make them more efficient and more useful in channeling money to cash-strapped South Korean investors.

Seoul's government planners are also undertaking a potentially far-reaching, if so far limited, economic "liberalization" program. More goods are being imported from abroad, and joint ventures with overseas firms, once discouraged by the government, are flowering. Daewoo has launched 13 ventures with foreign partners over the past five years, and Koo's Lucky-Goldstar has forged links with 46—including such hightech giants as AT&T, Honeywell and Dow-Corning in the United States and Japan's NEC. The benefits of these arrangements flow in two directions. For the Koreans, the attractions are Western know-how, equipment and investment funds. For the other partners, the bait is an able and still low-cost labor force and access to South Korea's surging consumer market.

"Sweat": In this sense, South Korea is treading a path not taken by Japan. While Japanese interests span the globe, few foreign firms have successfully penetrated Japan's home turf. Korea, too, has a legacy of xenophobia; and the Koreans are clearly wary of opening their markets to highpowered Western competitors. But they are tentatively doing just that, so far with a momentum unmatched by Japan. The aim is to defuse the protectionist pressures that have hobbled U. S.-Japanese trade relations and, in time, to enter the ranks of the world's developed nations. That's no small order, but the Koreans think it can be filled fairly simply. At bottom, says Nam Duc Woo, chairman of the Korea Traders Association, South Korea needs only "some degree of sweat and some degree of technological sophistication." And that's precisely what has already lifted Korea, Inc. into contention.

Michael R. Meyer with Tracy Dahlby and Patrick L. Smith in Seoul

—From *Newsweek* • May 13, 1985

Words and Expressions

Inc.	Incorporated 之缩写，股份有限的，一般用在公司名称后面，表示此公司是股份有限公司
hermit	*n.* 与世隔绝者
a hermit nation	一个闭关自守的国家
poised	*a.* 做好准备的
assault	*n.* 攻击
ritual	*n.* 仪式；程序；例行公事
filter	*v.* 透过
towering	*a.* 高耸的
corporate	*a.* 公司的
headquarters	*n.* （企业、团体、机关等的）总部，总机构
frock	*v.* 使穿长外衣（或罩衣等）
delve	*v.* 探索，钻研
sprawl	*v.* 向四周（扩展）延伸
petrochemical	*a.* 石油化学的
complex	*n.* 综合企业
reach	*n.* 所及范围；势力范围
harbinger	*n.* 前兆；预示
lieutenant	*n.* 副手，助手
prophecy	*n.* 预言
churn out	艰苦（费力）地做出
video	*n.* 录像的，录影的
mighty	*a.* 强大的
girdle	*v.* 围绕，遍布
auto	*n.* 汽车
rivet	*v.* 吸引住
colossus	*n.* 巨人；大企业

market	*v.*	推销
chip	*n.*	芯片
outstrip	*v.*	超过
might	*n.*	力量
label	*n.*	标签
trendy	*a.*	时髦的
buzzword	*n.*	时髦词语
forge	*v.*	锻造,使形成
heady	*a.*	使人兴奋的
rival	*v.*	与…匹敌
gantlet	*n.*	夹攻;重重困难
unwieldy	*a.*	(因机构庞大)难操作的;不灵便的
volatile	*a.*	变化无常的;不稳定的
chronicle	*a.*	长期的
flattery	*n.*	恭维的话
clout	*n.*	影响力、势力
justify	*v.*	证明…有理
target	*v.*	把…作为目标
all-out	*a.*	竭尽全力的
blitz	*n.*	闪电式行动
backlash	*n.*	强烈反对;强烈抵制
shudder	*v.*	战栗
suit	*n.*	控告,起诉
conspicuous	*a.*	惹人注意的
groundswell	*n.*	(舆论或情绪等的)迅速高涨
intrude	*v.*	侵扰
appropriate	*v.*	擅用;盗用
embargo	*n.*	禁运
enforce	*v.*	实施;强制执行
licenser	*n.*	许可证颁发者
lid	*n.*	盖子;禁止

edge	*n.*	优势
executive	*n.*	企业的经理人员
erode	*v.*	逐步毁坏;削弱(一点一点地)消失
emergence	*n.*	出现
power	*n.*	强国
startlingly	*ad.*	惊人地
scar	*v.*	给…留下伤痕(或创伤)
bereft	*a.*	失去…的;缺少…的
coup	*n.*	政变
hover	*v.*	盘旋;徘徊
bare-bone	*a.*	少得不能再少的;不充分的
commit	*v.*	把(军队)投入战斗
shower	*v.*	倾注;大量地给予
fledgling	*a.*	刚开始的;无经验的
fledgling industries	新兴工业	
bargain-basement	*a.*	(美)极低廉的,极便宜的
unabashed	*a.*	不加掩饰的,公然的
come up with	(针对问题、挑战等)提出,想出	
placard	*n.*	标语牌
exhort	*v.*	激励,敦促
boost	*v.*	增加,使增长
sincerity	*n.*	诚实,忠实
true	*a.*	忠实于
dazzling	*a.*	耀眼的;非凡的
sizzle	*v.*	显著增长
literacy	*n.*	读写能力,脱盲
poll	*n.*	民意测验
provincial	*a.*	乡气的
teem	*v.*	充满
pocket	*n.*	(与周围不同的或孤立的)一小群;一小片

glisten	*v.* 闪闪发光，闪闪发亮
jostle	*v.* 与…贴近，紧贴
warren	*n.* （兔子窝般）拥挤的地区（或房屋）
eke out	竭力维持（生计）；设法过（活）
subsistence	*n.* 生存，维持生活
subsistence level	勉强糊口的生活水平
nouveau	*a.* 新近产生的
nouveau riche	暴发户
elite	*n.* [总称]上层人士，掌权人物
beset	*v.* 困扰
found	*v.* 创立，建立
bonanza	*n.* 财源；繁荣
unsettling	*a.* 使人不安的
authoritarian	*a.* 独裁主义的
leisure	*n.* 空闲
press	*v.* 迫切要求
heavy-handed	*a.* 严厉的，苛刻的，压迫的
opposition	*n.* 反对党
pose	*v.* 造成
turbulence	*n.* 骚乱
unremittingly	*ad.* 持续地
bolster	*v.* 支撑
detract	*v.* 减慢
momentum	*n.* 动力；势头
change gears	调档
toe-to-toe	面对面地；直接地
negotiate	*v.* [口]顺利通过
brain trust	智囊团；顾问班子
technocrat	*n.* 技术专家政治论者，技术专家治国论者
chart	*v.* 指定
course	*n.* 行动方针

leapfrog	*v.*	跳跃
catapult	*v.*	一下把…推到高处
dwarf	*v.*	使矮小,使减少
development	*n.*	开发
commitments	*n.*	承担的责任
sister	*n.*	同类形事物;姊妹公司
revamp	*v.*	改组,把(旧物)翻新
envision	*v.*	想象
wholesale	*a.*	大规模的;全部的
chaebol	*n.*	大企业集团
unbridled	*a.*	不受控制的,不受约束的,放纵的
boil down to	归结为	
wield	*v.*	行使
awesome	*a.*	使人敬畏的
helter-skelter	*a.*	仓促忙乱的;无计划的
bluntly	*ad.*	直截了当地
rein (in)	*v.*	控制;放慢;止住
step on the toes (of)	触怒	
chieftain	*n.*	首领;领袖
rugged	*a.*	粗壮的;强健的
empire	*n.*	(由一人、一家族或一集团控制的)大企业
given	*prep.*	考虑到
routinely	*ad.*	经常反复的
break	*n.*	好运;优惠
tax breaks	税额优惠	
impede	*v.*	妨碍
stymie	*v.*	使处困境;阻碍
charge	*v.*	指控
proceed	*v.*	进行
eliminate	*v.*	消除;不加考虑

pointedly	*ad.* 直率地
bail (out)	*v.* 帮助…摆脱困境
insolvent	*a.* 无偿还能力的;资不抵债的;破产的
batter	*v.* 重创;连续打击
unique	*a.* 独有的;惟一的
bankruptcy	*n.* 破产
get the message	[口]领会
show	*v.* 显示;表现
cumbersome	*a.* 累赘的;麻烦的
float	*v.* 浮动
siphon	*v.* 吸收
cash-strapped	现金短缺的
bait	*n.* 诱惑物
tread	*v.* 在…上面走;沿…走
span	*v.* 横跨;跨越
turf	*n.* (黑势力的)地盘;势力范围
legacy	*n.* 遗传;遗产
xenophobia	*n.* 对外国人(或域外事物)的恐惧(或憎恨)
wary	*a.* 谨慎的;警惕的
highpowered	*a.* 强有力的;能力强的
tentatively	*ad.* 暂时的,初步的
defuse	*v.* 缓和;平息;使变得无害
hobble	*v.* 使跛行;阻碍
order	*n.* [口]难办的事;任务
at bottom	实际上
sweat	*n.* 艰苦的劳动;苦活
contention	*n.* 竞争

Notes to the Text

1. Newsweek　新闻周刊

美国综合性杂志。1933 年创刊,由华盛顿邮报公司在纽约出版,是美国发行量最大的新闻期刊之一。除国内版外,还有大西洋版和太平洋版。

2. conglomerate　跨行业公司

一般是通过兼并与本公司产品和业务无关联的若干公司而形成的大公司。它与持股公司有类似之处,但不同的是它在兼并其他公司时不受产品类别与业务性质的限制,而且它参与其子公司的经营管理。

3. Silicon Valley　硅谷

战后美国高科技发展的摇篮,美国电子工业的中心。硅谷坐落在加利福尼亚州旧金山市的南边沿海地区,以其最重要的发明——晶体硅芯片——计算机的心脏而闻名。按其产值,硅谷在美国为第九大工业中心。

4. Huntville, Ala.　美国阿拉巴马州北部城市

美国航空航天部的一个航天飞行中心所在地,人口142 513。

5. state-of-the-art　复合名词,在文中作定语用。

这一复合词的意思是"目前工艺水平"、"目前最先进的",即代表某一领域中的最新成就。

6. microprocessor　微信息处理机

具备完成数字计算的中央处理机功能所必需的算术、逻辑和控制电路系统的各类小型电子装置。

7. affiliate　联号

一个企业与另一个企业在管理上有一定的联系,如一公司是另一公司的"少数股东",或两公司有互兼董事的关系等,两者即互为"联号"。联号和附属公司相近似,但不同的是母公司对附属公司拥有实际的控股权,而有联系的企业之间没有这种关系。

8. “As with ‘Japan, Inc.’ before it, the new label ‘Korea, Inc.’ may be no more than a trendy buzzword.”

1) 如把从句补充为完整的句子，这句话应该是“As it (the new label) is with ‘Japan, Inc.’ before it, ...”

2) 这句话的意思是由于有日本在先已被称为“Japan, Inc.”(意指由政府倡导和支持的、大公司大企业进行的扩大出口运动)，与此类似的“Korea, Inc.”的叫法不会再让人感到新鲜和有趣。

9. dumping　倾销

以低于国内市场的价格，甚至低于生产成本的价格向国外抛售商品。

10. licenser　转让人

转让是以收费的形式允许另一公司使用某些权利，如专利、商标、技术等等。给予使用权的公司叫做转让人；接受这种使用权的公司叫做使用人(licensee)。

11. Sony　索尼公司

一家从事各类电子设备、器械装置的开发、制造以及销售的日本大公司。该公司成立于1947年，总部设在东京。其原名为东京通信工业株式会社。1950年该公司研制生产出世界上第一盘录音磁带和第一台磁带录音机。1959年，索尼公司试制出第一台晶体管电视机，接着该公司又于1961年和1962年推出了首台晶体管录音机和首台微型电视机。

索尼公司在经营活动中十分注重新产品的开发，并投入大量人力、物力和财力。从公司成立至今短短的40多年的时间里，索尼公司研制出许多“世界第一”。公司经营战略的另一重要原则是在主销售市场当地生产，在此原则指导下，索尼公司在世界许多国家设厂扩大生产，以扩大各类产品的生产能力。

12. Mitsubishi (Mitsubishi Group)　三菱财团

由独立的日本公司组成的松散的集团，主要特点表现在各公司总裁之间非正式的政策协调以及公司间金融方面一定程度上的互相依赖。三菱财团的主要公司都是以东京为根据地的跨国公司。这些公司在海外有自己的机构及附属公司，有些还与外国公司建立合资企业。

13. "... the chaebol, the closely held businesses that, ..."

指韩国的为少数人所有、控制的公司或企业。

14. insolvency *n.* 无偿还能力(课文中出现的是它的形容词"insolvent")

指企业或个人没有足够资金偿还所负的债务。它有两种含义:一种是负债额超过资产总值,资产不足以偿付所有的债务;另一种是对到期债务没有足够的现金来偿还,不论其全部资产是多于还是少于其全部债务。后一种是指某一时期没有清偿债务的能力。

15. market forces 市场力量

指市场上决定一商品或服务价格的力量,也就是供应和需求。

16. AT&T (American Telephone and Telegraph) 美国电话电报公司

美国电信业最大的垄断组织,1885 年建立,总部在纽约,由摩根、洛克菲勒等财团控制,除控制和经营美国大部分地区的电话和电话机生产外还从事导弹、核武器及反潜艇系统等的部件生产,在国外控制加拿大的电话公司,与美资国际电话电报公司(ITT)有密切联系。

17. Honeywell (Honeywell Inc.) 霍尼韦尔公司

美国公司,世界上电子控制系统最大的生产商。1970 年购得通用电器的计算机分部后,已发展为世界上第五大计算机生产商。该公司在 1885 年建立,总部设在明尼苏达州,明尼阿波利斯。该公司销售总额的 25%以上来自海外业务。

18. NEC (Nippon Electric Company) 日本电气公司

世界主要的电子产品生产商之一,其前身是日本电气有限公司。1899 年由日商和美国西屋电气公司合资兴建,主要生产电话,1983 年正式使用现名。战后,NEC 以开拓电子新领域和跨国经营为标志,进入全面发展的新时期。目前 NEC 主要经营范围包括通讯系统和设备、计算机与工业电子系统、软件产品、品种繁多的电子器械、电子元件和仪表、家用电子产品,以及提供相应的设备安装、保养等服务。

Questions on Content and Language Points

(for preview, discussion and review)

1. What is the implication of Korea, Inc.?

(Read the 3rd sentence of the 3rd paragraph and the 4th sentence of the 6th paragraph of the text for hints.)

2. "As one of Koo's lieutenants puts it: 'Our future lies in becoming a truly global company.'"

Paraphrase the lieutenant's quotation.

3. "For South Korea as a whole, that seems as much a prophecy as an ambition."

Rewrite the sentence in plainer words, having the central idea clarified.

4. "Another colossus, the $9 billion Samsung, has started marketing a 'supertech' 256K computer chip—encouraging some Koreans to speak confidently of the day when they will become the world's second largest manufacturer of basic electronic components, outstripping America and running just behind Japan."

What's introduced by "when" in the syntax? An adverbial clause, or an attributive one? How do you know?

5. "Still, the comparisons with Japan, Inc. are more than empty flattery; in fact, they signal Korea's gathering clout."

What's "gathering clout" in the given context?

6. "The once provincial capital of Seoul teems with energy and sophistication."

In what sense is the word sophistication used here? What might it refer to specifically and what has it to do with energy?

7. "For all the progress, deep pockets of poverty exist throughout the country."

1) What is the usual meaning of the expression "a deep pocket"?

2) What does "deep pockets" mean here?

3) Why is the expression used this way in the text?

It is used ironically here, isn't it?

8. "If South Korea is to carry its momentum into the next decade, however, it will have to achieve a huge economic leap forward."

"Such challenges and opportunities are to be expected as Korea enters a new era."

What do "is so..." and "are to..." mean respectively? Do they mean the same thing?

9. What does the writer mean by "the outer frontiers of high technology"?

10. How do you understand "Daewoo, Samsung and Dong Ah helped put Korea on the world's corporate map"?

11. "Given the stakes involved, ..."

1) What does "given" mean here?

2) What does "the stakes" refer to in the given context?

3) What's the meaning of "involved" here?

12. "That's no small order, but the Koreans think it can be filled fairly simply."

What's compared to an order in the given context?

13. "At bottom, says Nam Due Woo, chairman of Korea Traders Association, South Korea needs only 'some degree of sweat and some degree of technological sophistication.' And that's precisely what has already lifted Korea, Inc. into contention."

1) What does the writer mean by the word "sweat"?

2) What does "technological sophistication" refer to?

3) Can you explain "... lifted Korea, Inc. into contention"?

Topic for Summary

What are the problems left over by the South Korea's way of

"economic prosperity" as you have seen in the article?

Exercises

Ⅰ. Read the article given below and answer the following questions.

Taming the Chaebols

Having spent years fattening up its leading companies, South Korea is now forcing them to slim down. On January 18th the Ministry of Trade, Industry and Energy announced that the country's top 30 chaebols—the widely diversified and intricately interlinked conglomerates that dominate the country's economy—would do as the government had asked and concentrate on their core businesses.

The order to restructure came in the latest five-year economic blueprint, launched in July 1993. The ten largest chaebols were allowed to name three sectors each, the next 20 to name two sectors. They have now done so. Thus Lotte has chosen distribution, food and beverages, and chemicals; Samsung, which lobbied hard to be allowed to diversify into car making, eventually ended up with electronics, machinery and chemicals. Firms which play by the new rules will continue to receive preferential state-backed financing. Those which flout the rules will not.

The government claims it has three clear aims: to encourage competition and foster small businesses; to wrest power from the old industrial dynasties and hand it over to professional managers; and, above all, to stem the "octopus-like growth" of the chaebols into unrelated areas. The five largest chaebols are all involved in shipbuilding, semiconductors, financial services and textiles—industries with few obvious synergies. The top ten conglomerates each currently operate in an average of 11 different areas; the next

20 operate in an average of seven. By contrast, Japan's top 40 business groups on average operate in only five industries.

The chaebols' spectacular diversification, often driven by dynastic feuds as much as commercial sense, has chewed up funds for long-term research and development. Worse, these buying sprees were usually funded by debt—borrowed partly on the assumption that the government would not let the conglomerates go bankrupt. The debts of the average chaebol are 3½ times as big as its equity. At Kukje, which was briefly dissolved in August 1993 before being reprieved by the courts, the ratio was 9½。

Unfortunately, the government is partly driven by political grudges. Despite being the government's creations, the chaebols have become thorns in its side. Chung Ju Yung, the head of Hyundai, the country's biggest chaebol, had the temerity to challenge the president, Kim Young Sam, in the 1992 election. A stringent audit of Hyundai followed. Later, and separately, Mr Chung was accused of misusing company funds. He is now selling his family's controlling interest in Hyundai Heavy Industries and Hyundai Merchant Martine, and cutting all ties with the chaebol's insurance and hotel businesses.

To add to these political complications, the government's strategy is fraught with contradictions: while it talks much about the virtues of free trade, it also speaks of forcing companies to merge in order to avoid "excessive" competition. So far, no one has produced a detailed timetable for divestment to match the chaebols promises. Even if the government really means business this time, it is difficult to see who will buy the surplus companies, given the continued restrictions on capital flows, and the dominance of the chaebols in the economy. It could be a long wait.

—From *The Economist* • Jan. 22, 1994

Questions:

1. In what way did the government require the chaebols to slim down?

2. Can you explain the expression "octopus-like growth"?

3. What's the significance of a company's concentration on a few operations?

4. How was the chaebols' diversification financially supported?

5. What's the author's point of view over the government strategy?

6. Is company diversification a good choice or a bad one, according to your knowledge?

Ⅱ. Read the article given below and decide whether the following statements are true or false.

Asia, You Cost Too Much

By Mark Simon

The International Monetary Fund just predicted that Asia's economic boom will continue for the next several years. Sony just announced that it will no longer export TV sets from Japan because it's impossible to price the sets competitively. Which of the two should Asian business pay attention to?

Listen to Sony. Because even in a growing market, costs count. And for many businesses, Asia is beginning to cost too much.

The Asian economic miracle can be best summed up as the biggest price undercut in history. Asia grew because it was the cheapest source for the low-tech consumer goods that the West craves. Hong Kong and Korea didn't invent new or more efficient manufacturing techniques. They simply bought market share with low wages.

But that same market force—price—that enticed buyers from the U. S. and Europe to Taiwan and Japan 30 years ago is now working against Asian nations as they look to upgrade their industries. Years ago, an Asian factory turning out shirts was competing against huge, unionized factories in North Carolina and Manchester. Today, a shirtmaker in south China has to compete with 100 other guys in his own country, 20 factories in India, 5 in the Philippines and reinvigorated and highly efficient new plants in the U. S. and Europe.

Sony, Hewlett Packard and Ford need a competitive business environment that is based on more than a cheap pair of hands. Asia's poor infrastructure, high rents, shortages of managers, lack of natural resources, and—worst of all—official corruption are also deciding factors when companies such as Rubbermaid or Philips keep production in the U. S. and Europe rather than switch it to Asia.

Everyday, I see costs placing Asian nations at a disadvantage compared with their "cheaper" Western competitors. In shipping, for instance, terminal expenses in Japan and Hong Kong are two to three times higher than those of the U. S. A.'s busiest West coast ports. To truck a container 100 miles down from southern China to Hong Kong costs more than to ship that container from either the U. S. or Europe to Hong Kong.

Vietnam is trying to market itself as the future breadbasket of Asia. Really? According to a recent article in the Far Eastern Economic Review, it costs more to air-freight a load of lettuce from Ho Chi Minh City to Hong Kong than to fly in the same cargo fresh from Sydney. Australia may be four times farther away, but it doesn't have Vietnam Air and Cathay Pacific controlling the route.

If you still think Asia is cheap or even a bargain, compare office rents in Shanghai or Jakarta with those in Chicago and Paris. Or try to hold a qualified manager in China against the almost weekly job offers he receives due to the shortage of Chinese professionals. Since a happy employee is a productive employee, think about keeping someone in Singapore, where a 1,200 sq. ft. flat sets you back $2,000 a month, when for the same price you could be providing a comfortable 3,000 sq. ft. 4-bedroom house only ten miles outside Washington, D. C.

No wonder companies are voting with their feet in response to

Asia's rising costs. Matsushita, Sony and Honda continue to move production out of Japan. Taiwan's Nan Ya Plastic is establishing factories in North Carolina and Texas that will export finished products back to Asia. Germany's Siemens is dumping Singapore in favor of lower cost locations in the region. The way things are going, Siemens may have to move again before too long.

Take Korea, which has lost footwear and textiles to China and Indonesia because Korean wages kept climbing but productivity did not. Losing footwear may be nothing to cry over, but replacement gets less and less easy. What will Korea substitute for low-tech electronics? How do you replace lost airline customer service jobs in Hong Kong? Apple in Silicon Valley sprang up to provide new jobs as GM was shedding them in Detroit. What follows Samsung in Seoul?

It costs more to truck a container from south China to Hong Kong than to ship it from the U. S. to Hong Kong.

If Asia's definition of high-tech is TV sets, then the region's in trouble, because home appliances and computer boxes are not high-tech, they're old-fashioned commodities now. At a recent Hong Kong electronics show, while the Japanese and Korean exhibitors were marketing their audio visual equipment, U. S. and European firms were there selling technology, using the AV gadgets as simple host pieces.

The competition facing Asia is not going to let up, either. Local council representatives from Britain and U. S. state government officials are running all over the world advertising tax cuts, giving away state land and slashing bureaucracy in an effort to attract industry. Technological innovations and cost reductions in communications and transport mean that location (n. b. Hong Kong) isn't as important as it once was.

These days, the Philippines doesn't just have to compete with

India and Thailand for a semi-conductor plant—attractive bids are coming in from Texas and Spain as well. When it's time to commit, it won't be difficult to choose between government officials who offer a hand of assistance and government officials who have a hand out.

Good jobs come with a price now and the currency required is a competitive and open business environment. Only Singapore seems to understand that keeping up isn't good enough and that being competitive means forging ahead. It is not the uncertainty of 1997 that made Singapore a serious competitor with Hong Kong in the financial services sector. The Lion City made a concerted effort to open markets, cut government regulations and create transparency. All this cleared the path for Singapore's natural advantages, like lower rents and high quality of life, to carry the day.

But most Asian governments just don't seem to understand the relationship between high costs and low competitiveness. Otherwise, why would tariffs on agricultural imports be crippling the Korean and Japanese food processing industries? The oligarchical nature of trucking in Indonesia and Malaysia guarantees that high transport costs will drive business away.

Labor and transportation are not Asia's only problem areas. In terms of results, losing a company that pulls out of your country because of your corrupt bureaucracy is no different from losing the trade because you can't offer low enough wages. The old adage that corruption is a cost of doing business no longer applies. In today's free and open world, corruption is simply a cost.

It's not too late for Asians to reverse the trend and promote a market environment where internal competition keeps their countries competitive abroad. If they do, those automotive design jobs Tokyo sent to California should come back to Japan. Korea may be able to attract some investment other than knock-down IKEA furniture, and maybe Hong Kong can even keep its place in the sun as a trading hub. If they don't, well, they can always go back to making shoes.

Mr. Simon is a shipping manager based in Hong Kong.

—From *The Asian Wall Street* Journal · Oct. 30, 1995

True-or-false questions:

1. Mark Simon suggested that businesses should pay more attention to Sony's decision for the simple reason that Sony's idea actually represents that of the Japanese manufacturers. ( )

2. Asian economic growth was primarily based on their cheap exports rather than high-tech innovation. ( )

3. Some manufacturers of the advanced western countries were hesitant about moving to Asia only for there was a shortage of competent managers. ( )

4. When the author argued that to do business in Asia is too expensive, he was only making comparison between doing business in Asia in the past and today. ( )

5. Companies are fighting against the increasing cost in Asia by demanding with majority votes that the cost be lowered. ( )

6. Seimens would leave Singapore but find a better place in Asia and settle down there. ( )

7. According to the author, there exists even a big gap between Asian countries and the western industrial nations in the concept of high technology. ( )

8. Asian manufacturers now would have to face competitions not only from their neighbouring countries but those of the industrial nations. ( )

9. The 1997 return of Hong Kong to China would certainly make Singapore more attractive as an Asian financial center to foreign investors and businesses. ( )

10. When businessmen consider a location, the priority will be the cost of labor and raw materials, while bureaucracy is deemed

the natural cost everyone pays in order to get business done.

Ⅲ. Read the following picked passages from the article and put them into Chinese:

1. Sony, Hewlett Packard and Ford need a competitive business environment that is based on more than cheap pair of hands. Asia's poor infrastructure, high rents, shortages of managers, lack of natural resources, and—worst of all—official corruption are also deciding factors when companies such as Rubbermaid or Philips keep production in the U. S. and Europe rather than switch it to Asia.

2. The competition facing Asia is not going to let up, either. Local council representatives from Britain and U. S. state government officials are running all over the world advertising tax cuts, giving away state land and slashing bureaucracy in an effort to attract industry. Technological innovations and cost reductions in communications and transport mean that location isn't as important as it once was.

3. Labor and transportation are not Asia's only problem areas. In terms of results, losing a company that pulls out of your country because of your corrupt bureaucracy is not different from losing the trade because you can't offer low enough wages. The old adage that corruption is a cost of doing business no longer applies. In today's free and open world, corruption is simply a cost.

Supplementary Material for Free Reading

A. The Next Step

Amid a War on Corruption, South Korea Strives
to Remake its Economy

By Shim Jae Hoon in Seoul

It will be a watershed moment for South Korea when, later

this year, it achieves its long-held goal of membership in the Organization for Economic Co-operation and Development (OECD), the Paris-based club of the world's richest nations. The moment will be a recognition of how much this nation of 44 million people has achieved since it embarked on its first five-year economic plan in 1962 with a percapita income of just \$87.

South Korea certainly has a lot to celebrate: It has grown into the world's 11th-biggest economy and 12th-largest trading nation. In 1995, its per-capita income was \$10,000.

But in a larger sense, this economic success story stands at a crossroad that promises to make the coming years as much of a challenge as the ones just completed. Indeed, the price of admission to the OECD will be a profound change in the way South Korea conducts its business at home and abroad. But it's not just foreign pressure that's pushing open the doors to the economy—South Koreans' own desire for change is a big part of what's driving the liberalization process forward.

The need for reform is clear: Although South Korea's material achievements are impressive, the development of its political and economic organizations hasn't kept pace. In recent years, the government has come under more and more pressure from trading partners and has begun to open the gates to foreign investment. There's also strong pressure at home for leaders to keep up the fight against corruption, protect consumers and curtail the power of the huge business organizations that still dominate the economy. Keeping the reform process going and bringing the country's institutions up to the level of those in advanced countries has become the pivotal agenda of President Kim Young Sam's government.

And as always, the spectre of North Korea looms. Clearly, the worsening economic crisis gripping the North has implications for South Korea's long-term stability, adding additional impetus for structural change now.

"The years up to 2000 will be a critical time to determine our nation's destiny," president Kim said in a January speech. "Our ways of doing things—our institutions—must change so they become internationally competitive and earn the respect of the international community."

Indeed, South Korea is beginning to pare back the restrictions on foreign investment that have kept a heavy shield over the economy for so many years. The changes are gradual, but the process appears to be moving forward. By 2000, about 97% of South Korea's economy, including the ever-growing service sector, will be open to foreign investment, claims Park Jae Yoon, the minister of trade, industry and energy.

The last year has certainly brought some shocks for the nation. The sensational—and traumatic—trials of former Presidents Chun Doo Hwan and Roh Tae Woo continue to transfix the public, and the banner headlines haven't stated the desire for a radical break from the past. President Kim is hoping to parlay public support for reform into success in an even bigger fight—the push to curtail the power of the chaebols (big business groups) that have led the drive for economic success. With virtually all owners of the country's top 30 conglomerates now facing trial for their alleged contributions to Chun and Roh's slush funds, the time may be right for Kim to take on these mighty corporate organizations.

Luckily for the president, the economic surge of recent years has bolstered his popularity, improving his ability to effect change. The economy has grown by an average 7.7% a year since Kim came to office in February 1993. In 1995, growth was 9%, fuelled by a 30% increase in exports and spectacular domestic demand for capital investment. The general upsurge kept factories humming at close to 90% capacity and pushed unemployment down to 2.2%—a record low. Meanwhile, inflation has hovered around 5%.

Growth like that helps. But President Kim has also used his credentials as a corruption-fighter to build public support. Over 5,000 civil servants—from cabinet members to legislators in the national assembly—have been dismissed or imprisoned on graft convictions: "We will not relax our fight against corruption," Park Kwang II, the president's chief of staff, vowed recently.

Public sentiment favouring curbs on chaebol power runs strong, especially among younger voters. In the May 16 edition of *The Chosun Ilbo* newspaper, Hanyang University economics professor Ahn Suk Kyo wrote: "People dislike chaebols for the same reason they dislike dictators ... They have concentrated too much power in their hands ... Korean people have fought for political democracy in the past 50 years. Now it's time for the business community to seek a more democratic management style."

Remaking the country's industrial structure won't come easy. Opposition is stiff in both industrial and governmental circles. Centralization and close government-business ties have created personal fiefs for regulators and managers alike—all of which will be tough to tear down.

But reform is clearly needed. Rising wages, high interest rates and competition from newly emerging economies have combined to worsen the prospects of small firms, which employ around 70% of the total workforce. As many as 14,000 small businesses went bankrupt last year because of tight credit, primarily caused by the large portion of bank lending take up by chaebol-linked firms. "The gap between chaebols and small business is creating another gap in the distribution of wealth," says Lee Sung Chul, a *Hankook Ilbo* newspaper commentator.

Early this year, the Ministry of Trade, Industry and Energy

established the Small Business Administration to supply up to 2 trillion won ($ 2. 6 billion) in low-interest loans to small companies. But that emergency measure is seen as little more than a temporary step. Small businesses complain that deregulation is moving too slowly for them to benefit: Complaints range from the persistence of cumbersome zoning laws to the excessive licensing authority still held by government agencies.

The government has now fired its first salvo in its fight against the chaebols. On May 9, it stunned business leaders by issuing a policy paper seeking to impose more transparency on companies and cut into the groups' near-monopoly on bank financing. The paper was written by the government-funded Korea Development Institute and sponsored by the Fair Trade Commission; the government hopes to make its contents into a major legislative initiative in the coming year.

The report suggests revising existing laws to allow small stockholders in a company to bring lawsuits against majority shareholders. The owners of chaebol companies are often criticized for running their firms by whim and freely using company funds without approval from their boards. To prevent managers from improperly using company funds for political donations or bribery, the proposal suggests requiring chaebol owners to seek the consent of minority stockholders when using corporate money for non-business purposes.

But the paper's most controversial proposal is one that would phase out in five years the system that allows one chaebol-linked company to issue credit guarantees to another firm in the group. This change would effectively bar chaebol companies from monopolizing credit from group-linked banking institutions, as they do now.

The business community strongly opposes these changes, arguing that they increase government regulation of the private sector.

Another FKI executive, commenting anonymously to a local newspaper reporter, said the government's efforts could hurt South

Korean companies' ability to compete internationally. "It's like asking us to compete in a car race and then trying to control our gasoline supply," he said.

The debate has split policymakers into two diametrically opposed groups. In the reform camp are President Kim and his Blue House staff, who advocate speedy and substantial moves to dilute chaebol wealth and power. Among the leaders of the effort are Park Sell, the presidential adviser on social welfare; Lee Gak Bom, the presidential adviser on policy matters; and Kim In Ho, chairman of the Fair Trade Commission.

Allied against them is the bureaucracy of the Ministry of Finance and Economy, headed by Deputy Prime Minister Rha Woong Bae. The ministry, which still tightly controls bank operations down to personnel moves and loan-approval policies, is clearly reluctant to give up any of its turf. Rha has called for a "gradualist" approach to reform—meaning one that relies on the discretion of banking authorities.

Indeed, nowhere has the pace of South Korea's deregulation been as glacial as in the banking sector. Analysts of all stripes say the success of President Kim's deregulation policy depends on how swiftly the government loosens its bureaucratic control to give banks more freedom and autonomy.

Domestic banks are now burdened with massive loans to chaebol firms that carry preferential interest rate. But the opening of South Korea's financial markets will force the banks to enhance their competitiveness or face bankruptcy. If they are to strengthen themselves, the low-interest subsidy loans to affiliated companies must be eliminated: Chaebol reform would be the key step in allowing banks to tighten their belts.

If Kim succeeds in this fight, he will profoundly change South Korea's industrial landscape. Chaebols have long used their privileged access to credit to fund aggressive investment and expansion, regardless of the risk. With their access to unlimited capital curtailed by the new proposals, the business groups' empire-building heyday may be coming to an end.

Breaking up the tightly knit industrial structure will be a key part of vaulting South Korea into a position of maturity in the international economic community. An ambitious policy programme drafted by the government's KDI calls for South Korea to raise its GDP tenfold to $4.8 trillion between now and 2020. That dream, if realized, would place South Korea ahead of Britain among the Group of Seven industrialized economies.

But the country needs to do a lot more than simply replace old social and economic institutional frameworks to attain such goals. More and more South Korean industries are moving manufacturing operations overseas to avoid the rising cost of doing business at home. In the electronics industry, South Korean wages are twice the level of those in Britain. Industrial land prices are four times British levels.

South Korea's economy is also seriously over-reliant on a few industrial sectors in which chaebols have concentrated their development. The country still depends on heavy industry at the expense of light industry, and manufacturing at the expense of services. Exports are dominated by a few key items such as cars, ships, steel, petrochemicals and semiconductors. The top 10 export items accounted for 53% of the total value of shipments in 1995, up from a 50% share a year earlier.

This causes headaches for the economy, analysts say. Huge imports of machinery and equipment to expand and upgrade production facilities worsen the nation's trade balance: The trade deficit in the January-April period was $3.9 billion, up from $3.2 billion a year ago. The current-account deficit in the same period soared to $6.6 billion from $4.3 billion. The current-account deficit for the whole of last year was a record $8.7 billion.

Membership of the OECD, the Organization for Economic Co-operation and Development, carries other requirements. To keep pace with the standards of European countries, for example, South Korea is revising its restrictive labour laws. In early April, President Kim shocked businessmen by announcing his readiness to recognize a second nationwide trade union confederation comprised of centre-left political activists. This would reverse the Labour Ministry's long-held policy of recognizing only the Federation of Korea Trade Unions. Also to be discarded is the ban on union members from one company supporting strikers from another.

And then there's the troubling neighbour to the north. The KDI's ambitious 21st-century vision makes no mention of the possibility that North Korea's isolationist regime could crumble, forcing South Korea to take on the burden of a sudden reunification. With North Korea's economy tottering, nobody in Seoul underestimates the likelihood of some kind of implosion in the next few years.

That frightening scenario has forced the South Korean government to provide food aid to the North to help bring about an economic "soft landing". Anything less than success could wreak havoc not only on Seoul's current reform drive, but also on its long-term economic future. According to a presidential blue-ribbon committee, it could cost up to $1.2 trillion over several years to bring the North Korean economy up to the level of South Korea's.

—From *Far Eastern Economic Review* • June 20, 1996

B. What Asia—and the World—Must Do

There are moments in capitalism when financial plagues break out with such speed and intensity that the international economic community is astonished. The Asian financial collapse is one such event, as were the panic of 1907 and the failure of Austria's Creditanstalt Bank in 1931. In the first instance, J. P. Morgan stepped in and contained the infection. In the second, policy mistakes turned a serious recession into a long depression. Today, with a de facto debt moratorium in place and a recession under way, Asia is unleashing deflation into the world economy. Should China devalue its currency, the world could find itself in an agonizing slowdown.

The Asian crisis is a solvable problem. But serious blunders could allow it to spread in dangerous ways. Already, analysts have shaved as much as a full percentage point off their estimates for global growth for 1998. They have consistently underestimated the impact of the Asian crisis and it could get worse. The main trouble is that the aging Bretton Woods-era system, designed to counter-balance national trade deficits, is coming apart under the strains of hot-wired global capital flows. In the end, a commitment to changing the rules of the international economic game by all the players involved will be needed if serious trouble is to be avoided.

Plunging currencies and rising unemployment are quickly destroying the wealth of Asia, eroding the richest growth markets for Western exports and investments. There is a danger that Versailles-style austerity programs imposed on Indonesia, Korea, and Thailand by the International Monetary Fund and the U. S. treasury are dumping all the pain of restructuring on Asia's businesses and middle class while Japanese, European, and American banks get off free. So far, an Asian backlash has targeted corrupt politicians and crony capitalists. But angry nationalism is growing, and the backlash can easily shift to anti-Americanism or even anticapitalism.

NO RISK ANALYSIS. The Asian crisis, like all previous panics, has not one but many causes. Double-digit growth was based on cheap credit to friends, family, and favored businesses by politicians or bureaucrats. Japanese banks in particular, facing low interest rates at home and unwilling to write off the bad loans of the

1980s, sought salvation by lending massive sums in the region. German and U. S. banks piled on, as did pension funds and emerging-market mutual funds. It was a funny kind of capitalism. Local banks lent on the basis of contacts, not risk analysis. Foreign banks, projecting from their Latin American experience, looked at positive government budget numbers but not at negative corporate earnings figures. Huge overcapacity resulted.

A rolling bank panic brought an end to the party. The end began in Thailand. Devaluation by Japan in 1995 made Thai exports uncompetitive. The baht fell. U. S. hedge funds pushed the currency lower. The Thai central bank disclosed that it barely had any reserves left. Creditor banks were shocked and stopped rolling over short-term dollar loans to Thai companies. As each Asian currency came under pressure, new surprises surfaced. Indonesia's central bank had no idea what the country owed. Korean companies had quietly borrowed up to $150 billion short-term. Each crisis revealed more secrets. Credit dried up. Asia ground to a halt, dumbfounded.

What must be done now is clear. First, purchasing power and growth must be restored to Asia by restructuring the dollar liabilities of Asian corporations and banks. The IMF erred by first negotiating with Asian governments. It should have brought borrowers and creditors together immediately to bang heads. The IMF should have pressured the banking institutions to take a quick hit, securitize the bad debt, and extend short-term dollar liabilities to Asian corporations to stimulate growth again. Instead, the banks are now trying to offload their mistakes in extending bad loans to private Asian companies by getting governments and their taxpayers to, in effect, swallow a big chunk of the losses the banks themselves should take.

BOOST BUYING POWER. The most irresponsible player in this entire crisis has been Japan. To stem the currency slide, a lender of last resort should have immediately stepped forward. Japan is the natural choice to do this, just as the U. S. did in Mexico, but the Japanese Finance Ministry refused. Instead of providing Asia with backup credits in this time of crisis, it is being stingy. Amazingly, Tokyo is even depreciating the yen to gain advantage during the crisis, thus exacerbating it. Japan should be raising the value of the yen and cutting taxes to boost consumer buying power and absorb Korean and Thai exports.

Asia must realize that its old, secretive mercantilist ways have become the enemies of growth. The Japan model isn't working. If capital is to start flowing, there must be transparency to assess risk. Asia's central banks, like Mexico's, should publish honest numbers on their reserves on the Internet daily. Banks and mutual funds must insist on concrete numbers from Asian companies before they lend and invest. Rating agencies must get real. The high-octane global financial markets are clearly overshooting. Thanks to the lower cost of trading due to communications technology and the rise of derivatives and leverage, the magnitude and volatility of capital flows are rising. With enough data, markets can make the right decisions. Without it, capital flows can wreak havoc.

—From *Business Week* • Jan. 26, 1998

C. Less Cash Flow
——Currency Controls Gain a Hearing as Crisis in Asia Takes Its Toll

Curbs Seem to Limit Damage In Some Nations, Leading Opponents to Reconsider Jolt From Malaysian Leader

By David Wessel and Bob Davis

Staff Reporters of *The Wall Street Journal*

WASHINGTON—For better than a year, the Treasury and

the International Monetary Fund have lectured shaken governments that the only prudent response to their financial crisis is to move more rapidly toward unfettered markets, for everything from cars to currency. And until recently, those governments paid heed.

But it hasn't worked—at least not nearly as well as the advocates hoped.

Now, some of the afflicted countries are moving in the opposite direction, erecting new barriers to the free flow of money across borders. More appear likely to follow. The result is the most serious challenge yet to the free-market orthodoxy that the globe has embraced since the end of the Cold War.

Declaring that "the free market has failed disastrously," Malaysian President Mahathir Mohamad this week said his country will no longer allow its currency to trade outside its borders. Russia has unilaterally refused to pay some of its foreign debts. Some Latin American governments are flirting with new controls on the flow of money across borders.

"Historic Change"

Limits on the freedom of foreigners to lend and residents to borrow from abroad are "going to be tried in a lot of places," predicts Fan Gang, a economist who sometimes advises China's leaders. "It is a historic change that is taking place."

Rudiger Dornbusch, a Massachusetts Institute of Technology economist who considers capital controls harmful, now expects them to become "the fashion", And Chase Manhattan Bank economist John Lipsky sees Russia's refusal to pay some of its debts as "a harbinger of a more generalized recourse to debt rescheduling and the implementation of capital controls."

For at least the past decade, the prevailing view among the world's economic policy makers has been that money should move freely around the globe, allowing capital to find the most profitable and productive investments, no matter what country these happen to be in. And until last year, emerging-market countries thrived under that arrangement, attract hundreds of billions of dollars in foreign investment that fueled a remarkable increase in living standards. The market also imposed a discipline on governments, forcing them toward wise economic policies.

What Can Go Wrong

But it is now clear that relying on foreign money had its costs. Much of that money was in short-term investments, and could flee as quickly as it arrived. When it did, the result was to force up interest rates (as lendable money became scarcer), push down exchange rates (as the local currency was sold) and ultimately fuel the financial crises and recessions now so painful.

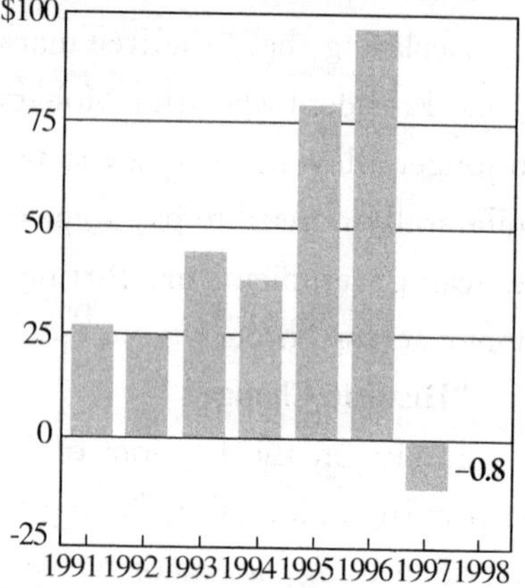

Forecast made April 30,1998
Source: Institute of International Finance

But some of the holdout nations that refused to adopt the free-flow-of-money or thodoxy of the 1990s—China, India and, to a lesser degree, Chile—now stand out as the countries least affected by the current crisis.

Because India never gave its own citizens and banks open access to foreign money, it is insulated from the tendency of financial markets to push currencies to extremes, says former Finance Secretary Montek Singh Ahluwalia, who helped craft India's market-oriented reforms of the 1990s and remains a strong advocate of free trade in goods and services. "In Indonesia," he adds, "the moment people knew the rupiah would slip, anyone with real money took their money out. In India, that can't happen: The rich in India couldn't move out $20 billion." Although he considers capital control "a nuisance," he says that "in this transition phase, it is necessary."

Wall Street Position Clear

Russia's Communists, who dominate the lower house of parliament known as the Duma, are keen on the Chinese model. Alexander Kravets, a Duma member who sits on the party's central committee, argues that Russia should reject IMF advice and adopt the "Chinese solution"—that is, to welcome foreign investment in factories and business but impose strict controls on currency trading.

All this hasn't been lost on Wall Street. As Goldman, Sachs & Co. economists note in their newsletter this week, "So far, countries whose currencies have not been freely convertible have done best. This raises the risk that at some point, other countries decide to impose capital controls. The exact consequences for the U. S. outlook are not clear, but they would certainly be negative." The Goldman economists see a threat to the profits of U. S. multinational corporations, particularly financial institutions, that have benefited from an increased openness to foreign direct investment.

Not all emerging market economic policy makers are leaping on the bandwagon, though. Just before Malaysia's move, the governor of the Philippines' central bank, Gabriel Singson, cited his country's bad experiences with capital controls earlier in this decade. "Controls are unmanageable and very susceptible to graft and corruption," he told reporters.

And one of the architects of Chile's successful attempts to discourage the inflow of volatile short-term money, former central banker Roberto Zahler has cautioned that controls should be used only as a preventive measure by countries that already have in place solid fiscal, monetary and exchange-rate policies.

At a conference of about 30 financial heavyweights convened in Washington this week by the Institute for International Economics, a private think tank, the costs and benefits of capital controls were much discussed. Wall Streeters knocked them as counterproductive and unworkable. David Folkerts-Landau, a former IMF official who heads emerging-market research at Deutshe Bank AG, says controls will drive away investment, because "the fear of being trapped is all-consuming for foreign investors."

But World Bank Chief Economist Joseph Stiglitz argued that controls should be considered, provided they can be designed to discourage short-term investments (such as bank loans or short-term currency trades) without disrupting foreign investment in factories and infrastructure. Mr. Stiglitz, a thorn in the side of former colleagues in the Clinton administration, has World Bank economists working on the particulars and reviewing the experiences of nations—such as Chile, Colombia, Thailand and the Czech Republic—that have experimented with such controls.

Controls come in various forms. Chile and Colombia have taxed short-term borrowing from abroad. Brazil once levied a 1% tax on foreign investment in its stock market to discourage short-term trading. Mexico, for a time, restricted the foreign-currency liabilities of its banks to 10% of their total loans. The Czech Republic levied a fee on all foreign-exchange transactions with banks. And Malaysia now limits the amount of cash its citizens can carry out of the country.

In the war of metaphors that often encapsulates academic debates, Deputy Treasury Secretary Lawrence Summers has likened the emergence of global financial markets to the invention of the jet airplane. "We can go where we want to go much more quickly. We can get there more comfortably, more cheaply and most of the time more safely. But the crashes when they occur are that much more spectacular."

In an op-ed piece in the Financial Times earlier this year, Mr.

Stiglitz fought back. A dramatic air crash is "an occurrence so rare that almost no one would question the superiority of air travel, especially for long distances... ," he said. "But the record of small planes traveling short distances is in greater doubt."

International flows of *short-term* capital, Mr. Stiglitz argued yesterday in a preliminary analysis of the Asian crisis he presented at the Brookings Institution, may expose developing countries to "unnecessary risks without commensurate returns."

Like a growing number of experts, Mr. Stiglitz sees merit in efforts to control the inflow of short-term money, such as Chile's tax on short-term foreign borrowing. But among economists and policy makers, the question of employing controls to block the *outflow* of foreign capital in a crisis, as Malaysia is now attempting, is far more controversial. Such controls may be much more difficult to enforce and may discourage sorely needed forms of foreign investment in factories and infrastructure.

But the alternatives—painfully high interest rates that still may not induce foreign and domestic owners of capital to bring their money back—aren't so pleasant either, as the Asian experience demonstrates.

International interest in capital controls picked up speed when MIT economist Paul Krugman made the case for controls in an article in Fortune magazine last week. The editors had asked him, before Russia imploded, to offer an answer to Asia's woes. He says in an interview that the best alternative he could conceive was to impose controls on currency trading to give troubled economies temporary relief from the pressures of the global economy so they can sort out their problems. "It's like Sherlock Holmes," he explans. "Eliminate everything is impossible, and what's left is probably the answer, however improbable it may seem." He had China's apparent success in mind.

Mr. Krugman says he was caught by surprise when Malaysia this week took his advice. In an open letter to Mr. Mahathir posted on his MIT Web site, Mr. Krugman said he "can't deny some responsibility." But then, clearly trying to put some distance between himself and the Malaysian prime minister, known for his vitriolic attacks on traders and Jews, Mr. Krugman laid out four principles for employing capital controls, none of which Malaysia appears to meet. He said the controls should disrupt ordinary business (such as foreign travel) as little as possible, clearly be temporary, be accompanied by a "highly competitive" exchange rate and be used "as an aid to reform, not an alternative."

While economists have argued for centuries for free trade in goods and services, the notion that government ought to permit—let alone encourage—free flows of financial investments is relatively recent. The architects of the International Monetary Fund—Britain's John Maynard Keynes and Harry Dexter White of the U. S. —feared that capital flows "would become an independent and disruptive force" that would interfere with trade, the IMF historian James Boughton has written. Mr. Keynes was unequivocal: "It is widely held that control of capital movements, both inward and outward, should be a permanent feature of the system," he wrote.

Notes Barry Eichengreen, a University of California at Berkeley economist: "Out of the collapse of the financial system in the Great Depression came profound distrust of both domestic and international financial markets." The response was tight regulation, both domestically and internationally.

For decades controls were, as Keynes had hoped, more or less permanent. With the dollar under pressure in 1967, President Johnson imposed a particularly stringent set of controls on outflow of capital by American businesses, banks and other financial institutions, including a now-unthinkable requirement that no dollars flow out of the U. S. to finance corporate investment in Western Europe and other developed nations.

The controls weren't fully lifted until 1974, and that move was controversial. In the talks surrounding the collapse of the exchange-rate rules that governed the world economy for the 25 years after World War Ⅱ, some nations sought, unsuccessfully, to give the IMF the power to require member countries to impose controls. At the beginning of the 1980s, only the U. S., Switzerland and Britain allowed the free flow of capital; Germany came along in 1984, and Japan eventually followed.

Gradually, says Mr. Eichengreen, the establishment of deposit insurance, securities regulation and sound monetary policy led to fewer restrictions on domestic financial markets; interest-rate ceilings were relaxed, for instance. Partly because of the changing ideology, and partly because freer domestic markets opened opportunities for international arbitrage among markets, the restrictions on international flows were eased. The advent of floating exchange rates in the early 1970s was also a factor, he says.

By last year, before the dimensions of the current crisis became clear, the members of the IMF agreed that there would be benefits to amending the organization's charter to make free flow of capital one of its major goals. (The existing charter allows countries to impose controls at will.) The proposed amendment, unlikely to win quick adoption now, would both push for fewer restrictions on capital flows and give the IMF the power to regulate their use.

The proposal has sparked a reaction from those who aren't convinced of the merits of unfettered capital flows. Danl Rodrik, a Harvard economist, finds it particularly galling that governments are forced to carry out policy based on "what 20 or 30 foreign-exchange dealers in London, New York and Frankfurt" think. In an influential study published earlier this year, he concluded that 23 countries that have experimented with lowered barriers to capital flows since 1973 — Malaysia among them — didn't enjoy faster growth or lower inflation than other countries.

One of America's most ferocious advocates of free trade in goods and services, Jagdish Bhagwati of Columbia University, worries that the case for free trade will be undermined by the damage done by the volatile flows of short-term money into—and now out of—emerging markets. Trade in goods and services boosts living standards without question, he says, but the case for free trade in currencies isn't so clear. Indeed, capital flows are characterized by "panics and manias," he observed in a May 1998 essay in Foreign Affairs.

Wall Streeters, Mr. Bhagwati notes, "have obvious self-interest in a world of free capital mobility, since it only enlarges the arena in which to make money." That may be a major concern of the Treasury, he argues, but not of emerging-market governments. "Any nation contemplating the embrace of free capital mobility," he wrote, "must reckon with the costs and also consider the probability of running into a crisis."

—Michael Williams in New York,
Marcus W. Brauchli in Shanghai, China,
and Darren McDermott in Singapore
contributed to this article

—From *The Wall Street Journal* • Sep. 4, 1998

Lesson 9

Newly-Emerging Trading Stars

Text

Prosperity Persists in the UAE

The profits of peace and prosperity

In the two years since Iraq was ousted from Kuwait, peace and prosperity have returned to the Gulf region, and the UAE in particular. Major development plans have resumed in Abu Dhabi's oil and gas sector and Dubai's trade figures are soaring as more companies adopt the emirate as their regional base. Yet, below the surface calm, defence is still of great concern. The topic dominated discussions at the GCC summit in Abu Dhabi in December, and in February the government announced its biggest-ever investment in defence equipment at IDEX 1993, an exhibition held in Abu Dhabi.

The huge purchases announced at IDEX include a \$3,500 million order for 436 of France's new generation Leclerc tanks and a \$300 million order for computerised air defence equipment from the US' Westinghouse Electric Corporation. Naval requirements are now being considered and could produce orders for six or seven vessels, including frigates, during the next three to four years.

The UAE remains wary about Iraq's threat to Kuwait and, therefore, to the Gulf, as well as the sovereignty dispute with Iran over the islands of Abu Musa and the Greater and Lesser Tumbs. Western diplomats say that, as Iraq has been neutralised for the moment, Iran is causing the greater concern. But they do not expect the dispute to revive, and conditions on the islands are said to be normal. "It is now a legal dispute," one says.

The appointment of an experienced UAE diplomat, Shaikh Fahim Bin Sultan al-Qassimi, as GCC secretary-general from 1 April will add weight to the UAE's voice in the organization. Shaikh Fahim has already shown in recent public statements that he is inclined to be forthright about the threat posed by the UAE's neighbours across the Gulf.

Domestically, the UAE is following the line of other Gulf states in promoting wider popular consultation. In January, the authorities announced that the federal national council, which last met in July 1991, would be revived. The council, made up of 40 nominees representing the seven emirates, has since met three times. It probably has more teeth than other consultative assemblies. It can reject or amend legislation according to the temporary constitution of the UAE, and it also has the power to summon ministers.

The local Arabic press has given full coverage to the council's debates and to a series of informal majlis discussions held weekly during Ramadan. In the latter, the issues of youth unemployment, drugs, the role of women and the size of the immigrant population were freely discussed. However, observers say Western-style democracy is not on the political agenda as the majlis system enjoys legitimacy and appears well-suited to the tribal traditions of Gulf society.

The wider publicity given to the council may be partly due to its first deputy speaker, Rashid Omran Tyriam, who is also the editor of the outspoken Sharjah-based newspaper Al-Khaleej. The editor of Dubai's Al-Bayan. Khalid Mohammed Ahmed, is also on the council. Both are newly appointed.

In Abu Dhabi, the economy is riding high on the spin-off from government plans to invest $5,000 million—6,000 million to increase oil output by 600,000 barrels a day to 2.6 million barrels a day by the late 1990s. The only sour note has been struck by new energy tax proposals in the US and the EC. Talks on the subject between GCC/OPEC oil ministers and EC officials are due to be held on 11 May. Diplomats say that OPEC is hoping to head off the threatened taxes, which may slow the growth in demand for oil and compromise Gulf capacity expansion plans. "It's a carbon tax, and the misunderstanding has arisen largely because the West has not thought it through properly," one diplomat says. "The inital reaction from OPEC was pretty tough but now seems to have softened a bit. Obviously they are reacting against a threat to their main source of livelihood," he adds.

Abu Dhabi is pressing on regardless, signing a contract on 10 March with a consortium led by the US' Bechtel for the biggest upstream hydrocarbons project in recent years. It involves a $1,350 million onshore gas project, known as 545, to develop reservoirs in the Bab gas field to produce dry gas, condensates and natural gas liquids.

Major projects outside the oil and gas sector in Abu Dhabi appear to be on hold. This applies to the Lulu island development and the third crossing project, for which tenders have been invited three times, although the prospects for medium-size infrastructure projects in Abu Dhabi are reasonable. "Look where the money is coming from, what really matters is oil and gas," a consultant says. The consensus is that these other projects will materialise; they are just not top priority at the moment.

Dubai is making progress in its efforts to promote international awareness of its attractions. The emirate is now firmly on the world sporting map and reaping the rewards of more publicity. Tennis has been added to the growing list of sporting events, with a BMW/Dubai Duty Free-sponsored tournament in February. This joins horse racing, golf, powerboat racing and snooker championships, which are all already established on the international tournament circuit.

Major investment is going into the Dubai-based Emirates airline, which added four new destinations last summer—Rome, Zurich, Paris and Jakarta—and on 14 April started operations to Dhahran, its 31st destination. Emirates now employs almost 3, 500 staff, making it one of Dubai's largest employers.

Soon, $ 2,000 million in financing will have to be arranged for the next phase of development, which will cover deliveries from 1996 to 2000. Firm orders have been placed for seven Boeing 777s with Rolls Royce engines and there is an option on a further seven.

Dubai's total non-oil trade grew by more than 23 per cent in 1992 to Dh 59,848 million and was seemingly unaffected by the recession. Abu Dhabi also achieved a 23 per cent increase in total non-oil trade, albeit with smaller volumes, from Dh 14,470 million in 1991 to Dh 17,860 million last year. And in Sharjah, which accounts for about 34 per cent of the UAE's manufacturing capacity, total foreign trade is expected to come to more than Dh 4,500 million, a rise of 10 per cent compared with 1991.

Surpluses

According to provisional estimates for 1992, the UAE's trade surplus was Dh 21,800 million, down from the 1991 figure, also provisional, of Dh 30,200 million. The drop is mainly because of a 25 per cent increase in imports to Dh 64,000 million from Dh 51,100 million. The current account surplus has risen to Dh 9,700 million from Dh 6,000 million, helped by a huge drop in government grants from Dh 17,000 million to Dh 2,700 million.

The central bank has begun to show new teeth with the announcement on 5 April of the rules defining capital and the ratio of risk-weighted assets to capital, which come into effect on 1 July. According to the new regulations, the minimum capital to risk-weighted assets ratio is to be 10 per cent—2 per cent higher than the minimum level recommended by the Basle committee on banking supervision.

Bankers say that the profits of some UAE banks will inveitably drop in 1993 as they will have to cut back on their riskier assets and will not be able to carry forward provisions to the next year. The rules have been welcomed as a clear sign that the UAE is determined to ensure its banking industry has soild, ethical foundations.

TRADE

China shows how it's done in Dubai

The Chinese city of Guangzhou, situated a mere 50 minutes flying time from Hong Kong, was expecting buyers from more than 400 UAE companies to attend its Chinese export commodities spring fair held from 15-24 April.

Interest in imports from China is high. The Chinese consulate's commercial section in Dubai reported a continual stream of visitors in the run-up to the exhibition from companies wanting to do business for the first time with China. More than 4,000 Chinese traders visited the emirates on government and private missions last year. As a result of this activity, China's exports to the UAE have almost doubled from $279.5 million in 1990 to $522.7 million in 1992, according to Chinese government statistics. Dubai's statistics show that China was the fifth largest supplier in 1990. Last year, however, it ousted the US to become the second largest exporter to the emirate with goods worth more than $1,000 million, or 8 per cent of Dubai's total import bill. The discrepancy in the value of imports compared with Chinese government figures is due to the fact that Dubai's figures show all goods manufactured in China including those by Taiwanese or Hong Kong joint ventures.

Either way, the increase is impressive. However, China is unlikely to challenge Japan's supreme position, with imports worth almost $2,000 million or 15 per cent of the total bill. Japan's chief exports to the UAE are vehicles, accounting for 20 per cent of the total, and consumer electronics, at more than 14 per cent. China's exports include textiles, ready-made garments, chemicals, food, household equipment and toys.

The UK, according to Dubai customs statistics, has slipped from second largest exporter in 1990 to fifth last year with Dh 3,402 million of exports or 7 per cent of the total. The UK embassy is quick to point out that the figures only show visible trade and the value of UK exports to the UAE is rising steadily—from £665 million ($1,024 million) in 1990 to £926 million ($1,426 million) in 1992, according to UK Department of Trade & Industry figures. The UAE was the UK's 25th most important export destination in 1991 and the 23rd most important destination in 1992.

UK exporters will be hoping that the trade fair, Britain & the Gulf, held in Dubai from 13-16 April, will help to boost UK market share. It is interesting to note that 14 per cent of British exports were tools and engineering equipment, according to Dubai customs figures. The biggest single category of exports was silver in semi-wrought or unfinished state, worth Dh 221.7 million or 6.5 per cent of the UK's total exports. Other commodities in the top 10 export list were medicine, vehicles, whisky and cigarettes.

The UAE's trade is conducted primarily through Dubai. Dubai accounted for approximately 77 per cent of UAE imports in the first half of 1992, 66 per cent of re-exports and 66 per cent of exports. Of Dubai's Dh 59,848 million total non-oil foreign trade in 1992, imports accounted for 79.5 per cent of the total, re-exports for 15 per cent and non-oil exports for just 5.5 per cent.

What the statistics do not reveal is how much is unofficially re-exported from the country. This is acknowledged by Dubai's customs department. "The re-export figures are indicative of markets rather than volumes," a spokesman says. "If you add up the import figures and work out that 85 per cent of it is supposed to stay in the country, then the UAE would be the best stocked warehouse in the world."

The number one re-export destination is Iran, with re-exports up 23 per cent on the 1991 figure to Dh 2,678 million—or almost 30 per cent of the total, according to official statistics. The top three re-export items are cars at 12.75 per cent, rice at 8.6 per cent and colour televisions at almost 8 per cent of the total. Dubai traders are not unduly concerned by the introduction on 21 March of an Iranian 20 per cent import surcharge as they consider demand for goods to be so strong that the surcharge will have little impact. If costs do rise sharply, the consequences are predictable. "Then the result will be a big increase in smuggling," commented one official as he gazed out of his window at dhows being loaded two and three abreast on the creek.

Other main re-export destinations are Saudi Arabia, with 8.4 per cent of the total, Kuwait with 8.41 per cent, and Qatar with 6.2 per cent. Re-exports to Kuwait have seesawed from Dh 183 million in 1990 to Dh 1 161 million in 1991 and Dh 757 million in 1992, reflecting the effect of the Iraqi invasion and the subsequent closure of Kuwait's ports. By far the biggest single re-export to Saudi Arabia and Qatar was synthetic fabric, while to Kuwait it was gold jewellery.

Dubai's biggest single non-oil export is aluminium, accounting for 44 per cent of the Dh 3,301.5 million export figure for 1992. The biggest single buyer is Japan, which bought aluminium, alloy and scrap worth Dh 538 million last year. Another major export item was clothing, at Dh 738.7 million. Main export markets for UAE-made garments were the UK, Germany and the US. The top three UAE export destinations were Japan, the UK and Oman.

It appears that the 23 per cent increase in non-oil trade registered by Dubai in 1992 will be repeated if not bettered this year. Says chamber of commerce director-general Abdul Rahman al-Mutaiwee: "According to the indications from the number of certificates of origin issued so far this year, we can look forward to considerable growth in exports and re-exports in 1993. Dubai's facilities, goods and services are becoming well-known all around the world."

INFRASTRUCTURE

The lure of the booming emirates

It is no coincidence that government departments in the various emirates are welcoming bids from consultants that are new to the area. Easily lured away from the recession-hit West by the notion that the streets of Abu Dhabi and Dubai are paved with gold, these companies are tending to submit very low offers to gain a foothold in the area. And, of course, the authorities are delighted to accept.

The esablished consultants are not quite so cheerful about this development. "There is a massive number of mainly British consultants coming in at silly prices to gain entry into the market," says one. "But they may well find that the loss leader philosophy only leads to more losses. There is a desperately competitive market out here."

The lure is obvious as both Abu Dhabi and Dubai are booming. In Abu Dhabi, the boom is driven by the government's plans to spend more than $5,000 million to raise crude oil output to about 2.6 million barrels a day by 1996. This is stimulating a very large spin-off in terms of an influx of people requiring accommodation and services.

In Dubai, the upward spiral in trading figures is fuelled by the large number of companies moving their regional head offices and distribution centres there, with a parallel spin-off in terms of demand for accommodation and services.

The most visible result of this buoyant market in both centres is a plethora of new multi-storey commercial and residential buildings. In Abu Dhabi, these projects are let through the Khalifah committee or the Department of Social Services to local consultants, but in Dubai there is more of an international spread. Such projects are not especially favoured by foreign consultants, however, as the profit margins are thin.

Building work apart, consultants predict a fairly wide spread of projects. "We expect the market to remain buoyant for the next couple of years. There is a fair bit of work at Mina Zayed coming up, a fair bit of road-working on the island and the hinterland, and we expect some airport development to rear its head in the not too distant future," says one long-established Abu Dhabi-based consultant.

New road projects are not likely to be in the same league as the two major ones already under way: the Dh 700 million Abu Dhabi to Al-Ain highway upgrading, and the Dh 300 million upgrading to a four-lane highway of the Abu Dhabi emirate section of the Dubai-Abu Dhabi road. However, new projects are expected around the developing areas of Liwa and Madinat zayed. Also, the Dh 500 million third crossing to Abu Dhabi island which so far has been tendered three times is expected to materialise at some point, as is the massive leisure and recreational development on Lulu island.

There will not be many new power and water projects in Abu Dhabi emirate. This should hardly be surprising as contracts worth more than $2,500 million have been let in the past 12 months. Consultants expect some transmission work in Abu Dhabi emirate to upgrade the system.

In the Dubai power and water sector, not a great deal is expected in the next couple of years. "Everything up for grabs is already secured," says one consultant. Consultants are now eyeing developments in Sharjah and the northern emirates with interest.

US' corporation was recently awarded the northern emirates unified water and electricity masterplan study. This covers requirements for the next 25 years, including the interconnection of Ajman, Umm al-Qaiwain, Ras al-Khaimah and Fujariah and the possibility of a central power and desalination plant which could cost up to Dh 2,500 million.

Less distant is the expansion of power generation and desalination capacity at Layyah power station, which has a capacity of 630 MW and 20 million gallons a day of desalinated water. The power station is handling arrangements to expand the desalination capacity by 15 million gallons a day and the power side by 66 MW as an in-house project. Tender invitations for the desalination plant are expected in two months and for a frame six gas turbine in three to four months. Road consultants are optimistic about work arising from Dubai municipality's masterplan which deals with requirements to 2011. They have heard unofficially that six or seven inter-changes may go to design tender this year. "If this programme goes ahead then there will be six to 10 years of work here. Dubai has great potential for us," says one foreign consultant. A precursor to this new work is the Dh 300 million scheme to convert the trade centre roundabout and two signal junctions into a combination of flyovers and underpasses. Construction tenders for this project are expected in the third quarter of 1993. The consultant is Italconsult.

Now that Sharjah has boosted its revenue from last year's gas and condensate discoveries, further infrastructure work can be expected there.

While there undoubtedly is work about and the outlook for the UAE is bright, the ever increasing competition among consultants and contractors means that margins are being squeezed. In the opinion of one major local consultant, the only way forward is to diversify: "International consultants, even well established ones, who want to secure definitive projects at lucrative fees are finding it harder and harder. Diversification into project management in the oil and gas sector is the only way to secure continuity of work and revenues and keep international calibre consultants on the ground."

—From *Middle East Economic Digest* • May 7, 1993

Words and Expressions

resume	*v.*	重新开始
emirate	*n.*	酋长国
frigate	*n.*	大型驱逐舰
sovereignty dispute		主权争端
neutralize	*v.*	使中立化,一般用被动语态
add weight to		扩大影响;增强优势
forthright	*a.*	直率的
nominee	*n.*	被任命的人
summon	*v.*	传唤
coverage	*n.*	报道
majlis	*n.*	(北非或中东国家的)议会
Ramadan	*n.*	斋月,赖买丹(月)
legitimacy	*n.*	合法(性);合理(性)
tribal	*a.*	部落的;家族的
publicity	*n.*	公众的注意
Sharjah		沙迦(市)(阿联酋东北部港市)
spin-off		派生产品;副产品
sour note		刺耳的音符
head off		阻止;防止…发生
head off a conflict		防止冲突发生
compromise	*v.*	危及;损害
carbon tax		双重税
press on		(不顾困难地)继续进行
consortium	*n.*	(国际性的)财团;联合放款团
upstream	*a.*	在(炼油等工业生产过程的)前阶段
hydrocarbon	*n.*	[化]碳氢化合物

reservoir	*n.* 蓄液槽
condensate	*n.* 冷凝液
on hold	等着
crossing	*n.* 渡口
tender	*n.* 投标
prospect	*n.* (成功、得益等的)可能性;前景
reasonable	*a.* 尚好的
materialize	*v.* 实现
Zurich	苏黎士
Jakarta	雅加达(印度尼西亚首都)
financing	*n.* 筹措资金
Dh (UAE Dirham)	迪拉姆(阿拉伯联合酋长国货币单位)
provisional	*a.* 临时的;暂时性的
grant	*n.* 授予物(如土地、权利、补助金等)
define	*v.* 限定
Basle	巴塞尔(瑞士西北部城市)
carry forward	把(账款)转入下期
provision	*n.* (尤指政府提供的)钱和设备
ethical	*a.* 合乎职业道德标准的
consulate	*n.* 领事馆
run-up	*n.* (事情的)序幕,前奏;前导期,预备期
discrepancy	*n.* 差异
supreme	*a.* 最高的
slip	*v.* 滑落;下降
destination	*n.* 目标
semi-wrought	*a.* 半成品
reveal	*v.* 展示;展露
indicative	*a.* 表示的,表明…的
unduly	*ad.* 过分的;过度的;不必要的
introduction	*n.* 采用
surcharge	*n.* 附加税

impose import	征收进口附加税	
impact	*n.*	冲击;影响
predictable	*a.*	可预料的
smuggling	*n.*	走私,非法私运
dhow	*n.*	(阿拉伯、印度、东非沿岸航行的)三角帆船
abreast	*a.*	[一般做表语]朝同方向并列的
creek	*n.*	通海的小湾
seesaw	*v.*	摇摆,涨落,起伏(不定)
coincidence	*n.*	巧合
notion	*n.*	观念
tend	*v.*	易于;往往会
out	*a.*	出现;外面的;外围的
lure	*n.*	吸引力;魅力
Dubai	迪拜(阿联酋东北部港市)	
Abu Dhabi	阿布扎比(阿联酋首都)	
boom	*v.*	兴旺发达;迅速发展
crude oil	原油	
influx	*n.*	涌进
accommodation	*n.*	住处;膳宿
spiral	*n.*	不断地急剧上升
fuel	*v.*	支持
buoyant	*a.*	活跃的
plethora	*n.*	过多
let through	允许通过	
apart	*ad.*	(撇开或排除)在一边
predict	*v.*	预测
come up	出现	
hinterland	*n.*	内地
rear its head	冒头;出现	
league	*n.*	种类;范畴

massive	*a.*	大规模的
let	*v.*	(招标后)被承包
transmission	*n.*	输送(电力)
up for grabs	供争夺的	
eye	*v.*	注视
municipality	*n.*	大城市,大都市
interchange	*n.*	(公路或高速公路的)互通式立体交叉(立交桥)
precursor	*n.*	前体;前身
roundabout	*n.*	绕行路
junctions	*n.*	交叉口
revenue	*n.*	(国家的)岁收
margin	*n.*	利润
diversify	*v.*	使多样化
definitive	*a.*	选定的;限定的
lucrative	*a.*	赚钱的;利润高的
calibre	*n.*	水准,程度
on the ground	当场	

Notes to the Text

1. Middle East Economic Digest (MEED)　中东经济评论

关于中东地区经济发展情况的重要刊物,自 1975 年由设在伦敦的中东经济评论有限公司出版。该杂志提供这一地区的经济建设、金融、贸易和其他商务活动以及重大政治事件的报道与评论。

2. Gulf region　海湾地区

Gulf 指波斯湾(Persian Gulf),阿拉伯语称"阿拉伯湾",是印度洋的一个边缘海,位于伊朗高原与阿拉伯半岛之间。海湾地区指波斯湾及波斯湾周围的一些国家(参考第 4 课注释)。目前海湾及周围国家石油产量占世界总产量的 31%,储量约占世界的 63%。

3. UAE (United Arab Emirates) 阿拉伯联合酋长国

位于阿拉伯半岛波斯湾南岸,由阿布扎比、迪拜、阿治曼、沙迦、乌姆盖万、哈伊马角和富扎伊拉七个酋长国组成,主要为阿拉伯人,信奉伊斯兰教,还有许多印度、巴基斯坦、伊朗等外籍人。首都阿布扎比。

阿拉伯联合酋长国的经济主要依靠阿布扎比和迪拜的石油。石油为主要出口项目;进口物资包括粮食、机器、建筑材料、军火、钻井器材和消费品等。迪拜为自由港。迪拜和沙迦是主要商业中心。

4. Abu Dhabi 阿布扎比

阿拉伯联合酋长国七国中最大的一个。其陆地和所属波斯湾底有藏量丰富的石油,为联合酋长国中最富有的两个酋长国之一。阿布扎比北邻波斯湾,西邻卡塔尔,东接沙特阿拉伯,东连阿曼。该国的经济几乎全部依赖原油生产,全国石油总蕴藏量估计为300亿桶。阿布扎比因其丰厚的石油税收而成为世界人均收入最高的国家之一。

5. Dubai 迪拜

阿拉伯联合酋长国中第二大国,位于阿拉伯半岛东部的海湾南岸,地处远东和欧洲之间,是中东的国际贸易中心。迪拜有泊位总数名列世界十大港口的希德港及杰贝勒阿里港。迪拜各港口驻有许多家国际航运公司,航线遍及世界各地。

迪拜是个拥有十亿人口的中东市场的大门,是海湾地区最大的贸易中心和转口市场,除输出石油外,还经手海湾地区20%的非石油贸易额,是该地区商业活动的晴雨表,中东最大的消费市场。中国目前主要向迪拜出口的产品是服装、手表和家具等轻工产品。中国在迪拜设有贸易中心,每年在迪拜组织展览会。这些对于扩大中国对这一地区的出口起了促进作用。

6. GCC (Gulf Co-operation Council) 海湾合作委员会

海湾阿拉伯国家建立的区域性政治经济组织。1981年5月25日由巴林、科威特、阿曼、卡塔尔、沙特阿拉伯和阿拉伯联合酋长国签署了《合作委员会章程》,次日宣布成立海湾合作委员会。其宗旨是加强成员国之间的密切合作,在自力更生基础上实现各方面更大程度的协调、统一和联系。委员会成立以来，在政治、军事、经济等方面进行了广泛的协调与合作，在共同发展经济方面取得了一定的进展。

7. IDEX 93 (1993 International Defense Equipment Exhibition)

1993 年国际国防设施博览会

8. Westinghouse Electric Corporation　威斯汀豪斯电气公司

又译为西屋电气公司。美国公司，产品有发电、配电设备、工业用电气装置、电器及航天和防务设备。总公司设在匹兹堡，公司创建于 1886 年。威斯汀豪斯的子公司，包括威斯汀豪斯广播公司（辖有若干电视台与广播电台，即美国国内通称 W 的集团），加拿大威斯汀豪斯公司（生产电气、机械电子产品和装备等），威斯汀豪斯信贷公司（向工业提供信贷），威斯汀豪斯电气供应公司（负责销售产品）和威斯汀豪斯升降机公司等。

西屋电气公司在 1995 年根据销售额排行的美国最大 500 家工业公司中名列第 35，销售额为 121 亿美元。

9. to be inclined to do　倾向于；想要

They are inclined to go there by train.

他们倾向于乘火车去那儿。

The administration is inclined to adopt fiscal retrenchment in the hope of reducing its huge budget deficit.

政府想采用财政紧缩的办法来削减其巨额预算赤字。

10. Ramadan　赖买丹月

伊斯兰教教历九月，是斋戒的圣月，即斋月。《古兰经》第二章第 185 节载，“赖买丹月中，开始降示《古兰经》，指导世人”。根据穆斯林教法，在赖买丹全月，每日从黎明到黄昏不得饮食。赖买丹月的开始和结束由教法当局根据可靠见证人见到新月的报告予以宣布，因此阴天可能推迟或延长斋月期。

11. Sharjah　沙迦

阿拉伯联合酋长国的成员国。部分国界尚未划定，国土主要部分为一形状不规则的地带，从西北的波斯湾延伸至东南的阿曼岬内地的中央。首都沙迦城，濒临波斯湾。城内有新建的房屋、国际机场、深水港；轻工业在发展中；有公路可通阿布扎比城。

12. “In Abu Dhabi the economy is riding high on the spin-off from government plans to invest ＄5,000 million—6,000 million to increase oil output...”

1) to ride high：to make great success。

2) spin-off：原意为纺线时飞出去的棉絮，在本文中指由政府投资增加石油产量的计划所提供的资金的一部分。

3) “... on the spin-off...”：依靠…；或靠…的支持。

4) 注题引文的含义是：政府投资扩大石油工业规模，为此，石油工业要从市场采购设备和服务，而很大一部分是来自本地市场，这就促进了整个酋长国的经济繁荣。

13. “... new energy tax proposals in the US and the EC...”

当时美国和欧共体提出的关于能源的新的税收政策，旨在促使削减能源（石油）进口，减少自身的贸易赤字。

14. OPEC （Organization of Petroleum Exporting Countries 的缩略语） 石油输出国组织

汉语音译其简称为“欧佩克”。该组织于 1960 年 9 月成立，总部设在维也纳，目前有 13 个成员国：伊拉克、伊朗、沙特阿拉伯、科威特、委内瑞拉、阿尔及利亚、厄瓜多尔、加蓬、印度尼西亚、利比亚、尼日利亚、卡塔尔和阿拉伯联合酋长国。石油输出国组织成立之后，不断与西方石油公司进行斗争，多次迫使它们提高石油税（外资石油公司向产油国缴纳的所得税）和原油价格并从国际石油垄断资本手中拿回了原油价格的确定权。

15. U.S. Bechtel

世界上最大的建筑及工程公司之一。曾承建的工程有 Hoover Dam，the San Francisco-Oakland Bay Bridge，the Alaska oil pipeline 以及旧金山和华盛顿特区的快速交通运输系统。

1936 年 Bechtel-McCone 公司成立，承建炼油厂及化工厂。第二次世界大战期间，他们制造轮船、飞机零件。战后重新组建的 Bechtel 公司在加拿大、中东和其他地方铺设管道，而且在世界各地建造发电厂。

16. tenders 招标

不经过磋商而由一方按照单方规定的条件公开征求应征人以进行交易的一种方式。在商业上，tender 一词意为正式或书面要求订约，包括要求订约购买或出售商品，to invite tender 或 invitation to tender 汉译为"招标"，而 to submit tender 或 submission of tender 为"投标"。

招标通常是一些国家的政府机构、市政当局、国营企业或公共事业单位用来采购物资、器材、设备或招商承建某项工程的一种常用方法。招标在发展中国家尤为盛行，有些国家规定凡政府机构采购物资达一定金额以上者，均须通过公开招标(public tender)进行。

对政府机关或私人企业的招标进行的工程建筑或订制大型设备，承包人提出的价格或承包条件叫做 bid，可简译为"承包(造)"或要价。"承包"或要价可以是应招标而出，也可以是像一般交易中的发盘那样主动提出(如 bid 被接受，得到承包项目，这时承包人叫 contractor)。招标购买商品时，如投标人愿按一定的价格供应商品，他提出的价格也叫 bid。

17. BMW/Dubai Duty Free-sponsored tournament

BMW—Bayerische Motoren Werke AG　巴伐利亚汽车厂，现名为宝马汽车有限公司

德国汽车制造公司。宝马公司以制造高品质赛车和摩托车而闻名，总部设在慕尼黑。公司成立于 1929 年，其制造的摩托车很快以在体育比赛中频破记录而出名。第二次世界大战中，宝马公司制造了第一台喷气发动机，由德国空军 Luftwatte 使用。

第二次世界大战后，公司试图进入小型汽车市场，但发现无法和大众汽车公司小型而廉价的产品竞争。1969 年公司濒于破产，当时欠巴伐利亚州政府相当于2,900万美元的债务。同年，公司推出的新车系列使公司得以从其金融危机中解脱出来。其新车系列设计为传统型，但其性能和价格如同赛车。公司同时还制造了新型摩托车，这些摩托车在美国非常受欢迎。

BMW/Dubai Duty Free-sponsored tournament 指由宝马汽车有限公司资助与迪拜政府共同举办的比赛。为了鼓励、支持公司资助这些体育活动，政府采取对由举办比赛而获得的收入(如门票等)

免税的做法。

18. Airbus　空中客车

1969年3月14日，欧洲空中客车公司宣告成立。法、德、英、荷兰和西班牙决定合作研制A300B2双发动机宽体客机。五年以后，1974年5月23日一架A300B2客机，搭载250名首航旅客，从巴黎直飞伦敦，开始了商业航班飞行。从此打破了美国公司在世界大型喷气客机市场上的一统天下。

空中客车公司为了密切同中国市场联系，成立了中国分支机构——空中客车中国公司(Airbus Industrie China)。

19. The Boeing Company　波音公司

1916年7月创立，原名太平洋航空产品公司，1917年改名为波音飞机公司，1961年因业务已超越飞机制造业的范围而改用今名。波音公司现从事设计和制造商用和军用飞机、直升机、航天器、导弹、水翼艇、火车车厢并提供各种地面站支援服务，此外还开展各种工程和建筑业务，特别是关于能源工厂，净水处理和供应等方面的业务。总公司设在华盛顿州西雅图。

20. Rolls Royce Ltd.　罗尔斯—罗伊斯公司

英国制造汽车的垄断组织，制造高级轿车、汽车和飞机发动机及其他工程技术产品。1906年3月成立，1971年2月破产。公司破产后改组成两家独立的公司。其一为罗尔斯—罗伊斯公司，内有前罗尔斯—罗伊斯公司的生产喷气式发动机的部分，1971年由英国政府投资设立，由国营企业局管理，总公司设在伦敦。另一为罗尔斯—罗伊斯汽车公司，1973年5月成立，包括所有原从事制造汽车和生产其他工程技术产品，如：内燃机、汽车和飞机部件、工业用机车、轻型飞机的部分，总公司设在德比郡德比。1998年，该公司售予德国大众汽车公司。

21. current account　经常项目

参考第4课注释。

22. "The central bank has begun to show new teeth with the announcement on 5 April of the rules defining capital and the ratio of risk-weighted assets to capital, ..."

central bank　国家中央银行，其职能主要包括：作为全国商业银行的管理与监督机构，收存与保管各商业银行的准备金；作为商业银行的最后贷款者，对它们提交的合理的商业票据和抵押品予以再贴现或给予贷款；协调或执行国家的货币和信贷政策。

这一段主要讲国家中央银行为了更好地控制资本，减少商业银行借贷风险，制定了新的规定，限定资本以及风险贷款与资本的比例。

23. Chinese Export Commodities Fair　中国出口商品交易会

简称"广交会"，是享有国际声望的交易会。创办于1957年，每年在广州春秋各举办一次，初期每届一个月，后缩短为15天。会上既展出各类产品，供客户选择并可当场进行交易，同时也接待洽谈其他进口业务，既有公司之间的往来，也有政府间贸易谈判。技术交流、期货贸易、签定长期供货合同、来料加工、合作生产、合作经营及补偿贸易等都可在交易会上进行。

24. visible trade　有形贸易

无形贸易(invisible trade，即劳务进出口)的对称，指商品的进出口贸易。由于商品是可以看得见的有形实物，因此商品的进出口被称为有形进出口(visible exports and imports)，亦即有形贸易(visible trade)。

25. reexports　再出口，复出口

指外国商品进口后未经加工又输到外国的一种贸易活动。

26. Saudi Arabia　沙特阿拉伯

位于阿拉伯半岛，首都利雅得。沙特阿拉伯的石油储量估计为220亿吨，占世界总储量的近四分之一。石油生产和出口为最大的经济项目。沙特阿拉伯是世界最大的石油生产国和出口国之一。其工业发展规划的主要项目是建造石油冶炼和加工厂。石油收入一般占政府总收入的90％以上。进口以各种制造业产品和食品为主。

27. Qatar　卡塔尔

阿拉伯半岛国家，与沙特阿拉伯和阿布扎比酋长国接壤。20世纪40年代因发现并开发丰富的油田使卡塔尔得以繁荣。石油工业的发展使该国在技术上进入20世纪，已建有现代化的公路、旅馆、政

府大厦和全国电视网。工业发展多样化，可生产化肥、水泥等。首都多哈有现代化国际机场。

28. Oman 阿曼

亚洲西部国家，位于阿拉伯半岛东南部。石油是阿曼惟一商业性矿产资源，占国家财政收入近 90%。商业为大城市马斯喀特和马特拉的主要行业。出口产品中原油占 90%以上，进口以制造业产品、运输设备及食品为主。

29. certificate of origin 产地证明书

出口国家的商会、有关协会或政府机构开出的证明所列货物是本国生产的证书。进口国对来自不同国家或地区的商品征收不同税率，或实行进口许可证或进口配额制，这就要求提供产地证明书，以便据以确定其关税待遇或是否符合许可证或配额的规定。

Questions on Content and Language Points

(for preview, discussion and review)

On "The profits of peace and prosperity"

1. According to the first paragraph of the text, what was the question that dominated discussions at the GCC Summit?

2. "Naval requirements are now being considered and could produce orders for six or seven vessels..."

In what sense is the word "produce" used in the sentence?

3. "Domestically, the UAE is following the line of other Gulf states in promoting wider popular consultation."

What does popular mean in the sentence? Does it mean "liked and admired by the people", or something else?

4. "It probably has more teeth than other consultative assemblies."

What does "to have more teeth" mean in the given context?

5. "The only sour note has been struck by new energy tax pro-

posals in the U. S. and the EC. Talks on the subject between GCC/ OPEC oil ministers and EC officials are due to be held on 11 May..."

1) What was the "new energy tax proposals in the US and the EC" about?

2) Why was the "tax proposals" "a sour note" for the oil producers, according to the given context?

5. "The emirate is now firmly on the world sporting map and reaping the rewards of more publicity."

1) What is the meaning of "more publicity"?

2) What's the good of being "firmly on the world sporting map" for a country?

(The answer lies in the rest of the sentence.)

7. "Tennis has been added to the growing list of sporting events, with a BMW/Dubai Duty Free-sponsored tournament in February."

Change the phrase introduced by "with" into an adverbial clause (of time or reason) for the same idea.

8. "Major investment is going into the Dubai-based Emirates airlines, ..."

What is meant by "Dubai-based"?

9. "Emirates now employs almost 3,500 staff, making it one of Dubai's largest employers."

What does "Emirates" stand for according to the context?

10. "Soon, $2,000 million in financing will have to be arranged for the next phase of development, which will cover deliveries from 1996—2000."

What does "which" represent in the sentence?

On "China shows how it's done in Dubai"

11. "China shows how it's done in Dubai"

What does the abbreviation "it's" represent? It is or it has?

12. Paraphrase the underlined part in the following sentence.

"The Chinese city of Guangzhou, situated a mere 50 minutes flying time from Hong Kong, was expecting buyers from more than 400 UAE companies to attend its Chinese export commodities spring fair held from 15-24 April."

13. Translate the following sentence into Chinese, paying special attention to the sentence structure.

"The Chinese consulate's commercial section in Dubai reported a continual stream of visitors in the run-up to the exhibition from companies wanting to do business for the first time with China."

14. "Last year, however, it ousted the US to become the second largest exporter to the emirate with goods worth more than $1,000 million, or 8 per cent of Dubai's total import bill."

1) According to the context, does "to oust" mean "to drive out" or something else more proper? If it does not, what does it mean in the sentence? What other word can be used to replace "ousted"?

2) What is the meaning of "bill" in the context?

15. Why is there a discrepancy in the value of imports between the figures provided by the Chinese government and Dubai?

16. "What the statistics do not reveal is how much is unofficially re-exported from the country. This is acknowledged by Dubai's customs department. 'The re-export figures are indicative of markets rather than volumes', a spokesman says. 'If you add up the import figures and work out that 85 per cent of it is supposed to stay in the country then the UAE would be the best stocked warehouse in the world.'"

1) Do the UAE's statistics on trade show the volume of all its reexports?

2) What is meant by "The re-export figures are indicative of markets rather than volumes"?

3) What does "stay" mean and imply in "... 85 per cent of it is supposed to stay in the country..."?

17. "The number one re-export destination is Iran, with re-exports up 23 per cent on the 1991 figure to Dh 2,678 million—or almost 30 per cent of the total, according to official statistics."

Translate the above sentence, paying special attention to the meaning and the usage of the prepositions: up, on, and to.

18. Why did re-exports to Kuwait between 1990 and 1992 experience sharp rise and fall?

19. What opinion does Mr. Abdul Rahman al-Mutainee have regarding 1993 non-oil trade?

On "The lure of the booming emirates"

20. "It is no coincidence that government departments in the various emirates are welcoming bids from consultants that are new to the area. Easily lured away from the recession-hit West by the notion that the streets of Abu Dhabi and Dubai are paved with gold, these companies are tending to submit very low offers to gain a foothold in the area."

1) What does "offers" refer to in the second sentence quoted above? Could you find the answer in the first sentence?

2) What is meant by "Dubai are paved with gold"?

21. What are "the established consultants" in Paragraph 2? Are they the same ones mentioned in Paragraph 1 of this section?

22. "There is a massive number of mainly British consultants coming in at silly prices to gain entry into the market," says one. "But they may well find that the loss leader philosophy only leads to more losses. There is a desperately competitive market out here."

1) Are "silly prices" high ones, or low ones according to the context?

2) What is the "loss leader philosophy"?

3) Why would "the loss leader philosophy only lead to more losses" in the case?

Try to find the answer within the above quotation.

4) What does well mean in "... they may well find that..."?

23. Translate the following into Chinese and then explain the underlined parts of the sentence.

"In Abu Dhabi, these projects are let through the Khalifah committee or the Department of Social Services to local consultants, but in Dubai there is more of an international spread."

24. Read the 7th paragraph carefully and then answer the following questions.

In what way are "the new road projects" different from "the two major ones"? Which word (an adverb) helps you find out the difference?

25. "Everything up for grabs is already secured..."

In what sense is "up" used here?

26. "This covers requirements for the next 25 years, including the interconnection of Ajman, Umm al-Qaiwain, Ras al-Khaimah and Fujairah and the possibility of a central power and desalination plant which could cost up to Dh 2,500 million."

What does the writer mean by "This covers requirements for the next 25 years"? What is the meaning of to cover in the context?

27. Read the first two sentences of the third paragraph from the bottom and find out the wording "the power side", and try to see what it stands for.

28. From the last sentence of the last paragraph, can you tell what's the way for the consultants to secure continuity of work and revenues, faced the severe competition?

29. After reading the whole article, do you think China should further develop her economic relations with UAE? And how could she increase her share in the UAF market?

Exercises

Ⅰ. Read the article given below and answer the following questions.

Smooth Ride on the Road to Success

The highway from Abu Dhabi to Dubai throws up its fair share of hazards for the unsuspecting driver. Apart from navigating the inevitable road works, cars have to jostle with huge trucks bound for Jebel Ali port or any of the numerous construction sites that line the highway. Perhaps the biggest challenge is presented by the speed ramps. Unless the ramps are negotiated in low gear at a snail's pace, both car and driver are in for a rude shock as they are tossed in the air before crashing back down to earth.

It is the good fortune of the UAE that the country and its economy are enjoying a much softer ride than is to be had on the local highway. The federation is functioning smoothly with few obvious obstacles on the path ahead. And the economy continues to cruise along, showing no signs of a slowdown. Indeed, economic grwoth in 1995 looks set to accelerate to a five-year high, supported by a year-on-year rise in the price of oil and vibrant activity in the non-oil sector.

The degree of political stability and economic prosperity looks all the more striking when set against the problems that affect some other Middle East states. One clue to the UAE's success has been the ability and willingness of Abu Dhabi and Dubai to maintain a high level of public spending, especially on capital projects in the two emirates.

And the happy circumstances seem set to continue. In early November, as Middle East news was dominated by the assassination of Israeli prime minister Yitzhak Rabin and a bomb explosion in Saudi Arabia, the two wealthiest emirates took the opportunity to remind the international business community of their continuing appeal. Abu Dhabi National Oil Company (ADNOC) informed a three-day gathering in the capital of its plans to spend $7,000 million over the next five years on upgrading its downstream oil capabilities and gas gathering network. At the same time Dubai was playing host to 25,000 business visitors at its biennial air show extravaganza and unveiling the designs for a $300 million expansion of its international airport and an estimated $500 million theme park on the creek.

UAE: FACT FILE, 1994—1995
($ million)

	1994	1995
Population (million)	2.2	2.3
GDP	36,700	38,500
GDP growth (per cent)	2.9	5.0
Inflation (per cent)	4.5	4.5
Exports	25,260	26,500
Imports	21,780	23,000
Trade balance	3,480	3,500
Current account	+450	+700

Sources: Central Bank, MEED estimates

Both events highlighted how the individual emirates are still building on their known strengths. Abu Dhabi, with oil production of about 2 million barrels a day (b/d) backed by almost 100,000 million barrels of oil reserves, has its sights set on becoming a major player in the downstream market. Accordingly, it is expanding refining capacity at the existing Ruwais facility and building a world-scale petrochemical complex in joint venture with a foreign partner.

Dubai is concentrating on consolidating its position as the regions leading location for trade, business and pleasure and entertains few thoughts of changing a winning formula. In early November, customs officials ruled out any increase in the current four per cent import tariff, even though other GCC members have been calling on the UAE to raise levies, so that a uniform customs duty can be established. Government officials have also been quick to dismiss any suggestions that the emirate plans to introduce some form of income tax.

As the heavy investment continues in infrastructure, tourism and business conferences, Dubai is working on polishing its image. On the business front, the government is leading by example. In the interests of greater transparency, state-owned organisations like Emirates airline have started to publish financial results. The authorities are also working to ensure that services are delivered professionally. In May, a fleet of new taxis owned by Dubai Transport Corporation hit the streets, offering uniformed drivers and metered rides.

Dynamic Dubai

Dubai is also projecting itself at an ever wider international audience. In the first quarter of next year the emirate launches two new events—the six-week-long Dubai shopping festival and the world's richest horse race—which should attract much attention.

Dubai has been accused in the past of being strong on style but weak on substance. Indeed, like the other six emirates, the government gives no details of its budgets or its oil production, which is estimated at about 300,000 b/d. Despite the discretion with the details there is little doubt that the high-profile strategy is paying off. Since the summer, nearly all the top hotels have been displaying no-vacancy signs. In addition, a steady flow of household name—the latest being IBM and Motorola—continue to set up shop in the eminate.

"A lot of the multinational companies have chosen Dubai to

target other markets," explains Anis al-Jallaf, managing director and chief executive of Emirates Bank International (EBI). "They recognise that here they can have the international exposure, the services and access to the storage and distribution networks. More and more companies are looking at Dubai as a distribution and management centre for the whole of the Middle East and the Indian subcontinent."

Developments in Abu Dhabi and Dubai tend to overshadow activities elsewhere. Sharjah, the centre of light industry, has this year sanctioned the creation of two new free zones, at the international airport and at Al-Hamariyya port. In Fujairah, a new tourism board has been established to promote the emirate as a holiday destination. while Ras al-Khaimah is setting up another cement company, its fourth, to build a 1 million tonne-a-year plant.

The range of economic activity remains one of the UAE's great strengths in combating the periodic downturns in the oil market. Nevertheless, it is widely acknowledged that the oil price continues to have a disproportionate bearing on the economy's well being and that further diversification is required. Strong emphasis is being attached to the development of non-oil activity, whether it be through joint stock investment companies, like the recently-formed Dubai Investments, government agencies such as the UAE Offsets Group or private sector initiatives.

The attitude of the local private sector towards industrial investment varies considerably, although there are signs that more investors are becoming aware of its commercial benefits. "The older generation is still into real estate." says EBI's al-Jallaf. "They see it and understand it... and whenever they have some spare cash they will invest it in land, as they consider it safe. But there is also a whole new, younger generation coming along, who know that industry can deliver. What they tend to do is to set up some venture which runs parallel to their trading activities."

It is a measure of the UAE's current prosperity, however, that other aspects of economic reform have hardly got onto the political agenda. "I have been here four years and really in that time very little has changed," says a foreign diplomat in Abu Dhabi. "Subsidies remain in place, there has been no privatisation and still there isn't a stock exchange. The only difference is that now, there is at least some debate on the merits of such issues."

Next year may see some action. Bankers say that the review of the draft stock exchange rules is nearing completion and that 1996 should see the publication of a stock exchange law. In addition, the coming 12 months could provide some indication on whether Abu Dhabi is prepared to hand over the Taweelah power and desalination complex to the private sector, as several international companies have proposed.

Yet, few expect a sea-change in economic policy. Says the diplomat, "I think the trend is towards economic reform, but it won't be rushed. And really it doesn't need to be: The UAE's foreign debt is nominal, its domestic debt is small. There is still enough money around to satisfy most people's expectations."

A similar assessment was made in a recent study by the Emirates Industrial Bank on the possibility of greater private involvement in infrastructure projects. "For the UAE, although these are not pressing policy concerns, it might be worthwhile to start looking at the best institutional arrangements from a medium to long term perspective for managing the infrastructure and reducing the state's fiscal commitment," it said.

The government is more immediately concerned by wider prospects in the Gulf, particularly the question of stability. It is keen to set a conciliatory tone. In October, President Shaikh Zayed Bin Sultan al-Nahyan expressed the UAE's desire to see sanctions lifted on Iraq, onces Baghdad has complied with UN conditions on destroying its weapons of mass destruction programme. In mid-November, the first meeting in three years took place in Qatar between UAE and Iranian officials to discuss the disputed Gulf islands of Abu Musa and the Greater and Lesser Tumbs. The simmering dispute dates back to 1992, when Abu Dhabi accused Tehran of annexing the islands in contravention of earlier agreements.

On issues other than foreign policy, the UAE can seem but a loose collection of seven individual emirates, all eager to maintain their independence and sovereignty. The present arrangements seem to suit most emirates well. Says one Dubai-based analyst, "There is nothing wrong with devolved government. Everyone within the federation has staked out a position, no one is jousting for power." And as one foreign diplomat notes. "Others would be prepared to forego almost anything to be in the shape the UAE is in today."

Exchange rate: US$1: Db3,673

Questions:

1. What do you think is the main contributor to the UAE's rapid economic growth in 1995?

2. Compared with other Middle East states, the UAE has fewer problems, doesn't it? How has the UAE smoothed its way to economic grwoth?

3. In what way is Dubai consolidating its position as the region's leading location for trade?

4. What are the purposes of Dubai polishing its image?

5. What is meant by "Dubai... being strong on style but weak on substance"?

6. What have had multinational companies decide to choose Dubai for their opeerations?

7. How is the UAE's current prosperity measured?

8. Do you believe, according to the information gained from the

article, that the UAE will become the paragon of the other emirates?

Ⅱ. Translate the short article "Economy: the numbers add up to prosperity" into Chinese.

Economy: the numbers add up to prosperity

The UAE is expected to enjoy growth of up to 5 per cent this year, on the back of higher oil prices and an increase in non-oil activity. The bullish forecast comes on top of the 2.9 peer cent rise in gross domestic product (GDP) recorded in 1994 and lends further credence to the claim that the federation has the best performing economy in the GCC.

Oil continues to be the pilot of the UAE economy, accounting for about a third of total GDP. This year, oil revenues are projected to rise to just under $13,000 million—up from the 1994 figure of $12,300 million—as a result of firmer oil prices. The performance will inevitably bolster export earnings and consolidate the current account surplus, which in 1994 dropped by half to $450 million.

The balance of payments situation will also be helped by a continuing rise in re-exports. In the first six months of 1995, total re-exports out of Dubai rose by 7.3 per cent to $1,582 million, compared with $1,473 million in the corresponding period of 1993. The increase was achieved despite a 22 per cent fall in re-exports to Iran, Dubai's most important trade destination, and a slight drop in volumes to Saudi Arabia. Slack demand in both countries was more than offset by increased trade with India, Hong Kong, Qatar, Pakistan and Somalia.

The improved economic climate has been reflected in higher demand for credit. In the second quarter of 1995, domestic Jending by banks operating in the UAE grew by $1,420 million to $19,537 million. Much of the increased lending in the March-June period was to the private sector. At the end of June, loans outstanding to business stood at $18,620 million.

Details about government budgets in Abu Dhabi, Dubai and Sharjah are still kept under wraps, although judging from the levels of infrastructure and construction activity, spending is being maintained. As for the federal government, it has continued with its tradition of releasing half-yearly updates on spending and revenues. The latest bulletin covering the first six months of the year showed that an improvement in revenues, coupled with a tight grip on expenditure, led to a surplus of $232 million. This was well ahead of budget, which had projected a deficit of $288 million for the whole of 1995.

—From *MEED* · Dec. , 1995

Supplementary Material for Free Reading

Why Africa Can Thrive like Asia
(slightly revised)

By Nicholas D. Kristof

Kisangani, Congo

One of the great paradoxes of Africa is that its people are for the most part desperately poor while its land is extraordinarily rich. East Asia is the opposite: a region mostly poor in resources that over the last few decades has enjoyed the greatest economic boom in human history.

The area around this river port city in eastern Congo, the former Zaire, is a case in point: it is dilapidated and impoverished yet studded with diamonds, like a billionaire on Skid Row. Back in the 1950's, when this country and several others in Africa were at the same income level as South Korea while blessed with far more natural resources, it might have seemed reasonable that Africa would soon leave Asia in the dust.

Now South Korea has a per capita income of about $10,000 a year, and Congo stands at $150 per person. Narrowing the gap is a fundamental challenge for Congo's new leaders as they try to rebuild their country after the overthrow this month of the long-time Zairian dictator, Mobutu Sese Seko. And a vital first step, not only for this country but for others across Africa—and for big aid donors like the United States—is understanding why such yawning disparities have occurred.

A wave of new research into the contrast between Africa and East Asia is producing some surprising findings. The most striking and reassuring conclusion is that although East Asia enjoyed some significant cultural and historical advantages, its economic boom relied on factors that probably can be replicated elsewhere.

In a nutshell, the formula was an outward-oriented, market-based economic policy coupled with an emphasis on education and health care. Countries in other regions like Chile have followed the strategy with great success. Several African countries, led by Congo's neighbor Uganda, are trying to learn from the Asian experience and are enjoying their own Asian-style boom.

Encouraging Signs

Uganda, a beautiful, vividly green nation on the banks of Lake Victoria in East Africa, with vast herds of antelope that graze beside modern highways, now has one of the fastest-growing economies in the world. Yet it is simply at the crest of a wave of African countries experimenting with privatization and stock markets—there are 16 so far in Africa—and trying to prove that rapid economic growth is not a prerogative of East Asia alone.

"This is still in the early days, and we're not euphoric and jumping up and down, but we think that parts of Africa are moving in the right direction," said Alan H. Gelb, chief economist for Africa at the World Bank. "I think there are grounds for optimism."

At last count, four countries—Uganda, Angola, Lesotho and Malawi—were enjoying growth rates of 10 per cent. That is about as fast as the peak growth rates for the Asian "tigers," Hong Kong, Taiwan, Singapore and South Korea.

"There's an emerging consensus that Africa is not hopeless, and that in fact there is an emerging renaissance going on in Africa," said Salih Booker, a senior fellow at the Council on Foreign Relations.

But to travel the back roads here and in Asia is to be reminded how many opportunities Africa missed over the last few decades, and how much it continues to mortgage its future by giving short shrift to education and health care. The new research suggests that a central feature of the successful East Asian model was a high level of education and public health—a level partly inherited from past centuries and partly nurtured in recent decades. Despite its own ancient educational traditions, Africa lags far behind in building this "human capital."

In the little village of Lalia, in eastern Congo, the principal of the mud-brick elementary school throws up his hands at the challenges he faces educating the barefoot children who swarm around him.

"We have no notebooks and no teaching materials, and some teachers don't come because we cannot pay salaries," said the principal, Bibi Masakama, an energetic 32-year-old, as he showed a visitor around the school. The mud walls leaned ominously, and light came from holes in the walls that functioned as windows. Lizards ran about on the walls and on the rough wooden planks that served as desks and benches.

"None of these kids has ever been vaccinated against any disease," Mr. Masakama added. "None has ever had a medical examination."

Many reasons have been cited over the years for the different economic trajectories of Africa and East Asia. Some said that the colonial burden on Africa was much heavier, or that Africa was troubled more by artificial boundaries and disparate tribes and languages. Others, including some Africans, pointed to climate or culture.

"In Africa the climate is such that there's always fruit around, in back of the house, and you just reach up and pick it when you're hungry," said Alauwa Lobela, the mayor of Kisangani. "But in Europe and Asia, the climate forced people to get food, to protect themselves from the cold in the winter, to develop a spirit of battle."

Such climate-based explanations are common, and analysts have found that the economies of tropical countries do indeed grow a bit more slowly than those of temperate countries, all other things being equal. But the statistical relationship is slight, and one study suggested that climate explains only one-twentieth of the difference in economic performance between Africa and East Asia since 1965.

Of course, East Asia includes North Korea, healthy and well-educated but an economic disaster area facing famine, while Africa includes countries like Botswana that have prospered over the years. But regionally per capita incomes grew about 11 times faster in East Asia than in sub-Saharan Africa in the years since 1965.

Educated and Healthy

Why? Economists point to a conjunction of factors associated with rapid growth: places like Japan, China, Taiwan and South Korea underwent land redistribution after World War II and became relatively egalitarian societies; they were relatively well-educated and healthy, and they experienced a sharp drop in birth rates. On top of that, economic policies were ideal: the East Asian countries sooner or later adopted relatively open, market-oriented policies emphasizing exports.

East Asian countries pursued various economic models, but there was also a common economic strategy, which countries like Uganda are now emulating. The strategy emphasizes fiscal prudence and avoiding inflation while vigorously promoting exports and keeping the currency undervalued. In the past, African countries often tolerated soaring inflation and overvalued their currencies, keeping exports uncompetitive on world markets.

The Path

A critical factor has been savings, which are needed to finance new factories and other investments that stimulate economic growth. Partly because of market incentives and government dictates, national savings rates have been much higher in Asia (more than 30 per cent of gross domestic product) than in Africa (about 12 per cent).

"Our problem is that we don't save," lamented Samuel Ndomba, a British-educated professor at the University of Kisangani in Congo. "When people get a bit of money, they just spend it to buy a beer."

That might change, though, were there more incentives for investment. There is nothing intrinsically Asian about high savings, for Japan had very low savings rates in the 19th century. They soared in part because of Government campaigns and the spread of deposit-taking institutions, and eventually financed Japan's industrial revolution.

One major reason not to save and invest in Africa has been inflation and instability: when people save money, it often ends up being confiscated. Victoria Baenongandi, for example, lasted just two weeks as an entrepreneur in eastern Congo. She bought a pile of merchandise to resell, but everything was seized by soldiers. So she returned home and gave up on business—and put her savings into beer.

Economic policy aside, East Asia enjoyed another crucial advantage over Africa, one that may be harder to replicate. Countries like South Korea or even China started the development process with citizens who were more literate and more healthy than those in other nations at their income levels, and they continued to improve. For all of China's persistent poverty, a child born in Shanghai in the early 1990's was more likely to learn to read and more likely to survive childhood than a baby born in New York City.

Some experts argue that East Asia's success in education derives not from government programs—Asian governments actually spend a smaller share of G. N. P. on education than do African governments. Rather, literacy and other education achievements in Asia may have been helped greatly by a culture of parental concern that supports enormous private spending on education, arising from a Confucian reverence for scholarship.

Because of Confucianism, China has had national exams and the rough equivalent of university graduates for 2,000 years. In contrast, Tanzania is said to have had only 13 university graduates at independence in 1961.

Their histories also meant that most Asian countries slipped farily easily into the form of the modern nation-state, for they had a sense of nationhood that in some cases went back for millenniums. On the other hand, some African countries—a hodgepodge of ethnic groups within borders drawn arbitrarily by colonial rulers—are still struggling to adjust to modern nationhood. Such instability has always been fatal to economic development, whether in Cambodia or in Mozambique.

Health problems have also been a greater economic burden on Africa than is often realized. Most Africans, for example, have stomach worms, and as a result millions of people cannot study or work energetically, and some children have their intelligence permanently impaired because of anemia caused by the parasites.

"From the age of two, most people here have worms," shrugged Bakondagama Barandala, a 24-year-old nurse at a shabby clinic in Mambasa, in northeastern Congo. The clinic is a metaphor for public health in Congo: it is the only clinic in the region, yet it has no doctor, no electricity, no drinking water, no instruments and no medicines.

The Graft Factor

For all the importance of education and health care, the cultivation of human capital seems to be effective only in tandem with the right economic policies. China was healthy and literate for its income level in the early 1960's when it underwent one of the worst economic contractions and famines in world history. Likewise, Tanzania for many years vigorously promoted education and health, but it stagnated because of catastrophic economic policies inspired by a quasi-socialist ideology.

One reason for some optimism about Africa now is its parallels with Asian countries earlier this century. Much like Asia was before its boom, Africa is relatively egalitarian in wealth, partly because land is not concentrated in the hands of a small elite (as in parts of Latin America). Similarly, in many African countries birth rates are dropping and literacy is rising.

Among the most important studies of the lessons of East Asia are a 337-page report edited by two Harvard economists and just released by the Asian Development Bank, and another major report published by the World Bank in 1993. Those studies and related research point to other factors that go along with the nurturing of financial and human capital—especially the effectiveness of Asian governments.

Asian governments have often been more effective than Africa's in part because they have been less corrupt. Asia has huge amounts of corruption by American standards, but for the most part graft there is just another cost of doing business; in Africa it often prevents business from being done at all. A joke heard in business circles makes the point:

An African visited an Asian friend, a government official, and admired the official's spectacular home and opulent life style. The Asian explained his wealth with a wink toward his "cut": "You see that highway out there? Fifteen per cent!"

Then the Asian visited the African, also a government official, and found that he was living just as lavishly. Asked how he had prospered, the African pointed outside, saying: "You see that highway out there?"

"No," the Asian said, peering helplessly out the window. "What highway?"

"That's just it. One hundred per cent."

—From *New York Times* • May 25, 1997

Lesson 10

On GATT—WTO

Text

Freer Trade, with Luck

In the past few days differences between the United States and the European Community on farm trade have narrowed almost to nothing. As a result the world is now close to concluding the Uruguay round of GATT talks. That deal is admittedly far from perfect, a series of messy compromises. The cause of free trade will have many more battles to fight. Never mind. On a conservative estimate the Uruguay round would permanently raise global welfare by more than $100 billion a year, spur economic growth everywhere (especially in the world's poorest countries) and extend competition to hither to sheltered, and therefore backward, parts of all economies. By any standards, it would be a hugely valuable achievement.

Such opportunities come too rarely to be squandered. Yet this one still may be. In the most recent talks about farm trade, America has shown a new willingness to compromise on details, doubtless reflecting George Bush's need for an economic success to boast of in his election campaign. Whatever the motive a spirit of compromise makes sense for America, since it stands to gain a lot more from a successful round than any other country. But the EC continues to hesitate—because of France. French farmers are violently opposed to the reform of the common agricultural policy (CAP) that Europe's governments agreed to last May. In certain respects, the farmers claim, the GATT deal now in prospect would take that reform further, damaging their interests even more.

If it is a small matter to France's farmers that the Uruguay round should fail, so long as they keep their subsidies, that is understandable. What is shameful is that their government appears to agree with them, even though most of the French economy (including many of the country's more efficient farmers) would gain handsomely from a successful round. Jean-Pierre Soisson, the farm minister ,has said France may block the EC's acceptance of a new farm-trade deal, and thereby wreck the round. This position is politically alarming as well as economically indefensible. Other EC governments must see off France, and start hailing a gain for liberal trade.

He carries his heart in his boots

Disputes over farm trade have bedevilled the current round of GATT talks from the start. That is unsurprising. For decades governments everywhere have suppressed market forces in agriculture with subsidies, tariffs, quotas, monopoly purchasing boards and all the other paraphernalia of mule-headed intervention. No industry in the world has been pushed further, or so needlessly, from the liberal ideal of guiding resources to their best use by means of prices set in markets. On one plausible estimate, consumers in industrial countries pay $300 billion a year in taxes and higher prices to support farming. Even allowing for the income transferred to farmers, the net welfare loss caused by the industrial countries' farm policies is $100 billion a year. Distortions on such a scale have given a comparative handful of people every reason to fight to the bitter end for economic lunacy. On October 14th French farmers held another "day of action" —blocking roads, planting wheat in awkward places and so forth—in protest at the planned reforms.

What exactly are those reforms? The benchmark remains the scheme set out by Arthur Dunkel, the GATT's director-general, in 1991. On cereals, where Europe and America have squabbled most fiercely, Mr Dunkel suggested cuts of 20% in the value of the CAP's production subsidies, 36% in the value of its export subsidies, and 24% in the volume of its subsidised exports. America said it would settle for nothing less. The EC then came up with a new plan to refrom the CAP. Its main idea is to replace some production subsidies with direct payments to farmers; these payments, though not entirely divorced from output, will be semi-detached. The value of the CAP's "subsidies" would therefore fall by enough to meet the Dunkel targets; but output would probably fall by too little to meet the target of a 24% cut in the volume of subsidised exports.

America objected to that, and asked whether the proposed "direct payments" were not really production subsidies in disguise. The talks have been snagged on those issues for the past four months. On October 13th, however, agreement on both points moved within reach. America's negotiators said that the CAP's new direct payments would not, after all, be regarded as production subsidies. And it seemed that a way could be found to satisfy America on the 24% cut in volumes. Several formulas are under discussion. (One would bind the EC to cut by 21%; another would allow it to cut by less than 24% in some crops if it cut by more than 24% in others.) Officials on both sides were optimistic that a deal on farming, which would unlock the rest of the round, was within reach.

A separate, long-running dispute over oilseeds does still pose a threat. Unlike cereals and other farm goods, which the Uruguay round aimed to bring within the GATT's jurisdiction for the first time, oilseeds (which are used for making cooking oil, margarine and animal feed) already fall within it. Twice America has complained to GATT that Europe is in breach of its undertakings; twice GATT has ruled against the EC. America wants the Community to cut its oilseeds output by nearly half over the next six years. The EC is willing to cut, but not by that much. Here too, the gap between the two sides appears to have narrowed a lot during the past few days.

Governments need to reflect on the broader deal that, because of this progress in the farm-trade talks, has once again moved within their grasp. In 1985, just before the round was launched, America's chief trade negotiator set out the administration's goals for the talks. They were suitably ambitious. On nearly every heading, the round as it now stands has delivered.

The draft agreement contains many sensible new rules for global trade (covering, for instance, the settlement of disputes, the protectionist use of technical standards, anti-dumping measures, subsidies, countervailing duties, government procurement and many other implicit barriers to trade). To promote trade and innovation, it offers new safeguards to owners of intellectual property. It brings trade in services into the GATT for the first time, opening new foreign markets to efficient producers of services in America and Europe. America's ambitious early goals for farm-trade liberalisation will not be fully met by the compromise that is now within reach; but even in farming, a half-successful round will deliver great benefits. And if this package can be banked, future rounds will be obliged to argue over how much to cut farm protection, not whether—an achievement in itself.

A recent study of the benefits of a half-successful round concluded that America would gain an annual $35 billion, Japan and Europe nearly $30 billion apiece, and the rest of world about $25 billion: a global gain of roughly $120 billion a year. These estimates are doubly conservative. They understate the effect that trade reform could have on long-term growth (which many economists believe to be substantial) and they take account of fewer reforms than the new compromise would include. True, "radical" liberalisation would more than double those figures, but that is no reason to sneer at a deal that can be done here and now.

Gattcha

America has shown some flexibility, and Europe should respond. Much of the EC would like to. Germany's willingness to embrace farm reform enabled the Community to produce its planned reform of the CAP last spring. Germany's role over the next few days will again be crucial, for it must tell France that its threat to block the Uruguay round is intolerable. To carry out that threat, France is likely to need German support. The Community decides its trade policy by qualified majority vote; France has no straight forward right of veto. Without allies, its only course would be to block the decision by citing "vital national interests"—the sort of profoundly unEuropean thing that Britain might do, but which France would rather not.

The GATT saga has dragged on too long already. But it might just have been worth the wait. A good agreement is there for the taking. If governments care for their citizens at large as opposed to noisy lobbies, they will grab it.

—From *The Economist* · Oct. 17, 1992

Words and Expressions

admittedly	*ad.* 公认地
spur	*v.* 促进;激励;鞭策
economic growth	促进经济发展
hitherto	*ad.* 迄今为止
squander	*v.* 浪费;挥霍
make sense	讲得通,有意义;言之成理,合情合理
prospect	*n.* 预期;展望
in prospect	期望中的,展望中的

subsidies	*n.* subsidy 的复数,津贴;补贴(本文中指政府给予农场主的农产品补贴)
wreck	*v.* 破坏;毁坏
the economy	破坏经济
an agreement	破坏协议
the round	破坏这一回合谈判
indefensible	*a.* 不可原谅的
bedevil	*v.* 使困惑;使受挫 a question that has long bedevilled the West 长期以来困扰西方的问题
carry one's heart in one's boots	吓得要命;焦急万分
paraphernalia	*n.* [复]复杂的程序;烦琐的手续
mule-headed	顽固的;固执的
plausible	*a.* 貌似有理的
stand	*v.* 定然会
distortion	*n.* 歪曲;曲解
lunacy	*n.* 疯狂愚蠢的行为;荒谬
benchmark	*n.* 基准尺度
squabble	*v.* (为琐事)争吵 squabble with sb. about (over) sth.
settle	*v.* 解决争端
replace … with	*v.* 代替;取代
detached	*a.* 独立的;分离的
disguise	*n.* 伪装;掩饰 in disguise 化装了的
snag	*v.* 被缠住;被绊住 The talks have been snagged on those issues for the past four months. 在过去四个月中,谈判一直在这些问题上纠缠不清。

pose a threat	形成一种威胁
jurisdiction	*n.* 管辖范围(联合国文件常用词)
be in breach of	违反…,与…相违背
implicit	*a.* 不言明的;含蓄的
deliver	*v.* 实现
apiece	*v.* 各个计算;逐一
saga	*n.* (口)一长串事件
for the taking	供自由拿取

Notes to the Text

1. 关税及贸易总协定(GATT, the General Agreement on Tariffs and Trade)

1947年,23个工业国家在日内瓦召开会议,讨论互相减少贸易壁垒事宜,最后他们达成了关税及贸易总协定。如今关贸总协定共有110多个签约国,其贸易往来几乎占世界贸易的90%。它的基本目的就是减少贸易壁垒。

关贸总协定的第一个协议于1948年1月生效。除了削减关税以外,它还制定了国际贸易的指导原则,如最惠国待遇。这些原则仍然是当前实行的各种贸易规则的基础。

关贸总协定最初是作为当时联合国筹建的国际贸易组织机构内部的一个具体贸易协议而提出的。该协议在国际贸易组织得到批准通过之前达成,为的是加快贸易开放进程。此协议只规定了最基本的组织安排,由于国际贸易组织的建立未能获得美国国会的批准,推行关贸总协定的工作实体就逐渐发展成为监督国际贸易的主要机构。

关贸总协定自1947年到目前已进行了8个回合的多边贸易谈判。

第一回合:1947年在日内瓦举行。23个创始国决定在世界范围内降低45 000种贸易关税；

第二回合：1949 年在法国阿讷西举行。参加这一轮谈判的 13 个国家建议再削减5 000种商品的关税；

第三回合：1950—1951 年在英国的托基举行。38 个参加谈判的国家对8 700种关税进行了削减；

第四回合：1955—1956 年在日内瓦举行。26 个参加国决定进一步降低总额达 25 亿美元的关税；

第五回合，即狄龙回合：1960—1962 年在日内瓦举行。26 个国家决定对4 400种关税进行削减；

第六回合，即肯尼迪回合：1964—1967 年在日内瓦举行。62 个参加国决定对所有工业品的关税进行大规模削减，并在粮油及化学品问题上达成一致；

第七回合，即东京回合：1973 年在东京开始，1979 年在日内瓦结束。99 个参加国决定把关税平均降低 20%～30%，并决定为世界贸易建立一个良好的框架；

第八回合，即乌拉圭回合：1986 年在乌拉圭埃斯特角城开幕，1993 年 12 月 15 日在日内瓦落下帷幕，历时 7 年 3 个月。

2. Uruguay round of GATT talks　关税及贸易总协定乌拉圭回合谈判

乌拉圭回合是关贸总协定建立以来的第八轮谈判，是内容最多，规模最大，最重要的，也是在关贸总协定监督指导下召开的最后一轮全球多边贸易谈判。这轮谈判发动的背景是：20 世纪 80 年代初，主要工业发达国家经历了严重的经济衰退，各国为解燃眉之急，争相采取贸易保护主义措施，世界贸易发展受到严重阻碍。为避免保护主义蔓延而导致 30 年代世界经济大萧条的重演以及全面贸易战的发生，在美、欧、日共同倡议下，1986 年 9 月关贸总协定在乌拉圭埃斯特角城召开部长级会议，发动了新的一轮多边贸易谈判。

乌拉圭回合谈判涉及到各种工农业产品的市场准入、服务贸易、建立多边贸易组织等 15 个领域。谈判原定在 1990 年 12 月结束，但欧美在农产品贸易问题上意见分歧严重，无法按时达成一致。

1993 年 7 月 1 日，新上任的总干事萨瑟兰要求在 12 月 15 日前必须结束谈判。美、欧、日之间虽矛盾重重，但彼此利益交织，谁也承担不起谈判失败的责任。经反复讨价还价，终于达成全面协议，致使这一回合的谈判于日内瓦时间 1993 年 12 月 15 日 19 时 34 分在日内瓦国际会议中心正式结束。

根据乌拉圭回合最后文本，117 个参加方的关税总水平将削减约 40%。农产品关税，工业化国家将在 6 年内削减 36%，发展中国家在 10 年内削减 24%。

最后文本规定建立世界贸易组织（WTO），取代关贸总协定。届时，WTO 将在联合国经济组织体系中取得与国际货币基金组织和世界银行同等的地位。

最后文本规定纺织品贸易自由化，多种纤维协议将在 10 年内废除。

1994 年 4 月 15 日，109 个政府在摩洛哥马拉喀什签署了最后文本——有史以来世界上最大的贸易协定，以消除贸易壁垒和推动全球繁荣。预料这项协定在 10 年内就能将全球收入提高2 000多亿美元。

与此同时，97 个国家的部长们签署了一份附加文件，宣布成立世界贸易组织——关贸总协定的新型的、得到改善的替身。

世界贸易组织已于 1995 年 1 月 1 日起行使其职能，负责管理乌拉圭回合谈判达成的各项协议。其宗旨是，提高生活和收入水平、实现充分就业、扩大生产与贸易和以最佳方式利用世界资源。

世界贸易组织还将与国际货币基金组织和世界银行合作，通过具有透明度的管理框架制定世界性的经济政策、取消妨碍世界贸易的种种壁垒。

3. “In the past few days differences between the United States and the European community on farm trade have narrowed almost to nothing.”

美欧之间在农产品问题上的争论持续时间最长，贯穿乌拉圭回合谈判始终，是妨碍谈判成功的主要障碍。

美国为与欧共体争夺农产品市场，要求双方至 2000 年全部取消对农产品的补贴和贸易壁垒，欧共体强烈反对，双方为此对峙数年。

进入1993年后,美国在农产品出口补贴问题上的立场没有改变,而在另一些问题上持强硬态度,向欧共体施加压力。为了使谈判不致破裂,造成两败俱伤,欧共体内部进行了紧张的协调,统一了立场。到1993年12月7日,美欧双方都做了让步,终于在农产品出口补贴问题上达成了协议。

4. "That deal is admittedly far from perfect, a series of messy compromises."

此句中的deal一词指整个乌拉圭回合谈判中的各项协议。乌拉圭回合谈判的有些议题是从双边谈判中他们之间的具体问题开始,不是从所有参与国的利害需求出发;而谈判又主要是在美、欧和日本等世界贸易大国之间进行,因此所产生的协议文件不能全面反映所有有关国家的意愿和充分体现所有参加国,特别是发展中国家的利益。因而作者用了a series of messy compromises (一系列混乱的妥协)来形容这次谈判所得到的结果。

5. on a conservative estimate　据保守估计

on one plausible estimate　据合理的估算

在此类介词短语中,on可以用at代替,意思不变。

如:at a rough estimate　据粗略估计

类似的短语还有:on current estimate　据目前估计。

6. George Bush　乔治·布什,美国第四十一届总统

7. "Whatever the motive, a spirit of compromise..."

这是一个用连接代词whatever (不论,不管)引导的表让步的状语从句,经常省略动词be(与no matter what...意思相同)。例如:

We will try to sell the product abroad, whatever the cost.

不论代价如何,我们要努力把产品销往外国。

Whatever the twists and turns (are), our future is bright.

不论道路多么迂回曲折,我们的前途是光明的。

8. "But the EC continues to hesitate—because of France."

农业是法国花大力气发展起来的产业,多年出口连续顺差,扶持农业是法国的重要国策。因此,法国在减少农产品出口补贴问题上一直持强硬态度。1992年11月20日欧共体和美国在华盛顿的布

莱尔宫就农产品贸易问题的协议一出台，法国立即表示反对，要求重新谈判。

9. Common Agriculture Policy (CAP)　共同农业政策

《罗马条约》中制定的农业政策。其主要目标是：提高农业生产率，保证农业社区的良好社会水平，稳定市场并确保按合理价格向消费者提供剩余物资。

共同农业政策的核心是产量不限，价格保证。欧共体以最低限价收购农场主的产品，即使是只能作为库存的剩余产品，然后在国际市场上按补贴后的价格销售。

共同农业政策的产量及价格保证在一些地区刺激了过剩生产，其结果是共同体的大部分资金用于补贴农产品出口，共同农业政策花费增加，而农场主的收入并没有增加。

1992年，共同体开始对其共同农业政策进行改革。改革的五个主要目标是：

1. 使农场主在国内及出口市场上更有竞争力。保持共同体作为主要农产品生产和出口商的地位。

2. 降低产量使其更加接近市场需求水平。但不能影响农场主的收入。价格方面的损失将由直接补贴抵消。

3. 对农场主的支持集中在最需要支持的收入方面。

4. 鼓励农场主从事农业。

5. 保护环境，开发农村的自然资源潜力。

10. "If it is a small matter to France's farmers that the Uruguay round should fail, so long as they keep their subsidies, it is understandable."

句中划线部分使用了虚拟语气(the subjunctive mode)的动词表示所说与将来事实可能相反。虚拟语气是一种特殊的动词形式，用来表示说话人所说的话不是一个事实，而只是一种愿望、假设、怀疑、建议、猜测、可能或纯粹的空想等。

11. market forces　市场力量

市场上决定一商品或服务价格的因素，主要指供应和需求。

12. allow for　考虑到，顾及，为…留出余地例：Allowing for the train being late, we should be back by eleven.

把火车晚点的可能性估计在内，11 点之前我们总可以到家了。

We must allow for the changes in demand when we make production plans.

在作生产计划时我们必须考虑到需求的变化。

13. Authur Dunkel 阿瑟·邓克尔

瑞士人。担任关贸总协定总干事 13 年，于 1993 年 7 月让位于彼得·萨瑟兰。这位资深外交家努力以妥协和务实的精神推进宏伟的世界贸易改革的谈判。他在任关贸总协定总干事一职期间，曾多次来中国参加各种会议，对中国进行友好访问。

14. "the protectionist use of technical standards"

一个国家或地区贸易集团为了抵制或控制外来进口产品施行贸易保护主义，可以使用技术手段达到目的，如：对进口品采用与其不同的技术规格检查，实行重复检查，设立高的检验标准等。

15. countervailing duty 反补贴税

又称"抵消税"，是指对接受过补贴的外国商品在进口时所征收的一种附加税。征收的税额应与其所接受的补贴数额相等，其目的在于抵消进口商品在降低成本方面所获得的额外好处，使它不能在进口市场上进行低价竞争或倾销，以保护进口国同类商品的生产。反补贴税是各国争夺市场的一个重要武器。

16. intellectual property right 知识产权

法律规定的人们对自己脑力劳动创造的精神财富所享有的权利，由版权和工业产权两大部分组成。按 1967 年在斯德哥尔摩缔结的"建立世界知识产权组织公约"的规定，它包括下列内容：关于(1)文学、艺术和科学著作；(2)演员的表演、唱片和广播；(3)人类致力于一切技术领域的发明；(4)科学发现；(5)工业品外观设计；(6)商标、服务标志、厂商名称和标记；(7)制止不正当竞争。目前世界上绝大多数国家对知识产权在不同程度上给予承认，并制定了有关法律加以保护。

17. trade in services 服务贸易

通常指国际服务贸易，即指国家间的服务输入和输出。服务贸易的内容很广，根据关贸总协定中的服务贸易总协定可将服务贸易的通常项目分为：国际运输，国际旅游，跨国银行，国际金融公司及其他金融服务，国际保险，国际信息处理和传递，电脑及资料服务，国际租赁，国际咨询服务，维修和保养、技术指导等售后服务，国际视听服务，教育、卫生、文化艺术的国际交流服务，商业批发和售后服务以及官方国际服务等。

18. "... the sort of profoundly unEuropean thing that Britain might do, but which France would rather not."

20 世纪 80 年代，英国在撒切尔夫人执政期间经常为了本国的一些利益，不顾欧共体大多数成员国反对，做出一些作为欧共体大家庭成员不应所为的事。英国在 80 年代初期为欧共体预算英国份额一事无休止的争吵，致使欧共体首脑会议无法正常进行，就是一个很好的例子。而法国一贯以顾全大局自誉，认为欧共体成员国应该团结一致对外，不应以本国的利益损害大家庭的利益。因此人们认为法国不会作出有损于欧共体整个利益的事。

19. "The GATT saga has dragged on too long already."

saga 一字在口语中指长篇记述、长篇故事、一连串事件等。GATT saga 在本文中具体指关贸总协定乌拉圭回合谈判自 1986 年 9 月开始，经历了不同时期各种这样的事件，到本文发表时仍未结束和取得预期的结果。

20. "If governments care for their citizens at large, as opposed to noisy lobbies, they will grab it."

lobby 原意为"走廊"，现用作"院外活动集团"之意，指常在议会走廊或休息室活动、游说，企图说服议员支持某项行动的社会势力的代表。

Questions on Content and Language Points

(for preview, discussion and review)

1. Interpret the title "Free Trade, with Luck" after your study

of the whole article.

2. "On a conservative estimate, the Uruguay round would permanently raise global welfare by more than $100 billion a year, spur economic growth everywhere (especially in the world's poorest countries) and extend competition to hitherto sheltered, and therefore backward, parts of all economies."

1) On what grounds does it say "the Uruguay round... would spur economic growth everywhere"?

2) What does "sheltered" mean here?

Why would an economy be backward once it is "sheltered"?

3. "In certain respects, the farmers clain, the GATT deal now in prospect would take that reform further, damaging their interests even more."

What part of the sentence is the participial phrase introduced by "damaging"?

4. What's the meaning of "so long as" in the first sentence of the 3rd paragraph?

5. What expression best replaces "see off" in the last sentence of the 3rd paragraph "Other EC governments must see off France, and start hailing a gain for liberal trade"?

And what is the exact meaning of "hailing"? Does it mean "welcome"?

6. "For decades governments everywhere have suppressed market forces in agriculture with subsidies, tariffs, quotas, monopoly purchasing boards and all the other paraphernalia of mule-headed intervention."

1) What does "market forces" refer to chiefly?

2) In what way could "subsidies" suppress market forces in the farm trade?

7. The word "awkward" in the middle of Paragraph 4 could mean "inconvenient, improper or embarrassing". Which of these

could best fit the context?

8. "What exactly are those (CAP) reforms?" This question is brought forth in the 5th paragraph of the text. Can you find the answer to the question?

9. "On cereals, where Europe and America have squabbled most fiercely,..."

In the above sentence quoted, the word squabble is used. Could you guess from his wording what the writer thought about the argument between Europe and America?

10. In Paragraph 5, the GATT director-general suggested cuts in the EC's subsidies to their farmers and on this "America said it would settle for nothing less."

What attitude do you think America took towards the reforms suggested by Dr. Dunkel for the EC? (What does to settle for some-thing mean?)

11. Why couldn't the target of 24% cut in the volume of the EC's subsidized exports be met?

12. Paraphrase the underlined part of the following sentence:

"On October 13th, however, agreement on both points moved within reach."

13. "Officials on both sides were optimistic that a deal on farming, which would unlock the rest of the round, was within reach."

1) What does "the rest of the round" refer to?

2) Can you find a word to replace "unlock?"

14. "... twice GATT has ruled against the EC."

What is the meaning of "to rule" in the given context?

15. "Governments need to reflect on the broader deal that because of this progress in the farm-trade talks, has once again moved within their grasp."

1) What does "to reflect on something" mean here?

2) What does "the broader deal" refer to?

16. "In 1985, just before the round was launched, America's chief trade negotiator set out the administration's goals for the talks. They were suitably ambitious. On nearly every heading, the round as it now stands has declined."

What does "heading" refer to here?

(Find out the answer within the passage quoted.)

17. "To promote trade and innovation, it offers new safeguards to owners of intellectual property."

1) Define "safeguards".

2) Why would trade and innovation be promoted with safeguards offered to owners of intellectual property?

18. "Gattcha" (the heading for the 2nd paragraph from the bottom.)

"Gattcha" is a compound word coined by the writer, which is supposed to be composed of 2 parts —Gatt and "cha". Cha-cha is a rhythmic dance originated in Latin America.

Could you make out what is meant by "Gattcha" here, with the information given above?

19. "... Without allies, its only course would be to block the decision by citing vital national interests—the sort of profoundly un-European thing that Britain might do, but France would rather not."

1) What does "course" mean here?

2) What is your understanding of the "unEuropean thing"?

20. Make a brief summary of the farm trade issue that bedeviled the Uruguay round of GATT talks and the way to settle it according to the text.

Exercises

Read the article given below and decide whether the following statements are true or false.

Greater Wealth of Nations

Conclusions of the Uruguay Round is truly a triumph in adversity. Securing agreement among so many countries on such a complex raft of trade agreements frequently seemed an insuperable challenge in the past seen years. To have done it at a time of sluggish growth, political uncertainty and protectionist pressures is an extraordinary achievement.

Whatever the shortcomings of the result, the original vision of a broad expansion of international trade law is now much closer to fulfillment. More remarkably still so is the dream that drove the founding fathers of the General Agreement on Tariffs and Trade: that of a liberal, rules-based international trading system overseen by an authoritative world trade organization. Just as the GATT helped foster economic integration and growth in the postwar decades, the new agreement should provide powerful underpinning for the world economy, fresh impetus to competition, fresh hope for those developing and former communist countries that have been opening up to international commerce.

Several individuals deserve credit. Mr. Peter Sutherland and before him Mr. Arthur Dunkel, Gatt directors-general worked tirelessly to cajole recalcitrants—especially the US and EU—into settling differences. Mr. Mickey Kantor, US trade representative, has dispelled the most serious doubts about his and the administration's commitment to multilateral free trade. Sir Leo Brittan, the European trade commissioner, played a difficult hand with consummate skill and by luring France into the fold, arguably saved the Union from a political crisis of alarming proportions.

Reduced Danger

The importance of the Final Act of the Uruguay Round is essentially threefold. First, as well as containing substantial tariff cuts, it promises to bring large areas of trade that have up to now been "outside the law" —above all in farm produce, services and textiles — within GATT disciplines. Inclusion of farm trade, though incomplete, will reduce the danger of international conflict over dumping of subsidised surpluses, reinforce market-based agricultural reforms that are gradually being introduced in the developed world, and give developing countries a better chance of exploiting their comparative advantage as food producers. The accord on services —though also not as far-reaching as hoped—begins the extension of rules to the fastest-growing sector of world trade, and in theory could generate gains as great as those stimulated by the establishment of multilateral disciplines for manufactures more than 40 years ago. In textiles, gradual phasing out of the protectionist Multifibre Arrangement will eventually allow greater international competition and force overdue restructuring of textile industries in the developed world.

Tougher Protection

Second, the agreement will deliver tougher protection for intellectual property rights, a source of increasing conflict between developed and developing countries. Third, it provides for a significant elaboration of rules designed to ensure that trade is air as well as free. It promises greater clarity concerning when and for how long countries will be permitted to resort to "safeguard" measures against imports, to impose anti-dumping duties and to subsidize domestic industries. While this does not go as far as intended in the previous draft Final Act of December 1991, the overall aim has not in the end been fatally compromised.

All this is not to say that a brave new world of perfectly liberal trade is at hand. Significant uncertainties remain concerning the trade policies of the biggest players, the US and EU, with the former reaching all too readily for unilateral instruments of "managed trade" and the latter increasingly following suit. At least one large, and rapidly growing, trading power—China—remains outside the multilateral framework. Moreover, yesterday's accord does not touch on emerging trade issues, from competition policy to the environment, which will offer ample potential for conflict in future. These matters will deserve urgent attention as soon as the ink from the Uruguay Round is dry. Before that, however, the signatories should celebrate a victory for the international rule of law, and concentrate on getting the accord ratified and implemented.

——From *Financial Times* · December 16, 1993

True-and-false questions:

1. It was not difficult for the member countries of the GATT to reach an agreement on trade. (　　)

2. Although the agreement reached in the Uruguay Round negotiation is believed to be a remarkable achievement, it offers nothing new to the world economy. (　　)

3. The member states of European Union, which negotiated as one party, took a unanimous stand on all questions from beginning to end in the Uruguay Round. (　　)

4. Many countries in the world subsidize their agricultural production and exports. (　　)

5. As the Multifibre Arrangement is an agreement reached between the textile producers and textile importers, it can satisfy the needs of both parties and help the world trade liberalization. (　　)

6. As the ultimate goal of the GATT is to achieve fair and free trade, no member country has the right to use protectionist measures under any conditions. (　　)

7. It is only the U. S. who reaches all too readily for unilateral instruments of "managed trade" in settling trade disputes with other countries. (　　)

8. Member countries should not take the Final Act of the Uruguay Round negotiation as the guarantee for the elimination of future conflicts in world trade. (　　)

Supplementary Material for Free Reading

Fifty Years On

LONDON AND WASHINGTON. DC

World leaders are about to celebrate the multilateral trading system's golden jubilee in Geneva. The past half-century has given free traders much to smile about. But their job is far from done.

In 1948 a club of 23 countries cut tariffs on each other's exports under the General Agreement on Tariffs and Trade, the first multilateral accord to lower border barriers since Napoleonic times. *The Economist*, we must confess, reacted somewhat equivocally. To assess the exact consequences of an agreement involving 106 sets of bilateral negotiations and two volumes of liberalisation schedules weighing eight pounds was, we concluded, "an impossible task". We feared that the GATT's complexity and its members' "caution and timidity" would hobble the intended growth of trade.

Our scepticism proved ill-founded. The GATT set in train a series of ever-thicker agreements that removed many of the shackles restricting trade. Today, average tariffs are a mere tenth of what they were when the GATT came into force. Ministers attending the World Trade Organisation's 50th-birthday jamboree in Geneva during May 18th-20th can therefore be forgiven a little mutual back-patting. But the mood of celebration ought not to obscure the fact that, 50 years on, the GATT's work is unfinished. A great deal of trade reform is still required, and by now is long overdue.

Since the GATT was implemented in 1948 there have been eight "rounds" of global trade talks, each involving more countries, and taking liberalisation further, than the last. The most recent of these, the Uruguay round completed in 1993, was also the most ambitious. Negotiators succeeded in crafting rules to govern trade in services and to protect intellectual property such as patents and computer software, matters which had previously been outside the GATT's purview.

The round's other success was the creation of the WTO. Unlike the loosely organised GATT, the WTO was set up as a permanent organization with far greater powers to arbitrate trade disputes. Under the GATT, any member-even one found to have violated the rules—could block a ruling that it had erected unfair trade barriers. In contrast, the findings of the WTO's dispute panels are not hostage to veto. Countries found to be in the wrong must change their ways or offer compensation; those that do neither face sanctions.

The prospect of swifter justice seems to have convinced governments to bring their trade disputes to the WTO instead of engaging in tit-for-tat retaliation. In just three years the WTO has dealt with 132 complaints; over its 47-year existence, the GATT heard only 300. The mechanism has not merely been used by big countries to trample small fry, as some feared: when Costa Rica asked the WTO to rule against American barriers to its exports of men's underwear, it won the case and forced America to change its import rules.

The WTO has been so successful that more than 30 countries, including China and Russia, are now queueing up to join. The membership has already grown to 132 countries. And the organisation has continued to oversee impressive growth in world trade (see chart on next page). Last year the volume of merchandise trade grew by 9.5%, over three times faster than global output. The East Asian crisis will slow things down this year, though growth in trade is still expected to outpace growth in production.

Fears that the Uruguay round would be followed by a prolonged lull in trade liberalisation have proved misplaced. Last year several strands that had been left dangling were tied, notably "sectoral" agreements to lower trade barriers in telecommunications, financial services and information technology. These deals were important for three reasons. They greatly increased the amount of trade covered by the WTO's rules and dispute-settlement procedures. They may lead to larger gains in trade volumes than the entire Uruguay round treaty. And they finished most of the round's left-over business, clearing the way for a new round of global talks to deal with obstacles that still inhibit trade.

Now Look Forward

With so much achieved, trade ministers might seem entitled to feel smug. They aren't. Protectionism, though waning, is still commonplace. In textiles and agriculture, tariffs remain high and progress in eliminating import quotas has been slow. Little advance has been made in lowering trade barriers in areas such as shipping and access for foreign workers.

The trouble is, many countries still think of opening their markets to more imports as a concession to be made reluctantly, not(as economists see it) as something that is good for them in its own right. Even America and the European Union, which have led the push for open markets, still shelter parts of their economies for fear of hurting workers in coddled industries.

Globalisation has aroused worries in many rich countries that free trade with much poorer countries threatens jobs and prosperity. This was plain in last year's debate in the United States over expanding the North American Free Trade Agreement, or NAFTA. The existing NAFTA, a 1994 pact covering Canada, the United States and Mexico, was viewed by many Americans as their loss and Mexico's gain. The idea that trade is desirable only if it happens among countries with similar wages dies hard. In a new poll by the University of Maryland, only 43% of Americans supported freer trade with "low-wage countries" which lowered their tariffs, compared with the 66% who supported freer trade in general.

This has dented the political commitment to free trade. Until recently, politicians in America set a global trade-liberalising agenda despite a doubting public. Nervous of stoking anti-globalisation sentiment, however, President Clinton made only a half-hearted effort to get congressional backing for "fast-track" authority to negotiate trade treaties. When the attempt collapsed, trade unions, environmentalists and many congressmen cheered. The same coalition has helped bring talks on a global foreign-investment accord to a halt.

Work in Progress

Against this background, the WTO faces several daunting challenges. The first is to continue bringing down tariffs on traded goods. Average penalties have fallen steadily since the GATT's formation but even the most open economies retain lofty barriers: for instance, America still charges a tariff of 14.6% on imports of clothing, five times higher than its average levy.

Resistance to tariff cuts is strongest in agriculture. According to Tim Josling, a trade expert at Stanford University, tariffs and other barriers on farm goods average a crippling 40% worldwide and create distortions that "destroy huge amounts of value". A new set of global farm talks is planned to start in 1999. At the least, you might think, these could lock in impressive reforms in Latin America and encourage further watering-down of the European Union's Common Agricultural Policy. But they will prove difficult: squabbles over agriculture almost sank the Uruguay round.

Round and round A GATT/WTO chronology	
1947	Birth of the GATT, signed by 23 countries on October 30th at the Palais des Nations in Geneva.
1948	The GATT comes into force. First meeting of its members in Havana, Cuba.
1949	Second round of talks at Annecy, France. Some 5,000 tariff cuts agreed to; ten new countries admitted.
1950—1951	Third round at Torquay, England. Members exchange 8,700 trade concessions and welcome four new countries.
1956	Fourth round at Geneva. Tariff cuts worth $1.3 trillion at today's prices.
1960—1962	The Dillon round, named after US Under-Secretary of State Douglas Dillon, who proposed the talks. A further 4 400 tariff cuts.
1964—1967	The Kennedy round. Many industrial tariffs halved. Signed by 50 countries. Code on dumping agreed to separately.
1973—1979	The Tokyo round, involving 99 countries. First serious discussion of non-tariff trade barriers, such as subsidies and licensing requirements. Average tariff on manufactured goods in the nine biggest markets cut from 7% to 4.7%.
1986—1993	The Uruguay round. Further cuts in industrial tariffs, export subsidies, licensing and customs valuation. First agreements on trade in services and intellectual property.
1995	Formation of World Trade Organisation with power to settle disputes between members.
1997	Agreements concluded on telecommunications services, information technology and financial services.
1998	Today the WTO has 132 members. More than 30 others are waiting to join.

The next challenge will be to assist trade in services, which is growing more quickly than trade in goods. A fresh round of services talks is due to start in 2000. The aim will be to strengthen last year's agreements on telecoms, financial services and IT, as well as completing an accord on accountancy services which is currently being negotiated. Rich countries want firm rules on government procurement, to replace the vague existing code. Some countries, but not America, are also keen to tackle other subjects that eluded agreement in earlier talks, such as shipping. These will prove thorny, too, as any global talks will have to cope with a spaghetti bowl of bilateral agreements dating back decades.

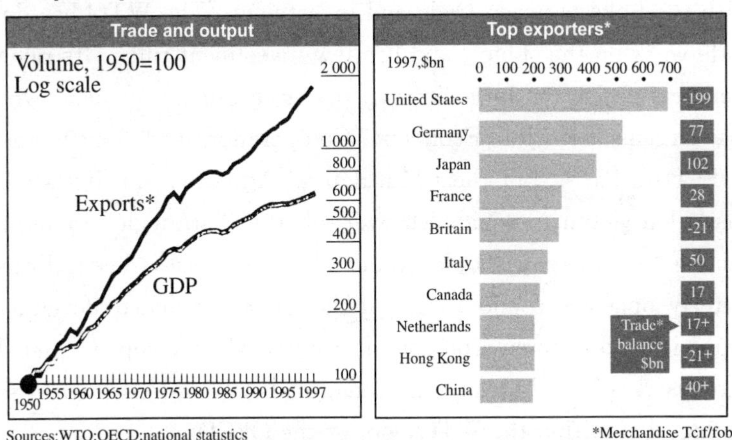

The WTO must also decide how closely to become involved in more esoteric issues, such as anti-trust rules, foreign-investment restrictions, workers' rights and environmental protection. These matters are conceptually complex and particularly contentious because they intrude on what many governments consider to be domestic policy. The WTO must strike a balance between attacking domestic policies that seriously distort trade and avoiding infringements of national sovereignty.

Anti-trust and trade overlap in all sorts of ways: when, say, a country's regulations prevent foreign companies from building factories or distributing their products through the same channels as local firms; or when governments turn a blind eye to international cartels in, say, oil or aluminium. So should the WTO be charged with drafting new rules that address this overlap? It is well placed for the task, having addressed complex competition-related problems in its telecoms-trade accord. If nothing else, it might hope to force the 60 or so WTO members that have no competition law to draft one. Alas, the biggest members cannot agree on whether the WTO should try to produce global competition rules. Europe is for, America against.

The members also disagree on whether the WTO should deal with the links between trade and investment. The WTO has done little work on the subject and has few investment rules. Its richest members decided to forge an investment agreement of their own at the Organisation for Economic Co-operation and Development (OECD) in Paris. But their Multilateral Agreement on Investment has fallen victim to squabbles over whether "strategic" industries such as broadcasting should be included (America is keen, France bitterly opposed), and over criticism from excluded developing countries and from environmental groups, which complain that the agreement is biased towards multinationals. The MAI is worth salvaging, but within the WTO, not at the OECD.

The trickiest and most emotive new issues, however, concern labour standards and the environment. These, unlike investment rules and competition policy, are of intense interest to a public worried about dolphins, rain forests, and maltreated workers. The WTO cannot afford to ignore them. But developing workable international rules that do not end up as tools for restricting trade will be difficult.

A first step in dealing with workers' rights, offering support for a set of "core standards", including pronouncements on child labour, was taken at the WTO's first summit, in 1996. The standards, pushed by rich countries, were not made binding, in part because some developing nations suspected that the real motive was to reduce their wage-cost advantage and to give rich countries an excuse to discriminate against poor-country exports—rather than to protect workers. They have a point: if poorer countires were forced to bring labour laws up to rich-country standards overnight, their exports would fall and their economies would be badly hurt. The WTO seems happy to let the International Labour Organisation lead the debate until there is a broader consensus about what sort of rules, if any, might be appropriate.

Going Green

The relationship between trade and the environment is the thorniest of all. The difficulty facing rule-makers is this: the benefits of trade depend on the assumption that relative prices in different countries reflect differences in factors of production, productivity and so on. However, if one firm is polluting freely while another bears the cost of cleaning up its pollution, then relative costs will fail to reflect these differences, and trade that looks desirable may not be.

So far, the WTO has shielded away from this. Its working group on trade and the environment has, the organisation itself admits, made little headway. Symptomatic of the confusion was its muddled reaction to a European ban on hormone-treated beef, contested by the United States. The WTO ruled last year in the Americans' favour, but let Brussels keep the ban while its scientists looked again for evidence to support it. Another example is the WTO's recent ruling against an American law blocking imports of shrimps from countries that do not use special nets to protect endangered turtles. The verdict was based on a narrow legal interpretation of trade rules with little regard for legitimate green concerns.

These new issues are likely to get even thornier as the WTO admits new members. By far the biggest wannabe is China. Without China, the world's second-largest economy and its tenth-largest exporter, the WTO cannot claim truly global status. The organisation had originally hoped to admit the Chinese at next week's summit, but this now looks unlikely before late 1999. Chinese officials hoping for quick entry point to concessions on their part: the closure of 54 factories producing pirated goods since 1996 and a promise to eradicate export subsidies and import quotas over several years, for instance. Rich countries reply that China has to lower border tariffs, free up trade in services and reform non-tariff measures such as licensing requirements before it can expect a seat.

Along with these challenges come two potential threats. The first is the rise of regional trade agreements. These have proliferated in recent years: in 1990 there were fewer than 25; today there are more than 90, including the European Union, NAFTA in North America, ASEAN in Asia and Mercosur in Latin America. Only last month, 34 countries from North and South America launched an initiative to free trade among them by 2005. Not to be outdone, the EU wants to form a bilateral economic partnership with America—though France may block the idea.

There is fierce disagreement about whether regional trade groupings are good or bad. Most are too new to analyse with much confidence. All of the groupings to date have tended to increase the flow of trade rather than to restrict it, which suggests at first sight that they are economically beneficial. None has yet adopted rules that are openly at odds with the WTO's.

There are, however, clear dangers. One is that regional agreements can divert trade, leading a country to import from a member of its trading block rather than from a cheaper supplier outside its region. Another is that regional groups might raise barriers against each other, creating protectionist blocks. (Recently, Mercosur raised its common external tariffs to avert an expected flood of imports from crisis-ridden Asia.) Also, regional trade rules may complicate the creation of new global rules.

The other threat to trade is a vacuum in political leadership. Sir Leon Brittan, the EU's trade commissioner, sings from a freetrade hymn sheet, but his constituency hardly leads by example. The EU's barriers against would-be members in Eastern Europe may be falling, but remain dauntingly high. Some EU countries, such as France and Italy, still preach protectionism in farming and car making.

Though less protectionist than the European Union, America is losing its way. Until recently wedded to multilateralism, under Bill Clinton it has focused on regional initiatives, such as NAFTA and the Free Trade Area of the Americas. This, and the failure to secure fasttrack, have raised concern that the government might soon buckle under pressure for protectionism from right-wing politicians, greens and unions. America's trade deficit is expected to widen as Asian exporters benefit from the recent currency devaluations. As it grows, so will protectionist pressure. Were America to halt trade liberalisation or raise import barriers, others would follow.

Keep Pedalling

How to prevent this? The best way would undoubtedly be to launch another round of global negotiations. A new round could balance the drift towards discriminatory regional tieups and reduce the risk that regionalism will become a source of conflict. With a broad agenda, the new round could enable governments to strike cross-sectoral bargains when negotiating sensitive issues such as farm trade: the Uruguay round would have achieved far less without links between assorted reforms in agriculture, textiles and services across many countries.

Sir Leon has already called for such an initiative. Before it stands a chance of sueceeding, however, governments will have to sort out their thinking on the new issues of trade—labour rights, the environment and competition policy. Talks that fail to address them are likely to face stiff political opposition on both sides of the Atlantic. Reaching consensus on these new issues among more than

100 countries will be no mean feat. But neither was the Uruguay round. It lasted eight years and was written off several times before reaching a successful conclusion. Another big push on trade would do the world economy a power of good, and the millennium round is such a fine name it would be a shame to waste it.

——From *The Economist* • May 16, 1998

Lesson 11

Barter Still in Use

Text

The Comeback of International Barter

It is a primitive, inefficient and expensive way of doing business—but the massive debts of developing countries and the world's oversupply of goods make it inescapable.

In 1983 the Saudi Arabian government decided to purchase ten Boeing 747-300s powered by 40 Rolls-Royce jet engines. But faced with declining revenues due to a worldwide surplus of oil, it was reluctant to pay $ 1 billion in cash. Instead, it offered crude oil. Neither the American aricraft manufacturer nor the British engine-maker wanted all that oil. But opportunities for such a big sale are rare. So the companies have arranged for an international financial institution to sell the Saudi crude on world markets. Boeing and Rolls-Royce will be paid in cash from the proceeds, and Saudi Arabia will get its aircraft without dipping into its currency reserves.

• To secure sales of its F—5 jet fighter to the Swiss government, the Northrop Corporation of the United States agreed to help the Swiss expand export markets for $200 million worth of goods. Northrop located a purchaser for Swiss elevators in Egypt, and steered the Swiss to a cement plant construction project in Indonesia. Over five years some 200 Swiss companies benefited from Northrop's assistance.

• In a hot contest the United States's General Electric Trading Co. won a contract for a $150 million turbine project in Romania—largely because it agreed to receive and market Romanian products of equivalent value. General Electric was able to use some Romanian steel products, and developed marketing programs to sell additional materials to the Middle and Far East.

Economists at the U. S. Department of Commerce estimate that up to 20 per cent of trade between nations is now subject to some form of countertrade—an outgrowth of the ancient practice of barter.

Barter endured for thousands of years as the primary means of trade. Colonial powers forced bilateral barter upon their client states, making the colonies take expensive manufactured goods in return for bargain-price raw materials, and prohibiting them from trading with other nations. International trade was supposed to be freed from bartering's constraints in July 1944, when diplomats and economists attending the United Nations Monetary and Financial Conference at Bretton Woods, New Hampshire, hammered out agreements that led to the creation of the International Monetary Fund (IMF) and regulation of the worldwide currency exchange system.

Commerce among nations entered a modern era; the constrained trading between imperial powers and their colonies began to break down. World markets opened to all countries, and multilateral trade flourished. Generally a country could sell its goods in the best market it could find, and buy what is needed from the least expensive supplier. Moreover, since currencies were convertible, most transactions could be completed with cash. Barter was as antiquated as the horse—soldier. Or so it seemed.

During the past few years, however, the international monetary system has begun to strain under a variety of economic changes. One important cause is the enormous burden of debt carried by Third World countries, today estimated at $800 billion. "The plain fact is that many countries are broken," says David Yoffie, assistant professor at Harvard University's Graduate School of Business Administration.

Nations with serious debt problems, such as Mexico, Brazil and

Argentina, have been compelled to devote almost all their export earnings to debt service, leaving themselves with virtually no surplus to pay for imports. With barter, however, debtor nations can continue to import goods while, in effect, concealing export earnings from creditors.

But countertrade is not the exclusive province of debtor nations. Says Yoffie, "Even countries with strong foreign exchange positions, such as Australia, Canada and Indonesia, are insisting on countertrade in certain areas. Linking imports and exports is a way to exert power over multinational corporations. Countries that lack expertise in international marketing try to use countertrade as leverage to tap the networks of global firms."

Nations also use countertrade as a camouflaged means of subsidizing exports. For instance, if a Middle Eastern country wanted to increase its oil exports, says Yoffie, it could simply lower its price. Such a move would, however, weaken the cartel. But if a country sells its oil at the OPEC list price, and in an interconnected deal quietly arranges to pay a premium for imported goods, both parties in the transaction benefit—at the expense, of course, of other oil producers. Up to a quarter of all OPEC oil transactions today have some kind of countertrade provisions attached.

Barter in its traditional form—the direct exchange of goods of equivalent value—is relatively rare. Its modern variants:

- Counterpurchase usually involves a supplier selling goods or services and in return ordering unrelated products, which essentially offsets the buyer's costs. For example, when McDonnell Douglas sold civilian aircraft to Yugoslavia in the 1960s, it agreed to purchase goods from that country—including hams that were then served in the company's cafeteria—and to market Yugoslavizn products in the United States. The firm also encouraged its employees to vacation in Yugoslavia; the tourist dollars spent served to offset the company's countertrade obligations.

• Compensation Agreements are often undertaken to win contracts for the construction of manufacturing plants. When Levi Strauss sold a blue jeans factory to Hungary, the American company agreed to market approximately 500,000 jeans per year in East Germany, Poland and Czechoslovakia.

• Clearing Agreements tend to be bilateral pacts between governments, an exchange of products to meet an agreed-upon value of trade. Large volumes of Western goods reach Russia through a clearing arrangement between the Soviet Union and India. Because India needs to export more to the Soviet Union to balance its imports, it has opened the door for some Western firms that otherwise might not be able to sell to the U. S. S. R.

Britain's Rank Xerox, for example, found it difficult to sell photocopiers to the Soviet Union because Moscow was unwilling to part with hard currency. But by opening a joint venture copier assembly plant in India, which sends the copiers to the U. S. S. R. through the clearing agreement, Rank Xerox has reached its market.

U. S. government officials worry that the explosive growth in countertrade will weaken the world trading system. By concealing the real prices and costs of transactions, says one U. S. trade representative, the various forms of barter may conceal and help perpetuate economic inefficiencies in the marketplace.

Barter can also be risky business. "Many companies," says David Yoffie, "suffer losses because they're stuck with products of poor quality or with the wrong specifications."

The structuring of countertrading deals is often Byzantine. In 1982 Chrysler Corp. set out to sell trucks to credit-starved Jamaica. To pull the deal off, the two sides arranged for the American and Canadian mining companies that dig Jamaica's bauxite and refine it into alumina to hand over about 50,000 tons of the refined product to the Jamaican government's Bauxite & Alumina Trading Co.

The trading company exported the alumina to Metallgesellschaft AG, a German metals company. Metallgesellschaft AG then sold the alumina to a refiner, which converted it into aluminum. The money the metal company got for the alumina went to Chrysler's bankers, the European American Bank. The bank paid part of the money to Jamaica's Bauxite & Alumina Trading Co.

The balance financed a letter of credit made out to Chrysler, which subsequently shipped trucks to Jamaica. Another government firm on the island took title, and sold the vehicles to a local Chrysler distributor. The mining companies got paid for their alumina and the Jamaican public finally got an opportunity to buy American trucks, to which they might not have otherwise had access.

International trade by barter is, in fact, an inefficient and expensive means of doing business compared to trading with money. Observes David Yoffie, "To cover the additional costs it incurs in handling goods it is forced to take in countertrade, a multinational company simply boosts the price of the goods it sells." Yoffie sees countertrade as a form of protectionism. "It can help one group and hurt another," he says.

On the other hand, Daniel Cecchin, director of Countertrade Services for Bank America World Trade Corp., asserts that the rise of countertrade provides practical solutions to the debt problems of the international monetary system.

—From *Reader's Digest* · August, 1985

Words and Expressions

barter	*n.*	易货贸易
primitive	*a.*	原始的

Saudi Arabian	沙特阿拉伯的
crude(oil)	*a.* 原油
proceed	*n.* 收入
dip (into)	*v.* 动用(款项等)
secure	*v.* 弄到;得到
locate	*v.* 找到
steer	*v.* 指导;指点
contest	*n.* 竞赛(尤指竞技者各自献技由裁判员择优的)
turbine	*n.* 涡轮机
equivalent	*a.* 相等的
the U.S. department of commerce	美国商务部
countertrade	*n.* 对等贸易;反向贸易
outgrowth	*n.* 分支;副产品
endure	*v.* 持续
primary	*a.* 首要;主要
client state	(在经济或政治方面依靠某一大国的)附属国
bargain	*n.* 低廉 bargain-price (用作定语)
prohibit	*v.* 禁止
prohibit sb. from doing sth.	禁止某人做某事
constraint	*n.* 约束;限制
Bretton Woods	布雷顿森林(美国一地名)
New Hampshire	(美国)新罕布什尔州
hammer (out)	*v.* 设计出
constrained	*a.* 强制的;被约束的
break down	崩溃
flourish	*v.* 繁荣;兴旺
convertible	*a.* 可兑换的
antiquated	*n.* 陈旧的;过时的

horse-soldier	骑兵
strain	*v.* 承受巨大的压力
plain	*a.* 简单的
broke	*a.* (俚语)[作表语用]破产的
Harvard University's graduate school of Business Administration	哈佛大学商业管理研究生院
debt service	=interest payment 利息付款
virtually	*ad.* 实际上
debtor	*n.* 债务人
creditor	*n.* 债权人
province	*n.* (活动)范围
exert	*v.* 施加
expertise	*n.* 专门知识
leverage	*n.* 杠杆机构
tap	*v.* 着手利用
camouflaged	*a.* 伪装的
subsidize	*v.* 补贴
cartel	*n.* 卡特尔;联合企业
premium	*n.* 加价
provision(s)	*n.* 条款
variant	*n.* 变体;变形
essentially	*ad.* 基本上
cafeteria	*n.* 自助食堂
undertake	*v.* 接受;同意
jeans	*n.* 牛仔服装
clearing	*n.* 清算
tend(to)	*v.* 易于;往往会
pact	*n.* 条约
part(with)	*v.* 花掉
perpetuate	*v.* 使长存;保持

stuck(with)	stick 的过去分词：缠住；陷入困境
Byzantine	*a.* 错综复杂的
set out	打算
Jamaica	*n.* 牙买加
pull	*v.* 努力实现
bauxite	*n.* 铝土
alumina	*n.* 矾土(氧化铝)
aluminum	*n.* 铝
finance	*v.* 供资金给
title	*n.* 所有权
take title	取得所有权
distributor	*n.* 经销商
access	*n.* 机会
cover	*v.* 支付
incur	*v.* 招致
assert	*v.* 断言

Notes to the Text

1. Reader's Digest　读者文摘

美国最成功的月刊之一。1922 年创刊时刊载一些从其他刊物缩写的有新闻价值和娱乐价值的文章。这种袖珍本杂志迎合广大读者的口味，自 1934 年起开始发表流行书籍的节录。至 20 世纪 70 年代晚期，读者文摘以 13 种文字出版，发行量高达3 000万份，居全世界期刊发行数量之冠。

2. Rolls-Royce Ltd.　罗尔斯—罗伊斯公司

英国制造汽车的垄断组织，制造高级轿车、汽车和飞机发动机及其他工程技术产品。1906 年 3 月成立，1971 年 2 月破产。公司破产后改组成为两家独立的公司：(1)罗尔斯—罗伊斯公司(1971)，1971

年由英国政府投资设立，由国营企业局管理，内有罗尔斯—罗伊斯公司前的喷气式发动机，总部设在伦敦；(2)罗尔斯—罗伊斯汽车公司，由前公司其余股东占有的公众性公司，1973 年 5 月成立，包括所有从事制造汽车和其他工程技术产品(如内燃机、汽车和飞机部件、工业用机车、轻型飞机)的分部，总部设在德比郡德比。

3. Northrop Corporation　诺思罗普公司

美国的跨国公司，生产航空航天设备、电子设备及通讯装置。它是美国无人驾驶飞机的主要制造商。总部设在洛杉矶。公司在美国有几家独资的子公司，在国外也有子公司和联号。

4. The United Nations Monetary and Financial Conference　联合国货币金融会议

会议于 1944 年 7 月 1 日至 22 日在美国新罕布什尔州的布雷顿森林举行，参加的有中国、美国、英国及法国等 44 个国家，就预期将德国和日本击败后战后的世界金融问题进行研讨，作出安排。会议拟出计划方案：(1)成立国家复兴开发银行，对急需外援的国家提供长期贷款；(2)成立国际货币基金组织，提供短期贷款，调剂国际支付方面的不平衡现象，以稳定外汇汇率。

5. "currencies were convertible"—convertible currency　可兑换货币

一种货币可以自由兑换为其他国家的货币，而不受到任何限制时，叫做可兑换货币。一种货币是否可自由兑换取决于它是否有足够的黄金储备或一些硬通货予以支持，因而可在任何时候兑换成大家所接受(公认)的一些具有永久价值的物品。在金本位制度下，货币可自由兑换成黄金。在最初的国际货币基金制度下，美元可自由兑换成黄金，所有其他货币可以兑换成美元，因此互相可按一定汇率通过美元进行兑换。货币的可兑换性对进行多边贸易是至关重要的。

6. "… the enormous burden … $800 billion."

据 1994 年有关国际组织发表的统计数字，第三世界国家所负外债已达14 500亿美元。

7. cartel　卡特尔

生产同类产品的若干独立的工业企业，为了共同获取高额利润和垄断某一市场，在划分产品销售范围、规定商品的产量和销售价格等方面通过建立协定而形成的一种垄断组织形式。卡特尔的参加者既有大企业，也有中小企业，而处于支配地位的是少数大企业。随着资本主义的发展，垄断资本的活动范围超越了国界，一些国家的垄断组织联合建立了国际卡特尔，成为国际垄断同盟的一种重要形式。

8. Levi Strauss & Co.　利瓦伊—斯特劳斯公司

美国和世界最大的裤子制造商，以其所制造的斜纹粗蓝布牛仔裤（称为利瓦伊裤，注册商标是 Levi's）而著名。现在也制造特定的便裤、茄克衫、衬衣、裙子、裤带。产品行销 50 多个国家。从 60 年代起，所产的利瓦伊裤及其他斜纹布裤已在全世界流行，成为时髦的东西。总部设在旧金山。

9. Rank Xerox—Xerox Corporation　兰克—施乐公司

是美国施乐公司与英国兰克组织合资组建的。

施乐公司是世界商用产品、系统以及金融服务市场上的一个跨国集团，首创静电印刷普通纸复印机。1906 年成立。1960 年首次销售 914 型复印机，大获成功。在与其他公司的竞争中，施乐公司依靠不断的新产品开发和旧产品改造，始终立于不败之地。公司目前主要生产商用设备，如复印机和其他现代化自动办公设备、计算机、人工智能系统等。施乐公司海外子公司遍布世界各地。公司总部设在康涅狄格州斯坦福。

10. "By concealing … in the market place."

由于种种原因，发展中国家生产的商品有相当一部分质量差，因而在国际市场上的竞争力较低。在一般交易中，买方对这类产品并不感兴趣。但在反向贸易中，贸易伙伴则不得不按市场价格接受这类商品。不然的话，他们就无法获得对方购货的定单。从长远的观点看，这无助于低劣产品的生产商，因为反向贸易不但掩盖了低效率而且解除了他们在生产中需要进行改善的压力。

反向贸易带来的另一个问题是交易的高额成本费用。尽管反向贸易看起来是发生在两个贸易伙伴之间，但一般情况下，这类交易都是多边交易。由于在反向贸易中买方得到的商品通常不是他们所需的商品，买方必须找到最终用户，把商品卖给他们。这一销售过程一般是通过中间人经过一系列的买卖才完成的。这就需要更多的推销、联系、旅行及其他费用。所有这些都将增加交易的成本，这也被看作是经济低效的一种形式。

11. "The structuring of countertrading deals is often Byzantine."

Byzantine 是形容词，意为具有公元五世纪拜占庭式建筑风格的。拜占庭式建筑的一个显著特点是其复杂的螺旋形建筑及塔尖。

在上面句子里，反向贸易的结构被比作拜占庭式的建筑群，实际上是强调其复杂性。

Questions on Content and Language Points

(for preview, discussion and reviews)

1. We are told in the first paragraph of the text that Saudi Arabia decided to buy 10 aeroplanes from Boeing then.

What was the purchasing price?

2. "International trade was supposed to be freed from bartering's constraints in July 1944…"

Paraphrase the underlined part of the aboved-quoted clause.

3. "Barter was as antiquated as the horse-soldier. Or so it seemed."

What difference does the use of the word "seem" make in meaning or tone between the above-given two sentences?

4. "Nations with serious debt problems, such as Mexico, Brazil and Argentina, have been compelled to devote almost all their export earings to debt service, …"

What is "debt service?"

5. "Countries that lack expertise in international marketing try to use countertrade as leverage to tap the networks of global firms."

1) What does "global firms" refer to?

2) What does the network of a so-called "global firm" usually

consist of?

3) What's meant by "tap the networks of global firms"?

6. "Yoffie sees countertrade as a form of protectionism. 'It can help one group and hurt another,' he says."

In what sense is countertrade seen as a form of protectionism? (Or in what way could it help protectionism?)

Protectionism (保护贸易制): the policy of controlling imports in an effort to achieve an specific objective, which is against competition.

Free trade (自由贸易): the policy of having no controls over imports or exports, which encourages competition.

Topic for Summary

What is the main content of the text?

Exercises

Read the article given below and do the following exercise:

Let's Make a Trade

In Tough Times, Swapping May Make Sense

By Alexanora A. Seno

Hong Kong

For cash-strapped businesses, barter trading may be a useful option. "Cash is king, but barter is smarter," says Hong Kong-based broker Brian Hodgson.

Barter used to mean swapping rice for a chicken, chickens for car repair. But with cash flow tight for many businesses in this economic climate, exchanging goods and services might be a trading method to consider as part of normal operations. "In times like these, cash is king, but barter is smarter," says Brian Hodgson, director of Hong Kong's Pacific Barter Company. Companies want to get rid of excess inventory and save cash. "Barter allows them to do this," reckons Hodgson. "It gives them a chance to try new goods and services at lower actual cost while meeting potential cash-paying clients."

Hodgson used to work in media advertising sales, where barter deals —ad space for air tickets, for example — are an accepted part of the business. He found that while there were dozens of barter brokers in the world, none were based in Asia. Yet the practice was gaining acceptance elsewhere. Even multinationals, mainly American companies such as Coca-Cola, Xerox and Ford, do a small percentage of sales this way. PepsiCo. has traded soft-drink syrup and beverage-making technology for Russian vodka. In Sri Lanka, carmaker General Motors has swapped locomotives for tea, selling the leaves in turn to English dealers for cash. The International Reciprocal Trade Association estimates that in the U. S. last year there were \$11 billion worth of swaps among 800,000 outfits.

In Australia and the U. S., barter has flourished in economic slowdowns when corporate budgets get slashed and customers are more careful about spending their cash. Brokers have made arranging deals much easier. Hodgson started his company in April 1997, just months before the crisis hit East Asia. "When we introduced the concept into the marketplace, people said: 'We don't want to barter, we have lots of money.' Now with the slump, they are telling us: 'We have warehouses full of things. Let's talk.'"

With over 60 members, ranging from major international conglomerates to small and medium-sized local firms, Pacific Barter handles about \$40,000 in deals monthly out of Hong Kong and China. Requests range from the mundane watches-for-computers to the more offbeat Eastern European hotel rooms-for-fertilizer. In a \$6-million deal Hodgson is putting together, one county government in China's Guangdong province is trading quality steel for scrap metal from a major Korean company.

Last month, Rudy Chan launched the Hong Kong operations of Australia-based Bartercard, the world's biggest trade exchange with 20,000 members. "Some large companies have whole departments specializing in this financially efficient practice," Chan says. "Our role is to provide smaller companies with similar services." Bartercard holders use "trade dollars" to purchase goods and services from other members. A security company for instance may buy $1,000 worth of uniforms from a garment maker. The seller is credited with 1,000 trade dollars by Bartercard, while the purchaser's account is debited the same amount. Straight swaps are not required. On joining, members are given a trade-dollar credit line. Chan hopes to sign about 1,000 clients in Hong Kong by next year. Members can take advantage of Bartercard's international network, which includes Sri Lanka and a month-old Thailand operation.

Pacific Barter charges a one-time $230 joining fee when the first deal is completed. On every trade, it also collects a cash commission of 5%～10%, depending on the value of the swap. Says Hodgson: "For cash-strapped companies, it's not a bad deal. For $100,000 worth of goods or services, the cash outlay is only $8,000." Bartercard has a similar initial membership charge and a 5% transaction fee payable in cash or trade dollars. "Barter allows profit from excess inventory and service dead time, and it can bring in more business," Chan explains. Sometimes, it pays to do things the old-fashioned way.

——From *Asiaweek* • May 15, 1998

True-and-false questions:

1. Barter is a new business practice which was invented during

the recent financial crisis. (　　)

2. Barter trade is popular with business companies because it can help them liquidate their stagnant inventory. (　　)

3. Barter trade is conducted only by those cash-strapped small-sized companies. (　　)

4. Barter trade practice had been widely accepted in Asia long before the Asian financial crisis. (　　)

5. "Trade dollar" is a financial means used to balance the accounts of members of Bartercard. (　　)

6. When a member of Bartercard purchases a batch of goods from another member, his account will be credited with the amount of the purchase. (　　)

7. Members of Pacific Barter do not need to spend a penny for business transactions among them. (　　)

8. Through barter exchange such as Bartercard and Pacific Barter, businesses can meet more potential clients and expand business opportunities. (　　)

Lesson 12

Market Competition

Text

Soft Drink Wars: the Next Battle

The reformulation of Coke has given the feuding cola giants a chance to go at each other again.

But Coca-Cola and PepsiCo are spoiling for yet another fight, and this time they're picking on the little guys: non-cola makers like Seven-Up and Dr Pepper.

By Monci Jo Williams

In the U. S. soft drink industry, where 1% of the market is worth $300 million in retail sales, Coca-Cola and PepsiCo don't wage mere market share battles. They fight holy wars. These days the fighting is on two fronts. One is on the vast plains of the cola business, where the reformulation of Coke has Pepsi on the defensive. The other is in the back alleys of the smaller, non-cola market. Until now these have been dominated by other companies. As growth of high-calorie colas slows, however, Coca-Cola and PepsiCo are invading new territory.

Coca-Cola is moving in with two new products: Cherry Coke, a canned version of the old soda fountain favorite, and Minute Maid Orange Soda, which contains orange juice. Pepsi's new product is Slice, a lemon-lime soft drink that also contains fruit juice. If these products live up to their early performance in test markets—a big if

—they could produce $ 3 billion a year in retail sales. The skirmishes between the cola giants will precipitate a battle for supermarket shelf space and for the loyalty of bottlers. The big guys will press bottlers to drop competing brands to make way for their new products.

It's too early to tell how the reincarnated Coke is selling, since many bottlers are still working off old inventories. But the company isn't leaving much to chance. Coca-Cola will back new coke with more than $70 million of advertising this year, vs. the $50 million or so PepsiCo will spend on its flagship brand. Over the long term, however, many industry analysts believe the Coke reformulation will do little to dramatically change either Coke's or Pepsi's market share. Says Joseph Doyle Harris Upham brokerage firm in New York: "Twelve months from now, we'll look back and see new Coke as a nonevent." In all its variations, Coke holds about 29% of the U. S. market, Pepsi 23%.

The company's new formula was designed partly to keep Coke's sales growing overseas. Compared with Americans, who guzzle more soda than water, the rest of the world is still in the sipping stage. Coca-Cola's goal is to kick up its slowing growth rate outside the U. S. from about 3% a year to 10%. Company executives think a less filling, more "guzzleable" new Coke will help.

Domestically, sales of soft drinks have been bubbling along nicely. They grew 6% last year, vs. 2% to 3% a few years ago. But the cola makers may experience more growing pains. at least with the high-calorie colas that account for half ofall sales (diet colas hold about 12%). Baby-boomers are showing a strong preference for healthier, less fattening drinks as they age — everything from diet soda to bottled water to fruit juice. For example, according to Beverage World, an industry magazine, fruit juice and fruit drink sales have grown from $ 1. 2 billion in 1976 to $8. 4 billion last year. John Costello, senior vice president of marketing and sales for Pepsi-Cola USA, thinks the popularity of fruit juices can be captured in new soft drink products such as Slice. "We want to take the vitality of the juice market and put it into soft drinks," says Costello.

Even without the new products from Coca-Cola and PepsiCo, the

Quenching the Cola Giants' Thirst

Coca-Cola and Pepsi Co have grown to dominate the soft drink business by selling colas. To satisfy their appetites for growth, they want to siphon sales from Dr Pepper and Seven-Up.

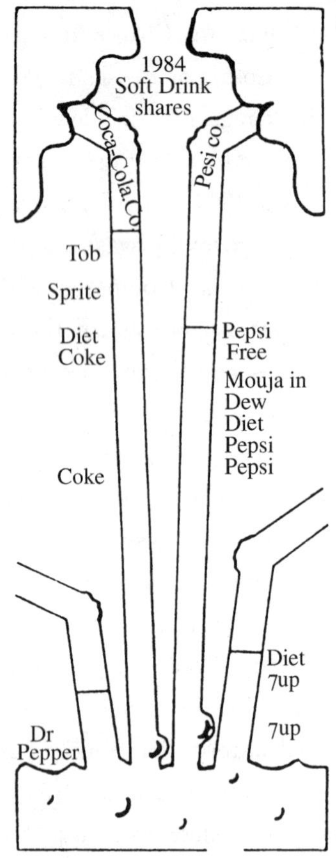

non-cola field is crowded. Indeed, with so many regional and national brands out there, it is sometimes hard to keep track of who owns what and who's competing with whom. But essentially the non-cola market can be divided into four segments: lemon-lime sodas, which account for about 12% of soft drink sales and include Philip Morris, 7 Up and Coca-Cola's Sprite: orange sodas (4% of sales), which include R. J. Reynolds's Sunkist and Procter & Gamble's Crush; mixers (2%), which include ginger ale, club soda, and tonic water and, finally, the Pepper category(7%), dominated by Dr Pepper, a non-cola drink based on a mixture of fruit flavors.

Although Coca-Cola and PepsiCo's new fruit juice sodas will compete with each other, they are more likely to steal market share from all those other drinks already on supermarket shelves. Slice, a lemon-lime soda that actually contains four juices—white grape, pear, lemon, and lime—poses a challenge both to 7 Up, the No. 1 lemon-lime soda (4. 4%)and sprite. Based on its performance in test markets, industry analysts say Slice could grab 3% to 4% of the U. S. market.

Coca-Cola seems determined that Slice's sales won't come at the expense of Sprite. This year the company hiked Sprite's advertising budget to $40 million, and boosted sales 25% in the first three months. Seven-Up, on the other hand, still seems to be searching for a defense. It is distributing more consumer coupons and giving bottlers bigger discounts, but has also unimaginatively returned to its 17-year-old "uncola" advertising theme. Says Jesse Meyers, publisher of Beverage Digest. "It's raining out there, and Seven-Up hasn't put up an umbrella."

Coca-Cola's advance into orange soda is bad news for Sunkist, which holds a 1. 5% share of the soft drink market, and Crush (around 1%) Coca-Cola began testing Minute Maid Orange Soda in Canada last summer. Some analysts think it will quickly challenge Sunkist as the top-selling orange drink.

The sleeper among the products might turn out to be Cherry Coke, which contains no fruit juice at all. Emanuel Goldman, a beverage analyst with Montgomery Securities in San Francisco, says Cherry Coke has captured shares of 4% to 8% in test markets. The drink probably won't do as well when it is rolled out nationally, since consumer coupons and price promotions have been helping it along. But Goldman believes Cherry Coke could eventually displace Dr pepper as the nation's fifth-best-selling soft drink.

Even if consumers swill the new sodas by the liter in test markets, however, Coca-Cola and PepsiCo still face a struggle in presuading bottlers across the nation to take the products. One of the biggest battles in the soda wars, in fact, may not be for drinkers but for bottlers. Bottlers have a symbiotic but occasionally fractious relationship with the syrup makers. Although Coke and Pepsi own some of their own bottling companies, most bottlers are still independent. They do the bulk of their business selling colas, counting on Dr Pepper, Sunkist, and other non-colas to fill out their line. But because exclusive contracts with the syrup makers prevent bottlers from distributing competing brands, the cola giants must persuade them to drop established products to take on Slice or Minute Maid Orange Soda.

The bottlers may not go along. Much of the expense of introducing a new product—blitzing consumers with coupons and offering deep discounts to retailers to get the product on the shelves—is borne by the bottler. He is reluctant to walk away from his investment in an existing brand to pony up for something new. That may be especially so in the case of the fruit juice sodas. Because syrups made with juices are more expensive than other syrups, Coca-Cola and PepsiCo will be charging bottlers more for them. But to boost Slice's sales, bottlers are discounting the drink. If they can't get the price up and keep it up, Pepsi—Co's new product will be less profitable to them than regular soft drinks that hold smaller market shares.

Contractual conflicts could hurt some new brands more than others. Minute Maid Orange Soda appears to face more trouble than Slice, since half of Coca-Cola's bottlers are pledged to distribute Sunkist or Crush; only 22% of PepsiCo's bottlers handle Slice's head-to-head competitor, 7 Up. Cherry Coke may have the easiest time. It will compete with Dr Pepper, for which Coca-Cola bottlers do more than 40% of the distribution. But Dr Pepper has told Coke bottlers that it doesn't see the new soda as a direct competitor, so they don't have to worry about losing the Pepper franchise if they take on the new drink. Is Dr Pepper being generous? Hardly. The company apparently fears that if Coke bottlers are forced to choose between Cherry Coke and Dr Pepper, they will let the doctor take a walk.

It's hard to gauge a bottler's loyalty. Coke's biggest bottler is John T. Lupton, chairman of JTL Corp., a $700-million-a-year Chattanooga company. Lupton also bottles Sunkist, but ask him if he's willing to drop it so he can take on Coca-Cola's Minute Maid, and he'll tell you, "I'll be glad to. All Coca—Cola has to do is give me a product that's competitive in price and quality, and I'll take it hands down." But not Charles Millard, chairman of the $600-million-a-year Coca-Cola Bottling Co. of New York, Coke's second-largest customer. Even though Coke owns 31% of his company, Millard says he will stick with Sunkist. "They have made a big investment in this market and in our business," he says. "The smart bottlers will leave the dance with the girl they came with."

HOLDOUTS LIKE MILLARD are likely to become targets of all-out sales campaigns. The hard sell won't come until later this year, since Coca-Cola is still in test markets with Minute Maid Orange Soda and Cherry Coke, and Pepsi is concentrating on distributing Slice through bottlers who have no conflict. But when the push does start, says a soft drink company executive, "Things are going to get very, very interesting."

To convince bottlers that the new products can match or exceed the sales of existing brands without heavy discounting or couponing, Coca-Cola and PepsiCo will have to cut back on special promotion, then ply the bottlers with the resulting sales data. But their most useful tactic will be to offer the bottlers generous cooperative advertising deals on the new sodas, and extra money to promote the old ones. Bottlers may come in for a little arm-twisting as well. "It's often very subtle," says an industry executive who prefers not to be named. "The Coca-Cola representative will say, 'That decision is not going to sit very well in Atlanta' or something like that."

If companies can't get their products distributed nationwide, marketing them will be more expensive. Buying local advertising is simply more costly than purchasing network spots. Brian Dyson, president of Coca-Cola USA, says that it generally doesn't pay to advertise nationally until a new product is in about 80% of the country. Costello of PepsiCo—whose Slice has been rolled out to 70% of the country—says Pepsi is willing to settle for the smaller profits that will result from partial distribution. Analysts believe that's because PepsiCo doesn't think it can persuade bottlers to dump 7 Up. Coca-Cola seems more confident about un seating Sunkist and Crush. If Coke proceeds beyond test markets with Minute Maid, Dyson's goal will be to distribute the drink across the country.

The battle to unseat smaller brands, dominate niches, and shove competing products out of distribution will be costly and exhausting, and could go on for years. But the large companies will surely squeeze into every market they can, hoping it will be worth the pinch.

—From *Fortune* • June 24, 1985

Words and Expressions

reformulation *n.* 重新配方

feuding	*a.* (个人或团体)仇恨的;长期不和的;争吵
be spoiling for	一心想;切望
guy	*n.* (口)家伙
wage	*v.* 进行
alley	*n.* 小巷;小街
calorie	*n.* 卡路里(热量单位)
minute	*a.* 微小的
lime	*n.* 酸橙
live up to	符合;达到
skirmish	*n.* (军事)小规模战斗;小冲突
precipitate	*v.* 促成;促使…加快
brand	*n.* (商品的)牌子;商标
reincarnate	*v.* 赋予(灵魂)以新的形体
advertising	*n.* (总称)广告;宣传
brokerage	*n.* 掮客业务;经纪业
guzzle	*v.* 狂饮
soda	*n.* 苏打水;汽水
sip	*v.* 小口地喝;抿
bubble	*n.* (口)沸腾;汩汩地流
diet	*n.* 平常营养;减肥
baby-boomers	生育高峰期出生的人
beverage	*n.* 饮料
vitality	*n.* 生命力;生机
track	*n.* 踪迹
keep track of	看清;跟上…的进展
segment	*n.* 部分
quench	*v.* 消除
siphon	*v.* 抽取;分出
ale	*n.* (原义为)淡色啤酒
flavor	*n.* 味道

pose	*v.*	提出(挑战)
hike	*v.*	(急剧地)提高;上升
coupon	*n.*	(附在商品上的)赠货券
sleeper	*n.*	[口]出乎意料的成功者
security	*n.*	有价证券
promotion	*n.*	推销活动
swill	*v.*	大口地喝
liter	*n.*	升(容量单位)
symbiotic	*a.*	共生的
fractious	*a.*	烦躁的;难驾驭的
syrup	*n.*	糖浆
fill out	凑足;补齐	
blitz	*v.*	(用闪电式行动)攻击
pony up	[美俚]付清	
pledge	*v.*	使保证
franchise	*n.*	(公司或制造商给予的在某一地区经营业务的)特许经销权
gauge	*v.*	测量;判定
holdout	*n.*	拒不合作者
ply	*v.*	不断提供
tactic	*n.*	战术;手段
deal	*n.*	协议;交易
come in for	受到;遭到;得到	
arm-twisting	*n.*	(口)强迫;压力
do a little arm-twisting	略施压力	
subtle	*a.*	微妙的
executive	*n.*	业务经理人员
settle for	勉强接受	
unseat	*v.*	使退位;使下台
proceed	*v.*	进行;开展
niche	*n.*	(原意为)壁龛;合适的地位

Notes to the Text

1. soft drink：软饮料，即不含酒精，一般经过碳酸化合的饮料。

2. Coke：Coca-Cola 可口可乐的俗称。

3. Coca-Cola Co.　可口可乐公司

美国和世界最大的软饮料公司，1892 年 1 月成立。现主要从事软饮料可口可乐的浆汁和浓缩品的制造和销售。同时也经营其他软饮料的浆汁和浓缩品、咖啡、茶、柑橘水、果汁和酒类。总公司设在佐治亚州亚特兰大。目前可口可乐公司通过其在全世界各国的独立的和控股的罐装厂经销软饮料。

4. PepsiCo，Inc.　百事有限公司

美国大联合企业，它所提供的产品和劳务有饮料、食品、运动用品、货物运输和建筑工程。现在的公司由百事可乐公司和弗里托—莱公司于 1965 年合并而成。此后，该公司开始进一步经营多样化，接连购入了北美长途搬运公司，威尔逊运动用品公司，亨利酒业公司和皮扎赫特公司等。百事可乐公司和百事有限公司的总部曾多次迁移，现设在纽约州珀切斯。

5. "They fought holy wars."

圣战(holy war) 最早指十字军东征，即西方基督教徒组织的反对穆斯林国家的几次军事远征，其目的是控制圣城耶路撒冷并夺取与耶稣基督尘世生活有联系的一些地区。在战争期间，只要十字军打赢了，他们就推翻当地政权，建立他们自己的统治。

本文中"圣战"的含义是可口可乐公司和百事有限公司对他们各自通过竞争取得的市场份额方面的增长都不满足，他们的最终目的是把他们的竞争对手全部赶出市场，建立自己的王国。

6. test market　试销市场；test marketing　试销

对于新的和经过改造的商品，在投入批量生产之前，制造商经常先在一个城市或地区进行小批量的销售，该城市或地区必须是能够

代表整个市场的，以此试探消费者对其产品的反映。试销结果将用来决定这一产品是否要大规模生产，取消，还是进行进一步改造。

这一调查过程叫做试销；用以进行试销的市场叫做试销市场。

7. bottler　装瓶商，经销商

对于美国的软饮料生产商来说，bottler 指他们产品的经销商。为了避免不必要的繁重的运输，软饮料制造商更愿意向他们在世界及美国各地的经销商提供浓缩饮料，然后由它们在当地稀释装瓶销售。

8. baby-boomer　生育高峰期出生的人

即第二次世界大战后 1947—1961 年间美国的生育高峰期出生的人。在本文中，baby-boomer 指的是可乐消费者中当时最年轻的那部分人，他们对软饮料的兴趣和口味随着年龄的增长而改变。

9. coupons　赠券，优惠券

向顾客散发用于促销的一种特别印制的票证，持有者在购买某种商品时能得到价格上的优惠。

在美国以及其他一些西方国家许多制造商和零售商通过邮寄或附加在报纸、杂志、广告上以及在店内发放优惠券等方式向消费者提供优惠价格或免费商品，以此促使顾客对其发生兴趣，多次购买，长期使用。

10. sleeper，在本文中的意思是出人意料的成功者，爆冷门的人或物。这是美国英语中一种非正式的用法。

11. exclusive contract　独家经销合同

在本文中指软饮料制造商与中间商之间的一种协议。此协议禁止中间人经营制造商竞争对手的同类商品。

12. franchise　特许专营权

制造商品或提供劳务的企业与零售商签定合同，授权后者在一定地区内用前者名义按合同规定的标准经营特准其经营的业务。其中后者就是“被特许人”(franchisee)；前者则是“特许人”(franchiser)。可口可乐公司与装瓶厂商之间是建立特许专营关系最早的例子。

Questions on Content and Language Points

(for preview, discussion and review)

1. "In the US soft drink industry, where 1% of the market is worth $300 million in retail sales, …"

How much is the total of the market worth?

2. "…The other is in the back alleys of the smaller, non-cola market."

What does "the back alleys" refer to? (The retail business or the distribution area? Don't make your choice till you have read through the text.)

3. "As growth of high-calorie colas slows, however, Coca-Cola and Pepsico are invading new territory."

Where is a hint dropped in the sentence as to the reason for the slow growth of the colas?

4. "If these products live up to their early performance in test markets—a big if—they could produce $3 billion a year in retail sales."

What does "a big if" mean?

5. "It's too early to tell how the reincarnated Coke is selling, since many bottlers are still working off old inventories."

Do you think that the new Coke would get into the market without difficulty, according to the lines quoted?

Why not? Why would "old inventories" prevent the new Coke's entrance?

6. "Compared with Americans, who guzzle more soda than water, the rest of the world is still in the sipping stage. … Company executives think a less filling, more 'guzzleable' new Coke will help (the increase of their overseas sales)."

1) What's the difference between guzzle and sip in meaning?

2) What does "less filling" mean in the given context?

Does the rest of the world like or hate more soda in Coke, according to the lines quoted? Who prefer more soda?

7. "But the cola makers may experience more growing pains, at least with the high-calorie colas, … Baby-boomers are showing a strong preference for healthier, less fattening drinks as they age—everything from diet soda to bottled water to fruit juice."

The slow increase of the sales of colas is repeated once and again in the text. Could you find some reason for that in the lines quoted? What is that?

8. "The drink probably won't do as well when it is rolled out nationally, since consumer coupons and price promotions have been helping it along."

What's your understanding of "price promotions" here?

9. "Bottlers have a symbiotic but occasionally fractious relationship with the syrup makers."

What's the "symbiotic" aspect of the relationship between the two? And what's its "occasionally fractious" aspect? (Study the whole of Paragrph 11 before you give an answer.)

10. "To convince bottlers that the new products can match or exceed the sales of existing brands without heavy discounting or couponing, Coca-Cola and Pepsico will have to cut back on special promotion, then ply the bottlers with the resulting sales data."

What is the implication of "resulting" here?

11. "Bottlers may come in for a little arm-twisting as well. 'It's often very subtle,' says an industry excecutive who prefers not to be named. The Coca-Cola representative will say, 'That decision is not going to sit very well in Atlanta,' or something like that."

1) Whose decision is "that decision"? (See the rest of the 3rd paragraph from the bottom of the text.)

2) Does "that decision" refer to something in line with Coca-

Cola's top leaders' opinion or conflicting to theirs?

3) Please paraphrase the underlined part.

Note: Atlanta is where Coca-Cola Co. is headquartered.

Topics for Summary

1. What is Coca-Cola's strategy for expansion of their market?

2. Why is Coca-Cola, the traditional, biggest Cola maker of the world, turning to the U. S. non-Cola market for expansion?

3. What is the key problem Coca-Cola has to tackle in invading the non-Cola market? Why?

Exercises

Read the following article and write a summary (about 200 words) on how Coca-Cola used marketing expertise to globalize its business and sustain rapid growth.

SYRUP-MAKER'S BOLD STRATEGY

Coca-Cola's success is often put down to its secret recipe. but Industry Editor Neal McGrath finds marketing is the key.

What would happen if someone got hold of Coca-Cola's secret recipe and published it for every soft drink maker in the world to read? Surely, it would spell the end of Coca-Cola's command of the global soft drink market as slews of cheap and close imitations flooded the market. Right?

Wrong. A recently released biography of the beverage included a Coke recipe, but so far Coke is going as strong as ever.

The secret of Coca-Cola's success is more than just the recipe. It lies in a strategy which has established the company so fimly in the minds of the world's consumers that no mere copy-cat could hope to displace it.

The company that started in 1886 when an alleged morphine addict began peddling the liquid in a drug store for 5 US cents a glass has grown into a US$55 billion multinational. Today, Coca-Cola has operations in 195 countries and claims to hold nearly half the carbonated soft drinks market outside the US.

Asia is a prime focus for the company and it recently announced a US$40 million deal that will be the first phase of a plan to re-enter India—one of the few major markets in which the company had no presence.

The key ingredient in Coke's recipe for success is marketing. Wherever Coke goes it spends heavily on every sort of promotion imaginable. Retailers are given menu boards, clocks, shop signs, banners and all manner of other items for use in their shops—all bearing the Coke logo.

"While the combination of tools and tactics we use varies from market to market, our overall strategy remains the same: To make sure the consumer cannot escape Coca-Cola," says Roberto Goizueta, chairman of the board and CEO of the Atlantabased Coca-Cola Company.

Alongside the promotional blitz, the factor enabling Coke to expand aggressively into every corner of the world is its policy of sharing the profit —and the expense—with local business partners. Most Coke bottlers are independent, but Coca-Cola goes to great lengths to help them develop their businesses.

Where there are no established bottlers, Coke helps new ones get started, works with them on quality control and contributes heavily to marketing by giving them advertising materials and subsidising promotion expenses. A subsidiary, the Coca-Cola Financial

Corp, offers loans to bottlers and other customers.

The reason Coke does this is simple. Coke makes its money by selling syrup concentrate. By helping bottlers sell more soft drinks, Coke strengthens demand for its concentrate.

Using independent bottlers has enabled Coca-Cola to continue growing without the mountain of cash that would be needed to fund its own start up operations in every new market. Without such a plan, Coke probably could not afford to expand as rapidly.

The approach also keeps the high profit-margin syrup concentrate business with Coke. Such is the importance of the concentrate business that Coke sets up separate syrup makers to supply the bottlers in each market—and insists on 100% ownership for this core business. When Coke left India in 1977, it was largely because the govenment demanded it sell at least 60% of its Indian syrup-making subsidiary to local investors.

The formula has proved profitable: Business has roughly doubled in each of the last two decades. Between 1980 and 1990, Coke sold some 20 billion gallons of syrup—4 billion more than in the entire history of the company before that. These impressive figures pose a tough challenge for Coca-Cola: How can it keep up this phenomenal pace of growth?

The solution is quite clear to Goizueta: Reach more people. "We are just beginning to reach the 95% of the world's population that lives outside the US," he says. "Today, (our) top 16 markets account for 80% of our volume, but cover only 20% of the world's population."

There are about 1. 9 billion people in what Coke views as its developed markets. That leaves a huge 3. 5 billion potential Coke drinkers in markets it sees as developing. Some 2. 2 billion of these potential customers are in Asia.

Coke has focused on Asia in the last decade and now hopes to cash in on its investment. "In the 1980s, major investment went into Asia-Pacific to put in place the infrastructure that now enables us to concentrate on volume growth. " says Douglas Daft, president of Coca-Cola International's Pacific Group. China and India, which together have almost 2 billion potential Coke drinkers, naturally figure prominently in these plans.

Coke sank US$250 million into China to establish 13 bottling plants in booming coastal areas and is planning to add more plants in the interior. Since 1988, sales of the drink in China have grown by 4 million cases each year to more than 70 million today.

Under Coke's recent deal in India, the company agreed to pay US$40 million to acquire five soft drink brands produced by Parle Exports, a massive company that commands 60% of the Indian soft drink market.

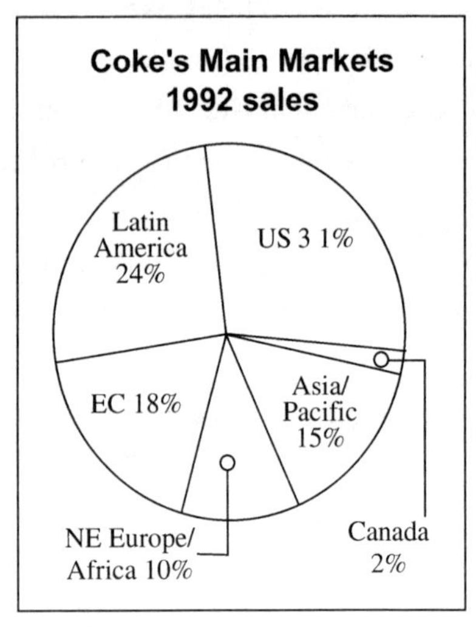

Source: company reports

It will use this acquisition as a springboard to re-launch its own products, using Parle as a marketing partner. There is irony in this partnership: Parle's owner and CEO Ramesh Chauhan once fiercely opposed allowing foreign brands into India and played a key role in driving out Coke.

Coke has supplemented core brands with local products in other markets as well. Georgia Coffee, developed by its Japan subsidiary, now commands 34% of Japan's canned coffee market. That's no small feat in Japan's fiercely competitive soft drink industry.

In Thailand, Coke bottlers sell Mello Lychee, while the Hong

Kong operation offers sweetened soy bean milk under the Hi-C brand.

However, this versatility has come about fairly recently. Until the 1950s, Coke was the company's only product. In the 1960s the Fanta line was introduced along with lemon-lime Sprite and a low calorie cola called TAB. Non-carbonated beverages were added with the Hi-C line of mostly fruit-flavoured drinks.

Coke's approach to dealing with bottlers also remained largely intact from the early days until the 1980s when it began causing massive problems. "Ten years ago they had a much more hands-off approach where they just started the bottler and then left them alone," says Paul Mc Donald, marketing director for Swire Bottlers in Hong Kong, which holds the Coke franchise for the colony, much of China and eight states in the US. That changed as Coke began to lose market share. "In local markets where they thought the poiential wasn't being exploited to the full, they went in with big guns,"he adds.

An example is the Philippines where Coke stepped in to assume greater control over operations after arch rival Pepsi reversed Coke's former two-to-one share of the Philippine cola market. Market watchers say local licensee San Miguel had been neglecting the franchise in favour of its core brewing operations. Coca-Cola shifted production away from San Miguel's soft drink division and into a new joint venture in which it has more say.

Coke still prefers to stay out of equity joint ventures but is now more willing to commit cash when necessary to ensure there are efficient bottlers in place to maintain demand for the concentrate. It spent more than US $1 billion on new plant and equipment in 1992 —nearly double the amount it spent in 1990. Coke owns equity in eight of its 13 China bottlers; high by its world standards but in line with its policy of taking equity where necessary.

Despite the challenge of matching the remarkable performance of the previous decades, Coke views its mission as straightforward:

To take a fairly simple refreshment to as many people as possible.

——From *Asian Business* • Jan. 1994

Supplementary Material for Free Reading

A. Pepsi and Coke Go to War Again, But This Time It's Over Orange Juice

Who's No. 1? Depends on the Drink.

Pepsi has long been second to Coke in the huge market for soft drinks. But it became the owner last July of the best-selling packaged orange juice when it acquired Tropicana, a much smaller business.

By Constance L. Hays

SOFT DRINK MARKET SHARE

Percentage of all carbonated soft drink sales based on number of cases shipped to distributors

TOTAL RETAIL VALUE $56.3 billion

TOTAL CASES 9.88 billion

ORANGE JUICE MARKET SHARE

Percentage of all refrigerated orange juice sales for the year ended Jan. 31, 1999

TOTAL $2.59 billion

* Pure Premium and Season's Best

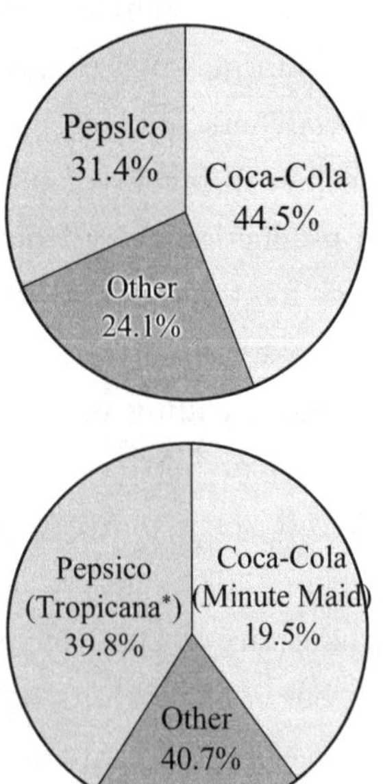

Sources: *Beverage Digest*; *Information Resources Inc*. The New York Times.

Coke promotes its "secret formula" for achieving uniformity of taste from Tuisa to Timbuktu. Pepsi scoffs, saying its product is just plain better and boasting that its market appeal gives it a big advantage over its archrival.

Nothing new in any of that — except that the soft drink giants are both talking about orange juice.

After Pepsico bought the Tropicana juice maker from the Seagram Company last July for $3. 3 billion, the spillover of the cola wars to America's breakfast tables was inevitable. The Coca-Cola Company has owned Minute Maid, the nation's No. 2 juice maker, for more than 35 years, and now the two companies have a new testing ground for their marketing arsenals.

Some analysts wonder whether the companies are indulging in overkill. Tropicana and Minute Maid are spending heavily to blast consumers with advertisements and promotions and are sniping at each other in the best Coke-Pepsi tradition. In February, Minute Maid trumpeted growing sales of its Minute Maid Premium even as "the Tropicana Season's Best line registered the largest decline in sales —down nearly 32 per cent —of all value brands." Not to be outdone, Tropicana has issued news releases comparing the taste of juices made from concentrates unfavorably with its "natural" brands.

All this, skeptics ask, for a market that is essentially stagnant? Indeed, the juice market, at about $3 billion last year, represents only a small corner of the companies' beverage empires — a small and highly volatile corner.

"There's very little synergy in terms of the economics," said Jennifer Solomon, a beverage analyst for Salomon Smith Barney and one of the early doubters about the wisdom of the Tropicana acquisition. "Pepsi now has to deal with refrigerated rail cars and perishable products. It's a whole level of complexity that you don't have in the soft-drink business."

Still, the Tropicana-Minute Maid clash makes for one of the more interesting side battles of the cola wars; Pepsi's purchase of Tropicana may have forced Coke to hold on to Minute Maid against its will, for example. And with orange juice, the tables are turned: Pepsi, the perennial No. 2 to Coke, has the best-selling brand for a change.

Coke and Pepsi argue that orange juice is a crucial element of their respective corporate strategies. And since both beverage giants are using the same basic techniques to sell orange juice that they use to market cola, any sudden reversals of fortune for Minute Maid or Tropicana could act as an early warning sign for the future of their other brands.

As does Coke, Minute Maid wants to convince consumers that no matter where they go, it will always give them the same familiar flavor. That is because both products are distributed as concentrate to all points of the globe.

"One of the hallmarks of a brand is consistency," said Ralph Cooper, Minute Maid's president and a former Coca-Cola president in Europe. "What we are trying to do with Minute Maid is make the taste the same everywhere. That was a conscious decision we made related to the brand building we are doing."

Minute Maid, based in Houston, adopted its concentrate-only policy in 1996 as part of an image overhaul that included the change of its name from Coca-Cola Foods. Along with a new package and a new name, the company also contended that it had come up with a formula to reproduce the taste of "biting into a fresh, ripe orange."

This was achieved, it said, through careful mixing of the orange juice, along with other "parts of the orange," that it buys from the United States, Brazil and other countries.

"It's a bit of secret formula," said Joe Scalzo, Minute Maid's marketing director, evoking the heart and soul of Coca-Cola, which still will not reveal how its cola is made. "The way we process orange juice gives us the ability to tweak the formulation such that you can naturally enhance some of the taste aspects of the product."

Taking a jab at Tropicana, Mr. Scalzo said consumers do not give a hoot how a product is made as long as it tastes good. "Our competition's approach is that they squeeze the orange juice during the season and then store it, either in tanks in Florida or frozen in big blocks,"he said derisively. "We process the juice the same way, year round. They are forced to vary the process based on the season."

In essence, the reconfiguration of Minute Maid mimics the model at Coca-Cola: Make a product that can be shipped worldwide, make people aware of your brand and drive demand for it through advertising.

Tropicana, of course, says Minute Maid's strategy is all wet, or rather, not wet enough. To the PepsiCo unit, it seems self-evident that consumers will prefer juice that is packaged just as it was squeezed out of the orange. And there is no longer any question that it can promote its not-from-concentrate juice as a premium brand or that consumers will pay another 10 cents a quart for it.

"Tropicana is the Michael Jordan of orange juice," said Emanuel Goldman, a global consumer-products analyst for Merrill Lynch. "That's why Pepsi bought it."

But Tropicana's real competitive advantage might be its parent company's extensive delivery networks. Pepsico plans to put Tropicana products in places they are not in right now—like additional convenience stores, airports and food-service companies. The company just introduced a 20-ounce Tropicana container, hoping to prod higher consumption with the large single-serving package.

Essentially, Pepsico wants to weld Tropicana with the other two components of its packaged-food empire: soft drinks and Frito-Lay snack foods. Pepsi senior managers, who have begun sitting in on strategy meetings at Tropicana's Bradenton, Fla., headquarters, believe the combination of the three lines creates a marketing appeal to both consumers and retailers that it calls "the power of one."

"We believe this is Pepsico's most important strategic initiative," Ms. Solomon of Salomon Smith Barney wrote in a recent report. "In test markets, Pepsico has found that Pepsi/Frito sales aisles have resulted in 30 per cent sales increases." At a recent food show in Chicago, Pepsi displayed combined soft drinks and snacks in various formats, clearly indicating this was the future.

In the first quarter of this year, Tropicana's sales grew $15 million, or about 3 per cent, from a year earlier, to $499 million, and its profits rose 29 per cent, to $35 million, from $27 million in 1998. "Tropicana frankly had a terrific quarter," Pepsico's chief financial officer, Michael D. White, told analysts in a conference call. "We have seen the benefit of the shift to Pure Premium and the reduction of our overhead costs."

The news at Minute Maid was even better: sales grew by 5 per cent over the same period, and the company turned in the best showing of any Coca-Cola unit in a quarter when Coke's volume worldwide declined by 1 per cent. Minute Maid does about $2 billion in sales annually, which includes products other than orange juice.

For all the impressive results at both companies, and for all their portrayal of their products as thirst-quenchers supreme, demand for orange juice remains lackluster. Only one in five Americans drinks it for breakfast. And both Tropicana and Minute Maid constitute tiny fractions of their parent company's total revenues: $22.3 billion at Pepsico; $18.8 billion at Coke.

"We've learned that it's in the refrigerator," Minute Maid's Mr. Scalzo said, sounding a little frustrated. "How do we get them to bring it out?"

It is not just Coke that feels his pain. Tropicana does, too.

"The big challenge is to get that segment of the population that is not starting their day with orange juice," said Brian Cornell, until recently Tropicana's senior vice president for sales and marketing and now president for Europe and Canada, "and, two, to get them to continue to drink orange juice on a regular basis."

The means to such an end, both juice makers believe, is adding more products. With its eye on young families, Minute Maid has begun packaging calcium-fortified juice in single-serving boxes for snacks and lunch boxes and is marketing new flavor mixes, also with added calcium. It has introduced an orange-passion fruit juice, Mr. Scalzo said, with "a more sophisticated taste" that is supposed to appeal particularly to older women.

Tropicana is leaning heavily on the calcium-added concept, with calcium-enhanced grapefruit juice as well as orange. There is also an orange juice with extra vitamin C, vitamin E and other additives. Marketing messages include comparisons between orange juice and bananas. "Few people recognize that a glass of orange juice has as much potassium as a banana," declares Mr. Cornell, the sales chief. And another thing: bananas may not be available in your local vending machine. Tropicana ads, with their "Perfect" slogan, are aimed at, among others, older women, whose worries about losing bone-mass because of menopause tend to be more urgent than those of other groups, Other ads focus on men and children.

Still, even if orange juice is fortified to the point that it packs all the wallop of an energy bar, consumers have dozens of other choices for a breakfast drink or midday pick-me-up, from competing juice blends to endless varieties of teas and coffees. Not to mention colas.

"You're not going to be able to sell orange juice like you sell Pepsi —price it low and stack it high," said Kevin Murphy, the chief operating officer for Ocean Spray, which has sued Pepsi, its distribution partner, over the Tropicana acquisition.

But it is not impossible to give old products a fin de siècle spark. "Look at milk," said Bob Vosburgh, who follows the business for Supermarket News, a trade publication. "There's a whole new aura for milk with these resealable single-serve jugs that were introduced by one of the big dairies. It's helped rejuvenate the whole milk category, even though it's the same thing in a new package."

Whether orange juice can pull off the same feat is unclear. "Everyone always points to what Quaker did with Snapple," Mr. Vosburgh said, referring to the cereal giant's purchase of Snapple for $1.7 billion and subsequent, humiliating sale of the beverage maker for $300 million. "What happens with Coke and Pepsi and orange juice remains to be seen."

——From *New York Times* · May 19, 1999

B. How the U.S. Helped Big Tobacco Crack Asia's Markets

By Glenn Frankel
The Washington Post

On the streets of Manila, "jump boys" as young as 10 hop in and out of traffic selling Marlboros and Lucky Strikes to passing motorists.

In the discos and coffee shops of Seoul, young Koreans light up foreign brands that a decade ago were illegal to possess.

And in Beijing, America's biggest tobacco companies are competing for the right to launch cooperative projects with the state-run tobacco monopoly in hopes of capturing a share of the biggest potential market in the world.

Throughout the bustling cities of a newly prosperous Asia — as well as the ruined economies of the former Soviet bloc — the American cigarette is king. At home, cigarette consumption has undergone a 15-year decline. Thanks to foreign sales, however, the companies are making larger profits than ever before.

But the industry did not launch its campaign for new overseas markets alone. The Reagan and Bush administrations used their economic and political clout to pry open markets in Japan, South Korea, Taiwan, Thailand and China for American cigarettes.

Waging the war

Many U. S. officials still see cigarette exports as strictly an issue of free trade and economic fairness, while tobacco industry critics and public health advocates consider it a moral question.

Even the Clinton administration finds itself torn: It is the most vocally antismoking administration in U. S. history, yet it has been in the uncomfortable role of challenging or delaying some antismoking efforts overseas.

At the same time, fledgling antismoking movements are rising up with support from American activists, passing restrictions that in some cases are tougher than those in the United States.

International epidemiologist Richard Peto of Oxford University estimates that smoking is responsible for 3 million deaths per year worldwide; he projects that 30 years from now the number will have reached 10 million, most of them in developing nations.

Asiais where tobacco's search for new horizons began and where the indutry came to rely most on Washington's help. U. S. officials in effect became the industry's lawyers, agents and collaborators. Prominent politicians such as Robert J. Dole, Jesse Helms, Dan Quayle and Al Gore played a role.

"No matter how this process spins it self out," George Griffin, commercial counselor at the U. S. Embassy in Seoul, told the public affairs manager of Philip Morris Asia in a January 1986, "I want to emphasize that the embassy and the various U. S. government agencies in Washington will keep the interests of Philip Morris and the other American cigarette manufacturers in the forefront of our daily concerns."

This was, U. S. officials insisted, solely an issue of free trade. But then-Vice President Quayle suggested another motive when he told a North Carolina farming audience in 1990 that the government was seeking to help the tobacco industry compensate for shrinking markets at home. "We ought to think about the exports," he said. "We ought to think about opening up markets, breaking down the barriers."

A handful of American health officials vigorously opposed the government's campaign, but were stymied or ignored. "I feel the most shameful thing this country did was to export disease, disability and death by selling our cigarettes to the world," said former surgeon general C. Everett Koop.

Clayton Yeutter, an affable, highoctane Nebraska Republican with a wide smile and serious political aspirations, came to the Office of the U. S. Trade Representative in 1985 with a mission: to put a dent in the record U. S. trade deficit by forcing foreign countries to lower their barriers against American products.

He took office when Washington was on the verge of declaring a trade war against some of its staunchest allies in the Far East. Asian tigers such as Japan, South Koresa, Taiwan and Thailand were running up huge trade surpluses with the U. S. on goods ranging from T-shirts to computer chips to luxury sedans. The U. S. annual trade deficit in 1984 totaled a record $123 billion.

So the Reagan administration turned to a small, elite and little-known federal agency, with a powerful weapon in its arsenal. Section 301 of the 1974 Trade Act empowered USTR to launch a full-scale investigation of unfair trading practices and required that Washington invoke retaliatory sanctions within a year if a targeted government did not agree to change its ways.

The U. S. tobacco industry had been trying for years to get a foothold in these promising new Asian markets. In 1981 the big three — Philip Morris Inc. , R. J. Reynolds Tobacco Co. and Brown & Williamson — had formed a trade group called the U. S. Cigarette Export Association to pursue industry-wide policy on the issue. But the companies had felt frustrated during Reagan's first term.

• Japan, the West's second largest cigarette market, remained virtually closed to U. S. brands because of high tariffs and discriminatory distribution.

• South Korean law effectively made it a crime to buy or sell a pack of foreign cigarettes.

• Taiwan and Thailand remained tightly shut.

All except Taiwan were signatories to the General Agreement on Tariffs and Trade, and Taipei hoped to join soon. Yet each appeared to viloate free-trade principles.

When Yeutter and his staff looked at the cigarette business in these countries, they saw hypocrisy. Each Asian government sought to justify its ban on imported cigarettes in the name of public health, yet each had its own protected, state-controlled tobacco monopoly that manufactured and sold cigarettes.

The state companies' marketing techniques were in many ways just as cynical as those of the American companies. In Taiwan, for example, the most popular state brand was called Long Life.

Health was simply a smoke screen, Yeutter quickly decided. "I would have had no problem with Japan or Korea or Taiwan putting up genuine health restrictions," he insisted. "But that's not what these governments were doing. They were restricting trade, and it was just blatant."

But the very flaws of the state-run monopolies were exactly what a doctor might have ordered: Their high price and poor quality had helped limit smoking mostly to older men who had the money and taste for harsh, tar-heavy local brands. The monopolies seldom, if ever, advertised and did not target the great untapped markets of women and young people. Per-capital sales remained low in every country except Japan.

Gregory Connolly, an antismoking activist who heads the Massachusetts Tobacco Control Program, has traveled throughout Asia and documented how U. S. companies skirted advertising restrictions by sponsoring televised rock concerts and sporting events, placing cigarette brands in movies and lending their brand names to products such as clothing and sports gear. A Madonna concert in Spain became a "Salem Madonna Concert" when televised in Hong Kong, while the U. S. Open Tennis Tournament in New York became the "Salem Tennis Open" in Malaysia.

Yeutter and his trade warriors saw foreign advertising restrictions as one more form of trade discrimination.

In January 1984 a letter to an official in the Commerce Department, Robert H. Bockman, then director of corporate affairs for Philip Morris Asia, described trade barriers against his company's products in South Korea. He then went on to discuss what he called "the politics of tobacco in this election year. Attached please find a listing of the 1980 election results in the major tobacco-growing areas in the United States. You will note that the margin of victory for the president (Ronald Reagan) was narrow in some key areas."

First Target: Japan

Republican Sen. Jesse Helms of North Carolina, who at the time chaired the Senate Agriculture Committee, also in tervened. In July 1986 Helms wrote to Japanese Prime Minister Yasuhiro Nakasone congratulating him on his recent election victory and pointing out that American cigarettes accounted for less than 2 per cent of the Japanese market.

"Your friends in Congress will have a better chance to stem the tide of anti-Japanese trade sentiment if and when they can cite tangible examples of your doors being opened to American products," Helms wrote. "I urge that you make a commitment to establish a timetable for allowing U. S. cigarettes a specific share of your market. May I suggest a goal of 20 per cent within the next 18 months."

At Yeutter's urging, Reagan decided not to wait for a formal filing from the industry against Japan. The White House filed three 301 complaints with USTR in September 1985, one of them against Japanese restrictions on the sale of U. S. cigarettes. Other U. S. bureaucrats began drawing up lists of products for possible retaliation.

In subsequent trade talks, Japanese negotiators hung tough through 14 sessions. Finally, a year after the 301 comolaint was filed the Japanese capitulated, signing an agreement allowing in American-made cigarettes.

Philip Morris aimed at Japanese women with Virginia Slims; Japan Tobacco fought back with Misty, a mild blend. When RJR wooed young smokers with Joe Camel, JT countered with Dean, named after fabled actor James Dean. Cigarettes became the second most—advertised product on television in Tokyo —up from 40th a year earlier.

Today, imported brands control 21 per cent of the Japanese market and earn more than $7 billion in annual sales. Female smoking is at an all-time high, according to Japan Tobacco's surveys.

Next, into South Korea

The next target was South Korea, with its $1. 7 billion domestic tobacco market. The U. S. tobacco industry filed a 301 complaint against Seoul in January 1988. USTR initiated an investigation a month later.

South Korea's state cigarette monopoly had done little advertising over the years, and a few months before the 301 case, the Seoul government had formally outlawed cigarette ads. But the U. S. insisted on defining "fair access" as including the right to advertise.

Even before the formal complaint was filed, tobacco state lawmakers had supported opening South Korea's market. Republican Sens. Robert J. Dole of Kansas, Helms and 14 others — including AlGore, then a Democratic senator from Tennessee — wrote to South Korean President Chun Doo Hwan in July 1987 demanding that tobacco companies be allowed "the right to import and distribute without discriminatory taxes and duties, as well as the right to advertise and promote their products."

In May 1988 Seoul formally agreed to open its doors to American brands. Cigarettes quickly became one of the most heavily advertised products in South Korea; from no advertising in 1986, American tobacco companies spent $25 million in 1988. Within a year, U. S. companies had captured 6 per cent of the market.

Fast work on Taiwan

On the heels of the Japanese agreement, Taiwan had agreed in October 1985 to liberalize barriers to wine, beer and cigarettes. But a year passed and the market remained effectively closed. Reagan then ordered Yeutter to propose "proportional countermeasures."

Six weeks later, Taiwan folded. "The atmosphere in the negotiations was very bad for us," recalled Chien-Shien Wang, then deputy minister of commerce, who was Taiwan's chief negotiator. "We were told the U. S. had lost patience with us and was about to put us on the 301 list. So we had no choice but to agree."

Following the agreement, consumption of imported cigarettes in Taiwan soared. According to one industry trade journal, foreign brands went from 1 per cent of annual cigarette sales to more than 20 per cent in less than two years.

New horizons

The 301 cases were a boon to the industry. The Boston-based National Bureau of Economic Research estimated that sales of American cigarettes were 600 per cent higher in the targeted countries in 1991 than they would have been without U. S. intervention.

When Yeutter moved to Agriculture, incoming President George Bush appointed Carla Hills, a highly regarded lawyer and former housing and urban development secretary, to succeed him at USTR. And the agency set its sights on opening more cigarette markets in Asia.

... and How Little Thailand Fought Back

BANGKOK, Thailand

The first thing Prakit Vateesatokit noticed were the billboards. The broad cowboy vistas and the chiseled features of the Marlboro Mansprouted in the summer of 1985 along the main highway to Bangkok International Airport, followed a few months later by full-color ads in Thai publications.

More disconcerting were the T-shirts, kites, baseball caps and school notebooks that began appearing with the Marlboro trademark. Philip Morris Inc. denied making or distributing these items and accused pirates of stealing the company logo. But it seemed to Prakit, a doctor and a leader of Thailand's fledgling antismoking movement, that someone was targeting children.

It was a bit strange because Thailand's rules effectively banned the import of foreign cigarettes, and the only American brands available for sale were either in the duty-free shop at the airport or smuggled packs sold under the table by small-time street vendors.

Then, in March 1989, Prakit learned to his surprise that after three years of secret talks, the Thai Finance Ministry was on the verge of approving a deal with the U. S. Trade Representative's Office that would open the country's markets to American brands. The U. S. bigthree cigarette companies —Philip Morris, R. J. Reynolds and Brown & Williamson — had targeted Thailand and enlisted Washington's help in prying it open.

They started by softening the Thai market with advertisements and sponsorships, then applied U. S. government pressure and the threat of trade retaliation as stipulated by Section 301 of the U. S. Trade Act.

It did not happen.

Instead a handful of determined Thai health officials and doctors resisted the assault and rolled it back. Led by Prakit and fellow physician Hatai Chitanondh, a senior official in the Thai Public Health Ministry, the counterattack was aided by antismoking activists from other parts of Asia and the United States.

Thailand won an enormous victory. Today it boasts some of the strongest antismoking laws in the world. And imported cigarettes still account for less than 3 per cent of the legal Thai market—a far cry from the 25 per cent anticipated by U. S. firms.

Thailand's resistance campaign played a crucial role in creating the antismoking movements that are taking root today throughout Asia.

Still, Asian public health activists contend that even under the Clinton administration Washington remains a reluctant ally of the tobacco industry when it comes to foreign markets. In recent years, U. S. officials retarded efforts to ban cigarette advertising in Taiwan and South Korea and opposed Thailand's attempt to require manufacturers to disclose ingredient information.

Judith Mackay, a Hong Kong-based antismoking campaigner, said the big U. S. tobacco companies "thought they could come in and have a free ride. But in the end the 301 cases probably did quite a lot of good because they galvanized people. They united people in Asia in outrage. And Thailand was the key."

The fight begins

The Royal Kingdom operated a typical, state-protected cigarette industry. The monopoly did not have to advertise or work hard for market share—indeed, in 1988 the government had banned all advertising of tobacco products. But more than 60 per cent of Thai men and 6 per cent of Thai women smoked, in effect a captive market.

Owen Smith of Philip Morris, a veteran trade lawyer, saw a sleepy, bloated state tobacco monopoly ripe for challenge. As in the past, his association turned to the office of the U. S. Trade Representative for help.

In March 1989, Hatai Chitanondh, then deputy permanent secretary in the Thai Public Health Ministry, was tipped off by a friend in the Finance Ministry about an impending deal with U. S. officials.

Hatai, who trained as a neurologist, had developed a hatred of tobacco in his job as a public health official. Acting on his own, he denounced "tobacco colonialism" at a news conference. Within days, Prakit and other antismoking activists had joined in protest, along with tobacco farmers and cigarette factory workers.

Bowing to pressure, the finance minister put the deal on hold. Shortly after, Smith's association filed an unfair trade practices complaint with USTR. The companies demanded the right to import, sell and distribute cigarettes in Thailand. They also insisted Bangkok lift its advertising ban so they could promote their products.

Carla Hills agreed with Smith. Like her predecessor. Clayton Yeutter, the new head of USTR was a nonsmoker; nevertheless, she believed Thailand was shutting out foreign cigarettes merely to shelter its own state-run monopoly. In April 1989 she accepted the case under Section 301, a provision that gave Thailand a year to comply or face retaliatory sanctions.

A veteran joins the fight

A few weeks after the complaint was filed, Prakit met a number of veteran antismoking activists for the first time, including Gregory Connolly, head of the Massachusetts Tobacco Control Program and a representative of the American Public Health Association, who had become an avowed enemy of the tobacco industry after his sister died of lung cancer.

Connolly listened to Prakit describe Thailand's struggles with the 301 complaint and urged him to hang tough. "Whatever you do," he told Prakit, "don't let the Americans in. They'll launch an incredible advertising campaign, and they'll get Thai women and children to smoke."

In August 1989, Prakit received a letter from USTR granting a public hearing and inviting him to appear. The hearing, held in September, was a turning point. Hills and USTR, usually lauded in the press, suddenly found themselves portrayed as handmaidens of Big Tobacco.

Faced with growing pressure and working for George Bush, a president who seemed less inclined than Ronald Reagan to go all out for tobacco, Hills broke precedent. She suspended the 301 procedure and referred the Thailand case to the World Health Organization in Geneva for adjudication under the provisions of the GATT.

It was the first clear break between Washington and the tobacco industry on a cigarette trade issue.

A victory for the crusaders

The U. S. delegation had not enlisted a health expert for its team in Geneva; instead, it marshaled the tobacco industry's standard arguments— claiming, for example, that American cigarettes were healthier than Thai products because they contained less tar.

Connolly, serving as an expert witness for WHO, replied: "It's like jumping from the 10th floor vs. the seventh floor. At the end, all cigarettes... will eventually kill you."

In November 1990 the GATT panel concluded that Thailand's failure to allow imported cigarettes was indeed a clear violation of Article XI, which prohibited discriminatory practices. At the same time, however, the panel ruled that smoking constituted such a serious health risk that Thailand justifiably could restrict cigarette sales and ban advertising, as long as it applied the rules equally to both domestics and imports.

Hills and USTR declared the GATT decision a victory. But they also quietly dropped their demand that Thailand allow cigarette ads. With help from Connolly and other American activists, Hatai and Prakit then drafted one of the world's strictest antismoking codes.

Thailand's Tobacco Products Control Act bans all cigarette advertising, as well as sales to young people. No cigarette promotions or free samples are allowed. Cigarette packs must prominently display one of 10 health warnings. The Non-Smokers Health Protection Act bans smoking in most public places.

Thailand's success reverberated throughout Asia.

By 1995, 33 of 35 Asian countries had tobacco control laws on their books according to activist Judith Mackay. (G. F.).

——From *The Japan Times* • Jan. 8, 1997

Lesson 13

Market Analysis

Text

Hong Kong is Tops at Cracking U. S. Shell Eggs

By Michael L. Humphrey

While most people think of Hong Kong as a small market, it is, in fact, the largest export market for U. S. shell eggs. In 1985, the United Sates exported over 7 million dozen shell eggs valued at $ 4 million for food use in Hong Kong. That market alone accounted for half of the volume and 40 per cent of the value of total U. S. exports of shell eggs for food use.

Hong Kong consumers enjoy a variely of shell eggs, including fresh hen and duck eggs, dyed eggs for special occasions, eggs cooked in salt or tea leaves, pigeon eggs and preserved duck eggs. Fresh hen eggs, however, are the most popular item.

Each consumer in Hong Kong eats an average of 215 fresh eggs and 20 preserved or dyed eggs each year. According to Hong Kong import statistics, the territory annually imports more than 1. 2 billion fresh shell eggs valued at $ 52 million. In addition, Hong kong produces 4. 5 million dozen hen, duck and goose eggs and 12 million dozen quail eggs annually.

Chinese eggs dominate the fresh egg market with more than an 80-per cent share. Thailand became the second largest supplier in 1984, following a nearly eightfold increase over 1983 shipments. The United States is currently the third largest supplier with a 7. 5-

per cent market share in 1985—up from 6.8 per cent in 1984. Egg imports from the Netherlands also showed a dramatic increase in 1985.

Chinese Prefer Brown Eggs

The Chinese, who constitute 95 per cent of Hong Kong's population, prefer brown eggs over white. In fact, 90 per cent or more of the fresh eggs consumed are brown. The major outlets for white eggs are hotels, western-style restaurants and fast food shops.

Chinese consumers prefer the deeper color of brown egg yolks—often considered essential to the color of many Chinese dishes. Chinese-style restaurants also find that brown eggs are more popular with customers.

Chinese eggs have a unique odor that can be an advantage or a disadvantage, depending on the consumer.

To the Chinese consumer, the odor is indicative of a "good egg" and is an important reason, in addition to a price advantage, for the popularity of Chinese eggs. The odor, however, is a major reason why Chinese eggs are not accepted by hotels, western-style restaurants and fast food outlets.

U. S. Brown Eggs Fail To Compete

Virtually all eggs imported from the United States are white. This is due in part to the fact that the availability of European brown eggs at lower prices has made U. S. brown eggs uncopmpetitive.

Packing and grading of U. S. brown eggs is also difficult beacuse unlike U. S. white eggs, U. S. brown eggs vary markedly in size. Eggs from medium to extra large are packed in the same carton, resulting in frequent breakage of larger eggs.

Wholesalers or retailers in Hong Kong also must sort the eggs by sizes, which creates extra work.

Importers point out that with alternative suppliers now available, U. S. brown eggs cannot compete without improvement in the method of packing.

In the white egg market, however, U. S. eggs have enjoyed a distinct advantage. Hotels, restaurants and institutions recognize the consistent high quality of U. S. eggs.

Another advantage is that U. S. eggs can be kept for a comparatively long time. The shipping time of 14 to 16 days from the U. S. West Coast, compared to 30 days from Europe, also has given U. S. white eggs a competitive edge.

However, U. S. white eggs now face growing competition from European eggs. The U. S. market share of the hotel and restaurant market dropped from 92 per cent in 1981 to 58 per cent in 1985, while the EC market share incrcased from zero to 28 per cent in the same period. Beacause of this loss of market share due to subsidized competition, USDA recently announced an Export Enhancement Program to facilitate the sale of 44 million eggs to Hong Kong.

Structure of Trade

Hong Kong has about 15 egg importers. The largest is the Hong kong eggs and Products Company, which monopolizes the import of Chinese eggs, both fresh and preserved. Others import from different sources.

There are 42 wholesalers under the Hong Kong Eggs and Products Company. Wholesalers are located in three small areas in Hong Kong: Egg Street and Saiyingpun on Hong Kong Island and Kam Lam Street in Kowloon.

Retailers, hotels and restaurants all buy from these wholesalers although some hotels and supermarkets buy directly from importers.

At the retail level, eggs are sold through the wet markets, hawkers, grocery stores and supermarkets. About 70 per cent of eggs are consumed in the home and the remaining 30 per cent goes to hotels, restaurants, fast food outlets and bakeries.

Most eggs on the retail market are not refrigerated and customers are allowed to choose each individual egg and examine the product under light. Some of the U. S. large white eggs, however, are offered in one-dozen packs in air-conditioned supermarkets.

Major Suppliers Compete

Major suppilers to the Hong Kong egg market are making greater efforts to increase the competitiveness of their products in order to maintain or expand market shares.

To promote sales of Chinese eggs, the Chinese Eggs and Products Company recently held a "luck draw"—a popular promotional activity in Hong Kong—with prizes in solid gold for winning retailers. Attractive posters are designed to promote both fresh eggs and preserved Chinese eggs.

The European countries apparently are trying to increase sales by maintaining low prices.

Although brown eggs continue to dominate the market, the rapid expansion of fast food outlets in the territory could help boost the demand for white eggs, making the prospects for shell egg imports brighter.

The author is the U. S. agricultural officer in Hong Kong.

—From *Foreign Agriculture* • October 1986

Words and Expressions

tops	*a.*	[俚]最能干的
account(for)	*v.*	(在数量、比例方面)占
item	*n.*	(商品的)品种
quail	*n.*	鹌鹑
shipment	*n.*	交运的货物量
the Netherlands	尼德兰(即荷兰 Holland)	
constitute	*v.*	构成
outlet	*n.*	(商品的)销售网络;市场
yolk	*n.*	蛋黄
essential	*a.*	必不可少的;非常重要的
unique	*a.*	独特的;仅有的
odor	*n.*	气味
indicative	*a.*	标示的
virtually	*ad.*	事实上;实际上
availability	*n.*	获得的可能性
packing	*n.*	包装
grading	*v.*	按级分类
carton	*n.*	纸(板)盒
wholesaler	*n.*	批发商
retailer	*n.*	零售商
sort	*v.*	把 … 分类
alternative	*a.*	供选择的;供代替的
distinct	*a.*	明显的
institutions	*n.*	(教育、慈善、宗教性质的)社会公共机构
shipping	*n.*	运输
subsidize	*v.*	给 … 津贴;资助

enhancement	*n.*	增加
facilitate	*v.*	使便利
monopolize	*v.*	垄断
supermarket	*n.*	超级市场
hawker	*n.*	沿街叫卖的小贩
grocery	*n.*	食品杂货
refrigerate	*v.*	冷藏
pack	*n.*	包装(容器)
competitiveness	*n.*	竞争力
promote sales	推销商品	
luck draw	幸运抽奖	
promotional	*a.*	促销的
poster	*n.*	招贴

Notes to the Text

1. Foreign Agriculture 《外国农业》

美国商业部出版的农业贸易月刊,其文章以农业部的官方资料为依据,主要向美国的出口商提供有关海外市场、购买趋势、新的竞争者、新产品、贸易政策的变化以及海外促销活动的信息。

2. "… dyed eggs for special occasions…"

按中国传统习惯,当一个家庭有新的成员诞生,为了庆祝这一喜事要向亲朋好友送红鸡蛋,其他喜庆的场合,也有类似的举动。许多居住在香港的中国人仍然保留着此习俗。

3. fast food shops 快餐店

以能够迅速将烹调食品送到柜台上出售为特点的商业单位,通常只有有限的几种预包装或预配料商品。快餐店提供的最常见的食品包括汉堡包,冰冻或夹馅的甜食及各种各样的三明治。美国的麦当劳快餐店(McDonald's)是最有名的,其国外分店达1 000多个。

4. USDA: 美国农业部,the United States Department of Ag-

riculture 的简写形式。

5. “Because of this loss … to Hong Kong.”

早在 1962 年，欧共体设立了“共同农业基金”，目的之一是为了向共同体成员国的农业经营者提供补贴，帮助他们在国际市场上同其他国家的农民竞争。凭借这些补贴他们便可以大幅度降低其农产品价格以打败对手。

向生产者直接付款并不是补贴的惟一办法。政府还可以通过自己承担损失向农产品出口商提供低息贷款或免费提供销售服务（提供信息，举办贸易博览会，建立商业联系等）来达到补贴的目的。

6. supermarket 超级市场

在自选售货基础上经营的大型零售商店，出售杂货、水果蔬菜、肉类、面包糕点和牛奶制品，有时也出售非食品货物。远在 20 世纪 30 年代美国即有超级市场，其主要优势是廉价售货。40 年代和 50 年代，超级市场在美国成为食品销售的主要渠道。50 年代超级市场遍布大部分欧洲。在发达国家，超级市场的发展是走向降低成本、简化销售方式趋势的一部分。60 年代超级市场在中东、远东、拉丁美洲欠发达国家中出现，主要为那些具有中上等收入的人们所欢迎。如今，超级市场几乎遍布全世界的每一个角落，已经成为人们生活中一个不可缺少的部分。

7. “… the wet market …”： 出售未经加工的肉、鱼、禽蛋的市场。

Questions on Content and Language Points

(for preview, discussion and review)

1. “Hong Kong is tops at cracking U.S. shell eggs.”

What's the implication of the heading of the market report?

2. “That market alone accounted for half of the volume and 40 per cent of the value of total U.S. exports of shell eggs for food use.”

Why did the market account for only 40 per cent of the value while it acounted for half of the volume of total U.S. exports of eggs?

3. What should be the objects of study when you make a study of a market, following the given market report's example?

4. What is the significance of studying your(potential) customers in market-research, as you have seen in the report?

5. Why should much of your interest be concentrated on your rivals and their products in the market, especially their advantages and disadvantages while investigating a market?

6. What constitue the marketing channel for eggs from the Mainland or abroad in H. K. ? Could you imagine how it operates?

Topic for Summary

What is the main content of the text?

Exercises

Read the article given below and do the following exercise.

A Healthy Appetite for World Markets

The food industry accounts for a quarter of exports
and has been hit by the recent Gatt deal. But there could
be new opportunities, writes Hilary Barnes

An English schoolgirl who was asked in the 1980s what she associated with Denmark, replied: "pig, pig, bacon, pig". This may not be an uncommon image, but there is much more both to modern Denmark and to its food industry.

Though it rears more than 20m pigs a year and still provides the best-selling imported bacon in Britain, Denmark, with only 5m people, produces enough food for three times that number. It also has a large share of world markets in other areas apart from pigmeat where it has specialised, such as cheese and fresh and frozen fish.

The food industry provides between 12 and 18 per cent of Denmark's domestic employment, (depending on the definition used), and accounts for about 25 per cent of the country's merchandise exports.

Denmark is the world's fifth-largest exporter of food products, according to a report produced for the Ministry for Industry last year, and a 16 per cent increase in output over the past 10 years has enabled it to maintain its share of world markets.

Manufacturing industry long ago overtook agriculture as the country's main export industry, and now provides about 70 per cent of the country's merchandise exports, but agriculture and fisheries still account for about 5 per cent of total employment and roughly the same share of total production.

The rise of the primary food industries—pigmeat, dairy products and fish—has been accompanied, too, by the development of companies in associated industries, many of them world leaders. These include Novo Nordisk, Christian Hansen Group and Grindsted Products, producers of food ingredients such as enzymes, emulsifiers, stabilisers and flavourings; Foss Electric and Radiometer in instrumentation; and APV Danish Turnkey Dairies and Niro Atomiser in food processing machinery.

Carlsberg has, of course, established itself, too, as a leading international brewing company. Danisco, the sugar, distilling, frozen vegetables and packaging group, is less well-known internationally but has become one of the largest European producers of beet sugar through acquisitions in Sweden and Germany, and is one of the country's largest listed industrial corporations.

The food and food technology industries, because of their vital importance to the health of the Danish economy, have been pinpointed by the government as one of the sectors on which Denmark's future growth and prosperity will depend.

For this reason the government is helping to finance a substantial programme of research, which, it is hoped, will enable the country to lift the quality of its products along the route from the farm to the table.

WORLD EXPORTS

Denmark's share

Pigmeat	26%
Frozen Fish	13%
Fresh fish	12%
Milk, cream	12%
Cheese	10%
Bakery products	10%
Total world exports	0.85%

Source:Kim Morer and Heook Pade. Industrial Success,Samtundslittevatur, 1988

The strong position which the country holds in the food industry goes back a long way. Denmark was one of a few countries in Europe which did not react to the challenge of cheap American corn in the 1870s by raising import barriers. Instead, its farmers had to find alternative sources of income, and as a result, developed a lucrative market exporting butter, eggs and bacon to the UK.

The country's food and food technology industry has never looked back. Since entry into the then European Communnity further support for Denmark's primary agricultural industry has come from the common agricultural policy, which subsidizes exports to non-member countries.

Yet, a threat of sorts does now hang over the sector in the shape of the recent GATT agreement, which calls for a reduction of 34 per cent in the volume of exports of subsidized products.

Mr Biorn Westh, minister for agriculture, sees the GATT agreement as a challenge, which opens up opportunities to win new markets. and he is calling for an attacking policy on the part of Europe to make the best of these opportunities.

Mr H. O. A. Kjeldsen, president of the Agricultural Council (an umbrella organization for almost all the Danish farmers' organizations) shares the minister's view, although, as he says, his members "face a harsh period of adaptation".

The rest of Europe has a special reason to be interested in the Danish food industry and its ability to adapt. A large share of Denmark's agricultural exports goes to non-European Union countries, especially cheese, a product in which Iran is the largest export market by tonnage. The Middle East is an important market for butter and milk powder and Japan has overtaken the UK as the most important market for Danish pigmeat (by value, though not by tonnage).

As Mr Westh points out, policies which allow Denmark to continue to export to third countries should be of interest to other European countries. Otherwise, the products concerned will be offloaded on to the European market, causing serious downward pressure on prices.

He wants the European Union to consider bringing the European corn price down to the world market level. This would eliminate the subsidy element in the production of pigmeat and poultry, which are fed on corn products. No quantitative restrictions, would as a result need to be imposed under the terms of GATT agreement, on exports.

Mr Kjeldsen also wants Europe to introduce B-quotas for milk production. The B-quota would be priced at the world market price and could be used to help Denmark to maintain its exports of cheese, butter, and powdered milk exports outside Europe.

Prospects for the primary food industry clearly depend on access to world markets, but Denmark has one important advantage. Pigmeat, the most important agricultural export product, is not directly supported under the common agricultural policy and its exports are therefore not threatened by the GATT agreement in the same way as dairy products and beef.

Though pessimists focus on the food surplus in European countries in considering the future of the agricultural food industry, others, such as Mr Erik Juul Jorgensen, head of the private Institute for Food Studies and Agro-industrial Development, in Copenhagen, focus on the global market. They predict a strong increase in demand for food, and see few limits to the potential for Danish production and exports, given a satisfactory world trading regime. In a 1992 report, Mr Juul Jorgensen argued that Denmark could double production by its agricultural, food processing and agro-technical industries between 1990 and 2001.

The pig farmers have shown the way. Between 1989 and 1993, pig production increased from 15.5m to more than 20m animals per year, or by 30 per cent. Pigmeat prices over the past year have been so low, however, that no further increase in production is expected.

Mr Bent Sloth, chairman of the Association of Danish Slaughterhouses and himself a pig producer, predicts that pig output will not rise from the present level for several years. However, Mr Westh believes production may well reach 25m by 2000, and Mr Juul Jorgensen sees no reason why it should not reach 30m during the first decade of the next century.

A feature of the agricultural sector is the domination by the co-operative movement. Two co-operative dairies, MD Foods and Klover Milk, account for 90 per cent of the milk produced on farms. Five slaughter-house groups account for almost all the pig production. MD Foods and the two largest slaughter-house groups, Danish Crown and Vestjyske Slagterier (West Jutland Abbatoirs) are among the largest companies in their industries in Europe.

The co-operatives, which are governed by a democratic system of one man, one vote, provide the dairies and slaughter houses with a unique degree of vertical integration from farmer through processing to export sales.

One of the disadvantages of the co-operative system according to its critics, is its inability to raise equity capital from external sources. The co-operatives have found a way round this limitation, however, through the establishment of MD Foods International in the dairy sector, and Tulip International in the meat sector.

MD Foods, which has invested heavily in the U. K. dairy industry, and Tulip, which is the processing arm of Danish Crown, (producing such items as minced meat and ham, as opposed to fresh and frozen cuts), are partly financed by equity from Danish institutional investors.

Critics of the co-operatives also say the industry has been slow in embarking on production of more highly processed foods, such as charcuterie products and convenience foods, but Mr Kjeldsen rejected that charge. "Most of our exports are high-quality, processed raw products. We obtain attractive prices, for example, for our pigmeat exports to Japan, because we make products with a uniform high quality. We would earn less if we went into highly processed convenience foods and sold them under our brand names, a business that required an enormous investments."

Although the farmers are enduring tough times at the moment, Mr Kjeldsen is not discouraged. "When young people ask me if there is future in farming, my answer is: Yes. There will always be problems, but there are problems whatever sector you are in. A well-educated farmer has a good future in Denmark," he says confidently.

—From *Financial Times* • June 7, 1994

Make the best choice according to the article:

1. We can understand the girl's reply in the sense that
   a. the only thing she knows about Denmark is pigs.
   b. Danish people use pigs to symbolize themselves.
   c. British people have a very easy access to Denmark's pigmeat.
   d. Danish food industry purposefully make pigs their image.
2. Denmark could produce enough food for as many as
   a. 20 million people.
   b. three times more than its own population.

c. its own population plus another 15 million people.

d. 15 million people.

3. The Danish primary food industries

   a. could not be developed without the rise of the companies in associated industries.

   b. have helped the associated industries develop.

   c. have developed with government subsidies.

   d. are so important that the government depends heavily on them.

4. Facing the challenge of cheap American corn in the 1870s, Danish farmers developed a lucrative market exporting butter, eggs, and bacon to the UK. Lucrative here means:

   a. smooth b. profitable c. substantial d. sophisticated

5. The development of Denmark's primary agricultural industry

   a. has been restricted by GATT regulations.

   b. does not meet the requirements of GATT agreement.

   c. has been challenged by products from other countries.

   d. has been promoted by EC policies.

6. As Mr. Westh points out, policies which allow Denmark to continue the export to third countries should be of interest to other European countries because otherwise

   a. they will have to import more Danish food.

   b. they will encounter a sharp price-cutting competition from Denmark in food trade at home.

   c. their own food products will be sold more easily overseas.

   d. every one will have to cut their own agricultural production.

7. Danish primary food industry

   a. relies very much on world markets for future development.

   b. can do very well without exploiting overseas markets.

   c. can count on its pigmeat to flourish.

   d. is supported by the Common Agricultural Policy and its exports are therefore heavily subsidized.

8. Some people are pessimistic about the futrue of the agricultural food industry because
   a. the whole world is having a grain glut.
   b. European countries all have too much food.
   c. the potential for Danish production and exports will be severely limited.
   d. because there is no sign of increases in demand for Danish food.
9. The argument against the charge that the co-operatives have been slow in embarking on production of more highly processed (convenience) foods is that
   a. it needs too big an investment.
   b. there is no potential market for the products.
   c. profits will reduce if they sell such products.
   d. to obtain the high-tech know-how for the food processing is impossible.
10. According to this article,
   a. Danish agricultural food industry has a bright future, which will help the country prosper.
   b. it is quite dangerous for Danish government to rely too heavily on food industry as it has many problems.
   c. most of the people are very much depressed by the prospects for the Danish food industry.
   d. GATT agreement will become the major obstacle to the future increases in Danish food exports.

Lesson 14

Commodities Market

Text

Soft Commodities

Many prices are at historic lows, and the IMF expects further falls. Yet there are signs that the worse may be over. One key commodity, sugar, has recovered.

Markets Have Lost Their Allure

For Most people involved in the production and trading of "soft" or agricultural commodities, this is proving to be a grim decade.

Prices are in many cases at, or near, historic lows in real terms as markets struggle to cope with floods of surplus produce. And—with most soothsayers forecasting flat, or stil lower, prices—the markets themselves have lost much of their allure.

Speculators who profited handsomely from the price volatility of the 1970s have deserted soft commodities for the newer excitement of financial futures or the security and big yields afforded by the equity and money markets.

The contrast with the "resources decade" of the 1970s could hardly be more marked. It is strange, indeed, to observe that only 10 years have elapsed since spiralling commodity prices were the focus of major international conccrn, and many respected forecasters were warning of impending global shortages of basic raw materials and foodstuffs.

The shortages never came, and the terms of trade have now

shifted dramatically against the commodity producers. Agricultural commodities have been particularly badly hit. Last year alone, the International Monetary Fund's indices of food prices and of agricultural raw material prices fell by 15 per cent and 12 per cent respectively. Commodity prices in general were about 35 per cent below their 1980 average in 1985 according to the UN Conference on Trade and Development (UNCTAD).

What is more, currency movements over the past year have unexpectedly made matters worse for many producers. In the first half of the 1980s, it was conventional wisdom to say that the exceptional strength of the dollar was partly responsible for——and helped to offset——the increasing weakness of dollar-denominated commodity prices. All other things being equal, so the argument went, a subsequent fall in the dollar might be expected to give a compensating boost to dollar commodity prices.

But now the dollar has fallen, and the very reverse has happened: commodity prices have continued to tumble from the peak they reached in the second quarter of 1984. When calculated in a more representative basket of currencies, such as the Special Drawing Right, the fall looks even more precipitous. In May of this year, for example, the IMF's food price index was a further 10 per cent below its level in the second quarter of 1985.

There are signs that the worst of the fall may now be over; indeed, one key commodity, sugar, has rebounded impressively from the lows of last year, though even the sugar price remains below the most efficient grower's cost of production, and its rally appears to have run out of steam. For the rest, nobody is bold enough to forecast a major improvement either this year or next. The IMF, for its part, believes that the prices of most commodities will fall substantially in 1986——with only sugar, tropical timber and hides among the softs likely to rise significantly.

"The behaviour of commodity prices is, to say the least, bewildering," remarked Mr Alister McIntyre, the acting head of Unctad, at a recent meeting of the body's commodities committee.

To many developing countries, the trend is deeply worrying as well as bewildering——the terms of trade have worsened dramatically for them. Between 1980 and 1985, their export earnings from an IMF-selected sample of 17 commodities dropped by 16 per cent.

For the industrialised world, by contrast, the drop in commodity prices has been a real boon in the fight against inflation. As Lloyds Bank commented recently:

"The weakness of dollar commodity prices, combined with the decline of the dollar, is having an important restraining influence on inflation in many industrial countries. Even in the United States, where a falling dollar would tend to boost inflation, weak commodity prices have helped to prevent relatively rapid GNP growth from being accompanied by accelerating inflation."

The explanation for the general weakness in commodity prices is complex, and the factors in play will obviously vary greatly from one commodity to another.

Coffee, for example, has proved to be an exception to the declining trend over the past nine months, because of a drought in the biggest producing country, Brazil.

In the case of some "temperate" agricultural products, such as the grains, on the other hand, there is a particularly severe glut of supplies, and world market prices are continuing to decline under the influence of a price-cutting war between the US and the EEC. The US is also setting out this year to arrest the decline in its exports of soyabeans, cotton, tobacco and rice—with potentially devastating consequences for many producers of these commodities in the Third World.

There are also deep uncertainties about the effects of the most dramatic commodity price crash of them all—that in the crude oil market over the last year. While falling oil prices ought to provide a fillip to western economic growth——and therefore, indirectly, to demand for other commodities——they are bound to have other, perhaps less desirable, spin-offs.

For producers of rubber and natural fibres such as cotton for example, the drop in the oil price is bound to mean increased competition from synthetic products. In tea and sugar, to name but two other commodities, it is already taking its toll in the from of reduced purchases by cash-strapped oil-producing states.

Nevertheless, several common features——which would apply to metals and minerals, just as much as to soft commodities——can be identified.

• First, world economic growth remains generally sluggish and has been at its weakest in manufacturing, as opposed to the services sector. Uncertainties over the future of the US recovery and slow growth in Europe are keeping demand for key industrial raw materials relatively depressed. In many of the newer and heavily-indebted industrial countries, commodity consumption has been squeezed, as a result of official austerity programmes.

• Second, developing states have had to maximize commodity exports in order to keep up their foreign exchange earnings and offset the decline in unit commodity prices. This, in turn, has aggravated over-supply problems. It is true of Chile in the copper market, as it is of Brazil in soyabeans or Malaysia in palm oil.

• Third, the world has got used to living with much lower levels of stocks than in the inflationary 1970s. On the one hand, the persistence of high real interest rates has in creased the cost of carrying large inventories, and consumers are, in any case, quite happy to defer purchase when prices are on the way down.

• Fourth, investment funds have moved out of commodities—which were bought in the 1970s as stores of value —and into more liquid assets. Traders complain about a lack of price volatility; several markets speak of the need to attract back speculative business—and of the difficulty of doing so in the present climate. Gone are the days when the focus was on possible market distortions resulting from excessive speculative activity.

• Finally, and perhaps most significantly, there is evidence of a more fundamental shift in the pattern of supply and demand for a number of commodities, and of a long-term downward trend in commodity prices. Looked at from this perspective, the scarcity worries of the 1970s were merely a temporary aberration resulting from a sudden spurt of economic growth and from the OPEC oil price shock.

The long-term downward trend, known among economists as the "Prebisch effect," is said to reflect increasing efficiency, both in the production and in the consumption of commodities. Increasing production efficiency would tend to increase supplies, while increasing efficiency in the way commodities are consumed tends to reduce demand.

Agricultural productivity has grown rapidly across the board, whether through new higher-yielding wheat varieties, or specially-bred hybrid cocoa trees or oil palms.

There is a constant shift in the soft commodities business, from the less efficient, higher-cost producers to their more competitive rivals: from Malaysia, say, to Indonesia in palm oil; from the US to Brazil in soyabeans; or from Ghana and Nigeria to the Ivory Coast, Brazil and——increasingly—Malaysia in cocoa.

Only protectionism, for many products, prevents this shift happening more quickly; or, in the case of coffee, the transition is impeded in normal times by the existence of a rigid export quota system.

Increasing efficiency, in both production and consumption, is clearly at work in the rubber market. Higher-yielding trees have increased supplies, while consumption in rubber's main outlet, the tyre industry, has been hit by the general reduction in the size of tyres.

Perhaps the 1990s will once again prove to be a decade in which resources look in short supply. That certainly seems to be the consensus about oil. But, for the moment, soft commodity producers seem more than capable of growing everything the world wants to buy.

——From *Financial Times* · July 23, 1986.

Words and Expressions

commodity	*n.*	商品;初级商品
recover	*v.*	(商品价格)回升
allure	*n.*	诱惑力;魅力
grim	*a.*	严酷的
decade	*n.*	十年
to cope with	(妥善地)处理;(成功地)应付	
soothsayer	*n.*	预言者
forecast	*v.*	预见
speculator	*n.*	投机者
volatility	*n.*	变化无常;不稳定性
desert	*v.*	开小差;逃亡
yield	*n.*	(投资等的)利润
afford	*v.*	给予
equity	*n.*	(常为 equities) 股票
elapse	*v.*	(时间)消逝
spiral	*v.*	不断地急剧上升
impending	*a.*	即将发生的
indices	*n.*	(index 的复数形式)指数
respectively	*a.*	分别地
average	*n.*	平均值
currency	*n.*	货币

conventional	*a.*	普通的
denominate	*v.*	表明;指明
dollar-denominated	以美元标价的	
subsequent	*a.*	继之而来的
compensate	*v.*	补偿;赔偿
boost	*n.*	增长
reverse	*n.*	相反情况
tumble	*v.*	(价格等)暴跌
precipitous	*n.*	急促的;猛冲的
rebound	*v.*	(价格的)回升;反弹
rally	*n.*	(价格的)止跌;回坚
tropical	*a.*	热带的
timber	*n.*	木材
hide	*n.*	皮革
bewildering	*a.*	使人困惑的
trend	*n.*	趋势
boon	*n.*	恩惠;及时的恩赐
restraining	*a.*	抑制(性)的
accelerate	*v.*	加速
factor	*n.*	因素
drought	*n.*	干旱
Brazil	巴西	
temperate	*a.*	不极端的;不过分的
grain	*n.*	谷物
glut	*n.*	过剩
set out	开始	
soybean	*n.*	大豆(黄豆)
potentially	*a.*	潜在地
devastating	*a.*	毁灭性的
crash	*n.*	坠落;暴跌
crude	*a.*	天然的;未提炼的

fillip	*n.*	刺激
spin-offs	*n.*	副产品;副作用
fibre	*n.*	纤维
synthetic	*a.*	合成的
take its toll	造成损失	
metal	*n.*	金属
mineral	*n.*	矿产
identify	*v.*	识别;确定
sluggish	*a.*	呆滞的
sector	*n.*	部门
depressed	*a.*	低下的;不景气的
indebted	*a.*	负债的
austerity	*n.*	(国家开支上的)紧缩
maximize	*v.*	使增加到最大限度
offset	*v.*	抵消
aggravate	*v.*	加剧
Chile	智利	
palm	*n.*	棕榈
stock	*n.*	库存
persistence	*n.*	持续状态
inventory	*n.*	(美)库存
defer	*v.*	推迟
assets	*n.*	资产
speculative	*a.*	投机的
distortion	*n.*	扭曲
evidence	*n.*	根据;证明
perspective	*n.*	(观察问题的)视角
scarcity	*n.*	短缺
aberration	*n.*	偏离;脱离正轨
spur	*n.*	突然加速进行
efficiency	*n.*	效率

productivity n. 生产率
yielding a. 产出的
variety n. 品种
bred a. (breed 的过去式)培育
hybrid n. 杂交的
rival n. 竞争对手
Malaysia 马来西亚
Indonesia 印度尼西亚
Ghana 加纳
Nigeria 尼日利亚
the Ivory Coast 象牙海岸(科特迪瓦)
protectionism n. 保护(贸易)主义
transition n. 变迁
impede v. 妨碍
rigid a. 僵化的
quota n. 限额;配额
outlet n. 销路;销售渠道
tyre n. 轮胎
consensus n. 一致的意见

Notes to the Text

1. Financial Times 金融时报

在英国伦敦出版发行的每日晨报,它被看作是英国最好的晨报之一,对英国政府的金融政策有很大的影响。

《金融时报》创立于 1888 年。它专门报道商业和金融新闻。其发行量是世界上金融类报纸中最高之一,仅次于《华尔街时报》。同时,它也是英国惟一一家每日报道伦敦股票交易所行情的报纸。

2. financial futures

futures(此义一般用复数):期货,指按购买时商定的价格而在将来一定时期付款交货的商品、货币或有价证券；financial futures 专指以期货方法进行交易的有价证券。

3. security（通常此义用复数 securities）：有价证券，即股票、公债、公司债券等证明所有权或借贷关系的书面凭证等的总称。

4. "... the equity ... market"

在商业英语中 equity 的含义之一是：以出售"普通股票"（英语为 common stock 或 ordinary share）的方法所筹措的公司资金。"the equity market"意指以此方法集资的市场，即一般的股票市场。

5. "the... money market"

"货币市场"，指短期资金的借贷市场；中、长期资金的借贷市场称之为 capital market"资本市场"。

6. United Nations Conference on Trade and Development (UNCTAD)：联合国贸易和发展会议，简称贸发会，是联合国大会审议和处理有关国际贸易和经济发展问题的常设机构，1964 年 12 月 30 日成立，秘书处设在日内瓦。贸发会的职能包括：促进发达程度不同、经济制度不同的各国之间的贸易活动；倡导贸易协定的谈判工作；制定国际贸易政策。

7. "All other things being equal, so the argument went, a subsequent fall in the dollar might be expected to give a compensating boost to dollar commodity prices."

"All other things being equal"，英语语法称之为"主格独立结构"（the nominative absolute construction）。这是英语动词分词短语的一种，特点是有自己的主语（而一般分词所表示的动作的逻辑上的主语即所在句中的主语）。

例：Weather permitting, the ship will leave the harbour at dawn.

This done, we went home.

8. Lloyds Bank P&C： 劳埃德银行，英国最大的综合性商业银行之一，总行设在伦敦，分支行遍布全英。以劳埃德国际银行为主的海外子行和联行经营多种货币存款贷款、外汇、投资和金融咨询业务。

9. "... some temperate agricultural products..."

temperate 的字意之一是"程度适中的"，或"非极端的"。在本文中指：有些农产品的价格并没有像咖啡和石油那样大幅度地涨落，只是在近几年中有时有些轻微的浮动。

10. "... the service sector..."

服务部门，即非产品制造专门提供服务的产业，如：金融、保险、交通运输、法律事务、广告、旅游、饮食业等。

11. Paul D · Prebisch

阿根廷经济学家，曾任联合国贸发大会秘书长。

12. "... in the case of coffee, the transition is impeded in normal times by the existence of a rigid export quota system."

"... export quota system"（"出口配额制"）指《国际咖啡协定》中的有关规定。该协定于1962年由美国等咖啡进口国和第三世界咖啡生产国签订，继而又在1963年成立了"国际咖啡组织"作为监督协定执行的机构。《国际咖啡协定》的宗旨是：在保持世界咖啡生产格局不变的情况下维持供求平衡和稳定价格。此协定已经多次续订、修改，据1975年达成的第三次协定，每一咖啡生产国都必须严格按照协定中出口配额规定的数量出口。

Questions on Content and Language Points

(for preview, discussion and review)

1. What are "soft commodities"? Could you name a few, according to the text?

What is the other category of commodities according to the text?

"And—with most sooth sayers forecasting <u>flat</u>, or still lower, prices—the markets themselves have lost much of their allure."

1) What does "flat" mean? Could you find a proper Chinese equivalent for it?

2) To whom had the soft commodity markets lost much of their allure? (To the buyers who would be end-users, or some other dealers?)

3. As pointed out in the text, the first half of the 1980s were

grim years for most commodities. When were they in strong demand and commanding escalating prices? Could you find some grounds within the text for your conclusion?

4. "In the first half of 1980s... the exceptional strength of the dollar was partly responsible for —and helped to offset—the increasing weakness of dollar-denominated commodity prices."

1) Why was then the ever rising dollar partly responsible for the increasing weakness of dollar-denominated commodity prices?

2) How could the same dollar, on the other hand, help to offset the increasing weakness of dollar-denominated commodity prices?

3) Could commodity-exporters profit much from importing from the U. S. in that period? Why?

5. "... <u>All other things</u> being equal, so the argument went, a subsequent <u>fall in the dollar</u> might be expected to give a compensating <u>boost</u> to dollar commodity prices."

1) What do "all other things" refer mainly to?

2) What was the "fall in the dollar" subsequent to?

3) Why should the "boost" have been a compensating one?

(If you find the questions hard to answer, read carefully the sentence preceding to the one quoted.)

6. "... When calculated in a more representative basket of currencies, such as the Special Drawing Right, the fall looked even more precipitous."

1) Why is S. D. R. adopted, generally speaking?

2) What does it imply that the fall looked even more precipitous when calculated in the Special Drawing Right—a stable composite currency?

Do you think that it is a question of currency, or a question of something else—demand and supply?

7. "... one key commodity, sugar, has rebounded impressively from the lows of last year, though... and its rally appears to

have run out of steam."

What do to rebound and rally mean in the text respectively? Could you find satisfactory Chinese equivalents for them?

8. "Even in the United States, where a falling dollar would tend to boost inflation, weak commodity prices have helped to prevent relatively rapid GNP growth from being accompanied by accelerating inflation."

1) Why would a falling dollar tend to "boost inflation"?

Would the same thing happen if the exchange rates of China's RMB were adjusted down somewhat? (China is primarily self-sufficient in industrial raw materials, foods and energy resouces, isn't it?)

2) How could weak commodity prices help the U. S. check inflation?

9. "... the world has got used to living with much lower levels of stocks than in the inflationary 1970s."

1) What is the implication of "inflationary"here?

2) Could you guess what manufacturers did in the inflationary 1970s'? Could they live with lower levels of stocks or just do the opposite?

Why?

10. "There is a constant shift in the soft commodities business, from the less efficient, higher-cost producers to their more competitive rivals:... ."

Only protectionsim for many products, prevents this shift happening more quickly...

What protectionist steps might be taken to prevent the shift happening more quickly?

Topics for Summary

1. How many questions are touched upon in the article?

2. What is the subject of this article?

Exercises

Read the article given below and do the following true-or-false exercise:

Review of Markets——Corn Futures

GRAINS: Futures markets for corn, wheat and soybeans have a tough act to follow in 1997.

The past 12 months featured some of the most volatile grain prices in recent history, as weather moved the market dramatically. Records were set for both price and volume.

The moves were considerable to say the least. Corn-futures prices marched up 57% from the beginning of the year to a record-setting $5.48 a bushel in July. But then prices plunged 51% to year lows in December of less than $2.60 a bushel. Wheat-futures prices also skyrocketed to an all-time high to about $7 a bushel, doubling in prices since early 1995. But better-than-expected weather and a significant increase in world-wide supply popped the overblown market in a matter of weeks, bringing prices down below $4 a bushel.

Agticultural trading volume at the Chicago Board of Trade increased dramatically in 1996 to record levels, up 40% on soybeans, 35% on corn, and 13% on wheat. On the Tokyo Grain Exchange, corn futures volume more than doubled and soybean volume more than tripled.

Increasing world-wide demand and an expectation of record-low crop production because of unfavorable weather led to high prices early in 1996. For wheat, conditions stayed dry through May, while for corn and soybeans, weather remained dry in key producing regions into June. Because of the weather early in the year, the nation's granaries held a precariously low amount—just 426 million bushels of corn at one point in September, the lowest level since the 1970s.

But just when supply concerns pushed prices into the record-breaking range, rains and international supply spoiled the bullish party. Analysts say farmers planted eight million more acres of corn alone in 1996, and large crops also came from Europe, Australia and South America. "The high prices encouraged shifts in planting-area and yield went up." explains Dale Gustafson, grains analyst for Smith Barney.

Weather also influenced supply and a crop that far-exceeded original expectations. Timely summer rains and warm temperatures late into the season boosted the 1996 U. S. corn and soybean crop to near record levels.

Several factors will add to further rebuiliding of supplies in coming years, analysts say. First, genetically enhanced crops could increase yields as the acceptance of the concept grows gradually. Also, freedom-to-farm legislation passed in the U. S. in 1996 and gaining momentum worldwide, will allow farmers to build up supplies when market conditions warrant.

Analysts expect 1997 prices to stay in ranges well below last year's unprecedented postings. Wheat is expected to average about $4 a bushel and corn about $2.60, on strong harvests and weaker export demand. On the upside, analysts say a growing livestock sector could increase demand for grains in the coming year.

Soybean demand could outpace its grain cousins because of the rapid growth in China, which recently switched from being an exporter to an importer of soybean products. "If there are any problems with production, the market is liable to have a large price advance. There's no cushion in supply," says Anne Frick, analyst for Prudential Securities in New York.

More bearish analysts say the price will generally stay below $7 a bushel on the likelihood that many U. S. farmers will shift production from corn to soybeans in 1997. Also, they say moist growing conditions in South America will lead to record crops there.

——From *The Wall Street Journal* • June 2, 1997

True-and-false exercise:

1. Futures markets for corn, wheat and soybeans would continue to be brisk in 1997. (   )
2. According to the context, "Records were set for both price and volume" means that in 1996 the prices for some grains and the quantities sold both reached the highest levels in recent years. (   )
3. Government policies such as "freedom-to-farm legislation passed in the U. S. in 1996" would be the main reason for "further rebuilding of (grains) supplies" in 1997. (   )
4. The prices of wheat and corn were expected to drop in 1997 because of their overstock. (   )
5. Many U. S. farmers were sure to shift production from corn to soybeans in 1997. (   )

Supplementary Material for Free Reading

Commodities Market, Despite Gains, Will Be Remembered for Its Losses

BY AARON LUCCHETTI
Staff Reporter of *THE WALL STREET JOURNAL*

While 1997 brought breathtaking gains to some individual commodity markets, the volatile and unpredictable year will be remembered most for its price losses.

A persistent trend of easing supply concerns hampered the gains of those betting on commodity price spikes, especially in industrial materials. With fears of inflation fading, the dollar soaring to new highs and faith in financial instruments remaining solid, commodities were relegated to the back of many investors' minds for yet another year.

"I can't think of any commodities that investors should have been buying" consistently through the entire year, says James Steel, commodities analyst at Refco Inc. in New York. "They should have been (buying) dollars."

The dollar posted solid gains for traders in 1997 as did stocks and bonds. But major commodity indexes fell, disappointing those investors who had predicted that stock-market jitters would push capital to alternative areas such as commodities. Ultimately, the Bridge Commodity Research Bureau Index slipped 9.8% from its springtime high, finishing the year at a three-year low of 229.14, down 4.4%. The energy-laden Goldman Sachs Commodity Index turned lower this fall and also finished the year down, losing 18.4% to 175.62.

While disappointing to some, the downward spiral was a soothing melody to those worriedly listening for inflationary peeps. Economists and analysts say commodities prices instead showed a trend toward disinflation, an economic environment without price increases. "It's become apparent that high growth rates don't necessarily mean higher commodity prices," Refco's Mr. Steel says. "Supply (of raw materials) is growing, and the world continues to be much more efficient in its use of commodities."

Last year's immediate trigger for price declines came from Asia, a major source of commodities demand growth in this decade. Much like multinational companies, commodities were hammered based on their exposure to the distressed region, which went through currency and stock-market losses through the second half of the year.

When Southeast Asian countries canceled or postponed metals-intensive infrastructure projects in an attempt to cut back spending, demand for industrial commodities dwindled and metals prices fell to four-year lows. The closely followed Journal of Commerce industrialcommodities index slipped below 100 for the first time since 1994, touching off an argument by some economists that deflation, or falling prices, had become a greater concern than inflation, the traditional nemesis of bull stock markets.

Asia's problems hurt a wide range of commodities, especially those with consumption heavily concentrated in the developing region's countries. From cotton and soybean meal to copper and platinum, beneficiaries of Asian growth were knocked back down to size.

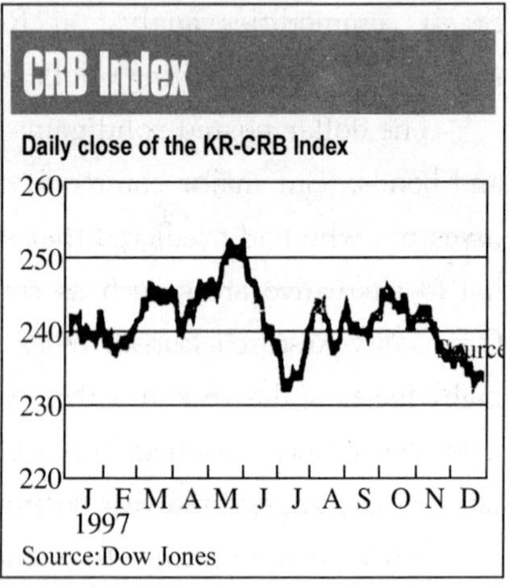

Source:Dow Jones

As Asian currency values plummeted throughout the fall, concerns built that Asian commodity buyers wouldn't have the cash to buy their usual load. Meanwhile, producers in the region eager to raise cash sought to take advantage of the local currency's weakness by exporting their own commodities, a decision that augmented world-wide inventories and drove down commodities prices further.

For exchanges and their trading members, increased volatility resulting from global financial uncertainties allayed fears about reduced business. Indeed, record annual trading volume was reported at several commodity and financial-futures exchanges, including the Chicago Board of Trade, the New York Mercantile Exchange, the New York Cotton Exchange, and the Coffee, Sugar and Cocoa Exchange. Meanwhile, the NYCE and the CSCE announced they would merge into one exchange, the New York Board of Trade, as cost pressures increased on commodities exchanges and futures brokers to consolidate.

In 1998, commodities investors will look for Asia to emerge from its troubles and start stockpiling material again. But forecasts for slower growth could bring formidable resistance to any major rallies, analysts say. "If you look at 1998 as a year of decelerating growth in the U. S. , a standstill in Europe and a question mark in Asia, it's hard to make a case for industrial commodities," says Dinsa Mehta, head of global-commodities research for Chase Manhattan Bank in New York. "We could be looking at a quite modest picture."

Here is a review of some markets:

PRECIOUS METALS: Gold investors would like to forget 1997 altogether. More than any other commodity, gold suffered from unfavorable economic trends, intense speculative pressure and a flurry of negative sentiment, emanating primarily from central banks, the official institutions that hold about one-third of the world's mined bullion.

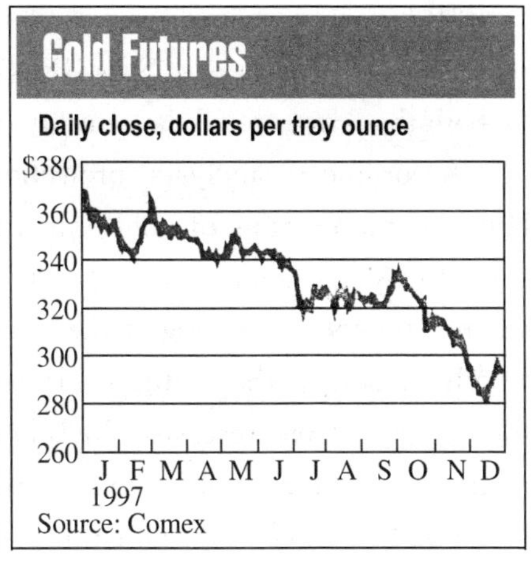

In December, spot gold prices hit an 18-year low and gold futures hit a 12½ year low, before ending the year at $289.90 a troy ounce, down a staggering 21% on the year. "Right now, gold is a dead asset," says Wiktor Bielski, senior metals analyst at Deutsche Morgan Grenfell in London. "I hate to say its's for good, but it's beginning to look like its role in the long run" is diminished.

Traders noted that 1997's debacle followed a lackluster performance in 1996, making gold one of the worst investments of the year. Failing to gain any ground in either bullish or bearish stock-market environments, gold mutual funds fell more than 40% for the year, according to Lipper Analytical Services. The American

Stock Exchange's gold-bug stock index fell 41%.

Other precious metals such as silver, platinum and palladium all diverged sharply from gold at some point in the year, staging their own rallies. Silver is more expensive relative to gold than at any point since the mid-1980s, and analysts have abandoned their models that suggested prices for the metals should move in the same direction day-to-day. Platinum prices skyrocketed more than $ 100-an-ounce higher than gold during the summer when Russian supplies of the white-metal were delayed. In December, silver prices shot up to an 8½-year high amid dwindling stockpiles.

Unlike silver or the so-called platinum group metals, gold has come under pressure from central banks, which have exchanged the metal in greater numbers for interest-bearing financial instruments such as Treasury bonds.

"It became a vicious cycle," says Stephen Yorke, a London-based preciousmetals analyst with Swiss Bank Corp. "Gold has been dominated by both the prospect and the actuality of central-bank gold sales."

According to analysts' projections, central banks will sell about 600 metric tons of gold onto the market this year, the most since 1993, and lend another 3,000 ounces, about three times the amount they were lending at the beginning of the decade.

In January, the Netherlands announced sales of 300 metric tons of gold from reserves. In July, Australia's central bank announced it sold most of its gold reserve. In November, Argentina followed with a similar announcement, sending prices even lower. The Swiss also sent prices reeling with a proposal to sell gold to fund a humanitarian program for Holocaust victims and with a proposal by government-appointed experts that the central bank sell more than half its gold. Germany meanwhile conceded it had loaned gold onto the market.

The injection of central-bank sales was tough for mining companies. With about two-thirds of all the world's mining unprofitable at current price levels, "A lot of people are trying to pick the bottom for the gold price," says William Byers, head of commodities research at Bear, Stearns & Co. He predicts gold will spend most of 1998 at prices between $250 and $300 an ounce, a range in which "there will be some mines closing up."

But any mine closings could help the metal's battered price. The faster mines surrender, the quicker excess supply will dry up, stabilizing prices. Gold bugs are also hoping for better growth in Asia and more signs of inflation in the U. S. Western investors tend to look upon gold as an alternative holding when dollar-denominated assets are being pounded by inflation. Eastern investors buy more gold when economic prosperity in their countries allows it.

Some analysts are predicting improvement for the metal's prospects this year. Many watch the amount of gold put into reserves by the proposed European Central Bank. If the bank allocates more than 10% of its reserves to the precious metal, analysts say the move would be viewed as a vote of confidence. The announcement, expected in May, "will have quite a big psychological impact," on gold prices, says Mr. Mehta of Chase Manhattan.

Analysts say gold is a little oversold at current bargain-basement levels. "In order for gold to stay at these prices, it would require more central-bank action." Mr. Mehta says. "I wouldn't be surprised to see a broader price range this year with shocks to the upside. I see a broad price range between $275 and $345 an ounce."

CRUDE OIL: For crude oil, 1997 was a slippery slope.

After ending 1996 at $25.92 a barrel, the nearby crude contract finished 1997 on the New York Mercantile Exchange near its year low of $17.50, at $17.64 a barrel, a 31.9% decline since the high in January. Most of the drop was attributable to two political situations: Iraq and the Organization of Petroleum Exporting Countries.

Crude began the year on a high note, with inventories lean and demand strong. But the weather warmed early, and inventories began to fill out in early February. Though late spring and early summer tensions with Iraq caused price spikes, ample supplies pushed the contract below $19 in June.

While prices surged again back into the low $20s after Iraq barred U. S. members of United Nations weapons-inspections teams this past fall, the tension dissipated just in time for more bearish news from OPEC's semiannual meeting in November.

Pushed by Saudi Arabia, the 11—country organization raised its production ceiling to 27. 5 million barrels a day from 25 million barrels. Analysts say that news was the biggest factor holding crude prices down at year end.

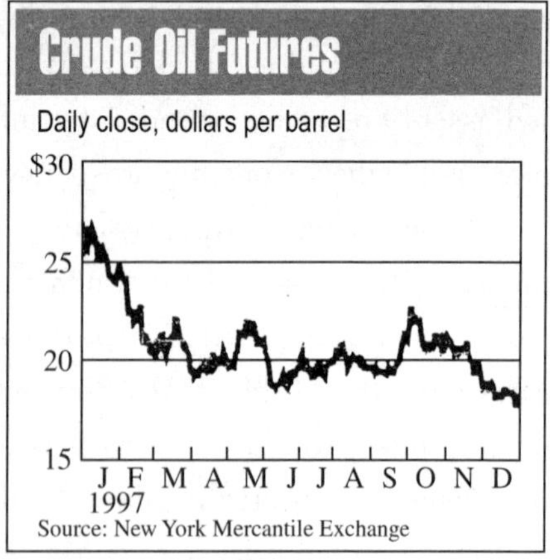

Nizam Sharief, an analyst with Houston's Hornsby & Co., says he expects the price of crude oil to slip even more early this year as weak Asian markets struggling with the region's financial collapse keep demand low. Meanwhile, the new production from OPEC, as well as a renewed oil-for-food deal with Iraq, will keep supplies high and prices down, he says. "I expect the price to be in the $17-a-barrel range."

The story proved bearish last year for heating oil, one of crude's chief products.

Low inventories had the nearby heating-oil contract riding high on the Nymex, at just below 73 cents a gallon at the end of 1996. But a buildup in inventories at the begininng of the new year coincided with the early end of winter, sending the contract down to the mid-50 cents range. It ended 1997 at 49. 08 cents. Mr. Sharief expects that situation to continue into 1998, particularly if the El Nino weather phenomenon results in an unusually warm winter in the Northeast as some observers expect.

Gasoline, in high demand particularly in the U. S. recently, is the only part of the crude complex expected to put in a bullish performance in 1998. Throughout 1997, refineries pumped out near-capacity levels of gasoline, barely enough to keep up with the gas-guzzling sport-utility vehicles trolling U. S. highways in greater numbers. The nearby gasoline contract ended 1996 at 54. 04 cents a gallon on the Nymex. It ended the year 1997 at 52. 81 cents a gallon.

Gasoline demand is likely to jump another 1. 5% in 1998, Mr. Sharief says. "The question is," he says, "can the refineries make the gasoline to meet that?"

BASE METALS: For seven months in 1997, copper was winning the battle to stay above $1 a pound. Then came a knockout blow.

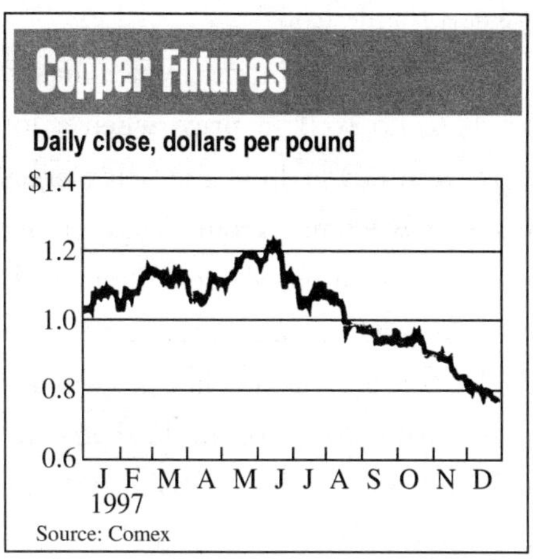

Financial problems in Thailand spread to Southeast Asia, then Hong Kong and Japan. Credit became tighter, firms were forced to close and countries suspended dozens of building projects. Demand for the metal in the rapidly building region ground to a halt and inventories poured out of the region, hurting prices almost immediately.

In 1997, aluminum, lead, zinc and tin all joined in on the sluggish second half. But copper's move was quick and painful. From its June peak of $1. 22 a pound, copper futures fell 37% on the Comex to 76. 9 cents, at one time in December hitting its lowest point in four years. "There's no bullish prognosis coming out of Asia," says Martin Squires, an analyst at Rudolf Wolff in London. "No one is seeing the light at the end of the tunnel. They just see the train hurtling downward."

William O・Neill, chief futures strategist at Merrill Lynch in New York, says he expects copper and industrial commodities prices to drift lower during the frist quarter of 1998, then to show some signs of life for the rest of the year, helped by continued strong growth in developed countries. "Copper was one of the first commodities to identify that there was going to be some crisis in Asia," he says. "It will also be one of the first to turn around and show that the worst is over."

But now that previous forecasts for booming Asian consumption have been wiped clean, many analysts agree that copper is set for a difficult year.

Unlike aluminum, which has more diversified uses, copper tends to do well in price when a lot of new buildings, telephone wires and power lines are being erected. Nearly 40% of copper demand now comes from Asia, compared with 23% in 1985, says John Gross, a metals consultant in Huntington, N. Y.

Amy Gassman, base-metals-mining strategist for Goldman, Sachs & Co., revised her projected copper price down to 85 cents a pound from 90 cents for 1998 and to 75 cents a pound for 1999 to reflect "concern that global metals demand... may no longer be adequate to offset the projected rise in supply in these metals through the late 1990s."

The wave of new supply in copper has already come on board, says Thomas McNamara, an analyst with CIBC Oppenheimer. "Asia is being blamed as the fall guy, but the real story is that increased refined production is up 7% through September," Mr. McNamara says. He projects copper prices will stay near the 80 cent mark this year.

NATURAL GAS: About the only thing that can be predicted about natural gas prices is that they will be unpredictable. The past year was no exception, with volatile natural-gas futures hovering near $3.50 per million British thermal units early in the year, only to sink below $2 per million BTUs and then rise again during the summer. The front-end contract closed 1996 at $2.757 per million BTUs and was quickly pushed higher on news of potential cold weather and concerns about tight supply. At the end of January, however, as it became apparent the winter wouldn't be as cold as expected, the contract went below $3 per million BTUs and fell even further, below $2, by the end of February.

Supply concerns arose again later in the year, when natural-gas producers, particularly those in the U.S., began to report production shortfalls as fields' reserves declined and rigs and other services became scarce. The contract rose to the $2.70 range in August and then above the $3 mark in September as winter loomed and natural-gas stockpiles began to look too meager. The bears held out hope, thanks to El Nino, the periodic warming of the Pacific Ocean that is said to cause—among other things—warmer than normal winters in the northern U.S.

Analysts expect production concerns that emerged this summer to continue into 1998, pointing to a bullish forecast. Demand also is expected to grow 3.1% in 1998 over 1997, according to the American Gas Association. Such strong consumption growth would likely exaggerate the effects of a supply crunch. "The million-dollar question next year will be whether production growth meets expectations or falls short like it did in 1997," says John Saucer, a natural-gas analyst with Salomon Smith Barney. Other bullish factors for natural gas could develop as well throughout the year, he says, including rail transportation snafus delaying coal shipments to the Southeast and longer turnaround times on nuclear power plants.

GRAINS: Corn and wheat settled down from a wild 1996, leaving soybeans to take the lead for the 1997 agricultural markets. In March, soybeans set an eight-year high near $9 per bushel, with the projection for year-end stockpiles hovering near a 20-year low. But the oilseed peaked too soon this year, as farmers planted soybeans enmasse, putting nearly 71 million acres of the plant in U. S. soil.

With favorable planting weather and an announcement during the summer that grain processor Cargill Inc. would take the unprecedented step of looking to South America to buy soybeans, prices eased. "When they said they'd import beans, the price crashed," says Bill Biederman, vice president of research for Allendale Inc. in Crystal Lake, ILL. "That fear driven through the countryside got enough farmers to step in and sell."

The price ended the year at $6. 705 on the Chicago Board of Trade, only 2. 9% less than where it started in 1997. Corn and wheat prices traded in a relatively narrow range, as prices were pressured by foreign-sales competition and fear toward the end of the year that Asian demand would be curtailed because of financial problems in the region.

This year, analysts are split on the outlook for crop futures. While soybean end-of-year stockpiles are set to increase, demand remains strong, even in beleaguered Asia. Corn and wheat, however, have garnered less export interest so far during the 1997—1998 crop year.

"The demand will certainly be in question because of the Far East currency crisis," says Dan Cekander, head of grain research for Fimat in Chicago.

But Mr. Cekander added that the highly touted El Nino weather phenomenon could wreak havoc with supplies, driving prices upward later this year. Already, it has delivered dry conditions to Indonesian oilseed producing regions and South African maize production areas. "Weatherwise, there will be a large expectation for some type of U. S. weather problem," due to fallout from El Nino, he says. "The market will put some risk premium into the price by springtime."

So far, El Nino has been unpredictable. Instead of having its usual effect drying out Australia's wheat growing regions, the dry weather spared that continent's farmland and instead damaged the corn crop in Northern China. But the reduced crop there has caused some analysts to predict that world corn stocks will tighten this year. "We expect corn prices to rise and lead the grain market significantly," said a recent 1998 grain analysis by Goldman Sachs.

Meanwhile Dan Basse, executive vice president of AgResource in Chicago predicted a drier spring in the U. S. Midwest will cause grains to rise over the first half of 1998. "There will be some concerns about dryness in the U. S. and China," he says, that will likely bring wheat prices to $4 a bushel, corn to $3, and soybeans to a level between $7.50 and $8.

TROPICAL COMMODITIES: Prices skyrocketed in coffee and climbed sharply higher in cocoa in some of the most volatile markets of the year. Coffee tripled in price, hitting 20-year highs of more than $3 a pound after heavy rains damaged the South American crop.

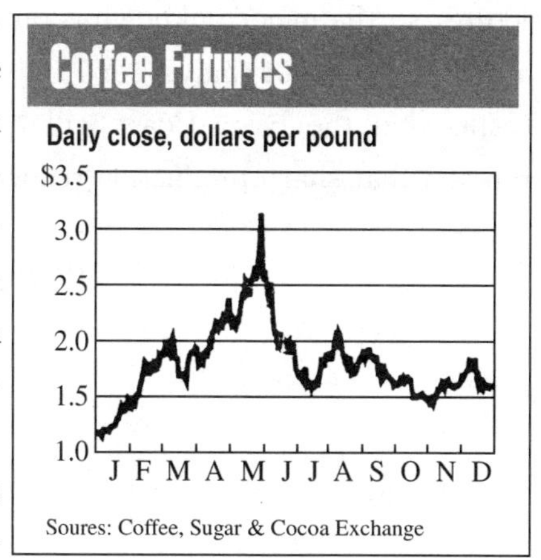

Repeated labor problems in Clombia triggered fears about delivery, while just-in-time inventory practices on the part of U. S. roasters added to the panic buying during the first six months of the year. A round of retail-price increases were put into effect by most major specialty chains and coffee roasters. Prices came back down, however, as producers unloaded much of their stored crop from 1997 and previous years. Roasters' restocking was illustrated by a bounce back in stockpiles at the Coffee, Sugar and Cocoa Exchange.

This year, the focus is turning to the possibilities of a large Brazilian crop from a smaller Brazilian crop in 1997. Meanwhile, Mexico and Central America, areas of increasing importance for U. S. coffee exports, have battled EL Nino related rains, hurricanes and frosty weather in December, all developments that could hurt supplies and prove supportive for prices. "It's been a roller-coaster ride, and it's going to continue to be that way," says Judith Ganes, an analyst for Merrill Lynch in New York.

On cocoa, the focus turned to the impact of El Nino on Southeast Asian production and the progress of the Ivory Coast crop. Despite heavy fund interest and sustained gains of 18.6% in 1997, not all analysts are convinced the small market can hold its gains in 1998. "The market had a more precise handle on the consumption picture, so the major unknown is on the production side," says Arthur Stevenson, an analyst for Prudential Securities. "The market accepts that the Ivory Coast will have a substantial 1997—1998 crop and that sharp production reductions aren't materializing."

——From *The Wall Street Journal* • Jan. 2, 1998

Lesson 15

Reports on Commodities Exchange in Telex

Text

Weekly Commodities(telex)

commodities 1

econews by kate kavanagh

oil prices seesaw to three-month low in "big bang week london", Oct. 31 (afp)—the attention of commodities dealers was last week captured initially by events on the stock exchange, where monday's big bang was muffled by computer failures, but turned later to the troubled oil market.

the unexpected departure of sheik ahmed zaki yamani from his post as saudi arabian oil minister aggravated existing uncertainty concerning the future direction of oil prices in view of severe world oversupply.

unstable crude prices in turn prompted falls in platinum and gold, the latter to its lowest since early september, aggravated by the withdrawal of investment support as the dollar regained ground.

sterling's decline lent some support to the base metal sector, where lead and zinc rallied on the continuing lack of a solution to the labour dispute affecting australia's broken hill mines.

coffee fluctuated wildly on uncertainty over brazil's role in the market but sugar and cocoa kept to a narrow range in quiet conditions.

the grain sector was dulled by the prospect of lower-than-expected soviet imports this season, despite improved british export figures.

commodities 2

econews(london)

gold: lower. after coming in for early support on news of strike action affecting mines belonging to gold fields of south africa, values declined in line with platinum and new york advices as miners were encouraged to return to work by management promises of negotiation. the fall in oil prices also brought pressure to bear but good resistance at around the 400 dollars per ounce level permitted a brief rally. however, values suffered a late decline to below 400 dollars per ounce in line with new york as the dollar strengthened on news of a decline in the u. s. budget trade and a cut in the bank of japan's discount rate.

Latest figures from the south african chamber of mines showed a 4. 6 per cent drop in gold production during the first nine months of 1986 to 481,854 kilos against 504,996during the same 1985 period.

silver: quiet. values fluctuated lower in line with other precious metals on both bullion and futures markets, the latter particularly affected by the low level of activity. London Metal Exchange (lme) stocks were down 100,000 ounces, at 25,148,000 ounces.

copper: easier. prices moved gradually lower following an early setback due to the 3, 825-tonne rise in lme stocks to 170, 625 tonnes, their highest level since february this year. but support was in evidence at lower levels.

commodities 3

econews(london)

lead: firmer. values moved up to their best level since april last year in the absence of a settlement at australia's broken hill lead-zinc-silver mines, currently operating on an interim labour-agreement that was extended indefinitely at the beginning of the week.

lme stocks were down 1,075 tonnes at 33,725 tonnes, the lowest level since july last year.

zinc: firmer. after a reasonably steady start due to the 350-tonne fall in lme stocks to 21,725 tonnes, the lowest level since july 1975, values eased back after the extension of the broken hill agreement. but fears of a tighter supply situation resurfaced in the absence of signs of a settlement there and as the dispute at Noranda's valleyfield (quebec, canada) plant approached its 20th week.

aluminium: lower. a sharp 3,375-tonne rise in lme stocks, to 125,725 tonnes dulled the market at the outset, as did the bleak outlook for aluminium prices in 1987 forecast by international traders shearson lehman. western world production, which is expected to result in a deficit of 220,000 tonnes this year after 370,000 last year, is forecast to rise next year, causing a surplus of 130,000 tonnes. news of a settlement at alcan's seebree (kentucky) plant, affected by strike action since june, further dampened sentiment.

merchants outside the lme quoted 1,230—1,250 dollars per tonne against 1,265—1,285 dollars per tonne the previous week.

commodities 4

econews (london)

nickel: slightly steadier. values fluctuated lower during the first half of the week on the lme in thin conditions, despite the 168-tonne drop in lme stocks to 8 172 tonnes. But a recovery was made on the back of sterling's weaker trend against the dollar. merchants' quotations moved one cent in either direction before ending the week at an unchanged 1. 63—1. 83 dollars per pound.

tin: firmer. the price of tin on the european spot market (basis rotterdam warchouse) rose to 4,400 pounds per tonne, some 400 pounds above the previous week's closing level and its highest level for seven months, reflecting widespread production cuts in the world tin industry. at a two-day meeting in Indonesia, the association of tin-producing countries, whose members represent 70 per cent of world tin output, decided to strengthen their co-operation in a bid to stabilize tin prices and to call on the united states to limit sales of tin from its strategic stockpile.

other metals: platinum progressed at the outset on concern about strike action in south African mines, but quickly fell victim and the dollar's late rally brought further pressure to bear. The metal was fixed at 572 dollars per ounce on friday morning against 570 the previous week or 408. 55 against 402. 85 pounds per ounce.

commodities 5

econews(london)

lower prices were quoted for tungsten, at 32—42 dollars per ten-kilo unit against 34—44 the previous week, cobalt 4. 50—5. 00 against 4. 75—5. 25 dollars per pound, cadmium 0. 90—0. 95 against 0. 92—0. 97 dollars per pound, and antimony 2,500— 2,600 against 2,600—2,700 dollars per tonne. buyers raised their bids for mercury from 150 to 160 dollars per 76-pound flask in reply to an unchanged sellers' quote of 170 dollars.

petroleum: irregular. crude oil prices fluctuated in nervous conditions throughout the week, beginning with losses in line with new york on reports of abundant supplies and rumours, later denied by saudi arabia, that it had offered a discount of 50 cents per barrel on sales of oil to the united states. the unexpected depature of sheik Ya-mani and bearish oil stock figures from the united states caused north sea brent prices to fall briefly to their lowest for three months at 13 dollars per barrel for december delivery but the market quickly recovered as it was thought that the new saudi oil minister, Hisham Nazer would put more emphasis on boosting oil prices. His call for an urgent meeting of the pricing committee of the organization of petroleum exporting countries (opec) took prices back up to over 14. 50 dollars, but resistance was in evidence at higher levels as the dollar strengthened.

gas oil futures were lower on prompt oversupply and trading ac-tivities on the two new oil products contracts were unchanged from the previous week's levels.

commodities 6

econews(london)

cocoa: quiet. terminal prices fluctuated in line with currencies in a quiet market due to the absence of many participants attending the annual cocoa dinner in hamburg.

but rumours of a shortage of nearby good quality cocoa prevented significant losses.

the announcement by lvorian agriculture minister denis brakanon that his county had produced a record 580,000 tonnes of cocoa in 1985—1986 (october—septermber) had been expected by the market.

The u. s. department of agriculture forecast a record world crop of 1. 97 million tonnes of cocoa in 1986—1987, which, it said, should result in a rise of 104,000 tonnes in world stocks.

the increase from 54,000 to 82,000 tonnes by the secretariat of the international cocoa organization of its estimate of last season's world cocoa surplus had little apparent effect on the market.

sugar: irregular. prices fluctuated under opposing factors, with reports that India had bought some eight to ten cargoes of white sugar, and algeria around 55,000 tonnes of the product, boosting sentiment.

but indications that around 20 cargoes were offered in reply to lndia's demand, and rumours that mexico intends to sell 150,000—200,000 tonnes of raw sugar on the world market put pressure upon values at higher levels.

commodities 7

econews(london)

coffee: irregular. prices continued to fluctuate wildly due to persistent uncertainty as to whether brazil intends to ship the coffee that it recently purchased on the london market or to resell it on the world market.

rumours that colombian coffee exports would not exceed 600, 000 60-kilo bags in november and december due to recent heavy rains underpinned sentiment at the outset. But gains were later wiped out due to heavy selling in line with new york.

exports of coffee by producing members of the International cof-fee organization (ico) to other members reached their highest level for 22 years during coffee year 1985—1986 (October—September) at 61. 2 million sixty-kilo bags, against 57. 5 million last season, according to preliminary statistics published by the ico Thursday.

oilseeds: firmer. prices continued to rise, underpinned by persistent demand for coconut oil on fears of supply shortages in certain areas, particulary the philippines, before profit-taking set in ahead of the weekend.

coconut oil was particularly strong, with palm and palm kernel oils gaining ground in sympathy. Rape and soya oils, in comparison, were relatively quiet.

the influential hamburg-based journal oil world estimated that European economic community (eec) rapeseed production could reach between 4. 3 and 4. 4 million tonnes in 1987, up from 3. 5 million this year and the record 3. 68 million in 1985.

ivory caost's oilseed production reached a record 225, 000 tonnes in 1985—1986, compared with 195,000 in 1984—1985, agriculture minister denis bracanon announced.

commodities 8

econews (london)

rubber: quiet. conditions prevailed on the physical market reflecting increased offers and a low level of enquiry. what little business was concluded was done at very competitive levels, in line with lower east asian advices, according to trade sources. futures activity re-mained at a virtual standstill.

cereals: irregular. prices on both wheat and barley futures markets went higher at the outset on encouraging eecexport figures showing that shipments since july 1 had reached 4. 96 million tonnes against 4. 72 millon at the same stage last year.

british wheat and barley exports had risen 164 per cent and 70 per cent respectively during the same period. reports of renewed soviet enquiry for up to one million tonnes of community grain added to the steadier undertone. but values were unable to maintain their best levels, following bearish reports from the International wheat council and the economist intelligence unit (eiu). the former lifted its esti-mate of world wheat production this season by four million tonnes to 515 million, against 506 million last season, and lowered its estimate of soviet grain imports by six million tonnes to 29 million, against 30 million last season. the eiu warned that soviet imports could fall to around eleven million tonnes a year by 1991, while annual world imports are likely to fall nine per cent to 86. 5 million, the lowest level since 1979—1980.

commodities 9

econews (london)

potatoes: irregular. values rose initially on poor weather but lost ground on expectations that the British potato marketing board would announce disappointing consumption figures. in the event, there was no publication, and values recovered before meeting resistance at higher levels.

wool: slightly steadier. extremrly quiet conditions prevented merchants from making more than very minor upward adjustments to wooltop quotations in line with firmer replacement costs at origin. bid levels remained very competitive. at the bradford (england) auction of british wool, 93 per cent of the offering was cleared, at mixed prices. The commonwealth secretariat raise its estimate of 1986—1987 world wool production from 2.96 million to 2.98 million tonnes (greasy) against 2.97 million last season.

cotton: irregular. the cotton index fluctuated narrowly on the liverpool (england) market, where interest was displayed in chinese, egyptian, turkish and peruvian styles. the international cotton advisory committee forecast world demand at a record 76 million bales this season against 74.25 million last season with production at 72.5 million, about six million down on last season.

jute and sisal: all sisal quotations remained unchanged, while raw jute and jute goods eased slightly.

commodities 10—last

econews (london)

tea: firmer. strong demand prevailed at the weekly auction where prices gained up ten pence per kilo in places. average prices in pence per kilo were: quality grade 198(195), medium 162(160) and low medium 136 (133).

Words and Expressions

seesaw	*v.*	玩跷跷板;(物价的)起伏不定
bang	*n.*	(突发的)巨响;爆炸声
initially	*ad.*	最初地
muffle	*v.*	使(声音)低沉;减弱;抑制
troubled	*a.*	混乱的
departure	*n.*	离开
sheik	*n.*	酋长;大人(伊斯兰教徒使用的尊称)
prompt	*v.*	引起;加速
platinum	*n.*	铂
sterling	*n.*	英镑
lead	*n.*	铅
zinc	*n.*	锌
dispute	*n.*	纠纷
fluctuate	*v.*	(市场)波动
dull	*v.*	使沉闷
prospect	*n.*	可能性;前景
come in	(潮)上涨	
advice	*n.*	(常用复数)报道;消息
resistance	*n.*	抵抗;抵制;反抗
ounce	*n.*	盎司(英制重量单位)
discount rate	贴现率	
chamber	*n.*	协会
bullion	*n.*	银块;银条
futures	*n.*	(商)期货(交易)
setback	*n.*	挫折
tonne	*n.*	公吨
interim	*a.*	临时的

extend	*v.*	展期
ease	*v.*	下降;呈下降趋势
resurface	*v.*	重现(原指潜艇等)重新露出水面
Quebec		魁北克(加拿大城市)
aluminum	*n.*	铝
bleak	*a.*	没有希望的;凄凉的
Kentucky		肯德基(美国州名)
dampen	*v.*	减少;降低
sentiment	*n.*	情绪
merchant	*n.*	商人
quote	*v.*	开价
nickel	*n.*	镍
pound	*n.*	磅(重量单位)
spot	*n.*	现货
Rotterdam		鹿特丹(荷兰港市)
warehouse	*n.*	仓库
closing	*a.*	最后阶段的
reflect	*v.*	反映
widespread	*a.*	分布广的;普遍的;广泛的
association	*n.*	协会;联盟
tin	*n.*	锡
stabilize	*v.*	使稳定
stockpile	*n.*	储备;存货
victim	*n.*	牺牲者;受害者
tungsten	*n.*	钨
cobalt	*n.*	钴
cadmium	*n.*	镉
antimony	*n.*	锑
bid	*n.*	出价
mercury	*n.*	水银
flask	*n.*	(运送水银用的)瓶状容器

petroleum	*n.*	石油
nervous	*a.*	神经质的;游移不定的
deny	*v.*	否认
barrel	*n.*	桶(装石油用的)
bearish	*v.*	行情下跌的
North Sea	北海(欧洲)	
Brent	不伦特(英国石油产地)	
delivery	*n.*	交货
prompt	*a.*	(货物)当场交的
Hamburg	汉堡(德国港市)	
crop	*n.*	产量
secretariat	*n.*	秘书处
cargo	*n.*	船货(一船所载的货量)
indication	*n.*	迹象
Colombia	哥伦比亚	
underpin	*v.*	加固 … 的基础;支持
preliminary	*a.*	初步的
the Philippines	菲律宾	
set in	到来;开始	
kernel	n. 果核或果壳内的仁	
sympathy	*n.*	协调;一致
rape	*n.*	欧洲油菜
journal	*n.*	刊物
prevail	*v.*	普遍存在
virtual	*a.*	实际上的
barley	*n.*	大麦
shipments	*n.*	交运的货物
renew	*v.*	重新开始
undertone	*n.*	[经](市场的)潜在倾向;市场动向
intelligence	*n.*	信息
in the event	[英]结果;到头来	

wooltop	*n.*	毛条
bid	*n.*	此处指卖方的索价;投标
auction	*n.*	拍卖
the Commonwealth	此处指英联邦	
greasy	*a.*	(羊毛)未脱脂的
Egyptian	*a.*	埃及的
Turkish	*a.*	土耳其的
Peruvian	*a.*	秘鲁的
jute	*n.*	黄麻
sisal	*n.*	即 sisal hemp 西沙尔大麻;波罗麻;剑麻
medium	*a.*	中等的

Notes to the Text

如对课文中描绘价格变化的词语的含义有疑问,请参阅注释后所附专业解释——《国际商品市场行情报道常用术语》

1. 总注——商品交易所

在资本主义国家的主要商业中心如伦敦、纽约、芝加哥,商品交易所——买卖初级产品的场所设立已久。第三世界国家也有几处,如:印度加尔各达的黄麻交易所,新加坡的橡胶交易所,但其影响尚未如上列几家那么重大。

商品交易所的买卖,投机活动占主导地位。不仅那些专门从事投机的商家买是为了价格升高后再卖或卖是为了价格低后再买,即使制造商和生产商基于实际供需关系的交易也是伺机成交谋价格变化之利。由于商品交易所的大量成交,交易所的价格已经成为国际市场上初级产品价格变动的一个重要指标,可以一时引导价格的升降。

世界上主要的新闻通讯社和商业杂志都报道交易所的情况。本课所录作为课文的电传报告是伦敦商品交易所一周变化的周末综述。

2. Telex： 用户电报，电传，是 teletypewriter exchange 的简写，可指传送文件的电传打字设备，也可指通过该设备传送的信件或新闻报道。

3. “Big bang”：“大爆炸”改革（bang 是拟音字，原意为“突发的巨响”），在本文中指 1986 年 10 月 27 日伦敦股票交易所在政策及经营方式上进行的彻底改革。

改革后，过去一直是保守排外的伦敦股票交易所现在打开大门，允许外国银行和经纪人作为会员加入，废除了买卖股票的固定佣金制度，并开始使用先进的电子交易系统。

这场改革的直接起因是英国政府坚持废除股票交易的固定佣金制度。采用这一制度在伦敦买卖股票比在纽约和东京贵 3—4 倍，因而使其失去很多宝贵的国际交易。这场改革是为了确保伦敦作为世界金融中心的地位而进行的。

4. AFP：法新社（Agency France—Press），世界主要通讯社之一，总部设在巴黎，创立于 1832 年。该社与美联社、路透社等世界各大通讯社签有交换新闻的约定，并向很多国家的新闻机构提供法国国内以及世界的新闻报道。法新社用 6 种语言发稿，在 165 个国家派驻有记者。

5. “The unexpected departure of Sheik Ahmed Zaki Yamani from his post as Saudi Arabian oil minister aggravated existing uncertainty concerning the future direction of oil prices in view of severe world oversupply.”

沙特阿拉伯是世界上最大的石油输出国，在“石油输出国组织”（OPEC）和国际石油市场上有很大的影响力。当时，在亚马尼任沙特石油部长的最后几个月中，沙特阿拉伯一直在强烈呼吁稳定和加强石油价格，而且成功地说服了其他 OPEC 成员国限制各自的产量从而使油价得以稳定回升。恰值此时，亚马尼突然去职，沙特对此也没有做出任何解释，一时离因不明。这一变动无疑地引起了世界石油商家的不安，他们担心重要的政策制定者的离去可能会导致沙特以至“石油输出国组织”现时经营战略和价格政策的改变，感到在本来就供过于求的形势下国际石油市场的价格动向更加无法预料。

6. “Unstable crude prices in turn prompted falls in platinum and gold,...”

沙特阿拉伯更换石油部长是这一连锁反应的背景。

亚马尼的去职被看作是石油价格将会下跌的信号(参注5)。因此,商品市场预料石油出口国的收入将会下降,这会使得经济上几乎全部依赖出口石油的中东国家有可能抛售他们的黄金或白金储备以支付其财政需求,而这样就必然要增加这两种贵金属的市场供应量并影响价格。以这种推断为指导的交易行为最终导致了白金和黄金价格的下跌。

7. “Sterling's decline lent some support to the base metal sector,...”

在伦敦商品交易所买卖的初级产品大都是外国提供的,用外汇成交,但以英镑标价。因此,当英镑对其它货币贬值时,以英镑标价的有关商品价格则会上涨。

8. “the U.S. budget trade”

指美国国家预算批准的政府海外采购。

9. Bullion:贵重金属金、银等的砖或条。银砖、条买卖用作工业原材料或制做个人装饰品。金砖、条作为银行间和政府间的支付手段进行交易,也可持有作为财富的保值和对纸币的支持手段。

10. “the price of tin on the European spot market (basic Rotterdam warehouse) rose to 4 400 pound per tonne,...”

1) spot market:现货市场,在现货市场货物售出后即行交付(比较期货市场)。

2) “...(basic Rotterdam warehouse)...”

括弧里的词语含义是采用锡的鹿特丹仓库交货现价作为伦敦五金交易所的锡价和欧洲现货市场不断变化的锡价的比较基础。

(Ex-warehouse [仓库交货]:价格条件的一种,按照该条件成交的货物,卖方不负担任何交付费用,而买方须至储存该批货物的仓库提货。)

11. “... the previous week's closing level”:伦敦五金交易所周

末最终交易的价格平均水平。

交易所常用的价格术语“closing price”（收盘价）通常指一天内收市前最后的交易价格水平。

12. “... terminal prices...”：期货价格。（期货市场[futures market]有时也称之为 terminal market）

13. International Coffee Organization（ICO，国际咖啡组织）

1963 年成立，监督《国际咖啡协定》的执行，总部设在伦敦，有 60 多个成员国。

14. “... the physical market...”：即 spot market，现货市场。

15. “Extremely quiet conditions prevented merchants from making more than very minor upward adjustments to wooltop quotations in line with firmer replacement costs at origin.”

1) replacement，文中用作“补充库存”之意，有时也用 replenishment.

2) “... at origin.”，即 at the place(s) of origin，place of origin 是产地。

15. auction：拍卖，在规定的时间和场所组织买者公开竞购把现货卖给出价最高的人。

Appendix：

国际商品市场行情报道
常用术语

资本主义国家的报刊和电讯在报道世界商品市场情况时，经常使用一些行情术语，如坚挺、疲软、活跃等等。这些名称的含义，有时理解各有不同。现根据英国路透社的解释介绍如下，以供参考。

十分紧挺（STRONG）：行市迅速及持续上涨。

很 坚 挺（VERY FIRM）：行市上涨，并继续趋涨。

软 坚 挺（FIRMER）：行市在徘徊后有了上涨。

坚　　挺（FIRM）：行市有上升表现。

活　　跃(BUOYANT)：活跃和坚挺。

很 坚 稳(VERY STEADY)：行市稳住在较高水平，并仍能支持。

较 坚 稳(STEADIER)：行市在稍有上升后，维持不变(特别是在出现了某些徘徊之后)。

坚　　稳(STEADY)：行市在目前水平上趋升而不趋落。

稳　　静(STEADY QUIET)：行市稳定，但成交很少(强调价格稳定)。

静　　稳(QUIETLY STEADY)：市场成交很少，但价格坚稳(强调成交少)。

勉强坚稳(BARELY STEADY)：市场表现下降趋向。

(成交)清淡(QUIET)：成交很少。

较 清 淡(QUIETER)：市场成交减少。

有行无市(NORMAL)：无成交，商人不愿出价或报价。

闲　　散(IDLE)：

停　　滞(STAGNANT)：全无交易兴趣。

不 活 跃(INACTIVE)：

呆　　滞(DULL)：只有很少成交，同时价有下降趋向。

很 呆 滞(HEAVY)：无生气，即毫无交易兴趣，同时价格有下降趋向。

趋　　疲(EASIER)：行市稍微下降，而且仍趋下降。

疲　　软(EASY)：行市下降而且继续趋降。

涨落不定(IRREGULAR)：行市先涨后落或先落后涨。

反复无常(ERRATIC)：忽涨忽落，变动无常。

曲折下降(IRREGULARLY LOWER)：

捉摸不定(UNCERTAIN)：

大致坚稳(ABOUT STEADY)：

——新华通讯社编译

Questions on Content and Language Points

(for preview, discussion and review)

1. "The unexpected departure of Sheik Ahmed Zaki Yamani from his post as Saudi Arabian oil minister aggravated existing uncertainty concerning the future direction of oil prices in view of severe world oversupply".

Which part of the sentence does "in view of severe world oversupply" modify?

2. "Unstable crude prices in turn prompted falls in platinum and gold, the latter to its lowest since early September, aggravated by the withdrawal of investment support as the dollar regained ground."

What was "aggravated by the withdrawal of investment support as the dollar regained ground"?

3. "Coffee fluctuated wildly on uncertainty over Brazil's role in the market..."

Why is Brazil's role usually so important for the world coffee market?

4. "After coming in for early support on news of strike action affecting mines belonging to gold fields of South Africa, values (of gold) declined in line with platinum and New York advices as miners were encouraged to return to work by managment promises of negotiation."

1) What is meant by "coming in for early support"? Does it mean that the price of gold fell more or less at the outset, or the opposite?

2) What meaning does the word advice carry in the given context? And what were 'New York advices'?

5. "... the dollar strengthened on news of a decline in the U. S. budget trade and a cut in the Bank of Japan's discount rate."

How could the above—mentioned developments help strengthen the dollar?

6. "Copper: easier. Prices moved gradually lower... But support was in evidence at lower levels."

Do you think that the price was likely to fall further or would stop falling to go up, according to the description ?

7. "LME stocks were down 1,075 tonnes at 33,725 tonnes, ..."

1) Paraphrase the sentence.

2) What is the correct pronounciation of tonne?

Could you recall the English equivalent of the French word? What is it?

8. "A sharp 3,375-tonne rise in LME stocks, to 125,725 tonnes dulled the market at the outset, as did the bleak outlook for aluminium price in 1987 forecast by international traders Shearson Lehman."

Paraphrase the underlined part of the sentence.

9. "Merchants quotations moved one cent in either direction before ending the week at an unchanged 1.63—1.83 dollars per pound."

Paraphrase the underlined part of the sentence, please.

10. "... its (the U. S.) strategic stockpile."

What is a "strategic stockpile"?

11. "... platinum progressed at the outset on concern about strike action in South African mines but quickly fell victim to profit-taking as work resumed."

1) What does to progress mean in the context?

2) What is profit-taking in the text?

12. "Crude oil prices fluctuated in nervous conditions..."

How would a price fluctuate "in nervous conditions"?

13. "But rumours of a shortage of nearby good quality cocoa prevented significant losses."

What is the implication of "nearby" in the given context?

14. "Sugar: irregular. Prices fluctuated under opposing factors,..."

What is the meaning of "opposing" here? Could you find a

substitute word for it?

15. "Rubber: quiet. . . . What little business was concluded was done at very competitive levels, in line with lower East Asian advices, . . ."

1) What does "at very competitive levels" mean?

2) Where (what countries) might the "East Asian advices" be from? (What countries are the major rubber producers in East Asia?)

16. You have seen in the report various reasons for the changes in price. Could you find out the root reason for the price fluctuation? What regulates the price movement in the market, fundamentally speaking?

Topics for Summary

1. What happenings or events could affect the price movement of commodities, as shown in the text?

2. What is the fundamental reason for the changes in price?

Exercises

I. Translate the following telex into Chinese:

Grains, soybeans suffer setbacks

Chicago (ap)—grain and soybeans futures prices retreated Wednesday on the chicago board of trade amid little new export news.

Soybeans futures prices initially gained on strong soybean oil prices tied to good world demand for vegetable oils. But investors became increasingly concerned about record U. S. supplies and the prospect of record brazilian supplies out of the Southern American country's harvest this month.

"Beans is a waiting game for south america." Said mickey luth, senior grains analyst for merrill lynch and co. In Chicago.

"We're all know it's around the corner."

"Buyers of soybean products are likely to wait for prices to come down before entering the market because of the expected record supplies", Luth said.

Wheat futures retreated on ideas that recent gains were overdone. Traders said the agriculture department's decision last week to expand its export subsidy program is useless unless major buyers like China ship the grain they have bought.

Wheat for march delivery fell 5 cents to dlrs 3. 66 1—4 a bushel • march corn fell 1—1 cent to dlrs 2. 34 a bushel • march oats was unchanged at dlrs 1. 19 3—4 b bushel • march soybeans fell 1—2 cent to dlrs 5. 58 a bushel.

Ⅱ. Read the following telex and write a summary on the trend of oil price fluctuation.

Oil companies act to save refining margins.

London, Jan. 27 (reuter)-major oil companies flexed their muscles to salvage profit margins from oil refining this week, supporting oil product prices and depressing crude oil.

World benchmark brent blend crude futures for march delivery traded 31 cents softer at 16. 36 per barrel by 1714 gmt on Friday, having fallen over 70 cents in the last two days.

By limiting the amount of crude oil running through their refineries, oil companies are hoping to eat away at burgeoning stocks of unused heating fuel and at the same time boost demand and prices for crude oil.

"By announcing run cuts, crude oil has suffered while oil products have held steady, "said anmed al-awa, a broker at prudential bache futures in london.

Stocks of heating fuel in the 12 European Union countries at the end of December were a mammoth 25. 17 million barrels above december 1993 levels at 304. 28 million.

Al-awa added that throughout reduction at european refineries was ultimately a bearish signal for all oil prices, products and crude.

"there may well be less output from refineries, but if demand is weak, that's still bearish for prices, "he said.

Brokers cited tumbling gasoline prices in new york as another negative influence.

Traders on new york's futures trading pits sold gasoline futures heavily on news that new jersey may not enforce the use of a new cleaner grade of gasoline in its sales at the pump.

State officials in new jersey argued that they have almost attained their pollution targets and are unwilling to enforce expensive winter regulations controlling fuel quality.

"we feel we've done a lot to improve our air quality, if we're not in attainment, we're very close,"said amy collings of the new jersey department of environmental protection.

Traders said that if new jersey does not enforce clean gasoline regulations, demand for the grade will fall.

On the New York mercantile exchange, unleaded gasoline futures for february delivery traded 1. 24 cents down at 56. 40 cents per gallon by 1711 gmt.

Index

Notes on Technical Terms & Introductions to International Organizations and Enterprises

A

B

C

Capital market
Capital stock
Cartel
Cash crops
Central and Eastern Europe
Central bank
Certificate of Origin
China Export Commodities Fair
China Now
China Resources Inc.
Chrysler Corporation
China International Trust and Investment Corporation (CITIC)
Closing price
Coca-Cola Co.
Comecon
Commodity exchange
Commodity market
Common Agricultural Policy (CAP)
Conglomerate
Consortium
Constant (dollar) terms
Continental Europe
Convertible currency
Cooperative enterprise
Counter-trade
Countervailing duty
Coupons
Current account

D

E

F

G

H

I

J

L

M

N

O

P

R

S

T

U

V

W

Brief Answers or Clues to Questions on Content and Language Points

(Easier questions are left to your sole efforts)

&

Key to Exercises

Lesson 1

I

1. "The pattern of China's foreign trade" refers chiefly to the commodity structure of China's foreign trade and her trade partnership with the outside world.
2. An attributive clause.
3. More foreign exchange is required for more imports. All sections of China's national economy would have to work harder and better to export and earn more for the imports increased.
4. "A net grain exporter" should be one who has done both imports and exports of the item, but finally exported more than imported within a period of time.
5. Foreign capital has flowed into China mostly in the form of foreign direct investment. This type of investment requires foreign industrial investors to set up production facilities locally together with their Chinese partners or alone. For production efficiency and other reasons, as a rule they bring in technology and equipment from abroad to equip themselves. Thus it would result in a rise in imports.
6. China is a developing country with her own economic conditions. In introducing advanced technology into our country, we

would first choose those most needed and applicable at the present stage of our economic development.

7. China's financial borrowing is for industrialization and modernization. Without well-developed transport network and enough energy supply, however, industry and the entire economy could not be further expanded successfully. Therefore it's no time for borrowing them then, which could not be effectively used and result only in heavy interest payment.
8. "Commercial" carries the meaning of having profit-making as the aim. "To borrow on commercial terms" is to borrow at the regular business interest rates (without any special favor received from the bank). China borrows from the World Bank Group for lower interest rates and other favorable conditions.

II

1. T 2. T 3. F 4. F 5. T 6. F 7. F 8. F
9. T 10. T 11. T

Lesson 2

I

1. The country is fully confident in her social system—Socialism with Chinese characteristics when China is opened to the outside world though it seems unavoidable that all sorts of Western ideas and their way of life are to be brought in together with the inflow of the needed capital and technology.
2. Here tax (a noun) is used as an attribute to modify "incentives".
3. At the time of writing the article (1984), the reform of China's economic structure just began, and most of her own enterprises were not quite self-responsible yet for gains and losses in their business operation. In contrast, the enterprises with foreign

funds were organized on the principle of the market economy and they had to be active in competition for survival, with no "same big pan" to eat from. In this sense, they were considered "a real element of competition."

4. drive (n.),运动
5. "better" implies that they had already had things like radios, bicycles and clothing, but expected to have better ones.
6. In the given context the meaning of sales is quantities to be sold.
7. If Gu Mu's statement is understood in the word-for-word way.
8. Administrative setups responsible for absorbing foreign direct investment and relevant local rules and regulations.
9. Source here is used in the sense of a source of information, which might refers to a person or an organization. "A well-placed source" should be an official who is well-informed because of his special position.
10. The reason for the decision was the determination.
11. together.
12. Throw carries the meaning of doing that with force—determination in the sentence quoted above.
13. According to the author's own understanding, as the 19 open areas and cities were competing actively with one another for more foreign direct investment, they made their preferential systems more and more attractive and thus complicated, hard to operate.
14.
15. key projects, 重点(工程) 项目
16.
17. an attributive clause.
18.
19. reviewing (reexamining) of the open policy.

II

I.

1. China's fast economic growth has attracted many international companies to make investment here.
2. Yes.
3. "... economic planners in Beijing are determined to channel foreign money more explicitly to the projects and regions that meet their own needs." "We need to guide foreign investment so that it goes to sectors that are conducive to our economic growth plans."
4. Lucrative short-term property development such as urban real estate development and fairly basic low-technology manufacturing plants such as shoes-making sector.
5. Because these projects bear heavily on the future of China's economic development. High-tech projects such as telecommunications can help improve China's economic structure and raise the productivity, while the infrastructure construction can lay a sound foundation for the development of the other sectors of the economy.
6. The policies to be passed by the NPC would help create favorable conditions for foreign investment in the targeted sectors by providing tax, investment and import-export benefits and more foreign investors would be attracted to these sectors.
7. Yes.
8. It is implied here that the Chinese authorities would not merely be satisfied with short-term visible financial benefits but also attach importance to the fundamental interest of the national economy in absorbing FDI, such as improvement of productivity, operation efficiency, labor force quality, etc. that could be brought about by technology transfer, sharing management know-how and employee training and so on. These benefits might not be visibly reflected in money terms, but could actually upgrade and strengthen the national econo-

my and sharpen the competitiveness of Chinese enterprises, and thus, more vital to the sustained development of the economy.

9. Yes.

Ⅱ.

Ⅰ)

Ⅱ)

Ⅲ)

1. 跨国公司所进行的直接投资正成为世界经济中的一股十分重要的力量。
2. 外国直接投资增长的根本原因没有改变。从本质上讲,各种因素相结合,比如全球通讯的发展和对跨国公司的政治气候的改变等正带来一个真正的全球化生产时代。
3. 外国直接投资往往将资产从发达国家转移至发展中国家,但直接投资的格局(注:产业和地区的分布,见下文)并不完全简单。
4. 公司经常寻找的是三个要素:当地有技术劳动力;基础设施(特别是通讯设施)良好;政府对外国公司持欢迎态度。能得到前两者是一收获,而第三个方面至少也是可以争取的。

Lesson 3

I

1. "Highway 204 out of Shanghai" is one leading out of Shanghai. (Try to work out Sub-question 2 on your own.)
2. "Shoulders" here mean the edges of a road.
3. 1) To give way to something means to make room for something (让位于某物) in the sentence.

   2) Eventually sometimes implies an inevitable result.

4. According to their respective contents, "dynamic economy" refers to an economy full of energy and activity; "the world's dominant economy" means the world's major economic power.
5. China is short of technical and management professionals.
6.
7.
8. (Hint: "a work" here is used in a sense like that of a work of art; "a work in progress" is that in the progress of making.)
9. 1) What the author meant to say is that moving on Highway 204 were both local old-style vehicles and foreign autos of the latest fashion, and like that in China's economy co-exist her national enterprises originally founded for the planned economy and other businesses founded for or adapted to the market economy: the structure of China's economy is under change but not decided definitely yet.
   2)
10. to clear: to gain as a profit. • • •
11. On here is used in the sense of according to or on the basis of • • •
12.
13.
14. (Hint: though is used as an ad. here.)
15. One country's trade surplus would be some other country's trade deficit. If it's too big, it would be a loss for the importer, both financially and economically.

    The country with huge trade surplus might be accused of dumping or using other's import quota illegally as in the textile trade.
16.

II

I.

1. T　2. F　3. T　4. F　5. T　6. T　7. T　8. F　9. T　10. T

Ⅱ.

1. China's economy is rising fast and has a great impact on the Asian economic development. Aware of this, the other Asian countries such as Japan, South Korea and Singapore are seeking to establish economic and trade contacts with China for their own sakes.
2. China is becoming a motive force for Asia's economic development. Although the US is still the largest export market for Asian countries, much larger than China's market for imports, and Japan keeps the strongest economy in Asia, China is now so deeply involved in the regional economic and trade activities that many people in Asia believe that China's role in Asian economy and the world economy at large will become as important as that of the old economic powers such as United States and Japan.
3. Foreign and Hong Kong and Taiwan's investors benefit tremendously from their direct investment in China by expanding their exports to the world with the local low-cost labour.
4. The demand of Japan's domestic market is not very active and the strength of Japanese yen resulted in the high production cost and the high export price. In contrast, China's market is large and thriving and the cost of production there is much lower.

Ⅲ.

1. 中国拥有12亿人口,其经济发展速度大大超过该地区的其他任何成员,中国作为一个贸易国、制造国和投资国,其重要作用正在增强。这为那些曾严重依赖对美贸易的中国的邻国提供了一个机会,使它们得以减缓西方经济的减速给其带来的不利影响,继续实现迅速发展。
2. 对于那些疲于应付日元坚挺(所带来的不利影响)的日本企业来讲,中国特别有吸引力。日本的国内市场疲软,以日元为基础的生产成本太高,致使其出口产品价格过高。中国可以给它们提供一个繁荣的市场和低成本的生产基地。据一种估算,今年日本公司所做的投资当中,每10日元中就有一个日元是投向中国的。

3. 可以肯定地说，中国的贸易增长并非一帆风顺。今年，中国政府解决了与美国就版权和专利保护方面的一项争议，从而避免了美国的制裁。而且，如果中国不进一步开放市场达到国际标准，它就不能加入世界贸易组织。

Appendix to Lesson 1—3

1. 1) ideas of little value.
   2) The "left" political line in the Party that was dominating in China from the late 1950s to the late 1970s.
2. It's similar in meaning to "I should like to say", one polite way of expressing one's idea.
   我想说・・・
3. The nominative absolute construction (独立分词结构)。
4.
5.
6.
7.
8. RMB 200 yuan and RMB 400 yuan respectively.
   "增加三倍"
9. Anywhere in China the Party's leadership must be kept up and the socialist system must be maintained.
10. 1)
    2) They pay foreign exchange for the imports they need in production—machinery, technology, materials and so on.
11. "日新月异"
12. 1)
    2)"政治上可靠(忠诚)"。
13.

Lesson 4

I

1. Aggregate (adj.): made of separate parts, total.
2. • • •

   ", compared with 3. 8 per cent during the 1980s" in the sentence is an adverbial modifier for comparison.
3. That is that in estimating the GDP growth by group, the countries were not classified definitely by the level of industrialization into developing countries, developed ones etc. as often.
4. After World War II, the economic growth of many developing countries depends substantially on export. With the Western economies slackening then, they could not enjoy as much as overseas markets as before.
5. The basic meaning of grip (v.) is to hold firmly. In the given context, it implies that the recession was hard for the countries named to get rid of.
6.
7. "the improvement".
8. arrangements.
9. To edge down is to decelerate slowly.
10.
11.
12. 1) Less credit limited investment and consequently the demand for some assets had to be reduced, which would result in lowered prices for the items.

    2) Consumption of both capital goods and consumer goods.

    3) The tightening of credit and a weak market means less funds for enterprises in investment and reduced income for either bosses or workers, which would affect consumption.

13. 1)The effect of trade as a cause of the deficit.

    2)For the exporter, lower inflation at home could help cut down the cost of their exports and enable them to lower prices for competition abroad; a national currency's depreciation could reduce prices of their exports in forex automatically and legally, in favor of their competitiveness overseas.

14. An appreciation of the national currency usually hampers one country's exports as it lifts the prices of their products in international trade.

15. "accommodative" means "helpful", "cooperative".

16. 1)GDP of the developing countries (see Table 2-3 attached).

    2)Ease here carries the meaning of beginning to fall.

    3)In the given context, "broad-based" factors refer to those applicable to many or most cases; "more specific" ones should be those just applicable to a few cases or even just some particular one.

17. Merchandise usually includes all items for sale. In the text it refers specially to physical goods for export as a contrast to services exported.

18. A change in the political and economic systems.

19. 1) Estimates of GDP for each grouping of the world countries which are categorized on the basis of their geographic positions.

    2)The pick-up enabled China to absorb more imports from abroad, including Asian countries.

20.

21.

22.

II

I.

1. 需求疲软并不是反通货膨胀的后果,更多的是由于失去了从 1983

年就开始的长期扩展时期形成的动力。

2. 苏联及其后所建立的各共和国的经济形势正在恶化，它们外汇日益短缺使其减少了从东欧的进口，也使其加速出口某些初级产品（如铝，金和铅等）来赚取硬通货。这些情况使这些趋势更加复杂化。
3. 造成这一大趋势的原因是美国和英国经济复苏大大出乎预料地遇到了障碍，而且日本和德国已明显开始进入经济较缓慢增长的时期。
4. 这两个国家的金融机构采取了更加保守的借贷政策，削减了对商业建筑这类风险较高项目和对公司依靠大量借贷进行的交易的融资。
5. 在债务重组的支持下，在财政调整、贸易与投资自由化、金融部门、公营企业结构调整和私有化等方面进行的政策改革已然促使该地区缓和了通货膨胀压力，强化了国内需求。

Ⅱ.

1. 在加拿大和英国，商业也正在复苏。加拿大今年的实际增长率预计为 2.7%左右，英国本周公布的新预算推定明年该国的实际增长率为 2.5%。
2. 麻省理工学院的经济学家们批评法国政府为使法郎对德国马克保持坚挺而采取的高利率政策抑制了经济的增长。因此，Dornbusch 预测，1993，1994 和 1995 年，法国的失业率会上升，而大量的失业将使法国的预算赤字扩大，通过减税或增加政府开支来刺激经济的前景也更暗淡。他得出的结论是："法国的情况将会很糟。"
3. 加拿大的通货膨胀率比美国的低，这使加拿大银行可以在明年降低利率而不会出现外汇市场上加元大幅波动的风险。

Ⅲ.

1. T　2. F　3. T　4. T　5. T　6. F　7. T　8. F
9. F　10. F

Lesson 5

I

1. They meant that they would insist on their demand regardless of the consequences (at any expense) until it was satisfied.
2. A market with the least trade barriers against American exporters.
3.
4.
5.
6. 1) Agreements.
   2) Attaching great importance to results.
7. 1) What is implied by "tactical" here is that the US "tough talk" was merely a method, adopted to attain their goal of expanding exports, with no attempt to touch off a trade war.
   2)
8.
9.
10.
11.
12.
13.
14. "his trading signals".

II

Lesson 6

I

1.
2.

3. At the start of the single market one could not see much change and many Europeans would look at it with reservation, according to the writer.

4. 1) Drastic.

   2) The writer feared that making drastic changes in such a large and wealthy area might sharpen interest conflicts between EU member countries, if handled improperly, and arouse unexpected confusion.

5.

6. "The new world of competition" refers to the newly-established single market in the text.

7.

8.

9. 1) Two.

   2) An appositive clause and an attributive one.

   Both are used as attributes in the sentence.

10. In the given context, the word translate means to change from one form to another. Its Chinese equivalent might be 转化, or just 变。

11. Adjustment to the market has dragged on rather long and won't be (could not be) completed very soon.

12. The business circles.

13.

14.

15. When the leaders of some EU countries felt weak politically at home, to improve their domestic positions, they would try harder in dealing with the EU common questions to protect and promote each of their own national interest, instead of the common good, which could lead to more fighting among them than compromise.

16. Legal framework: a set of outlined laws; blueprint: a detailed plan for actual work.

II

I.

1. Because the bulk of the exports of the Eastern European countries flow to the Western European market. If protectionism ramps there they would encounter severe setback in their exports and their economies would suffer a lot.
2. With the introduction of protectionist measures by Western European countries on the export of Eastern European countries, the latter suffered a lot in their foreign trade. To protect themselves, they had to adopt temporary import quotas and impose indirect barriers within their own block because the other trading partners are much stronger than them, and they were not in a position to retaliate against their protectionist measures. Meanwhile, as the four Eastern European countries were bidding for EC membership, they didn't have much interest in promoting free trade among them. Instead, they opted to setting up trade barriers.

II.

1. d　2. a　3. d　4. c　5. b　6. b　7. d　8. c

Lesson 7

I

1. To draw the line: to set limits, to set a limit on what one is willing to do.
2. 1) According to the context of the article and the developments in international trade in recent years, the "pressure" mentioned here should include mostly economic sanctions or threats of that.

   2) To give in: to yield, surrender.

   3) Fuss: nervous activity or excitement (complaint, annoyance etc.)

"... the fuss would die down". is that that would become weak.

3.

4. Multipartite (having many sides).

5.

6.

7.

8.

9. No.

II

Ⅰ.

in, with, on, at, to, in of, for, from, of, before, at, in, to, by

Ⅱ.

trade, market, excessive, surplus, increase, order, counter, raised, going, imposed, is, should, mother, leading, enough

Appendix to Lesson 7

1. 1) Here move means to change the position of something.
   2) The Japanese government's trade policy.
2. Yes.
3. "A pace too slow for the eye to follow" means that the speed of the changes taking place in Japan is so slow that one can hardly notice them.

   这种既得利益正在动摇并慢慢地减少,但其改变的速度如此之慢,以至于人们根本注意不到。
4. It implies that in Japan people are very loyal to the established relationships and practices and their ways of doing things are not easily changed by some new ideas or policies even if they might

be better or more rational than the tradition. The word "transactional" is used here basically in the sense of negotiable.

5. It means "stop thinking about cultural factors and the existence of 'Japan Inc.'..."
6. It refers to the big Japanese business firms.
7. 1) It refers to Japan's foreign trade system, which spares no efforts to support and promote their own export expansion on the one hand, but pursues protectionism in their imports on the other.
   2) As it protects the interest of their own industry, agriculture and other economic sections. But it is unfair to their trading partners and against the universal trading principles of equality and mutual benefit.

Lesson 8

I

1. It implies that the South Korean government favored the country's big conglomerates with preferential policies so as to sharpen their competitiveness in the world market and aimed at establishing a strong national economic machine based on their strength, which would propel forward the whole of the economy. "... Inc."refers to the collaboration.
2. They pinned all their hopes of success and prosperity on the overseas expansion.
3. "For South Korea as a whole, that seems both aprophecy and an ambition."
4. An attributive clause, for it modifies a noun —"the day".
5. Clout (n.): power and influence.
6. In the given context, it means the advancement of technology. It refers specifically to their (technically) modernized municipal facilities, which helps give people the impression that it's a place

full of “energy”.

7. 1)“a deep pocket” usually means “a large sum of money”.
   2) Here “deep pockets” means serious problems, a terrible state.
   3) It is used ironically to indicate that in spite of fast economic growth in South Korea, sad poverty still exits throughout the country.
8. “... is to ... ” means “... plans to... ”; “... are to... ” means “... should be... ”
9. The most advanced high technologies.
10. Those companies' successful expansion overseas helped Korea begin to take rank among the trade powers with numerous giant multinationals & global economic influence.
11. 1) Considering or in view of.
    2)“The stakes” refers to the personal interests.
    3) Concerned.
12. Here “order” is compared to task or requirement.
13. 1) It means to make great efforts —slave.
    2) It refers to the advancement of technology.
    3) What's meant is that it's those things mentioned above that has made Korea a rising world trade power and able to compete with countries like the U. S. and Japan in the international market.

II

Ⅰ.

1. The government required the *chaebols* to concentrate on their core business by allowing the ten largest *chaebols* to name three sectors each and the next 20 to name two sectors.
2. “Octopus-like growth” here means to grow in nearly all directions and different fields without proper planning and control.
3. By concentrating on a few operations, a company can utilize its resources more efficiently, strengthen its research and develop-

ment capability, improve management and sharpen its competitiveness in the market.

4. It was funded by debt—borrowed partly on the assumption that the government would not let the conglomerates go bankrupt.
5. The author thought that the government's strategy was partly driven by political conflicts between the government leaders and the powerful chieftains of the *cheabols*.

Ⅱ.

1. F　2. T　3. F　4. F　5. F　6. F　7. T　8. T

Ⅲ.

Lesson 9

I

1.
2. Result in (something)
3. Here popular means: carried on by the people.
4. It has more effective means to have the relative laws enforced.
5.
6.
7. ... as a tennis tournament was held (there), which was sponsored by the BMW/Dubai Duty Free(the name of some enterprise).
8. With their headquarters (head office) in Dubai.
9.
10. "Which" stands for "$2 000 million in financing".
11. It has......
12.
13.
14. 1)Replace.

2) Spending.

15.

16. 1) No. The unofficial re-exports' figures were not included.

2) The re-export statistics could inform you only of the destination countries, but not of its actual volumes as the figures of the unofficial re-exports are not given there.

3) To be kept for re-export.

17.

18.

19.

20.

21.

22. 1)

2) The loss leader refers to an article that is sold at a price well below its cost in order to attract customers. The loss-leader philosophy is the idea of that held as a marketing strategy in the article given.

3)

4) With reason.

23.

24.

25. "Up" is used here as an adj., meaning "ready".

26.

27.

28.

29.

II

I.

1. The rise in the price of oil and vibrant activity in non-oil sector.
2. Yes. The UAE has maintained political stability, and a high

level of public spending, especially on capital projects.

3. By keeping the current 4% import tariff unchanged and refusing to introduce some form of income tax.
4. To attract more foreign investment, tourists and businesses, etc.
5. It means that outwardly Dubai appeared strong in economy but actually was not so.
6. In Dubai, they can have the international exposure, the services and access to the storage and distribution networks. To some extent, Dubai can function as a distribution and management center for the whole of the Middle East and the Indian subcontinent.
7.
8. Yes.

Ⅱ.

继1994年阿联酋的国内生产总值增长了2.9%之后,今年,基于油价较高和非石油部门的活动有所增加这两个因素,对该国经济增长的预测更趋乐观,可望高达5%。这一乐观预测使人们更加相信阿联酋是海湾合作委员会国家中经济表现最好的这一说法。

石油在阿联酋经济中仍占主导地位,其产值占其国内生产总值的大约三分之一。由于油价较坚挺,预计今年该国的石油收入将从1994年的123亿美元增至略低于130亿美元。这必将增加该国的出口收入,巩固经常项目顺差。1994年该国的经常项目顺差降低了一半至4.5亿美元。

再出口的持续增长也将有助于该国的国际收支。1995年前六个月,迪拜的再出口总额上升了7.3%,达到15.82亿美元,而1993年同期为14.73亿美元。尽管迪拜对其最主要出口市场——伊朗的再出口下降了22%,对沙特阿拉伯的再出口额也有所下降,但其再出口总额还是增加了,这是因为这两个国家需求的疲软被阿联酋对印度、香港、卡塔尔、巴基斯坦和索马里的贸易的增加完全抵销了。

对信贷需求的增加反映了阿联酋经济状况的改善,1995年第二季度,在阿联酋开展业务的银行所做的国内贷款增长了1.42亿美元，达195.37亿美元。在三至六月这段时间里所增加的贷款中大部分都是贷给了私营部门。到六月底，给企业的贷款总额达186.2亿美元。

在阿布扎比、迪拜和沙加，有关政府预算的具体信息还未公开，但从基础设施和建筑活动的规模来看，政府的支出仍将保持下去。至于联邦政府，它仍坚持传统做法，每半年公布一项关于政府开支和收入的最新数字。有关今年前六个月的最新公报显示，由于收入的增加和紧缩开支，出现了2.32亿美元的盈余。这比预算的情况要好，对1995年全年的预算有2.88亿美元的赤字。

Lesson 10

I

1.

2. 1) According to the doctrines of absolute advantage and comparative advantage, international trade could help a country make better use of its advantages and thus "spur economic growth", and the Uruguay round could promote trade between countries.

   2) "Sheltered" here means "protected" (economically).

   When one country's economy is "sheltered" and with little competition, it's most difficult for them to make good use of their absolute and comparative advantages, leaving the country far behind in economic development.

3. An adverbial modifier of result.

4. If only or on condition that...

5. "... see off..." here means to make a clear break with (France on the question of farm trade).

6.

7.

8.

9. Squabble: to fight or argue, often about unimportant things.

10.
11.
12.
13. 1)The other problems of the round.
    2)To solve.
14. To adjudicate (裁定).
15. 1)To consider fully.
    2)
16.
17.
18. Trade talks under GATT should be conducted in good order and harmoniously to end with success, though unavoidably with rise and fall, just like a nice cha-cha featuring strong rhythm.
19. 1)Policy or principle.
    2)Acts against the unity and the unified interest of the European Union.
20.

II

1. F　2. F　3. F　4. T　5. F　6. F　7. F　8. T

Lesson 11

I

1.
2. "... was supposed to... ":... was required by law to...
3. The basic meaning of to seem is to appear to be. When it's used in a sentence like the one of the text, it implies that the speaker (writer) is not quite sure of what he says, or speaks(writes) with some reserves.
4. Here it refers to loan payments.

5. 1) Multinational corporations.

   2) The network of a multinational corporation usually consists of the headquarters, their home and overseas branches, subsidiaries and their affiliates. Normally each is independent in operation and self-responsible for their own gains and losses, but they tend to do business with one another whenever it is possible and beneficial to the entire firm.

   3) To find access to "the network"—"the global firms'" internal market.

6. Countertrade involves conditional buying or allows no free choice in importing. That's both against competition and free trade.

II

1. F 2. T 3. F 4. F 5. T 6. F 7. F 8. T

Lesson 12

I

1.

2.

3. "High-calorie".

4. "If" here is used in the sense of possibility. "A big if " is a very or rather doubtful possibility.

5.

6. 1)

   2) (The beverage) filled with less soda, making one not feel so full in drinking.

7.

8. "Price promotions" is to promote sales by means of various price reduction.

9. The symbiotic aspect of their relationship is their interdepend-

ence on each other in business—without the syrup makers' regular supply, the bottlers would have nothing of this kind to sell, and without the collaboration of the bottlers, the syrup makers would have no ready access to the market, but sometimes their interests conflict with each other, as described in the text(Paragraph 11), when the bottlers would become "fractious" to the syrup makers.

10. (The sales data) resulting from sales with the "special promotion" cut back.
11.

II

Your summary should include the following points:

1. Coke's strategy of winning the retailers and the consumers(Paragraph 6,7),
2. Its expansion strategy for bottling(Paragraph 8,9,10,11),
3. Its strategy in syrup concentrate business (Paragraph 12).

Lesson 13

I

1. (To be tops at doing something: to be excellent at doing something; to crack: to break with the pieces remaining together.)

   The heading means literally that Hong Kong is very good at cracking—consuming US shell eggs, with the implication that H. K. is a big market for the eggs from US.
2. It is a matter of difference in price between the US eggs exported to H. K. and those sold elsewhere.
3. Following the example of the given market report, a survey of the market might take as its objects the items below:

   1) The general quantity demand(size) of the market for the subject article;

2) The market response to each of the different kinds of the article and their respective market shares;

3) The distribution of the market—the share for each supplier;

4) The competitors, their advantages and disadvantages as compared with your own, and their market strategies.

5) The operating mechanism of the market.

6) The prospects for the market.

7) Suggestions and proposals.

4.

5.

6.

II

1. c　2. d　3. a　4. b　5. d　6. b　7. a　8. b
9. c　10. a

Lesson 14

I

1.

2. 1) "Flat prices" implies that the prices were inactive remaining at the same level and showing a tendency to fall.

2)

3.

4. 1)

2) There might be reasons like this:

a. The lowered prices of those commodities caused by the appreciation of the USD could also promote exports and their losses from reduction of the unit price would be compensated for by their increased earnings from the export expansion.

b. With the appreciation of the USD, many countries' currencies depreciated, but to different levels. And their dollar-denominated commodity prices declined accordingly—some more, some less. Those countries whose prices dropped less could benefit, even a lot when they imported from some others with their commodities' prices depressed more.

3)

5. 1) The market forces—chiefly demand and supply (which determine market prices combined with the currency movements).
   2) It was subsequent to the rise in the dollar described in the above lines of the same paragraph.
   3) The usage of compensating in the context implies that once the US currency movement had the dollar commodity price suffer a loss.
6. 1) For a currency unit stable in value.
   2)
7. To rebound: (of price) to rise again usually with force after falling to a certain level, 反弹.
   To rally: (of price) to stop dropping and become firm, 止跌回坚。
8. 1)
   2)
9. 1) The implication of "inflationary" here is that the decade was a period with inflation as a leading feature.
   2)
10. Higher import duties, restrictive import quota or license systems, irrationally high quality standards for import inspection or subsidies to local producers, for example.

II

1. T 2. T 3. F 4. F 5. F

Lesson 15

I

1. The predicate verb "aggravated".
2. The"falls in platinum and gold".
3. Brazil is the biggest producer and exporter of coffee of the world.
4. 1) To rise.

   2) When advice is used in its plural forms, it refers to news from a distance, esp. commercial.

   "New York advices" were some news report on the business developments of the New York Exchange.
5. "A decline in the US budget trade" indicated that less dollars would be sold for foreign exchange for imports, thus changing the pattern of demand and supply for the USD in the currency market in favor of the dollar;"a cut in the Bank of Japan's discount rate" means that the interest rate in Japan would have to be lower than before and that would drive investors to places like the US offering higher rates for better yields and more dollars would be needed in the market, which was to result in strengthening the USD as well.
6.
7. 1) LME stocks had been reduced by 1,075 tonnes to 33,725 tonnes...

   2)
8. (Hints: before paraphrasing, you have to see whether the sentence order is normal and find out the sentence elements.)
9.
10.
11. 1)

    2) Profit-taking: to profit in a price fluctuation on an exchange by selling what one has bought at a lower price when the

price goes up.

12.

13. The meaning that nearby carries here is close in time. “Nearby... cocoa” actually refers to goods for prompt delivery.

14.

15.

16.

II

Ⅰ.

谷物、大豆价格受挫

芝加哥(美联社消息)——由于少有新近出口的消息,星期三在芝加哥商品交易所谷物和大豆的期货价格回落。

由于世界市场对蔬菜油的需求大,豆油的价格坚挺,因此,大豆的期货价格最初有所上升。但由于美国大豆的供应量创下纪录,而本月南美洲国家大豆收获后巴西的供应量也可能创下高纪录,投资者们对其日益越发担心。

“就南美洲而言对大豆可以采取伺机而动的策略,”位于芝加哥的 Merrill Lynch 公司的高级谷物分析家米基·路斯说,“而我们都知道情况很快就会明朗。”

路斯说,因为预期大豆的供应量会创最高水平,所以大豆制品的购买者们可能要等到价格下跌后才会进入市场。

由于人们认为最近小麦价格的上升过高,所以其期货价格已有回落。交易商们说,除非像中国这样的大买主将其所购的谷物运走,否则农业部上周所做的扩大出口补贴计划的决定是没有用的。

三月交货的小麦价格下跌了五美分,为一蒲式耳 3.661—4 美元;三月交货的玉米价格下跌了 1—2 美分,为一蒲式耳 2.341—4 美元;三月交货的燕麦价格没变,仍是一蒲式耳 1.193—4 美元;三月交货的大豆价格下跌了 1—2 美分,为一蒲式耳 5.58 美元。

Ⅱ....

Thesis for Reference——

"The Content Constitution and Language Features of Journal Articles on World Economics and International Business"

附录

西方报刊经贸文章的内容构成和语言特点

史　天　陆

报刊选读课在中国外语院校和其他高校外语专业的高年级已开设多年，近年来又普遍开设，受到高度重视。据 1983 年英语专业高年级教学座谈会的统计，当时开设报刊选读课的就有 14 所大学，其中有 10 所（包括北京大学、复旦大学、北京外国语言学院和对外经济贸易大学）是把这门课作为必修课开设的。1990 年经国家教委批准发布的《高等学校英语专业高年级英语教学大纲（试行本）》明确要求在高年级要开设“外国报刊选读课”。

报刊选读课受到如此重视是中国改革开放方针实施的需要和结果。改革开放各项政策的推行大大增加了我们的对外交往和合作，我们只有了解、熟悉我们的外国伙伴，对手和国际环境，才能完成各项任务，“知己知彼，百战不殆”。对于对外经贸工作者来说，信息尤其重要。这是由于当今世界市场竞争激烈，情况瞬息万变，不及时了解最新的情况，就很难做出正确的决策。阅读外国报刊是了解有关信息的一条重要途径。我们的“外国报刊选读”课就是为了培养学生的阅读，理解外报外刊的基本能力而开设的。

一、文章内容专业化

主要是关于国际贸易、世界经济方面的，也涉及国际商务（international business）的其他方面，如：国际信贷、直接投资、证券投资、技术转让，劳务出口等。这些文章说明，分析问题的理论依据是西方经济学。

由于这类文章内容高度专业化，理解起来往往比较困难。一位外语造诣高但不从事经贸研究的学者，面对一篇西方报刊文章会不知所云。其实这是不足为怪的正常现象。因为他不是不知其文——基本的语法和词汇，而是不解其意——专业的内容。

出现这种情况，有时是由于对文章中出现的单个专业词汇的含义即所代表的概念不清楚，尽管整个句子很简单，也不知道这句话要说的到底是什么，

如：

British GDP should rise 3.6% in real terms in 1985, vs. 1.6% last year.

In the past three years, the terms of trade and curent-account balances of the Asian newly industrialized countries have improved dramatically.

Because syrups made with juices are more expensive than other syrups, Coca-Cola and PepsiCo will be charging bottlers more for them.

显然，理解上列各句的关键在于是否理解其中 4 个专业名词所表达的概念(有关解释请见文后附注 1),2),3),4))。

有的人可能认为，既然专业词汇也是由普通词汇演变而成的，那就可以顾词思义，即根据原词的基本词义来解释专业词汇而得其梗概。其实这是很不可靠的，而且往往造成大错。如上例第二句中有“terms of trade”一词，就词释义似乎应是“贸易条件”，特别商业英语中又有“terms and conditions”(“条款”)一说，但国际贸易中只作“进出口比价”解(见注 2)。所以专业词汇词义的确定只能以专业知识为基础。

知文而不解其意，这种情况出现的原因还可能是更深一层的。有时句中并没有出现什么含义复杂或生僻的专业用语，主要是有一两个既是专业词汇也是普通词汇的词语，如：inflation/labour dispute 等。对单个专业词汇的理解可能问题不大，但有可能就是看不清句中或上下句中各个概念之间的关系，因而对整句或一个段落似懂非懂。

例如：

West Germany is still congratuating itself on its success in combining real GDP growth of 2.6% with only 2.4% inflation last year.

（西德仍然为去年得以使国内生产总值实际增长 2.6%的同时将通货膨胀控制在 2.4%沾沾自喜）。

But in looking for explanations and remedies, only Mitterrand in France tried the Keynesian response of pumping more monoy into the system. The result was a surge in inflation, a big current-account deficit and falling currency.

（但是在寻求原因和解决办法当中，只有法国的密特朗试用了凯恩斯的对策，增加对整个经济的货币供应。其结果是通货膨胀增长，经常项目的巨额赤字和货币贬值。）

Sterling's decline lent some support to the base metal sector, where lead and zinc rallied on the continuing lack of a solution to the labour dispute affecting Auslralia's broken hill mines.（电传文）

（英镑比价的下落有助于贱金属类价格的上升，这类商品中的铅和锌的价格由于澳大利亚布罗肯山矿区的劳资纠纷仍未得解决而回升了。）

第一例中虽出现了两个专业名词 GDP（gross domestic product）和 inflation，但这两个词都是为大家所熟知的，不会给理解造成多大障碍。那么是不是知道了这两个词本身的含义，这句话就算懂了呢？不见得。用心的读者会发现，这句话说的不是西德分别欢庆国内生产总值的实际增长和通货膨胀得以控制两件事，而是要讲清：西德在使国内生产总值得到可观增长的同时居然还把通货膨胀率压得相当低这件事值得一庆。至此已很明确，要想弄清这句话的真正含义，就必须理解为什么同时做到这两件事就很不容易，它们两者之间到底有什么联系或关系。而要认识到这一步,那就不是略知皮毛就能解决的,而是要有一定程度的经济学专业知识。第二例也是如此,要想弄清全句的意思光知道什么是"货币供应"、"经常项目"、"货币贬值"(实际上这里指的是汇率的下降)是不够的,还要明白:为什么增加货币供应就可能引起通货膨胀,继而造成经常项目赤字并导致本国货币的汇率下降,即这些经济现象之间的联系。第三例理解的关键在于:英镑比价和伦敦商品交易所贱金属价格之间的联系;文中提到的船、锌价格的起落与产地发生的劳资纠纷的关系。

综上所述可以得出一个结论:了解并初步掌握西方经济学以及国际商务的基本知识是阅读和研究经贸类西方报刊文章的必不可少的条件。

二、文章内容涉及到的背景复杂多样

报刊文章是述实论事之文,经贸类文章自不例外,报道和评论的都是正在发生或发生不久的实事。这些经济情况和商务活动都必然在某时某地某种环境的特定背景下发生的,并且受到错综复杂的经济和非经济的——政治、历史以至文化、科技发展等各个方面因素的影响和制约。为了深刻地揭示内容,表现主题,这些背景也就往往理所当然地成了经贸类报刊文章的重要组成部分。

经贸类文章的这一特点常常成为阅读理解的障碍。首先,由于这些背景因素是非经济性的,如果读者对这些经济以外的大大小小的背景的有关情况不熟悉,即使是英语和经贸专家也难以理解;而不了解事物发生的背景,就无法摸清其来龙去脉,深入、透彻的理解主题内容。

例如:

Most economists believe, that the relatively modest growth of China's imports since 1980 cannot be sustained. The 1983 level of \$18.1 billion was lower than 1980 figure (\$19.6 billion). The need for stepping up capital goods imports, the slow growth in domestic steel and synthetic fibre output are just some of the more compelling reasons for higher spending on imports. But the historical and political aversion to running large visible trade deficits is likely to keep this growth in check.

（然而大多数经济学家认为，1980 年以来中国进口增长较为缓慢的情况不会继续下去。1983 年 181 亿美元的进口水平较 1980 年的数字（196 亿美元）为低。对增加生产资料进口的需要，国内钢铁和合成纤维产量增长的缓慢只是更为紧迫地要求在进口上花更多的钱的部分原因。但历史上对负有巨额有形贸易逆差的反感多半会使这一增长受到限制。）

上文中"历史上和政治上……的反感"指的是什么？如果对这一点不了解，就无法理解为什么这种"反感"会制约中国进口的扩大，以及在多大程度上会起到限制作用。这就需要有经济领域之外的背景知识（"反感"的解释请见文后注 5）。

又如：the unexpected departure of Sheik Shmed Zaki Yamani from his post as Saudi Arabian oil minister aggravated existing uncertainty concerning the future direction of oil prices in view of severe world oversupply.（电传文）

（沙特阿拉伯石油部长亚马尼酋长意外的去职使得由于（石油的）世界性的严重供过于求而对油价走势本来就拿不准的看法更加捉摸不定了。

亚马尼的去职是一项政治上的人事变动，然而以此为背景，国际市场上对石油价格变化的预测就更加摇摆不定。为什么他的去职对石油市场会有这么大的影响呢？要看清这一疑点，就要了解这位世界石油输出第一大国的石油部长在沙特和石油输出国组织（OPEC）的作用、影响和他当时所执行的政策这一系列政治性或带有政治性的背景（有关资料，请见文后注 6）。

文章内容的背景之所以难于理解还在于：西方经贸类报刊文章的作者在写作中对背景的提及一般总是很简略的，难得详加描述，提供一个理解的基础。所以即使是一种经济性质的背景，只具有一般专业知识也可能仍不能理解。作者对背景情况介绍得比较简单可能是由于：专门写给某一种行业的人士看的，涉及的背景在这个范围内是个常识而不要解释；或某一背景情况在作者下笔的时候在彼时彼地是众所周知的，无需详介。

例如：

The attention of commodities dealers was last week captured initially by events on the stock exchange, where monday's big bang was muffled by computer failures, but turned later to the troubled oil market.（电传文）

（做初级产品生意的商人的注意力上周一开市先为股票交易所的盛况所吸引，那里订于周一开始的"一鸣惊人（的改革）行动"，由于计算机系统失灵给弄得黯然失色，尔后注意力就转向了混乱的石油市场）。

文中所谓"Big Bang"是指英伦股票交易所的对外政策，管理收费以及交易方式于 1986 年进行的一次改革。在这里，改革实施第一天开始的情况用作背景，衬托初级产品交易所当日开市由静到动的状态，背景本身也是经济性质的。但这样的事有很大的行业局限性。"Big Bang"主要是交易所这一行内部的变化，不可能像 GNP（国民生产总值），the Great Depression（1929 年资本主义世界的经济大萧条）或 Uruguay Round（乌拉圭回合）那样的经贸基本常识为从事国际经贸各行业的大部分人所了解。由于伦敦股票交易所的股票销售对象主要是与交易所业务有关的商家，"Big Bang"之类的背景他们必然是知道的，因而对此未加任何解释。而这就给其它读者出了一道难题，使之困惑不已。

再如：

Despite the assurances given at <u>the Plaza Hotel conference</u>, as long as the U. S. budget deficit persists and real interest rates remain high stateside, foreing goverments will be under pressure to hold down monetary growth to protect their currencies from falling against the dollar.

这句话摘自 1985 年 11 月《幸福》杂志的一篇文章。这句话以所谓“广场饭店会议”为背景，对“外国政府”的金融行为做出预测。为了完全、深入地理解这句话的内容，有一系列与背景有关的问题需要弄清：为什么“外国政府”“减少货币供应”和他们曾做出的“保证”相矛盾呢？他们的“保证”是什么？“广场饭店会议”有哪些国家参加？讨论了什么问题？做出了哪些决议？会议的结果对有关国家政府的经济政策有什么影响和约束？这就需要对“广场饭店会议”这一背景有足够的了解。然而，在上述那句话的前前后后都没有再提及这一会议。原因何在呢？情况如下：“广场饭店会议”于 1985 年 9 月在纽约举行，同年 11 月，美国《幸福》杂志就发表了这篇文章，时隔还不到两个月。对于美国以至西方经贸界有关人士来说，看到这篇文章的时候会议的情况仍然记忆犹新，没有必要详加解释。而面对不了解该会议情况的读者来说，阅读理解此文就颇感困难，需寻根求源，做一番探索（“广场饭店会议”简介请见文后注 7）

由于西方报刊经贸文章具有上述特点，即主题内容的表述都是以一定的历史条件为背景的，研读这类文章除去要有西方经济学理论的基础知识和一般的经贸知识外，还应从下述几方面努力：

1. 不断扩大知识领域，涉猎与国际经贸活动有关的政治、历史、文化、科技等诸方面知识；

2. 注视国际经贸实际和理论的不断发展，及时了解新情况，补充必要的新知识；

3. 严谨治学，遇到不清楚的背景问题，要追索查询，务求水落石出。

本文以上对西方报刊经贸文章的内容构成进行了分析，现再就其语言方面的特点做一些探索。

西方报刊国际经贸类文章所使用的语言有鲜明的特色，除了新闻语体的简练、明确、灵活等特点外，最显著的特点是专业性强。

(一)文章内容高度专业化导致专业用语的大量使用。

例如：

The productivity improvement has been a reaction to crisis. Many companies were in difficulties in the recessionary years of 1980,1981 and 1982. They had to rationalize and modernise or die. Many collapased, but those which survived are now much more efficient than they were. Jaguar, the British luxury-car manufacturer, was a loss-making part of a nationalised company in 1980. It produced fewer than two cars a year per manufacturing worker. Now the company is independently quoted on the stock exchange and made a 54 million (US$77 million) profit in 1984. Production per man has more than doubled.

这段文章约 100 字，粗略统计专业词语就有 20 个(productivity improvement, crisis, company, in difficulties, recessionary, rationalize, modernise, efficent, manufacturer, loss-making, nationalize, produce, manufacturing worker, independently quoted, stock exchange, £(pound sterling), US$ (US dollar), profit, production, man)，单词 27 个，有的还重复出现，更值得注意的是，这段由 8 个句子组成的文章内含有 10 个主谓结构，而 10 个主谓结构中就有 6 个主语和 8 个谓语是由专业词语组成的，也就是说，这段文章的主要意思是通过这些专业词语表达的。

由此可见，为了理解西方报刊经贸类文章的内容，就必须了解，熟悉一些经贸专业词语的含义。而要做到这一点，必须深入学习和研究有关的经贸知识。

在辨认、理解经贸专业词语当中，要特别注意那些普通英语常用字演化而来的词语，稍有疏忽就会造成曲解、浅化而不得真意，如在上面所引段落中“productivity improvement”里的“improvement”，转化后的确切含义应为“提高”而不是大家在普通英语中所熟悉的“改进”；“in difficulties”意为“有财政困难”，而不是一般的“有困难”；“rationalize”不是一般的“合理化”，而是专指近来西方世界以解决 19 世纪 30 年代的资本主义国家经济危机的方法为借鉴，采取以优劣汰，以大兼并小的办法改组企业提高效益度过经济衰退的做法；“manufacturer”不是一般的“制造者”，而是“厂家”、“工厂”；“production”不是指“生产（过程）”，而作“产量”解；“man”不是“男人”或泛指“人”，而指“工人”或“参与生产的人”。

（二）西方报刊经贸文章内容的表达，除了通过专业词语外，一部分普通英语的词语也被大量地、频繁地使用，从而形成了带有专业词语色彩的准专业词语群。

比如，很多经贸问题的研究都离不开考察有关方方面面的增减；如看一国，一地区乃至世界的经济情况，必须要了解其生产总值是增长了还是减少了；看市场的变化就一定要知道价格是涨了还是落了；看国际投资形势就得清楚资本的流动是增加了还是减少了。为了表达这些内容，表示“增”、“减”或“升”、“降”意思的词语以及与其相关连的词语在报刊经贸文章中经常、反复地使用，有时密度还很大，

如下例：

The US dollar value of Chinese exports increased at an average rate of almost 18 per cent per annum between 1978 and 1983, while imports increased by aproximately 11 per cent per annum. As a result, the visible trade surplus rose sharply from US$1.4 billion in 1981 to US$4.4 billion in 1982 and US$3.7 billion in 1983. Exports grew much faster than imports during this period not only because of the strong emphasis placed on exporting by China's economic planners, but also because a number of industrial projects were postponed in 1979. Official recogintion that foreign technology could play a major role in modernising the Chinese economy had caused imports to rise by more than 50 per cent in 1978 placing undue strain on the national economy. China became a net grain exporter in 1984 and in 1983 the country started to export soyabeans and cotton.

在上面这段约160个字的文章中,表示"增长"的词共出现了5次(引文中下加横线的字),为了避免重复,使用了3个同义词(increase, rise和grow),其中仅两个字重复了一次。与此同时,和这些词相关连的词语(引文中下加浪线的字)也得到了使用。如:at a rate of... per cent, per(time), between(time) and (time), by... per cent, approximately, sharply, from (an amount) to(an amount), in(time), during (a period)等,其中by... per cent还重复了一次。

又例:

Commodity markets are relapsing. After two years of holding steady, though at depressed levels, commodity prices have fallen 10% this year in SDR terms. The terms of trade of exporters of primary products(measured by the IMF's commodily price index deflated by the export price of manufactures) have fallen to their lowest level since the series was first compiled in 1957. The combination of sluggish demand and over-production suggests that commodity markets may remain weak for a long time. The best hope for producers is that if the dollar continues to slide then commodity prices may rebound, in dollar terms at least. But there is scant sign of this happening yet.

在这一小段约110字的文章里,表示"下降"这个概念的词用了4次。为了避免同一词语频密的重复,使用了3个同义词(relase, fall和slide),其中仅fall重复使用了一次。与此同时,"下降"的关联词出现了3个。

从上面的例子可以初步看出,西方报刊国际经贸文章所使用的这部分准专业词语的两重性:

1. 像rise和fall这类词语,不同于那些专门用来表达专业内容的词语,如 productivity、stock exchage 等。rise 和 fall 的基本含义("上升"和"下降")可以用来反映社会生活各个方面的情况,大至航天,小至日常生活,一概通用。从其适用的广泛性来看,这部分词语应该归入称之为"common core" 的共核语言的范围。

2. 尽管 rise 和 fall 这类词属于通用词语,但这些词语在西方报刊经贸文章中却大量使用,经常用来表达专业内容或与专业相关的内容,因而被着上了浓重的"专业词语"的色彩。

在西方报刊经贸文章中经常见到的这类词语还有表示比较或对此意义的一些词语,

如:

The 1983 level of $18.1 billion was lower than the 1980 figure ($19.6 billion). The need for stepping up capital goods imports, the slow growth in domestic steel and synthetic fibre output are just some of the more compelling reasons for higher spending on imports with an unemployment rate of about 13%, the highest in Europe, consumer spending will remain depressed.

(Telex) ivory coast's oilseed production reached a record 225,000 tonnes in 1985—1986, compared with 195,000 in 1984—1985, agriculture minister denis Bracanon announced.

During the past few years a major objective of the Chinese authorities has been to reduce the proportion of agricultural exports, while increasing that of industrial and mineral products.

显而易见,表示比较与对比意义的词语,如上面例中的 lower, higher, more compelling, highest, compare, while 等都是普遍使用的通用英语词语,然而由于这些词语在西方报刊经贸文章中经常大量地使用,表达有关专业内容,已经成了这类文章写作手段不可缺少的一部分。

在西方报刊经贸文章中频繁使用的另一组通用英语词语是表示"估计"和"预测"意义的词语,

例如：

It is estimated that between 1970 and 1983,39.2 million workers found jobs in the urban areas—7.83 million jobs a year!

Many prices are at historic lows, and the IMF expects further falls.

Consumer prices in the EC rose an average 12.8% in 1980. They are expected to rise only 5% in the current year.

(Telex) Potatoes: irregular. Values rose initially on poor weather but lost ground on expectations that the British potato marketing board would announce disappointing consumption figures.

The IMF, for its part, believes that the prices of most commodities will fall substantially in 1986.

Energy production and telecommunication are likely to be major bottle-necks for some years to come...

In fact these sums are unlikely to be borrowed in the foerseeable future...

For producers of rubber and natural fibres such as cotton for example, the drop in the oil price is bound to mean increaced competition from synthetic products.

Reduced imports should give France close to a $3-billion surplus in 1986.

上面列举的3组词语只是通用英语常用于西方报刊经贸文章的一小部分。实际上这类文章的语言构成，除去表达专业内容的专业词语之外，通常大部分是共核语言。外贸函电所使用的英语大体也是如此，其他学科（包括自然科学）的专门用途英语的基本情况也大致相同。但需要注意的是："共核语言"或通用英语在西方报刊经贸文章或其他专业英语当中的使用是不平衡的：大部分是偶尔用之，只有一小部分使用得多而频，已经成为表达类文章内容必要的语言手段。从这个意义上讲，这部分词语应该归在专业英语的范围之内，实际上该部分词语和专业词语组成了这类文章的语汇主体。

从西方报刊经贸类文章的语言特点，可以得到一点启示：所谓专业英语，是以通用英语为基础为依托的，因而专业英语水平、包括阅读能力的提高，是与通用英语即基础英语水平的提高相伴相随的，并是以基础英语水平的提高为前提的。

（三）西方报刊经贸类文章，总其类是对世界经贸问题的述评，可以说是叙述文和论说文的结合体，简明的陈述、概括的提法和抽象的说理应是其固有的特征，但近年来这类文章往往倾向于使用形象的表达方式，如此喻，象征、文学式的具体描写等，而且有日渐增多之势，表现如下：

1. 在用字遣词中，用形象化的词语代替概念化词语。

U. S. imports have fueled much of the recent economic growth among the major industrial nations.

（“fuel v. ”原意为“向……提供燃料”，现用作“支持”之意，本来可以用 support 之类概念化的词来表达。）

The Hungarians commenced with the reform of the price mechanism and moves towards a less centralised economic decision making process were also put in train.

（“put s. g. in train”原意为“将东西装上火车”，现用作“把一切准备好”之意本来可以用 get s. g. ready 之类的概念化的词语来表达。）

Some 400 joint ventures have been set up within the Special Eeonomic Zones (SEZ) which are receiving the lion's share of new investment.

（“the lion's share” 原意为兽中之王狮子获取的那一份儿，现用作“最大的份额”之意，本来可以用 most 之类的词来表达。）

… adamant support for import restrictions among Japanese farmers, one of the most powerful political forces.

（adamant 原意为“（金刚石般）坚硬的”，现用作“坚定的”之意，本来可以用 firm 之类的词来表达。）

（Telex） coffee fluctuated wildly on uncertainty over brazil's role in the market...

("wildly"原意为"任性地",现用作"剧烈地"之意,本来可以用greatly之类的词来表达。)

2. 使用比喻,象征等修辞手段,使内容表达得具体、生动。

如:

Nakagama says that the "rapid growth pace for China has enormous implications for the rest of the world on both sides of the iron curtain. It is like a giant elephant running ahead of a pack of smaller animals in the zoo."

(以"巨象"比喻经济上日益强大的中国。)

For foreign investors, the prospect of having access to a market of 1 billion consumers no longer seems like a pipedream.

(以鸦片吸食者吸毒后的幻觉——pipedream,比喻不能实现的空想。)

Stock-taking of the policy will come later this year when the National People's Congress discusses the seventh five-year plan, which will run to the end of the decade.

(以"盘点货物"比喻对一项政策实施情况的检查。)

The view is echoed by a U. S. diplomat closely involved in the efforts to open Japanese markets to American goods, Washington's stock solution to the ballooning trade imbalance.

(以"(气球的)迅速升高"比喻贸易逆差的激增。)

Simple loyalty to long-term domestic clients is enough to dissuade retailers from putting foreign products on the front shelves.

(以"把外国货陈列在前面的货架上"表示积极推销之意,使用了象征的表现手法。)

"We Japanese are traveling abroad more and more these days, learning of other countries," he says. "But we still travel in groups, and we still want to eat sushi."

（以“日本人（在出国观光中仍）坚持集体行动、吃日式餐”表示日本人对自己民族传统的执著，也是一种象征的表现手法。）

比喻、象征在西方报刊经贸文章中使用最多的地方是标题，如以“China in the Market Place”为题的一篇文章，讲的是中国参与国际贸易的情况；以“A New European Accent（强音）”为题的文章讲的是西欧近年来经济复兴之势；题为“Toyota Fast Lane（快车道）”的文章讲的是日本丰田汽车公司先进的、高效率的经营方法；题为“Soft Drink Wars”的文章讲的是美国可口可乐和百事可乐两大饮料公司之间的竞争。

3. 不时使用具体的、文学式的描写代替笼统的表述抽象的说理。

例如：

The ritual begins shortly after dawn. As the early morning light filters through the windows of Lucky-Goldstar's towering corporate headquarters in Seoul, Koo Cha-Kyung, chairman of the $8 billion conglomerate, issues instructions that echo around the world. In Huntsville, Ala., 200 factory workers are producing a million Coldstar color televisions yearly. In California's Silicon Valley Koo's whitefrocked research scientists delve into the mysteries of state-of-the-art semiconductor technology. In Jubail, Saudi Arabia, the company is putting the final touches on a sprawling new petrochemical complex. It is an impressive display of global reach, and a harbinger of things to come. As one of Koo's lieutenants puts it: "Our future lies in becoming a truly global company."

以上这段的主要意思是：南朝鲜的大企业正在努力向外扩张，开展跨国经营。按照报刊述评的传统写法，说明这样一个意思只要简明地列举几个事实和数字，再加以归纳总结就可以，而这篇文章却对提出的事例进行了具体，形象的描写：描绘了晨曦映入塔式建筑物内的总裁办公室的情景以及他们海外科研人员的衣着等细节，采用了报告文字和电影蒙太奇的表现手法,给人以生动,具体而更加可信的印象。

西方报刊经贸文章重视形象化表达的趋势,很大程度上恐怕与资本主义报刊企业以盈利为主要目的的经营高度商业化相关连。采用形象化的表达会使艰深,枯燥的专业文章比较易于理解,也增加了阅读的趣味性,从而可以扩大报刊的读者面、拓宽销路。与此不同的是,官方拟稿的同一题材、同一内容的报告和分析,如世界银行和各国政府编写的材料,却没有明显地采用形象化的表现手法,这固然可能是出自保持官方文件的严肃性,也是由于没有商业上的需要。

西方报刊经贸文章采用形象化的表达方式使文章写得具体、生动,一般来说会减少理解上的困难,但对外国读者来说同时也可能会增加一些困难,这是由于英语中不少形象化的表达方式是以西方的文化、历史为背景的。

如:

Domestic demand in Japan remains weak. Wages grew slowly during the first half of this year, holding down purchashing power. Consumption should increase no more than last year's 2.8% gain. A one-trillion-yen(about $4.5-billion) personal income tax cut is in the works, but it probably won't have much effect. Ryo Watabe, senior economist at Nomura Rescarch Institute in New York City, says:"One trillion yen is peanuts."

"one trillion yen"在这里比喻成"peanuts",如果不了解在英国人的文化里"几粒花生米"可以代表"一小笔钱"这样一个意思,就无法理解这句话的确切含义。又如:

In the U.S. soft drink industry, where 1% of the market is worth $300 million in retail sales, Coca-Cola and PepsiCo don't wage mere market share battles. They fight holy war.

在这个句子里,把两个可乐公司在市场上的竞争比作"holy wars",可以看出是以典故作喻来揭示他们所进行的竞争的性质和特点。如果要弄清他们竞争到底具有什么性质和特点,就必须对西方

历史上的“圣战”有足够的了解。(“Holy wars”请见篇后注 8)

4. 西方报刊经贸文章惯于使用较为高深的英语。除了经贸文章本身内容复杂需要有与之相应的表达形式这一因素外,另一个重要原因是:文章的读者主要是资本主义大、中企业的高、中级经营管理人员,政府的经贸官员以及专业研究人员,而他们所受的教育程度一般都在大学以上,很多人还有硕士甚至博士学位,他们的阅读水平、风格、喜好和要求对报刊文章的文字取向起着很大的影响,致使文章所用的英文比较高深,大体表现在三个方面。

1)综合运用复杂,高级的语法手段。

如:

In the meantime foreign capital is expected to play a greater role(1) in the shape of investing(2)in China, training (3)its managers,providing(4) it with modern technology and helping (5) to play a greater role in the international economy by increasing (6) trade. Some 400 joint ventures have been set up (7) within the Special Economic Zones (SEZ') which are receiving the lion's share of new investment (8). Shenzhen, in Cuangdong province is the best known of these with over 200 joint ventures in operation (9).

引文中第一句,谓语动词(1)被动语态出现并带一复合宾语;修饰复合宾语不定式动词的作状语的前置词片语的宾语是动名词 investing(2),其本身又用三个现在分词((3)(4)(5))作表明行为方式的状语来修饰,三个分词各带各自的宾语、状语,而最后一个分词片语里又包含着一个动名词(6)作前置片语的宾语。第二句,主句谓语动词(7)同时使用了现在完成时态和被动语态,套一定语从句(8)。第三句的整个结构看似简单,但带了一个由 with 引导表原因或理由的前置词片语,其宾语和所带的前置词片语“in operation”形成复合结构(9),在意念上起主谓语的作用,代替一个从句。

2)经常使用多义词、变义词,并时有生僻词语。

例如：

One wheel on the commodity price cycle is still spinning forward the other is in reverse. Food crop prices continue to soar, while industry's raw materials have cheapened dramatically. That heady spell in 1973 and the first months of this year, when all commodily prices shot up at an unprecedented rate together, is over.

The great snag of the early 1970s was that all the world's major economies boomed in unison, sharpening demand for industrial raw materials just when major crop failures were causing shortages of grain and agricultural commodities. This led to the fashionable theory that commodity markets were somehow irrevocably linked together by speculators governed by a single stock-exchange-like mood.

西方报刊经贸文章为了深刻地表达内容和表现自己的风格，经常使用含义丰富或词义多变的词，理解和确定这些词义需要深入研读并有厚实的语言和有关的知识功底。以引文中的"the great snag"中的"snag"为例，这个字的基本意思是"断根"，有时也用作"暗瞧"解，以此为基础在本文中被引伸为"造成问题的隐蔽的原因"之意；又如"that heady spell"中的 spell(n.)的根意(root meaning)是"轮班"，几经引伸有了"(病的)一次发作"之意，在这个基础上引文又将其用作"折腾"解，指文中提到的 20 世纪 70 年代初期两大部类初级产品的价格失常和轮番上涨。引文中属于这种用法的词还有 cycle，spin，shoot up，boom 等。这类词的多种词义有的是相对固定的，选择、确定一个词在所读文章的上下文中的词义时有所依据还比较容易。但在不少情况下，词义的演化是作者的创造，因此词义的确定也主要靠读者的思考和推理。

此外，西方报刊经贸文章由于文体上的关系不时使用比较生僻的词语，如引文中的 unprecedented，in unison，irrevocably 等。

3)语言运用高度灵活，有所创新。

西方报刊经贸类文章有时为了深刻地揭示内容，文字的运用不受常规约束，赋予词、句新意。

举例如下：

The thrust of EC policy is beginning to reflect the changed mood of the individual countries. No longer are subsidies io“sun-set” industries and support for agricultural prices at well above world levels seen as the top priorities. Instead, the priority now is on such things as the elimination of barriers to trade within the EC.

thrust(n.)的基本意思是“插”、“刺”，由此衍生的一系列用法均可见诸辞书，但无一解释在此适用。引文在这个字所用意思上的创新是：基于这个字的根义，把这个字的含义引伸为“锋芒所向”，在本文中与 policy 连用就有了“主要目标”的意思即下文的“priority”，显然这儿用“thrust”来强调目标的所在，劲透纸背，很有力度。又例：

There is on doubt that the economic planners are making haste slowly after some early blunders which came about through over ambitious projects.

按照通常的理解，make haste 和 slowly 显然不应该放在一起使用，这是两个刚好相反的概念，实际上在这里文章予 slowly 以新意，和 make haste 搭配用作“谨慎地”、“慎重地”解。但用 slowly 和 haste 一下子就会引起读者的注意，促使探其究竟。这一反常组合的妙处就在于 slowly 和 haste 的明显对照，恰如其分地揭示了“the economic planners”主观上急于发展经济，而在实践过程中又坚决严格按客观规律办事既矛盾又统一的心态，如果这里换用 prudently、cautiously 之类的字则平淡无奇，难以达到现在的效果。

本文从阅读和理解的角度对西方报刊经贸文章的主要特点做了初步的探索和总结。然而，这些特点在文章中不是各自独立存在，分别发挥作用的，而是紧密地结合为统一体。西方报刊经贸文章的实质是专业知识、背景知识和语言的复合。因此，正确地理解一篇文章必须具备这三方面的知识和综合运用这些知识进行研究的能力，其中经贸专业知识和语言知识是主要的。所以，能否读懂一篇西方报刊经贸文章，不简单地是一个语言问题，但也不完全是一个专业知识及背景知识的问题，任何一个方面都不可忽略，不可偏废。这是一个在教学和实践中都必须注意的根本问题。

（本文引用的例句选自《经济学家》、《金融时报》、《幸福》、《商业周刊》、《新闻周刊》、《美国新闻与世界报导》、《基督教科学箴言报》、《远东经济评论》、《现代中国》和法新社商情电传稿等西方报刊在1985～1986年期间刊载的文章。）

1996年10月整理于日本东京　国分寺

东京经济大学

注

1)In real terms:(studying an economic problem) with all the monetary aspects removed. In the given context what it means is allowing for price changes resulting from inflation.

2)Terms of trade (进出口比价):the relation of export and import prices of a country represented by a ratio(terms-of-trade index $=\frac{\text{export price index}}{\text{import price index}}$).

When the prices of imported goods fall in relation to the prices of exported goods(the index above 1), the terms of trade of the country is said to be more favourable since it means it can obtain more goods from abroad than before in exchange for a given quantity of exports.

3)Current account (经常项目):part(one item) of the balance of payments, consisting of statements of money paid and received for both goods and services imported and exported.

Balance of payments(国际收支):

International trade and other financial dealings(chiefly service transactions and capital transfers) between countries make it necessary for them to make payments to one another. The balance of payments shows the relationship between one country's total payments to all other countries and its total receipts from them. It is thus a sort of statement of income and expenditure on international account.

4)Bottler:

For American soft-drink makers, it refers to the distributor of their products. To avoid unnecessary heavy transportation, the manufacturers prefer to supply powdered drinks to their distributors in different parts of the country and the world for them to have the products liquefied and bottled locally.

5)"The historical and political aversion to running large visible trade deficits."

When a nation runs "large visible trade deficits" regularly, they would have to borrow heavily (usu. hard currency) from foreign sources to pay for their excessive imports. Thus they would be exposed to the danger of becoming dependent on international financial powers and the latter would be in a position to exercise their influence on the nation's economic and political developments. China has suffered long from that in her modern history when the country was ruled over by warlords and the Kuomintang Govenment. For all that, China always guards carefully against "large visible trade deficits"。

6)"The unexpected departure of Sheik Ahmed Zaki Yamani from his post as Saudi Arabian oil minister aggravated existing uncertainty concerning the future direction of oil prices in view of severe world oversupply."

Saudi Arabia is the biggest oil exporter of the world highly influential in the OPEC and the international oil market.

During the last few months when Yamani was at the post of oil minister, the country had been strongly advocating stablizing and strengthening the oil price and succeeded in having the other OPEC members restrain their own outputs for price gains. At this moment Yamani was dismissed abruptly, without giving any reason for a while. It aroused suspicion undoubtedly among global oil dealers that Saudi's and the OPEC's current operating strategies and their policies in price might be changed with departure of one of the leading policy-makers, and the oil price would contiue to fall further. They felt more uncertain about the future direction of oil prices.

7)"The assurances given at the Plaza Hotel conference":

On the 22nd of September, 1985, the financial ministers of the United States, Japan, West Germany, Britain and France met at the Plaza Hotel, New York. After a day-long conference, a statement was issued declaring that the five countries were to join their efforts to encourage a lower value for the dollar so as to mitigate protectionism in the United Ststes and elsewhere.

Assurances were also given in the statement by the U. S. allies that they would stimulate non-inflationary growth in their economies, expanding potential markets for U. S. exports which had recently been damaged by the strong dollar.

8)"They fought holy wars."

Holy wars originally refer to the Crusade (十字军东征). The Crusade was that in Middle Ages (1096—1291) the West European Christian rulers in collaboration with feudal lords and big merchants invaded frequently the east-Mediterranean coast countries in the name of recovering the Holy Land (today's Palestine) from the Muslinms. During the war, wherever they won they eliminated the local rule and set up a new state for their own.

In the text the implication of holy wars is that neither Coca-cola nor Pepsi is satisfied with their increased market shares captured in competetion and their final goals are to drive all their rivals out of the markets and establish their own domination.

附

外刊经贸知识选读
自学考试大纲

全国高等教育自学考试指导委员会　制定

出版前言

为了适应社会主义现代化建设事为对培养人才的需要，我国在20世纪80年代初建立了高等教育自学考试制度，经过近20年的发展，高等教育自学考试已成为我国高等教育基本制度之一。高等教育自学考试是个人自学，社会助学和国家考试相结合的一种新的高等教育形式，是我国高等教育体系的一个组成部分。实行高等教育自学考试制度，是落实宪法规定的“鼓励自学成才”的重要措施，是提高中华民族思想道德和科学文化素质的需要，也是造就和选拔人才的一种途径。应考者通过规定的考试课程并经思想品德鉴定达到毕业要求，可以获得毕业证书，国家承认学历并按照规定享有与普通高等学校毕业生同等的有关待遇。

从80年代初期开始，各省、自治区、直辖市先后成立了高等教育自学考试委员会，开展了高等教育自学考试工作，为国家培养造就了大批专门人才。为科学、合理地制定高等教育自学考试标准，提高教育质量，全国高等教育自学考试指导委员会（以下简称全国考委）组织各方面专家对高等教育自学考试专业设置进行了调整，统一了专业设置标准，全国考委陆续制定了几十个专业考试计划。在此基础上，各专业委员会按照专业考试计划的要求，从造就和选拔人才的需要出发，编写了相应专业的课程自学考试大纲，进一步规定了课程学习和考试的内容与范围，有利于社会助学，使自学要求明确，考试标准规范化、具体化。

全国考委根据国务院发布的《高等教育自学考试暂行条例》，参照教育部拟定的普通高等学校有关课程的教学大纲，结合自学考试的特点，组织制定了《外刊经贸知识选读自学考试大纲》。现经教育部批准，颁发试行。

《外刊经贸知识选读自学考试大纲》是该课程编写教材和自学辅导书的依据，也是个人自学，社会助学和国家考试（课程命题）的依据,各地应认真贯彻执行。

全国高等教育自学考试指导委员会

2000 年 2 月

I 课程性质与设置目的

《外刊经贸知识选读》课程是全国高等教育自学考试国际贸易专业的必考课和英语专业的选修课，是为培养和检验自学应考者的阅读和理解西方报刊经贸文章所需的专业英语的基本知识和应用能力而设置的一门专业英语课程。

这一课程是英语阅读和理解课的一个专业分支。其特点是：阅读材料以当代国际经贸活动为主要内容和背景；文章是用相关的英语表达的；课程的设计和教材的编写着力于提示和总结这类材料的语言运用规律和启发有关经贸知识的应用。由于课程内容的高度经贸专业化，学习本课程之前应完成经济学和其他国际贸易基础课程的学习。

设置本课程的具体目的和要求是：使自学应考者初步掌握使用英语从西方报刊或相类的材料中直接了解并获取经贸信息的基本知识和技巧。

II 课程内容和考核目标

一、课程内容和目的

本课程所用教材以课文为核心，选文题材包括与我国经贸研究与实际工作有关的几个主要方面：中国对外贸易与吸收外资的概况以及其改革开放的大背景，国际经贸的宏观形势，世界经济和贸易大国的贸易政策和问题，亚洲新兴经济的状况和问题，日益激烈的市场竞争，从关贸总协定到世界贸易组织，初级产品市场的前景预测和市场变化的微观报导等。这些课程内容的表达在语言上则提供了大量的、丰富的经贸研究与实际工作经常需用的词语、句式和文体及其应用的范例。

本课程的教学目的是：通过课程的学习，认识和掌握有关的语言工具达到阅读和理解相应程度的经贸报刊文章或相似文字材料的能力水平。

二、考核知识点与要求

1. 认知、记忆课文所含新的词、语、句型并掌握其在文中所表现出的用法，特别注意在报刊经贸文章等材料中经常出现的部分(见附录 I)。

2. 熟悉课文所用不同文体(如：报导、评论、述评、官方报告、电传等)及其特点。

3. 参照课文注解，了解与课文内容有关的经贸知识。

4. 正确、深入地理解每一篇课文，能将其译成通顺的汉语并做出简要的内容小结。

5. 参照“课文问题”及其答案，思考和研究课文中内容和语言的重点。

6. 在学通课文的基础上，认真按照要求完成课后练习和补充材料的阅读，检验和提高自己的实际应用能力。

7. 运用通过本课程学习所获取的知识和技能解决新的问题，处理新的材料，而不是简单地重复课内所学。

III 有关说明和实施要求

一、实现课程设置目的在学习中需要达到的具体目标

如前所述，本课程的设置目的为：使学员初步掌握使用英语从西方报刊或相类的材料中直接了解并获取经贸信息的基本知识和技巧。

为了实现这一最终目的必须在学习过程中切实达到下列目标：

1. 熟悉并掌握课文中出现的经常用于报刊经贸文章(或相类材料)的词、片语和句型；

2. 能比较熟练地运用这些语言知识并结合所学的经贸业务和背景知识正确地理解教材中的课文练习用文、补充阅读材料等，并能得其要旨。

二、本课程所用教材为《外刊经贸知识选读》，全国组编本，史天陆主编，中国人民大学出版社出版。

三、教材的构成与使用

教材的每一课由课文、词表、注解、课文提问、练习和补充阅读材料组成，并备有课文提问和练习的答案附在教材后部。

每课书学习和研究的核心应该是课文，入选的课文都是典型性较高的文章以资举一反三，学懂学通了课文就会对这类文章语言的使用规律和语言与专业知识的结合有一定的认识和掌握。

词表和注解基本上属于辅助性资料的部分，是学习和研究课文的工具。

有关课文内容的提问，是用来启发、诱导以使理解和研究深入到课文中各个语言和内容的重点或难点。

练习，是把所学的阅读技能和技巧应用于实践的训练和对学习成绩的检验。

补充阅读材料，主要是用来做阅读练习的补充，可藉以进一步提高阅读能力，要求可因人而异。

后附课文问题和练习答案，对自学者很重要，可以用来查对自己读解和练习的正误，同时深化原有的知识并开启新的思路。

四、自学方法

学习这门课程：

1. 首先要反复认知和记忆教材中出现的在西方经贸报刊文章(英语)中经常使用的词、片语和句型，了解其含义，掌握其用法，能够熟练地运用在阅读理解之中；

2. 在初步掌握了有关语言知识的基础上，在阅读中要结合所学文章的上下文和内容背景运用这些基本语言知识去正确、深入、灵活地理解。

这里所谓“灵活”，就是说一个词、片语或句型具体用在一句一段一篇里时其含义以至其用法经常有所变化，报刊文字尤其如此，而读者在理解上也要有随机应变之巧，不可一味墨守而不得其真义。

3. 报刊经贸文章的内容就是述评世界经济和国际贸易，极具专业性。读懂这种文章仅具一定的英语水平是无法深入的，必须有必要和充实的经贸知识和应用这些知识认识问题的能力。

五、关于社会助学

社会助学是推行高等教育自学考试的必要条件，社会助学单位和辅导教师应注意以下几项要求：

1. 社会助学单位和辅导教师应根据自学考试大纲规定的课程(考试)内容和考核目标，认真研究指定教材，明确本课程的特点、学习范围和学习要求，结合自学应考者的实际需要进行切实有效的辅导，并从学习方法上给以指导。

2. 要正确处理有关语言以及经贸的基础知识和应用能力的关系，努力引导自学应考者将识记、理解同应用联系起来，在牢靠掌握知识的基础上，着重培养和提高自学应考者的分析问题和解决问题的能力。

3. 要正确处理重点和一般的关系。课程内容有一般和重点之分，但两者是密切联系，不可分离的，不掌握全面就不可能深入重点，而考试的内容是覆盖全部课程的。因此，社会助学单位和辅导教师都应指导自学者全面系统地学习教材，全面掌握课程内容，在此基础上再对重点问题深入研究，要注意引导，防止自学中的各种偏向。

六、考试命题原则

1. 本课程考试的命题，应根据本大纲所规定的各章学习(考试)内容和考核目标，确定考试 范围和考核标准，不要扩大或缩小考试范围，也不要提高或降低考核标准。考试内容要全面覆盖，并适当突出课程的重点内容，难易程度要适中。

2. 试题要合理安排题目的能力层次结构。本课程在试题中对不同能力层次要求的分数比例，一般应为：识记占 10%；理解占 35%；简单应用占 30%；综合应用占 25%。

3. 试题要合理安排题目的难度结构。题目难易程度分为易、较易、较难、难四个等级。每份考卷中各种难易程度题目所占的分数比例一般应为：易占 20%；较易占 30%；较难占 30；；难占 20%。

试题的难易程度和能力层次是两个不同的概念，在每个能力层次的题目中，都会有难易程度不同的问题。

4. 本课程试卷采用的题型一般包括：常用词语的英译汉，常用词语的汉译英，正误判断题，单项选择题，课文句、段的英译汉、任选文章的英译汉以及任选文章的内容提问(用英语答题)等。

题型举例见附录Ⅱ。

附录：

Ⅰ. 课文中出现的报刊经贸文章常用词、语和句型

“在报刊经贸文章等材料中经常出现的”词、语、句型，首先指在教材中每课注解和课文问题中提出的各课语言重点，同时包括下列逐课补充部分。

补充部分引用包含重点词、语、句型的课文原文的全句或句中有关的部分，重点在底部划线标出。

Lesson 1

1. the overseas economic links
2. The pattern of China's foreign trade has changed substantially...
3. ...China exported agricultural products to the USSR and East European countries in return for manufactured goods...
4. The Great Leap Forward of 1958—1959 initially produced gains in agricultural and industrial production...
5. ...the volume of foreign trade contracted...
6. The withdrawal of Sovitet economic and technical aid in the early-1960s caused trade to shift away from the USSR ant its Comecon partners towards Japan and Western Europe.
7. ...industrial production fell sharply
8. Foreign trade ... has grown rapidly over the past few years.
9. The Sino-USA agreement ... came into force ...
10. ... fuels accounted for 24 per cent of total exports in 1982...
11. the leading categories of imports
12. light manufactured items
13. The US dollar value of Chinese exports increased at an average rate of almost 18 per cent per annum
14. ...the visible trade surplus rose sharply ...
15. ... foreign technology could play a major role in modernizing

the Chinese economy...

16. ... China became a net grain exporter in 1984...

17. The pattern of foreign trade growth was reversed in 1984...

18. ... imports jumped 38 per cent...

19. the visible trade account was in deficit...

20. buoyant economic activity

21. ... much is re-exported to other destinations...

22. the leading export markets

23. ... the portion destined for the Comecon countries declined from almost 15 per cent in 1978 to 6 per cent in 1983.

24. The most important suppliers ... were Japan,...

25. The successful outcome to negotiations... [1)] is expected to[2)] boost trade...

26. The value of Chinese exports... recovered strongly in 1983...

27. Chinese officials stress the importance of introducing advanced technology to domestic industry,...

28. varying degrees of sophistication.

29. earnings from tourism

30. ... the current account has been in surplus ...

31. Foreign exchange reserves

32. ... [1)] the balance is controlled by the Bank of China which [2)] specialises in foreign exchange business.

33. Individual cities must try to balance their foreign exchange earnings and requirements.

34. ... to permit a run-down in the country's international reserves...

35. ... to mount exhibitions...

36. trade fairs

37. foreign trade practices

38. exemption from customs duties and taxation

39. A series of polices designed to encourage foreign investment

40. raising substantial sums of money
41. the transfer of technology
42. practical bottlenecks
43. China's access to substantial sums of money from the World Bank
44. figures compiled by the OECD
45. the bulk of China's foreign obligations
46.... to undertake profitable business...

Lesson 2

1. ... tax and other[1)] incentives for the foreign investor... to[2)] attract foreign investment.
2.... a tax law for joint ventures was promulgated.
3. ... Chinese leaders were[1)] growing impatient with the rate of progress in the [2)] showpiece SEZ—Shengzhen.
4. ... thus introducing a real element of competition into the country's economic-development programme.
5. Even local factories are taking note of the vast potential sales in their own domestic market.
6. The central govemment's determination to raise the level of industrial technology is clearly behind the decision to open the 14 coastal cities.
7.... repay in Renminbi.
8. The need to upgrade industrial equipment...
9. The combined industrial output of the 15 coastal areas...
10. the preferential systems
11. the intensity of competition
12. private-housing estates.
13. wholly foreign-owned operations
14. a uniform 15% income-tax
15.... plant is being upgraded by foreign investment...

16. ... waive the usual 10% profit-remittance tax.

17. A joint venture outside the zone... is liable to the standard 33% tax rate.

18. Tourist enterprises and any other service industry outside the zone ... are not entitled to any special status.

19. ... who has the authority to approve projects.

20. the consultancy arm

21. rules and regulations

22. ... it will be some time before the dust settles ...

23. Stock-taking of the open policy

Lesson 3

1. the most dynamic economy

2. Its boom radiates from Guangdong, its richest province...

3. China's economy[1] bounced back mightily, reaching a recent[2] peak of 13 per cent growth last year.

4. the world's dominant economy

5. a huge boost for a low-wage export economy

6. Last year China's trade surplus[1] surged, [2] buoyed by exports of toys

7. Its[1] trade surplus with the United States hit a[2] record $18 billion.

8. the renewal of China's most-favored-nation trade status

9. "After Japan, we'll be first in line for retaliation."

10. ... America has an increasingly large stake in good relations with China.

11. more than $30 billion worth of contracts

12. 30 times more than the 1987 record for annual foreign investment in South Korea

13. McDonnell Douglas... has contracted to build 40 more.

14. Other state-affiliated companies ... are branching out from

Hong Kong...

15. Inflation has recently [1] climbed back into[2] double digits,...

Lesson 4

1. In 1991, for the second year [1] in a row, the economies of low-income and middle-income countries virtually [2] stagnated, as measured by an increase in [3] per capita gross domestic product (GDP).
2. [1] Aggregate output for developing countries [2] advanced by slightly less than 2 per cent during 1991(similar to the [3] weak performance of 1990), implying an [4] easing in per capita income of 0. 1 per cent.
3. Excluding Central and Eastern Europe, [1] growth in developing countries in 1991 was 3. 4 per cent,[2] compared with 3. 8 per cent during the 1980s.
4. ... an[1] increase in China's growth rate helped to[2] sustain high rates of growth in the East Asia region.
5. International conditions for growth in developing countries deteriorated in 1991.
6. The seven major industrial countries (the G-7) experienced a significant slowdown in GDP growth....
7. ... it also[1] contributed to a [2] drop of over 6 per cent in nonoil commodity prices...
8. These trends were compounded by worsening economic conditions in the Soviet Union and its successor states,...
9. Policy reforms in Latin America helped to moderate inflation and domestic demand...
10. robust domestic demand
11. the third consecutive year
12. There were no breakthroughs in the Uruguay Round of GATT negotiations on key elements,...

13. Growth in the G-7 countries decelerated . . .

14. The broad trend was the outcome of largely unexpected[1] setbacks to recovery in the United States and the United Kingdom and the apparent [2] onset of a slower period of economic growth in Japan and Germany.

15. a slump in construction of rental housing

16. . . . expectations of profitability were dampened by higher wages and high short term nominal and real interest rates.

17. Inflation as measured by the GDP deflator slackened in most of the G-7 countries.

18. It continued to decelerate in North America and edged down in Japan.

19. curtailing financing of higher-risk projects

20. These developments played some part in the general tightening of credit during 1991. . .

21. a narrowing of current-account imbalances

22. dollar depreciation

23. the earlier appreciation of the deutsche mark,

24. The slope of the Japanese yield curve

25. primary commodities and manufactures

26. merchandise exports

27. the spike in oil prices

28. the sharp compression of imports

29. the severely adverse effects of the Gulf crisis on the economies of Middle Eastern countries

30. a pick-up in China

31. significant gains in the export of manufactures

32. a double-digit rates

33. market diversification

34. reining in of its budget deficit

35. exchange-rate devaluation

36. a bottoming-out

Lesson 5

1. a tougher U. S. policy on trade
2. ... the U. S. trade representative, moved quicly to...
3. ... discrimination against U. S. companies...
4. The administration will begin retaliating in six weeks...
5. ... to impose sanctions on major trading partners to reduce trade barriers abroad,...
6. ... this more aggressive policy could escalate into a full-fledged trade war...
7. ... to ease frictions on a range of issues.
8. the highest trade priority
9. Some representatives of U. S. business,
10. government procurement
11. Anyone who thinks Europe and Japan will be bullied into meeting American deadlines and priorities isn't awake to the changes that have occurred.

Lesson 6

1. the European Community's vast single market
2. ... political and economic integration ...
3. As Europe's economy has soured,...
4. ... much of that will already have been translated into national law,...
5. In addition, economic growth is skidding to an anticipated 1 per cent next year.
6. Business investment, which had been [1] flat for the five years preceding the decision in 1985 to create the single market, [2]

soared to a 7 per cent annual growth rate from 1985-90.

7. 1) budget cuts, 2) deregulation, 3) privatization

Lesson 7

1.... to meet import targets...
2. this new thrust of American trade policy
3. Japan's average tariff on mining and manufactured goods
4.... the country is once more exporting its way out of recession.
5.... Japan has seen a decline in expensive imports of luxuries,...
6. America's strengthening economy
7. their firms' market share
8. In the past, that is, Japanese firms have been export-driven...

Lesson 8

1. Lucky-Goldstar's towering corporate headquarters...
2. Its 1) surging $81 billion economy is 2) churning out a flood of increasingly sophisticated products,...
3.... the Koreans are aggressively targeting Western markets...
4. And in the United States, 13 antidumping suits were brought against Korean firms.
5. Sooner or later they will begin to lose their edge,...
6.... yearly per capita income hovered at a bare-bones $100.
7. For years, relatively cheap labor has been the driving force behind Korea's export boom.
8.... the chaebol,... have long powered Korea's growth.
9. an overwhelmingly large share
10. ... the chaebol have grown increasingly vulnerable to business setbacks and changes of economic climate.
11. the lion's share of the nation's new wealth

12. Seoul now hopes to become more self-sufficient in capital.
13. It has allowed official interest rates to [1)] float more freely, largely in an effort to [2)] siphon funds out of the country's illegal but sprawling "curb money" market.
14. cash-strapped South Korean investors
15. ... few foreign firms have successfully penetrated Japan's home turf.

Lesson 9

1.... Dubai's trade figures are soaring...
2. a $3,500 million order for 436 of France's new generation Leclerc tanks
3.... the economy is riding high...
4. It involves a $1,350 million onshore gas project,...
5.... these other projects will materialise...
6. Major investment is going into the Dubai-based Emirates airline,...
7. Soon, $2,000 million in [1)] financing will have to be arranged for the next[2)] phase of development, which will cover[3)] deliveries from...
8. Dubai's total non-oil trade grew by more than 23 per cent in 1992 to Dh 59,848 million and was seemingly[1)] unaffected by the[2)] recession.
9. .. which accounts for about 34 per cent of the UAE's manufacturing capacity ...
10. ... it ousted the US to become the second largest exporter to the emirate...
11. The UK, according to Dubai customs statistics, has slipped from second largest exporter in 1990 to fifth last year...
12.... the value of UK exports to the UAE is rising steadily ...

13. The UAE was the UK's 25th most important export destination in 1991...

14. The biggest single category of exports...

15. The UAE's trade is conducted primarily through Dubai.

16. Then the result will be a big increase in smuggling

17. Re-exports to Kuwait have seesawed from Dh 183 million in 1990 to Dh 1.161 million in 1991 and Dh 757 million in 1992,...

18. It appears that the 23 per cent increase in non-oil trade registered by Dubai in 1992 will be repeated if not bettered this year.

19. certificates of origin

20. ... to gain a foothold ...

21. There is a massive number of mainly British consultants coming in at silly prices to gain entry into the market,

22. In Dubai, the [1] upward spiral in trading figures is [2] fuelled by the large number of companies moving their regional head offices and distribution centres there,...

23. this buoyant market

24. Such projects are not especially favoured by foreign consultants, however, as the profit margins are thin.

25. contracts worth more than $2,500 million

26. lucrative fees

Lesson 10

1. ... [1] differences between the United States and the European Community on farm trade have [2] narrowed almost to nothing.

2. ... spur economic growth...

3. its subsidised exports

4. production subsidies

5. A separate, long-running dispute over oilseeds does still pose a threat

6. The draft agreement

Lesson 11

1. Boeing and Rolls-Royce will be paid [1] in cash from the [2] proceeds...
2. To secure sales of its F-5 jet fighter to the Swiss government,...
3. Northrop [1] located a purchaser for Swiss elevators in Egypt and [2] steered the Swiss to a cement plant construction project in Indonesia.
4. Over five years some 200 Swiss companies benefited from Northrop's assistance.
5. a hot contest
6. Romanian products of equivalent value
7. ... [1] up to 20 per cent of trade between nations is now [2] subject to some form of countertrade...
8. the [1] primary [2] means of trade
9. bargain-price raw materials
10. ... multilateral trade flourished.
11. ... currencies were convertible.
12. ... many countries are broke...
13. debt service
14. debtor nations
15. creditors
16. expertise in international marketing
17. to tap the networks of global firms
18. the OPEC list price
19. at the expense, of course, of other oil producers
20. Counterpurchase usually involves a supplier selling goods or services and in return ordering unrelated products, which essentially offsets the buyer's costs.
21. Because India needs to export more to the Soviet Union to balance its imports,...

22. with the wrong specifications
23. The balance financed a letter of credit made out to Chryslcr,...
24. Another government firm on the island took title ...

Lesson 12

1. retail sales
2. on the defensive
3. Until now these have been dominated by other companies.
4. If these products live up to their early performance in test markets...
5. ... to make way for their new products
6. ... many bottlers are still working off old inventories.
7. its flagship brand
8. Harris Upham brokerage firm
9. ... Coke holds about 29% of the U. S. market, Pepsi 23%.
10. Company executives
11. But essentially the non-cola market can be divided into four segments:...
12. Although Coca-Cola and PepsiCo's new fruit juice sodas will compete with each other,...
13. bigger discounts
14. Some analysts think it will quickly challenge Sunkist as the top-selling orange drink.
15. distributing competing brands
16. offering deep discounts
17. If they can't get the price up
18. a product that's competitive in price and quality,
19. all-out sales campaigns
20. heavy discounting

Lesson 13

1. the largest export market for U. S. shell eggs.
2. the most popular item.
3. a nearly eightfold increase
4. The United States is currently the third largest supplier with a 7. 5-per cent market share in 1985—up from 6. 8 per cent in 1984.
5. The major outlets for white eggs
6. [1)] Packing and [2)] grading of U. S. brown eggs
7. Wholesalers or retailers
8. ... U. S. eggs have enjoyed a distinct advantage.
9. growing competition
10. the remaining 30 per cent
11. the competitiveness of their products

Lesson 14

1. Many prices are [1)] at historic lows, and the IMF [2)] expects further falls.
2. One key commodity, sugar, has recovered.
3. surplus produce
4. ... most soothsayers forecasting flat ...
5. ... big yields afforded by the equity and money markets.
6. spiraling commodity prices
7. currency movements
8. ... commodity prices have continued to tumble...
9. ... one key commodity, sugar, has rebounded ...
10. ... its rally appears to have run out of steam.
11. The explanation for the general weakness
12. a particularly severe glut of supplies

13. The U. S. is also setting out this year to arrest the decline in its exports...
14.... they are bound to have other, perhaps less desirable spin-offs.
15.... it is already taking its toll...
16. cash-strapped oil-producing states
17. First, world economic growth remains generally 1) sluggish and has been 2) at its weakest in manufacturing,...
18. In many of the newer and heavily-indebted industrial countries, commodity consumption has been 1) squeezed, as a result of 2) official austerity programmes.
19.... to maximise commodity exports...
20. unit commodity prices
21. Third, the world has got used to living with much lower levels of stocks...
22. the cost of carrying large inventories
23.... when prices are on the way down.
24. stores of value
25. liquid assets
26. price volatility
27. the pattern of supply and demand
28. Agricultural productivity has grown rapidly across the board,...
29. competitive rivals
30. a rigid export quota system
31. Increasing efficiency, in both production and consumption, is clearly at work in the rubber market.
32.... resources look in short supply.

Lesson 15

1. oil prices seesaw to three-month low in "big bang" week
2. 1) unstable crude prices in turn prompted falls in platinum and gold,

the latter to its lowest since early September, [2] aggravated by the withdrawal of investment support as the dollar regained ground.

3. Sterling's decline [1] lent some support to the base metal sector, where lead and zinc rallied [2] on the continuing lack of a solution to the labour dispute affecting Australia's broken hill mines.
4. the grain sector was dulled by the prospect of lower-than-expected Soviet imports this season,...
5. gold: lower. after [1] coming in [2] for early support on news of strike action affecting mines belonging to gold fields of South Africa, [3] values declined in line with platinum and New York [4] advices as miners were encouraged to return to work by [5] management promises of negotiation.
6. the fall in oil prices also [1] brought pressure to bear but [2] good resistance at around the 400 dollars per ounce level permitted a brief rally.
7. ... the dollar strengthened...
8. values fluctuated lower in line with other precious metals...
9. london metal exchange (lme) stocks were down 100,000 ounces, at 25,148,000 ounces.
10. prices moved gradually lower following an early setback due to the 3,825-tonne rise in LME stocks to 170,625 tonnes, their highest level since february this year, but support was in evidence at lower levels.
11. values moved up to their best level...
12. values eased back...
13. a tighter supply situation
14. a sharp 3,375-tonne rise
15. the bleak outlook for aluminum prices
16. news of a settlement at Alcan's Seebree(Kentucky) plant, affected by strike action since june, further dampened sentiment.
17. in thin conditions,

18. ... but a recovery was made on the back of Sterling's weaker trend against the dollar
19. the previous week's closing level
20. platinum progressed at the outset
21. crude oil prices fluctuated in nervous conditions...
22. bearish oil stock figures
23. his call for an urgent meeting of the pricing committee of the Organization of Petroleum Exporting Countries (OPEC) took prices back ...
24. nearby good quality cocoa
25. some eight to ten cargoes of white sugar,
26. boosting sentiment
27. rumours that colombian coffee exports would not exceed 600, 000 60-kilo bags in November and December due to recent heavy rains underpinned sentiment at the outset,
28. profit-taking
29. ... with palm and palm kernel oils gaining ground ...
30. futures activity remained at a virtual standstill.
31. ... shipments since july 1 had reached 4. 96 million tonnes
32. [1] renewed soviet enquiry for up to one million tonnes of community grain added to the steadier [2] undertone
33. values rose initially on poor weather but lost ground on expectations...
34. making more than very minor [1] upward adjustments to wooltop [2] quotations
35. the cotton index fluctuated narrowly on the liverpool(england) market,
36. strong demand prevailed at the weekly auction...

附录　题型举例

1. 常用词语的英译汉

Put the following phrases into Chinese：

Gross National Product

public works

2. 常用词语的汉译英

Put the follwing phrases into English：

外汇储备

物价指数

3. 正误判断题

Read the following passages and decide whether the statements are true or false：

Changing Face of World Trade

In 1995，the merchandise imports of the US were ＄770.8bn，the European Union's ＄736.1bn and Japan's ＄355.9bn. These are impressively large figures，but the three giants still only purchased 47％ of world imports. Meanwhile，the imports of the ten leading Asian developing economies amounted to＄748.4bn. Asian developing economies have become the fourth focus of global commercial activity. They are also the fastest growing.

In order of their importance as markets for merchandise imports，these ten leading economies were South Korea（with imports of ＄135.1bn），China（＄132bn），Taiwan（＄103.8bn），Malaysia（＄77.7bn），Singapore（＄76bn），Thaiand（＄69.1bn），Hong

Kong ($53.7bn), Indonesia ($42.2bn), India($31.7bn) and the Philippines ($27.1bn). To put these figures in perspective, the imports of South Korea alone were half those of France and 40% of Japan's.

The trade of Asian developing countries is not just large. It is also dynamic. The volume of imports into Asia as a whole grew at an annual rate of 10% between 1990 and 1995—which gives a rise of more than 60% in just five years.

The volume of the region's exports grew more slowly, at only 7.5% a year. For those concerned about the overall effect of Asian growth on demand in the rest of the world, the relative sluggishness of exports should be quite encouraging. Similarly, the merchandise imports of the ten leading Asian developing countries exceeded their exports by $41.1bn in 1995.

1) The merchandise imports of Asian developing economies became the largest in the world in 1995. (   )
2) The exports of the Asian economies grew with the same dynamism as their imports. (   )
3) South Korea's imports in 1995 were nearly half as large as those of France. (   )
4) The rest of the world is encouraged by the news that the Asian economies have a trend of strong import demand and slow export growth. (   )

4. 单项选择题

Choose one answer that best explains the underlined part or what is required in the following statements.

1) A real economic growth rate of 4% in fiscal 1986 was <u>viable</u> for Japan.

a. able to succeed　　b. likely to fail

c. hard to predict　　d. vulnerable

2) Official discount rate is usually used to refer to the interest rate charged by ________.

a. commercial banks to their correspondent banks

b. commercial banks to the central banks

c. local banks to foreign banks

d. the central bank on loans to commercial banks

5. 课文句、段和任选文字的英译汉：

Translate the following passages (some are selected from the textbook and some are tree-choice writings) into Chinese.

1) Speculators who profited handsomely from the price volatility of the 1970s have deserted soft commodities for the newer excitement of financial futures or the securities and big yields afforded by the equity and money markets.

2) With 1.2 billion people and an economy growing more rapidly than any other in the region, China's rising importance as a trader, manufacturer and investor offers neighbors once heavily dependent on U. S. trade a fast-growing cushion against slowdown in the West.

6. 任选文章的内容提问(英语回答)

Read the following passage and answer the questions in English:

France has had a recovery that barely deserves the name. Real GDP rose only 1% in 1983 and slightly more than that in 1984. Net exports accounted for over half the increase. Low growth has been a consequence of the Mitterrand government's fiscal austerity, which has, to give it credit, gone a long way toward solving the problems it was designed to overcome. Government spending is under better control, and inflation has dropped from 12% in 1982 to 6.2% this year; it will probably edge down to below 6% in 1986.

1) What is "a recovery that barely deserves the name"?

2) What was the reason for the "low growth"?

3) Did "the Mitterrand government's fisical austerity" have any positive effect on the French economy? What was that?

后　　记

经全国高等教育自学考试指导委员会同意，由经济管理类专业委员会负责高等教育自学考试经济管理类专业课程大纲的组编工作。

《外刊经贸选读自学考试大纲》由对外经济贸易大学史天陆教授负责编写。大纲写成后，参加审稿的有：经贸部经贸管理干部学院陆祖汶教授、《国际商报》副总编王学文教授和对外经济贸易大学王关富教授。在此一并表示感谢。

全国高等教育自学考试指导委员会
经济管理专业委员会
2000 年 2 月